Practical Forensic Pathology and Toxicology

Practical Forensic Pathology and Toxicology is a companion to the authors' original book on the subject, *Forensic Toxicology: Mechanisms and Pathology.*

This new volume addresses issues that forensic pathologists face when confronted by the suspected or demonstrated presence of drugs or toxins in their cases. Since such considerations include the need for a basic understanding of the direct physiological effects of potentially toxic agents, the authors highlight various connections and interaction between forensic pathology and toxicology. The book is written for both the practicing pathologist, and those in training, who may already have some knowledge of forensic medicine but are on occasion faced with issues that reach beyond a basic determination of cause and manner of death.

Pathologists are expected to provide informed, well-reasoned opinions explaining *how* a person died—which includes questions about any drugs, prescription medications, or otherwise that may have caused or contributed to death. As such, this book looks at the direct physiological effects of drugs and toxins, answering questions such as "Why does hypernatremia cause seizures?" or "Why can synthetic cannabinoids cause fatal complications, yet THC does not?" or the very timely "What is the mechanism by which an opiate overdose causes death?" Coverage primarily centers on the pathological derangements and physiological consequences of the actions of drugs and toxins, and the cellular mechanisms by which those pathological consequences arise.

Organized using an organ system approach, sections are divided into major target organ systems and sections included for affected organs and tissues. While some drugs affect more than one organ system—and some patients will have multiple drugs present—the book's categorization and organization take this approach to be readily usable for the reader. Case reports are included with additional patient data to show the effects of specific toxins and poisons both alone and in combination with natural disease. Color figures illustrate all aspects of drug or toxin impact on postmortem casework including the scene of death, the deceased persons, and the organs and tissues affected.

Practical Forensic Pathology and Toxicology is an invaluable resource for practicing pathologists, toxicologists, and those training for those fields. It also serves as a useful reference for lawyers, judges, insurance companies, and other medical professionals who need to know, in light of what drugs are present in a particular case, what such compounds do, and how their presence (or absence thereof) is—or is not—related to an individual's death.

Practical Forensic Pathology and Toxicology

Dorothy E. Dean and Robert H. Powers

CRC Press
Taylor & Francis Group
Boca Raton London New York

CRC Press is an imprint of the
Taylor & Francis Group, an **informa** business

Designed cover image: Dorothy E. Dean and Robert H. Powers

First edition published 2025
by CRC Press
2385 NW Executive Center Drive, Suite 320, Boca Raton FL 33431

and by CRC Press
4 Park Square, Milton Park, Abingdon, Oxon, OX14 4RN

CRC Press is an imprint of Taylor & Francis Group, LLC

Library of Congress Cataloging-in-Publication Data
Names: Dean, Dorothy E., author. | Powers, Robert H., author. | Powers, Robert H. Forensic toxicology.
Title: Practical forensic pathology and toxicology / Dorothy E. Dean and Robert H. Powers.
Description: Boca Raton FL : CRC Press, 2025. | Companion to Forensic toxicology / Robert H. Powers, Dorothy E. Dean. [2016]. | Includes bibliographical references and index.
Identifiers: LCCN 2024027520 (print) | LCCN 2024027521 (ebook) | ISBN 9780367638610 (hardback) | ISBN 9780367638627 (paperback) | ISBN 9781003121060 (ebook)
Subjects: MESH: Forensic Toxicology—methods | Forensic Pathology—methods | Toxicological Phenomena
Classification: LCC RA1228 (print) | LCC RA1228 (ebook) | NLM W 750 | DDC 614/.13—dc23/eng/20240725
LC record available at https://lccn.loc.gov/2024027520
LC ebook record available at https://lccn.loc.gov/2024027521

ISBN: 9780367638610 (hbk)
ISBN: 9780367638627 (pbk)
ISBN: 9781003121060 (ebk)

DOI: 10.4324/9781003121060

Typeset in Berling
by codeMantra

PREFACE

Practical Forensic Pathology and Toxicology has been written primarily for the practicing pathologists and those in training who already have some knowledge and experience in forensic medicine but are, on occasion, faced with issues that reach beyond the simple determination of cause and manner of death. Questions such as "Why does hypernatremia cause seizures?" or "Why can synthetic cannabinoids cause fatal complications, yet THC does not?" or the very timely "What is the mechanism by which an opiate overdose causes death"? can lead to the fascinating common ground between pathology and toxicology. We also hope that forensic toxicologists will find this book provides interesting and useful insights into the practice of forensic pathology.

This work is intended to be a companion to the authors' first book on the subject, *Forensic Toxicology: Mechanisms and Pathology*. The reader may recognize some material from that first book, which was written to accompany and complement a course in forensic toxicology and is, therefore, heavily weighted toward toxicologic considerations, mechanisms, and questions. This book places more emphasis on the questions and issues the forensic pathologist addresses when confronted by the suspected or demonstrated presence of drugs or toxins in their cases. Such considerations include the need for a basic understanding of the direct physiological effects of drugs and toxins.

The worlds of forensic pathology and forensic toxicology are well recognized as having significant overlap. In many medical examiner and coroner's offices, there can be many opportunities for useful and interesting exchange of information and ideas between pathologists and toxicologists. Clearly, the ability of the toxicology laboratory to provide reliable qualitative and quantitative information regarding the drugs and toxins that may be present (or absent) in forensic casework has become an essential tool for the pathologist. Beyond simply the information regarding what drugs were present and in what amount, the toxicologist may, in some cases, be able to offer useful information regarding effects, interactions, and physiological consequences. Similarly, the opportunity for forensic toxicologists to gain knowledge and insights with regard to their analytical challenges can be an interesting and rewarding aspect of their career and allow them to provide a higher degree of support and useful information to the pathologist. Both fields can clearly benefit from an attitude of collegial mutual interest and interdependence. The authors have been collaborating for over two decades and firmly believe that the quality of overall work product is greater as a function of cooperation and collaboration than would have been achieved working without the exchange of ideas and information that characterizes any practice of good science. In short, by working together, the forensic pathologist and the forensic toxicologist are both able to have a better understanding of the cases presented to them. Furthermore, the pathologist will be able to make better decisions about sample testing and interpretation of toxicologic findings, leading to better cause-of-death statements, and the toxicologist will be a more knowledgeable, helpful, and reliable resource for that determination of the final diagnosis.

Forensic pathologists are often called upon to explain findings to the general public as well as to the end-users of our product. Lawyers, judges, insurance companies, other medical professionals, and family and friends of the deceased want to know or *need* to know what drugs are present (or, in some cases, critically absent), what they do, and how their presence or absence is related to the death, if at all. Pathologists are expected to provide well-reasoned and well-informed opinions explaining, in a comprehensible manner, how a person died. Similarly, they should be able to comfortably field questions about drugs that caused or contributed to death, or were otherwise present, such as prescription medications, including at least in a generalized sense of how those drugs function in the body. The more we understand the mechanisms of drugs and toxins and how their presence leads to physiological effects, the better prepared we will be to provide useful, relevant explanations.

CONTENTS

ABOUT THE AUTHORS

Dorothy E. Dean obtained her MD from the University of Toledo Medical Center in Toledo, Ohio, acquiring additional training in general pathology at the University of Cincinnati and a fellowship training program in forensic pathology at the Hamilton County Coroner's Office in Cincinnati, Ohio. Dr. Dean is board certified by the American Board of Pathology in anatomic, clinical, and forensic pathology and is currently a Deputy Coroner at the Hamilton County Coroner's Office in Cincinnati, Ohio. Prior to her medical training, Dr. Dean was a high school mathematics and physics teacher.

Dr. Dean is a member of several professional organizations including the American Academy of Forensic Sciences and the National Association of Medical Examiners. She is a member of the federal Disaster Mortuary Operational Response Team (DMORT) and its Ohio counterpart (OMORT). Her special interests include teaching medical students and medical residents, identification of unidentified remains, and the evaluation of drug- and poison-related fatalities. She is an adjunct assistant professor in the Department of Pathology at the University of Cincinnati.

Robert H. Powers completed his PhD in biochemistry at Michigan State University under Dr. Steven Aust, working on the mechanism of dioxin, PCBs, and similarly acting toxins. Dr. Powers has directed several forensic toxicology laboratories around the country and retired from that role to become a professor at the University of New Haven, Department of Forensic Sciences, where he has taught forensic toxicology at the graduate level for over 10 years. Dr. Powers' and his graduate students' research projects at the University now include the effect of ethanol on phase I and phase II metabolism of selected drugs and drug classes, decompositional drug metabolism, and related postmortem changes.

Dr. Powers is active nationwide as a forensic consultant and expert witness for civil and criminal cases, with a particular focus on questions related to the potential of drug involvement in death cases, and drug- and alcohol-related impairment issues.

INTRODUCTION

The core of this book is the pathological derangements and physiological consequences of the actions of drugs and toxins, and the cellular mechanisms from which those pathological consequences arise. We did not consider analytic techniques or methodologies, recognizing that the rich field of analytical toxicology upon which we rely for accurate and reliable results, is more than adequately addressed in other works. Nor did we attempt to provide an understanding of toxin action at the molecular or biochemical level. For example, the fact that a particular drug is considered a "GABA receptor agonist" and the physiological consequences of that action is the target depth for this book. The focus of this book is on the physiological consequences of that agonistic interaction with the receptor, rather than the actual nature of the molecular interaction between the toxin and the receptor at the biochemical level.

We have also concentrated on the acute effects of drugs, while recognizing that drugs can and do have cumulative effects, such as ethanol-related cirrhosis of the liver and cardiac hypertrophy consequential to sympathomimetic amine abuse. Nevertheless, it is the nature of forensic pathology that our casework concern is often primarily that of the acute drug action leading to a cardiac or respiratory collapse or CNS depression to the point of death. Chronic toxin exposure will often be discernable by pathological clues and may not be supported by analytic demonstration of the presence of a particular toxin.

We have organized this book along an organ–organ system approach. While some drugs affect more than one organ system and some patients will have multiple drugs present, we felt this approach provided a reasonable means for categorization. We have organized the sections into major target organ systems and added sections for those organs and tissues "also affected." While there are multiple ways in which this material could have been organized, we have chosen this approach with a hope that it will be readily usable for the reader.

Finally, both forensic pathology and forensic toxicology are fascinating fields. This book is written for the curious as well as the serious. Both authors continue to thrive on the ongoing challenges of new and different cases and circumstances in specific and learning and exploration in general. We hope, in addition to being a useful resource for the practicing pathologists, toxicologists, and those training in those fields, that this book will provide a basis for the readers to build upon their own knowledge base and to encourage life-long learning, just the inherent enjoyment of seeing new connections and learning new things.

DOI: 10.4324/9781003121060-1

SECTION 1

GENERAL CONSIDERATIONS

DOI: 10.4324/9781003121060-2

1.1 INTRODUCTION

We have chosen to begin this book with an overview of the general approach used by forensic pathologists and toxicologists to address the basic overarching challenge of the profession, the scientific and legal determination of the "Cause and Manner" of death. We recognize that many readers of this book will be very familiar with the standard processes and procedures of the autopsy suite, and, to some extent, the toxicology laboratory. However, we also recognize that some may be relatively new to the field or otherwise be interested in our view and approach to both pathologic considerations and the manner in which toxicologic findings may play a role in that process of determination of the "Final Diagnosis." We also wish to emphasize the potential for overlap and interaction between the roles of the forensic toxicologist and pathologist. It is our view that the ultimate challenge of the forensic pathologist (FP), that being the determination of cause and manner of death (COD & MOD), can often benefit from the incorporation and consideration of information from the realm of the toxicologist – beyond the simple determination of what drugs, and in what concentration, may be present in postmortem samples.

Perhaps the most basic and common drug-related question arising in postmortem considerations for the FP is: "Did the drug(s) found during postmortem toxicology testing, considered with the background of underlying medical issues, and/or pathologic findings, cause or contribute to the death in this case?" Recognizing that the determination of COD and MOD is the sole responsibility of the FP, the potential for valuable insight or contribution from a toxicologist to the considerations leading to those conclusions should not be overlooked or underestimated. As we discuss in subsequent sections questions regarding the role that a drug or drugs may have played in a particular death cannot always be reliably resolved by a simple reference to a table of therapeutic, toxic, and lethal drug levels. Similarly, the assumption that postmortem values necessarily or reliably reflect antemortem levels or can be utilized to infer an amount of drug(s) that had been taken or administered may be significantly flawed and lead to erroneous conclusions.

Based on knowledge of the individual mechanism of action of the drugs that have been detected in postmortem samples and the uncertainty associated with inferences based on the postmortem toxicologic results in a specific case, a toxicologic perspective may provide some valuable insight into the interpretation of drug findings. An example of this process is presented in Sidebar 1.1: A Methadone/Benzodiazepine Challenge.

Sidebar 1.1: A Methadone/Benzodiazepine Challenge

A 47-year-old man was found dead in his apartment by a friend at about 8:30 AM on a welfare check because he didn't show up for work. He was seated on a couch slumped to his left side, toward the middle, and away from the arm of the couch. The television was in the "on" position as though he had died while watching a television program. He lived alone and his home was neat and tidy. The coroner's investigator assessed the scene, and his body and found no illicit drugs, drug paraphernalia, or medications. There was no sign of a struggle or foul play. His clothing was appropriate for the season. Livor mortis was purple, blanching, and consistent with the position in which he was found dead. Further investigation revealed that he was last known to be alive at about 7:30 PM the evening before.

An autopsy conducted 2 days later (refrigerated in the interim) revealed the following:

Body length: 67 inches,

Body weight: 195 pounds,

Heart: 400 g; left ventricular free wall thickness 1.5 cm; 75% narrowing of the left anterior descending and circumflex coronary arteries,
Lungs: 1,430 g combined, and
Brain: 1,510 g, not edematous.
Toxicology results from peripheral (femoral) blood:
Alprazolam 0.104 mg/L,
α-hydroxyalprazolam 0.006 mg/L,
Diazepam 0.010 mg/L,
Nordiazepam <0.005 mg/L, and
Methadone 1.71 mg/L EDDP 0.874 mg/L.
The decedent's past medical history was significant for opioid addiction for which he had been receiving methadone maintenance therapy, with records indicating that he had been given 110 mg of methadone in liquid form daily for at least the previous 24 months, receiving one at-clinic and one take-home dose from his treatment provider every other day. This schedule had been adopted by the clinic to minimize interpersonal contact during the COVID-19 pandemic. There were no other prescriptions given by this facility or any other medical provider; therefore, it was assumed that the benzodiazepines were illicitly obtained.

The challenge in this case arises from the presence of three potentially "adequate" causes of death: underlying cardiac pathology, the elevated opiate (methadone) levels (alone), and the combined effects of elevated alprazolam [a non-opiate-based central nervous system (CNS) depressant)] and methadone. At first consideration, the apparently elevated methadone level is compelling, (potentially fatal at levels ~0.4 mg/L and up) and when combined with another CNS depressant, perhaps even more so (alprazolam can be considered "toxic" at levels above ~0.1 mg/L; therapeutic 0.005–0.05 mg/L). On the other hand, the position in which the decedent was found along with his cardiac findings seems suggestive of a sudden cardiac death. There is also the issue of the combination of elevated opiate and benzodiazepines. Would it have been reasonable for the decedent in this case to have overdosed on both drugs, as opposed to just the methadone? One is tempted to attribute the elevated drug levels to postmortem redistribution (PMR), but the blood collection was unquestionably femoral and done in a proper manner.

In our opinion, the key to providing a reasonable understanding of the death in this case lies in the nature of the PMR process (see Sidebar 1.5: PMR: How and Why) and understanding the implication of the body's semi-reclined position for an extended interval after death. Specifically, the physical positioning of the body placed the internal organs (liver specifically) considerably closer to the eventual blood draw site than would have been the case had the body been reclined, making the probability of the draw site being within a "diffusion front" as methadone (and alprazolam) concentrated in the liver during life, diffused out and away from the liver during the postmortem interval. It is significant that both drugs were significantly elevated over therapeutic levels; since in the case of a specific drug overdose, one would expect therapeutic levels of drug not taken in excess. If the levels of all the drugs determined to be present were relatively similarly elevated, PMR becomes, in many cases, the more reasonable explanation. The physical and temporal circumstances of the death in this case strongly suggested that the quantitative toxicologic findings were artifactually elevated and, hence, unlikely to be reflective of the true antemortem concentration of the drugs. As such, the cause of death in the case was considered to have been primarily a function of the decedent's underlying cardiac disease, and the suggestion that the drug levels reflected an antemortem overdose was discounted.

1.2 FORENSIC POSTMORTEM EXAMINATIONS

The responsibility of a forensic postmortem examination is to determine the COD and MOD in cases where the death was unexpected, suspicious, unattended, the result of criminal activity, accidental, a suicide, or when there is no treating physician willing or able to sign the death certificate. Such cases then become the legal responsibility of the office of either the coroner or medical examiner (ME), depending on the local jurisdiction. Both systems are currently in use in the United States and are based on the English "Coroner" system, (see Sidebar 1.2: Origin of the US Coroner System and Inquests in England). Our current ME system has evolved from that model. Coroner systems were, at their inception, managed by people with generally the same degree of knowledge about forensic pathology as fully trained physicians. In the early days, non-medically trained people would determine the cause and manner of death and complete the death certificate the best they could, given the information they had. As medicine advanced and became more specialized, so did the coroner system, becoming more organized and transitioning to a forensic medicine specialty operating within governmental structures. The first medical examiner system to be developed based upon advanced, specialized knowledge in the United States was in Massachusetts in 1877. Currently in the US, the death investigation system is composed of multiple jurisdictions, be it ME or coroner divided by geographic boundaries (state, county, parish, etc.). All jurisdictions employ or have access to medical doctors specifically trained in forensic pathology. In a general sense, the roles and responsibilities of the two types of offices are the same, but the educational backgrounds of the coroner v. ME may be different. The organizational criteria and oversight authorities for the systems are dictated by statute.

Sidebar 1.2: Origin of the Coroner System in the US and Inquests in England

The role and position of "Coroner" arose in medieval England with the dual responsibility of holding inquests regarding individuals who had died by accident or violence and maintaining the rights of the Crown with regard to tax and property matters. In essence, the role at that time was that of law and tax enforcement. The title was not initially "Coroner", but "Crowner" or "Coronator" as an homage to the Crown.

In modern times, coroners in England are lawyers who investigate deaths and call upon FPs for examinations of decedents. There are approximately 100 coroners in England (and Wales) with geographically defined responsibilities. These coroners have jurisdiction over the same types of cases as they do in the US: when no doctor has examined the patient in the 14 days before death (the time frame is variable in the US); or when the death was sudden, unexpected, unexplained, apparently caused by unnatural means; or when further investigation is needed. The pathologist then offers an opinion as to the medical cause of death, but it is the responsibility of the coroner to determine the manner thereof. Hence, the coroner relies upon the reports of the experts involved in the case before making a ruling.

Inquests are still held in England when a death is presumed to be unnatural or otherwise likely to be of public interest. These procedures are essentially a non-adversarial inquiry, open to the public and the media. The purpose of the inquest is for the coroner to gather information and is limited to the following: who is dead, when, where, and under what circumstances did the death occur; discussion of negligence or blame is forbidden (issues of culpability are dealt with in the civil or criminal courts, if warranted). The process allows the coroner to hear from witnesses in the case and allows interested parties to raise questions. Participants in the inquest procedure are the coroner, witnesses (expert and fact), and any interested parties including family members or organizations implicated in the death. The coroner usually presides over the procedure alone, but an inquest may require a jury of 7–11 people when the case involves issues of public interest. Coroner juries must be empaneled for inquests regarding deaths while in "the care of the state" (i.e., prison, police custody, or detention in a secure mental-health facility).

The coroner or ME may be an elected official or appointed at the local governmental level. He or she is responsible for issuing death certificates and is often a doctor if not a forensic pathologist (FP). There are some jurisdictions in the US in which a lay person may serve as coroner. (However, many such coroner's offices either have FPs on staff or send cases as appropriate to neighboring jurisdictions for autopsy procedures which are then performed by FPs.) In contrast, an ME is often an appointed position, and the office is generally filled by an FP. Regardless of the organizational structure, forensic death investigations and autopsies will ideally be performed by trained FPs and staff. For simplicity, we will refer to the responsible authority for COD and MOD person as the MEand the organization as the "ME Office" throughout this text.

Modern medicolegal death investigation practice in the US is routinely a cooperative venture between law enforcement, prosecutors, and ME offices. Examination of a body *in situ* is normally performed by investigators from the ME Office, although the circumstances under which a decedent is discovered may dictate the extent to which preliminary or additional scene investigation will be carried out by law enforcement personnel. Scenes at which a body has been discovered and reported directly to law enforcement will routinely result in ME Office personnel also being called in to declare death; perform a preliminary evaluation regarding the nature of the death; and, potentially, take custody of the case. Many ME Offices will only respond to death scenes when law enforcement personnel are already on scene (to ensure both the safety of responders and that the scene and potential evidence will not be compromised).

1.2.1 Role of the Medical Examiner

As noted above, the essence of the role of the ME is to determine the cause of death and the manner by which the death has occurred. In so doing, it is their responsibility to ensure that a death that has resulted from criminal action or activity is recognized as such and is then brought to the attention of law enforcement personnel. It is this key societal role that provides the basic justification for the office and for the ability of the office to override potential objections to either investigation or autopsy. Naturally, the consequences of accurate assessment of COD and MOD can have significant benefits beyond the realm of law enforcement: from the proper settlement of death benefits (e.g., insurance, etc.) to recognition of workplace hazards, evaluation of the efficacy of medical treatment, the discovery of unrecognized medical issues, etc.

While the essence of the postmortem examination is the autopsy, the modern ME Office has the advantage of a wide variety of informational sources to aid in the determination of COD and MOD, including access to crime laboratories with their analytical and related investigational expertise. In many cases, the eventual determination regarding a case will reflect the collation and consideration of many different bits of information and observations from multiple sources, with the ME functioning as a central organizing element, with the task of weighing all the information in an effort to reach an appropriate and accurate final determination. It is also the responsibility of the ME to properly identify the deceased person. If the deceased person cannot be visually identified by a friend or relative (e.g., died at home with family or friends), a scientific method of identification is needed whereby antemortem data are used to compare with postmortem features, such as fingerprint comparison, medical and dental radiograph comparison, or serial numbers on implanted medical devices. Circumstances requiring a scientific identification include when the body is not physically recognizable, there is no one available to do so, or the circumstances around the death indicate that a scientific identification is necessary (e.g., a body in a dumpster, burned beyond recognition, homicide victim).

The concept of an in-depth, invasive examination of a deceased person may be only a curiosity or even a repulsive thought for some people who are uninitiated to the medical field. The justification for the practice is, of course, the potential for significant information regarding a death to become available during a thorough and potentially complex examination of the decedent. Traditionally, this process was termed "necropsy," as derived from the Greek words for corpse (nekros) and view (opsis). Necropsy is now more commonly used for the postmortem analysis of animals, with "autopsy" used to describe the examination of human remains. This term is derived from the Greek words for self (autos) and view, yielding "autopsy" or "see for oneself." An autopsy, or the dissection and examination of the body, and the subsequent secondary examinations (e.g., microscopic analysis of tissues) and analyses (e.g., toxicologic analysis of blood or other tissue samples) includes the primary mechanism by which the FP gains the information required to determine the cause and manner of death.

1.2.2 Scene Investigation

The evaluation of a death that has been determined to be or is being considered as potentially within the jurisdiction of the ME Office will almost always include some degree of scene investigation, usually by personnel specifically trained for that process (e.g. "medicolegal" or "death scene" investigators). Scene investigation can be brief and perfunctory or, in the case of an apparent or suspected homicide (which may have already been recognized as a crime scene), may be extensive and complicated. Many crime scenes require considerable expertise from investigative personnel both for the recognition of potentially important evidentiary materials as well as the proper collection, preservation, and labeling thereof. Information from this process can eventually be of considerable use and interest to the FP and toxicologist and may include such information as medical history and prescription information, clinical and medication history just prior to death if the decedent was hospitalized, medications present (and associated pill counts), illicit drugs and/or paraphernalia found at the scene, and any other information that may help guide the toxicologic investigation, and eventual characterization of the nature of the death.

1.2.3 Types of Postmortem Examinations

Forensic pathologists have a range of possible approaches for the examination of the body of the decedent. The extent of the postmortem evaluation may vary, depending on the nature and circumstances of the case. Not all cases accepted into an ME Office will receive an autopsy. COD and MOD can be determined, and a death certificate is completed in a case without an autopsy if, in the opinion of the ME or case pathologist, such an examination is not necessary for an accurate determination thereof. Some cases may be satisfactorily resolved simply by an evaluation of medical records; others may require an examination of the outside of the body only; and some will need a full autopsy examination. In many, if not most or all (depending on the office practice, cases, in which an autopsy is not performed, toxicologic analysis may be done on specimens obtained postmortem specifically for that purpose, or on samples that had been collected by medical services prior to death and retrieved by ME Office personnel for toxicologic testing.

A comprehensive review of medical records, coupled with pertinent investigative information, may provide the pathologist with adequate information to satisfactorily resolve a case even without the actual examination of the deceased person. This approach might be employed in situations when there are no forensic concerns, other than a possible drug overdose (for which samples for toxicologic examination will presumably have been collected and preserved for analysis). For example, if a person dies after a week of hospitalization following an apparent drug overdose, with hospital drug screening consistent with the clinical course and diagnosis, the body of the deceased may not be autopsied. Further toxicology testing may still be requested if samples proximate to the day of hospital admission are available (or have been requested by the ME Office to be reserved for forensic analysis).

In cases where the decedent has a documented medical history, a terminal, or other recognized disease process that may reasonably have become fatal, and there are no concerns of foul play, the pathologist may choose to limit the examination to the outside of the body (variably called an external examination, view, inspection, etc.). An external examination may also be adequate when the decedent's treating physician is not available to sign the death certificate, there are no apparent forensic concerns, and the patient's medical history is well documented. Biological samples from the deceased can be collected and reserved for toxicologic examination if determined as warranted by the FP. As for other medical procedures, the decision whether to conduct an autopsy or limit the examination to the outside of the body is a medical one, which may vary by jurisdiction, personal experience, and administrative factors.

1.2.4 Autopsy Procedure

The autopsy procedure is a complex physical examination of the body, accompanied by written and photographic, and, occasionally, as necessary, radiologic documentation. The process begins with a thorough examination of the outside of the body followed by the evaluation of the internal tissues and organs. The usual autopsy procedure includes the examination of the head, the thorax, the abdomen, and the pelvic organs. Rarely, a partial autopsy will be performed, limiting the examination to one or several body regions, usually in response to an objection raised by the family of the deceased person. In any case, the nature and extent of any injury and natural diseases are noted and documented. Radiographs may also be obtained to assess for retained projectiles, medical devices, surgical hardware, fractures, accumulations of air or gas, or any other feature that may be of potential interest or relevance to the case. Radiographs are especially useful to capture and preserve images of portions of the body that will be altered during and as part of the autopsy process. Comparisons with antemortem images may then facilitate a positive identification of the decedent, if not already known. Clothing, personal effects, and medical devices (e.g. IV lines, tubes, leads and telemetry equipment, etc.) and their specific locations are documented (for hospital patients whose death has been deemed, as within the jurisdiction of the ME, all medical devices that are in place on the body at death are left intact).

After the assessment of the outside of the body, the pathologist examines the inside of the body, including the condition of the internal organs and tissues. During this process, the individual organs are removed, weighed, and examined. Gastric and intestinal contents are examined (pills or pill fragments can be recovered and reserved for analysis). Samples of body fluids and organs are taken and reserved for toxicologic, microbiologic, and microscopic analysis as necessary, per the discretion of the FP and standard practice of the office. Blood samples are also collected for genetic analysis for inherited conditions that may have significant implications for the family of the deceased person. Microbiological analysis can confirm or identify disease processes that may not be immediately apparent upon gross exam (e.g., viral pathogens, such as COVID-19; bacterial pneumonia; bacterial meningitis; sepsis). Microscopic analysis of tissue sections can allow the pathologist to identify diseases that are not evident grossly (e.g. myocarditis, dysplasia of the AV nodal artery, amyloidosis, and tuberculosis). Items of potential evidentiary value recovered during the process are retained, including medication patches (on or in the body), pills, tablets (or fragments), projectiles, bullets, etc. Indwelling devices, such as pacemakers/defibrillators and drug delivery systems, are removed at autopsy, photographed, and then evaluated by the manufacturer. Information obtained may assist in determining the cause and/or manner of death.

To many people, it may seem unnecessary to perform an autopsy where the cause and manner of death are apparently obvious, such as on victims of a drug overdose, motor vehicle accidents, or even gunshot wounds. However, there may be more questions or issues surrounding a particular case other than an apparent final mechanism. The autopsy process may provide unexpected or unanticipated information about pre-existing or underlying medical issues and the extent to which such conditions may have contributed to the death. Many cases have been initially expected to have been the consequence of a drug overdose, but upon autopsy, significant underlying disease (e.g., coronary artery stenosis) coupled with therapeutic levels of prescribed medications (as opposed to illicit drug use) has presented an alternate explanation for the death.

Similarly, toxicology testing can provide information about drugs that may have affected the decedent at the time of death, even to the point of being the major causative factor, despite such a potential role not being apparent or anticipated during the investigation and the autopsy. In this sense, routine toxicologic investigation provides a "safety net" ensuring that the FP will have all the pertinent information regarding a case, so that they may appropriately determine the cause and manner of death.

In many cases, the FP may not detect significant disease at autopsy and become suspicious that the cause and manner of death may be related to drugs present in the decedent. For example, in the case of an apparent drug overdose, the death may have been the consequence of an unusually concentrated dose or even contaminated illicit materials [e.g., highly concentrated heroin or mixture with a potent fentanyl analogueanalogue or a "club drug" containing unexpected (and toxic) byproducts of the drug synthesis procedure]. One of the more frequent, but unexpected findings in forensic medicine is the detection of apparently high levels of one or more prescription medications in the bloodstream of a person for whom they were (or not) prescribed. An apparent overdose of prescription medications may represent an inadvertent consequence of a prescribed dose, an effect on drug metabolism, or a conscious departure from the prescription regimen (e.g., in an abuse or suicide scenario). In motor vehicle crashes or other accidents, drugs found in the crash victim, and particularly the driver, may be significant with regard to considerations of impairment. A homicide victim may have been impaired or affected by drugs at the time of death, which may impact the interpretation of the event. The information that may be generated during a death investigation can have very significant legal consequences, depending on the nature of the case.

1.2.5 Autopsy Findings and Reports

The findings and opinions of the ME, including the autopsy and toxicology results, will be presented in a summary report detailing the assessment of cause and manner of death. That final report will be issued after all relevant examination results (including microscopic and toxicology testing) have been obtained and considered. Reports are routinely considered public records and are readily available (however, reports regarding homicide victims are generally available only after the case has been adjudicated). Governmental agencies directly involved in a case (e.g., law enforcement, prosecutor, and defense team) will have access to autopsy findings, toxicology results, photographs, and associated opinions. Autopsy findings and reports may also be used by medical services attempting to correlate clinical information with autopsy findings (e.g., hospital morbidity and mortality review panels). Autopsy reports are regularly requested by family members for resolution of insurance matters. This varied array of users necessitates that pathologists write reports in typical medical language with appropriate explanatory notes for specialized language or provide a distillation of findings in an "opinion" section, allowing people without specialized medical training to understand the findings and conclusions.

1.3 THE ROLE OF THE TOXICOLOGIST IN POSTMORTEM FORENSIC EXAMINATIONS

In many cases, the role that drugs or poisons may have played in a death represents an obvious and essential question and issue for the case FP and therefore requires a reliable analysis of samples collected at autopsy and, where present and appropriate, at the scene. Information regarding what drugs were present (and in some cases, absent) in the decedent can be a significant factor in facilitating the eventual determination of COD and MOD. In such cases, there may be extensive and specific toxicologic analysis and interpretation. When appropriate, final autopsy reports may be withheld until the analytical work is completed and interpreted. In many offices, there can be considerable interaction between the case FP and toxicologists, particularly when questions regarding the mechanism of action, interaction between drugs, and consideration of validity or utility of postmortem concentrations are important to the resolution of a case.

Cases in which drugs may have caused or contributed to the death can present unique and interesting challenges for forensic pathologists and toxicologists. The need for reliable chemical analysis of samples collected after death has long been a driving force within the field of toxicology, with a unique set of challenges that serve to make this subdiscipline a fascinating field in its own right. An understanding of the postmortem procedures (potentially including examination, autopsy, embalming, cremation), as well as the complex and chaotic process of decomposition to which the body may be subjected after death, is essential for the toxicologist to appreciate and fully use the information they provide and to communicate their findings in a useful manner to the case pathologist. It is also important for the toxicologist to understand that biochemical changes occurring in the postmortem interval may also impact their toxicologic findings, from the artifactual generation of target analytes [e.g., ethanol; γ-hydroxybutyric acid (GHB)] to the equilibration (postmortem redistribution) within the body of drugs that were concentrated in specific organs or tissues during life. Underlying the considerations of the potential for the effects of drugs on the body is the need for the toxicologist to have an understanding and appreciation for mechanisms of action of drugs, and the pharmacologic and physiologic processes leading to toxic mechanisms and consequences.

1.3.1 Samples and Sampling

With current analytical procedures and approaches, essentially, any body fluid or tissue could be utilized for toxicologic analysis; however, blood is the most commonly collected, reserved, and analyzed body fluid. There is a generalized (and commonly valid) expectation that levels of drugs in blood will correlate with the magnitude of pharmacologic/physiologic effects, and such levels provide the basis for the comparison of drug levels between cases. Tables of therapeutic, toxic, and potentially fatal blood concentrations along with monograph collections containing similar information can be of significant utility in evaluation of toxicologic data (with caveats discussed below; Section 1.4.2.) Standard practice for what specific samples are routinely collected for particular types of cases will vary somewhat with different offices and occasionally between different FPs but are nevertheless generally collected in a routine or standardized manner. As in all forensic processes, there is an expectation of clear and accurate sample labeling, documentation of chain of custody, and proper storage.

Blood is generally collected from either a central source (heart or large vessels close to the heart) or a peripheral source, one outside the central trunk of the body (usually the femoral vein as it is the largest vein distant from the central body organs). For toxicologic purposes, a peripheral collection site is generally preferred so as to avoid questions regarding postmortem redistribution (addressed in Section 2). The use of (even properly collected) heart or "central" blood for the determination of most drug levels is generally considered unreliable as an accurate reflection of antemortem levels due to the expectation of postmortem redistribution, (unless the sample has been collected quite proximate to the time of death). Occasionally, blood will be collected from the subclavian vein (located just beneath the clavicle or collarbone) and is often considered as "peripheral". However, while containing venous blood, the location of the vessel in the chest cavity makes it "central" from a toxicologic perspective. Some facilities routinely collect blood from both central and peripheral sites and may use central blood for screening purposes and peripheral blood for quantitative analysis. Standard practice in most offices is to collect blood for toxicologic analysis in "gray top" vacutainer tubes, containing sodium fluoride and sodium oxalate. The fluoride acts as an enzyme poison, minimizing metabolic degradation that might occur, and the oxalate acts as an anticoagulant. Samples maintained in gray top tubes may be valid for a considerable amount of time, particularly if refrigerated.

Heart blood may be collected through the intact skin or from the heart using a large bore needle and inserting it directly through the torso prior to autopsy. While blood samples may be readily obtained with this method, the specific sample site and integrity of the sample may be subject to question. Such blind taps may result in getting blood contaminated with fluid from the chest cavity, from within the pericardial sac, or even from the lumen of the esophagus. In some cases, "blood" from the chest cavity is collected for analysis. Such fluid is of questionable toxicologic value because of its undefined character but may be useful for screening. Other sample types may be collected routinely as a function of the practice of individual pathologists or ME Offices. Urine samples are collected in many offices via direct extraction from the bladder, by a suprapubic tap, or from a urinary bladder catheter pouch. Urine samples generally reflect drug exposure/use for days prior to the death, and while not reliably predictive of true antemortem drug concentrations, urine samples may provide useful information about the drugs in the body during life. Historically, some toxicologists have participated in sample collection; however, this practice is increasingly unusual, and most often, samples are collected by medical or morgue personnel.

Extensive tissue sampling and quantitative analysis of drugs used to be regularly performed as part of routine toxicologic examination, particularly in cases where drug overdose was suspected. A correlation between elevated drug levels in the blood and correspondingly high levels in tissues (primarily liver) was expected. However, in a case where the drug has only been present in the body for a relatively short time before death, there may not be adequate time for tissue levels to rise to those normally seen in overdoses of individuals who are acclimated or are otherwise regularly exposed to the drug. Most often collected and analyzed organs are liver, kidney, brain, spleen, and lung. While such analyses can provide useful and instructive information in many cases (particularly those that for one reason or another are challenging with regard to assessment of COD and MOD), most cases are resolved by qualitative and quantitative analysis of blood samples. Of tissues, the liver is probably the most commonly examined and often reflects the presence of drugs at concentrations considerably greater than that found in the blood, as a function of the active uptake of drugs, toxins, and xenobiotics in general by specific and active protein-based transport. Bile is occasionally collected and submitted for analysis; however, because of the mechanism of its generation, the ability of bile to be reflective of the drug composition is somewhat compromised (many relatively low-molecular-weight drugs are not significantly excreted in the bile). Bile can be somewhat viscous, and its analysis can require special treatment before it is introduced into an instrument. Similarly, samples of gastric contents can also be analyzed for ingested substances. Finally, vitreous humor (VH) can be a very useful sample, particularly with respect to alcohol-based or related deaths (e.g., motor vehicle crashes); in that, the concentration of drugs in general and alcohol, in particular, tends to lag somewhat behind the blood concentration and can therefore be a valuable sample from decedents in the early postmortem period (see Sidebar 1.3: Vitreous Humor Testing).

Sidebar 1.3: Vitreous Humor Testing

Vitreous humor VH, the viscous fluid in the eye, can be a particularly useful forensic sample due, in part, to its location in a somewhat protected space within the body and its source as an ultrafiltrate of blood. Vitreous humor is readily and routinely collected at autopsy using a small gauge needle and a 5 mL syringe. Vitreous humor samples can often be collected even in cases of severe trauma or from decedents with some degree of decomposition. Because of its location, drug concentrations present in VH are not likely to have been affected by postmortem redistribution and may reasonably be assumed to have been present in the blood at the time of death. Vitreous humor levels of ethanol lag in time somewhat behind the blood level, and this relationship is often used to infer whether an individual's blood alcohol concentration (BAC) was rising or falling at the time of death. Vitreous humor is also used as a "blood substitute" for blood chemistry for some analytes. While the levels of some analytes tested are reflective of antemortem levels, there are some whose concentrations are predictably different.

The circumstances of postmortem testing occasionally require that less-than-optimal sample materials be used, e.g., samples recovered from bodies in some stage of decomposition. In cases of suspected overdose, or those where there may be a question as to whether a drug had been present in overdose levels, tissue samples may also be analyzed. In such cases, either relatively low or high tissue levels might be significantly misleading, reflecting either drug loss (e.g., from microbial degradation) or drug concentration (e.g., as a function of desiccation). It is generally understood that quantitative results in even early decomposition may be reflective of significant uncertainty, and drawing any inference beyond simply the presence or absence of a particular drug would be expected to be accompanied by an adequate and clear justification. As the decomposition processes proceed, the potential for misinterpretation of any quantitative information correspondingly increases. In essence, toxicologic results from decomposed samples should generally be considered as providing information regarding only the presence of the drug, and hence antemortem use, rather than any quantitative inference, or utilization of such result to determine a toxic level (or indeed, lack thereof).

1.3.2 Scope of Testing

Postmortem toxicology testing is driven by need, standard practice, case circumstance, and case-relevant available information. Most offices utilize a standard menu or panel for routine analysis of postmortem samples with the extent of testing determined by the type of case. Within the toxicology laboratory, samples are commonly screened and tested in batch processes for efficiency. If a case warrants a particular analysis that is not part of the usual practice, the laboratory either performs it "a la carte" or arranges for the analysis to be performed at an outside ("reference") laboratory.

Testing in most laboratories utilizes a combination of broad-spectrum screening procedures, usually immunologically based, followed by, as necessary and appropriate, specific confirmatory procedures that are usually performed as quantitative analyses, utilizing high performance liquid chromatography (HPLC)- or gas chromatography (GC)–mass spectrometry (MS) instrumentation (discussed in Section 2). Many laboratories are increasingly shifting to newer analytical instrumentation that allows mass spectrometry methodologies to be incorporated in the "screening" stages, thereby increasing the scope and reliability of such testing (Table 1.1).

Table 1.1 Generalized Toxicology Approaches, Based on Autopsy Protocol and Case Circumstances

"View" no autopsy deemed necessary	Alcohol+Immunoassay Screen [Screen positive results may or may not be confirmed, depending on case specifics]
Autopsy, no expectation of drug/pharmaceutical involvement	Alcohol+Immunoassay Screen [Screen positive results may or may not be confirmed, depending on case specifics]
Autopsy, suspicion of drug/pharmaceutical involvement, unspecified	Alcohol+Immunoassay Screen General Drug Screen; confirmatory unspecified procedures as appropriate
Autopsy, suspicion of drug/pharmaceutical involvement, specific target analytes identified	Alcohol+Immunoassay Screen General Drug Screen; Confirmatory procedures as appropriate Specific confirmatory procedures as appropriate

In many cases, there may be specific questions regarding whether or not the patient had either overdosed on or, in contrast, failed to take medication(s) as prescribed. In such circumstances, specific quantitative analysis, and a clear understanding of the potential uncertainties associated with the results, can be crucial to the eventual determination by the FP.

As an example, consider a 55-year-old woman who suffered a sudden collapse and died. Her past medical history included chronic obstructive pulmonary disease, hypertension, depression, and schizophrenia, as well as illicit drug use. Routine medications include clozapine, citalopram, and lorazepam. Expected results (assuming a cardiac-related death) would be negative alcohol, positive immunoassay screen for benzodiazepines (all others negative), both clozapine and citalopram levels within therapeutic levels on an HPLC- or GC–MS-based "General Drug Screen." (To the extent that recreational drugs may have been present, the relevant immunoassay screen positive results would be confirmed, with quantitative analysis, allowing the FP to evaluate the potential for such analytes to have played a causative or contributory role in the death.) Any significant departure from the expected results would reasonably result in the re-evaluation of the death in light of the toxicologic findings.

1.4 CHALLENGES AND CONFOUNDERS OF POSTMORTEM TESTING

The problems and difficulties that can arise with the analysis of biological samples for postmortem testing are easily divided into two general categories: analytical and interpretive. Clearly, the ability to detect and accurately quantitate drugs in the postmortem setting is an essential and limiting factor in the use of toxicology findings to facilitate an understanding of the cause and manner of death. However, equally important is recognition of the potential uncertainties and limitations associated with those determinations when trying to explain or understand antemortem behavior, based on results from postmortem samples. In essence, the ability to quite reliably acquire an understanding of what drugs are present in a compromised or questionable sample, even coupled with accurate quantitative results, might not make a sample any more useful than simply as an indicator that a drug was present or absent.

1.4.1 Analytical Challenges

The analytical challenges faced by the forensic toxicologist tend to be primarily a function of the nature and/or the amount of sample available for analysis rather than the availability of reliable methodology for the detection and quantitation of a particular species. In many cases, there is an ample supply of blood, urine, and even vitreous fluid such that multiple tests can be run with confirmatory procedures as necessary, particularly with increasingly sensitive analytical instrumentation available to the toxicology laboratory. Often, postmortem samples are in excellent condition, having been collected shortly after death, or are hospital-derived antemortem samples. Samples routinely arrive in the laboratory in appropriate tubes for preservation (e.g., fluoride/oxalate "gray tops"), are not hemolyzed, and are of sufficient quantity. However, the nature of postmortem work is such that some samples are less than perfect. Most laboratories will attempt analyses on samples that may be challenging, recognizing that the information that may be gained could be of significant value to the investigating pathologist.

Postmortem samples can be of limited volume because the patient had very little obtainable intravascular blood (e.g., small pediatric patients, patients in hemorrhagic shock). Samples can also be of undefined composition (e.g., fluid collected from decomposed or partially decomposed bodies) or significantly contaminated by nonbiological materials. Such samples may not behave in the extraction and analytical schemes as well as the typical sample materials or as the corresponding control materials used. Occasionally, only tissue samples are available, and they may not be of a consistency that is easily handled (e.g., desiccated, decomposed, or otherwise degraded), or the only samples available have been collected from an embalmed body. While "less-than-optimal" samples can be analyzed, there may be questions regarding the degree to which target analytes are extracted from compromised sample materials. It is the responsibility of the testing facility to clearly communicate any unusual level of uncertainty in the analytical process due to the sample conditions to the FP. [see Sidebar 1.4: Embalmed Remains with Subdural Hematoma (SDH)].

Sidebar 1.4: Embalmed Remains with Subdural Hematoma

Toxicologic analysis of SDH has traditionally been used as an indication of antemortem drug levels, including for ethanol and other alcohols. Drugs and alcohol in SDH are contained in a somewhat protected space in the body; sequestered from the intact circulation; and, as such, are less subject to metabolism than drugs in circulation. In the early postmortem

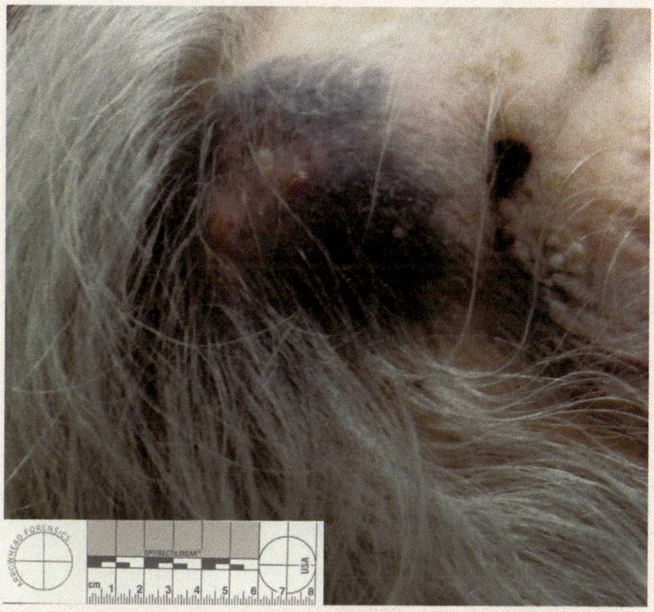

Figure 1.1 A purple contusion two inch in diameter associated with intense subcutaneous edema and ecchymosis located on the right side of the forehead.

period, drugs in the SDH are less exposed to enzymatic degradation than drugs in the intravascular blood. Analytical findings derived from hematomata are therefore presumed to more closely resemble drug or alcohol concentrations at the time of formation of the clot (during the traumatic event) than those determined from postmortem blood, especially when the patient has survived for some period of time. We have reported a case of an elderly woman whose death had not been reported to the coroner's office until after her body had been embalmed. She had received palliative care at the time of her demise for debilitating cardiovascular disease. Approximately two weeks following the initiation of the "Do Not Resuscitate-Comfort Care Only" order, she was found next to her bed by nursing staff during morning rounds. She reported to them that she had fallen from her bed and struck her head on the bedside table. The fall resulted in a scalp hematoma and a contusion on her right knee. Nursing staff helped her back to bed, and family members arrived at the facility, stayed with her, and requested an evaluation for hospice care. Later that day, she became somnolent, eventually completely unresponsive, and expired shortly thereafter. The attending nurse was initially unaware that the fall from her bed was a situation that was required to be reported to the coroner's office. This error was corrected several days later, and her embalmed body was retrieved for autopsy.

Gross autopsy examination of the decedent revealed significant hypertensive cardiovascular disease as well as a traumatic brain injury with an SDH causing a mass effect. The most significant findings at autopsy were related to the decedent's fall on the day of her death, which included a 2 inch (5 cm) in diameter purple contusion associated with intense subcutaneous edema and ecchymosis on the right side of the forehead (Figure 1.1). This injury was associated with a 6 inch (15.2 cm) in diameter subgaleal and subcutaneous hemorrhage (see Figure 1.2) and an ~250 mL SDH compressing the brain by 1–1/2 inches (4 cm) from right to left. The hematoma was acute, composed of coagulated, gelatinous, blue-red blood that was not adherent to the dura. The surface was light-reflecting, and there was no evidence of organization. Interestingly, the SDH appeared similar to those observed in

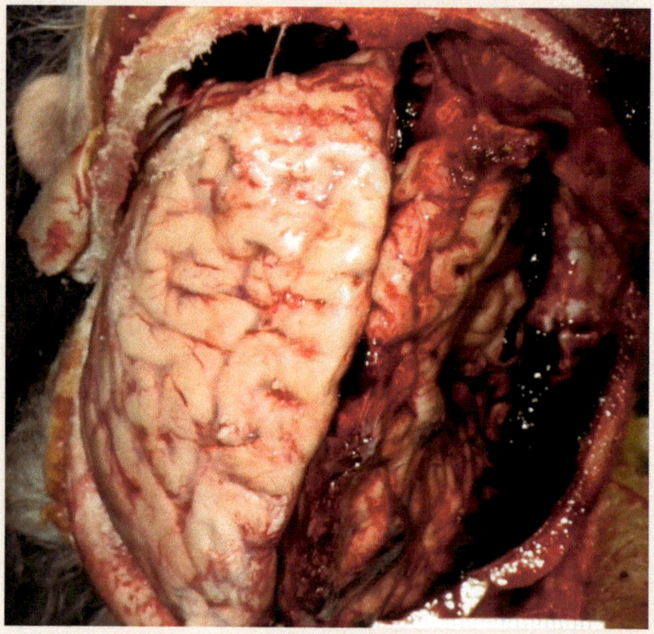

Figure 1.2 An ~250 mL SDH compressing the brain by 4 cm from right to left, as viewed from behind with the skull cap removed.

unembalmed decedents and had not apparently been perfused by embalming fluid (despite the well-embalmed appearance of the rest of the body, with body organs and tissues, including the brain, firm throughout). The brain was markedly edematous, with flattened gyri and narrowed sulci. The cerebellar tonsils were herniated. The right lateral ventricle was completely compressed. The left lateral ventricle and the remaining ventricular system were markedly narrowed. Multiple small contusions of the head, face, chest, and extremities were noted, consistent with her reported single fall event.

1.4.2 Interpretive Challenges

One important issue, or concern, in the field of forensic toxicology is the potential for inaccurate conclusions to have been drawn regarding antemortem drug levels based on postmortem drug level analyses. Perhaps the main problem that has been recognized over the last several decades is "Postmortem Redistribution". When PMR has occurred, drugs that have become concentrated in tissues during life diffuse away from such tissues in the postmortem interval, resulting in artifactually high drug levels in blood samples drawn proximate to the organs. The results would not be reflective of true antemortem blood concentrations. The potential for erroneous conclusions to be drawn regarding COD and MOD are obvious. (How and why PMR occurs is addressed in Sidebar 1 of Section 2.)

Second (and also a potentially compounding problem with PMR) is the application of toxicokinetic calculations to postmortem values. These calculations generally take two forms: the first being an extrapolation from postmortem values to antemortem levels and the second being a calculation or attempt to determine if the "amount of drug" administered serves to explain either the postmortem levels or the levels expected to have been present at time of death. While the calculations and kinetic parameters underlying these processes are clearly well established and relied upon in the realm of clinical toxicology, historically, there has been a failure to appreciate the extent to which uncertainty or variability in key underlying assumptions will affect the magnitude (and even overall applicability of the calculations) when applied to postmortem circumstances. In short, while the calculations themselves may be quite good and accurate, the uncertainty associated with those calculations, and in particular the values upon which they are based, may be of such magnitude as to render them useless. On the other hand, toxicologists must be cognizant that there may indeed be cases in which PM toxicokinetic calculations can provide reasonably reliable values with which to assist the FP with the determination of COD and MOD. Neither blanket acceptance nor rejection of toxicokinetic calculations reflects a reasoned scientific evaluation of the data and the case circumstances. What is called for on the part of the forensic toxicologist is a reasoned, justified consideration of the variables and assumptions underlying a particular case and an equally reasoned evaluation of the uncertainty associated with any final value, or range thereof, to be communicated to the case FP.

1.4.2.1 Decomposed Samples

Decomposition of the decedent poses additional complications regarding the toxicologic analysis and interpretation, depending on the extent and circumstances of the process. Obviously, in such cases, the supply of usable specimens may be limited, and the composition of samples can be significantly different from those normally analyzed. Blood from deceased people who are slightly or moderately decomposed can be more viscous than blood obtained from a decedent in the early postmortem period. Blood from decomposed sources is also usually hemolyzed, and intracellular components released into the liquid portion of blood can interfere with some analyses (particularly enzymatic-based alcohol or immunologic drug screen analyses, but generally not HPLC- or GC–MS-based confirmatory analyses). Microbial metabolism can produce chemicals adding to the potential for matrix effects affecting target drug analysis, and the appearance of microbial metabolic products can be difficult to interpret in some circumstances. Drug residues that are actually present may be diminished due to microbial activity or concentrated due to dehydration (which may lead to artificially high and potentially misleading drug levels) (see Sidebar 1.5: Ethanol in Decomposed Cases). In a practical sense, any inference beyond the identification of the drugs present may be questionable, and further, the absence of expected or suspected drugs may not be reliably indicative that a particular drug had not been administered or used.

Sidebar 1.5: Ethanol in Decomposed Remains

Ethanol can be produced in significant amounts during the process of decomposition by bacterial fermentation of native sugars, and levels in excess of 0.1 g/dL have been reported. Because ethanol is water soluble and not specifically concentrated in any tissue, it is generally not subject to postmortem redistribution, and a central blood sample (e.g., from the heart) would be expected to provide a result as valid as one drawn from a peripheral source. An antemortem concentration of ethanol in the stomach can, however, provide a reservoir from which postmortem redistribution can occur. In practical terms, microbial production of ethanol via fermentation or other processes will also produce other short-chain alcohols and aldehydes, and a characteristic pattern of products of decomposition can be readily recognized via headspace GC. Nevertheless, attempts to distinguish between antemortem ingestion and postmortem production of ethanol in decomposed remains must be carefully considered. While such a distinction may be important for the determination of cause and manner of death, and perhaps to answer ancillary questions, the inherent uncertainty in the process is considerable, and a strong opinion should be accompanied by corroborative analysis of a VH sample if possible.

1.4.2.2 Pediatric Cases

The pediatric population is recognized as representing the potential for significant challenges for the toxicology community. In essence, the pharmacologic parameters associated with drugs in adults cannot automatically be applied to children as if they were merely miniature adults. While drug absorption, distribution, metabolism, and elimination follow the same general patterns in children, the rates of these processes can vary significantly from the adult. The adage "children are not just small adults," popularized by toxicologists with extensive experience in this area, is particularly apt, and care should be taken in drawing any conclusions regarding drug levels in the pediatric population when using toxicologic parameters developed from an adult population. Neonates and children generally have a higher percentage of body water than adults and, as such, may have a slightly different volume of distribution for some drugs as they would for adults. Likewise, protein binding can be less in children than in adults, yielding a higher active (free, unbound) drug concentration in circulation than would be found in an adult with a similar weight-based dose, potentially resulting in greater tissue uptake. Metabolism of many drugs occurs primarily in the liver, catalyzed by cytochrome P450 and similar enzymes. In children, the expression of these various metabolizing systems may not be at the levels expected in adults, resulting in significantly slower elimination rates than would be expected in the adult population. Neonates and infants generally have a lower glomerular filtration rate (GFR) than do adults, and drugs eliminated by the kidney may have a lower elimination rate than expected in adults. Neonatal GFR is only about 50% of that of adults but usually approaches adult rates by the end of the first year of life.

An adage that might be helpful for both pathologists and toxicologists in the consideration of such cases is "pathology trumps toxicology" with the interpretation that the totality of the medical evidence in a case, including medical history and records, clinical parameters, and autopsy findings, will often provide the best information as to the physiological processes that had occurred in the child. An understanding of the mechanism of action of a drug or mix of drugs in a case may help inform consideration of clinical and pathological findings, which are, ultimately, the expression of toxicity.

1.4.2.3 Geriatric Cases

The geriatric population also presents issues for the toxicologist to consider regarding the interpretation of drug levels. As with the pediatric population, the same basic pharmacologic processes continue to operate in older patients as in adults; however, rates of such processes may be affected as organs become less efficient as a function of the normal aging process or are otherwise affected by the disease. Often, older adults can have digestive issues resulting in either rapid or slow absorption of drugs. Elderly patients often have a lower percentage of muscle mass and body water and a higher percentage of body fat. Drugs that are primarily lipophilic will have an effectively lower volume of distribution for these patients. Liver function may be impaired leading to significant effects on metabolism and elimination. Elderly people more commonly have some degree of compromised kidney function, with a reduced GFR, leading to a longer drug half-life and blood concentration for some drugs. The geriatric population is also apt to be prescribed more medications than younger adults, complicating interpretation of toxicologic findings and raising the potential for drug–drug interactions. The relatively large doses of analgesics that may be used in the hospice setting, particularly in the hours proximate to death, may also raise concerns and issues in some cases. As such, in some laboratories, postmortem opiate levels in patients receiving palliative care are reported without quantitative values.

1.4.2.4 Embalmed, Entombed, or Buried Remains

Occasionally, questions will arise regarding a death for which the only logical recourse is a reexamination of the body or examination of a body that has been buried. In such cases, the body may be disinterred and autopsied (or re-autopsied), and new samples may be collected for toxicologic analysis. During the embalming process, venous blood is withdrawn from the body via a catheter that has been inserted into the vascular system, while, at the same time, embalming fluid is injected, replacing much of the intravascular blood. Embalming fluid may also be injected into the organs of the torso via a trocar. Following some period of equilibration, the fluid that may be collected during a reexamination, or re-autopsy, can, due to the presence of heme compounds, look like blood and may be presumed to be so by a laboratory in the absence of proper identification. Such misinterpretation has occurred in more than one laboratory. Interpretation of "blood" ethanol can then be problematic, depending on the nature of the embalming fluid utilized (many embalming formulations contain some percentage of ethanol). However, within the toxicology laboratory, the appearance of methanol, isopropanol, and acetone in addition to ethanol is considered strongly suggestive of an embalmed body.

The analysis of "blood" and body tissues from embalmed remains can pose a serious problem for the toxicology laboratory. Many laboratories will decline to analyze samples from embalmed bodies, but occasionally a case may arise where the simple demonstration that a particular drug or poison was present can provide useful forensic information. However, in such circumstances, the failure to demonstrate a drug is not necessarily definitive proof that the drug had not been present. During the embalming process, drugs or volatile compounds present in the blood and vascular system are effectively removed, and some degree of extraction of drugs from tissues can be reasonably expected. However, following the completion of the process, some degree of re-equilibration would be expected, as drugs remaining in the tissues diffuse into the fluid remaining in the body, (as somewhat of a variation of the postmortem redistribution process). Analytical procedures then performed on samples derived from an embalmed body, while potentially qualitatively useful, will have a considerable uncertainty associated with any quantitative drug findings, and any inferences based on the concentration of drugs in such cases are likely to be meaningless at best, and significantly misleading at worst.

Bibliography

Britannica. (27 September 2007). The Editors of Encyclopedia. "Coroner". *Encyclopedia Britannica.* https://www.britannica.com/topic/coroner. Accessed 23 March 2021.

DiMaio V., DiMaio D. (2001). *Forensic Pathology*. 2nd ed. Boca Raton, FL: CRC Press.

Dolinak D., Matches E., Lew E. (2005). *Forensic Pathology Principles and Practice*. New York: Elsevier.

Knight B. (1996). *Forensic Pathology*. 2nd ed. London: Arnold.

Powers R.H., Criss B.E., Topmiller R.G., Dean D.E. (2019). Methanol detected in a subdural hematoma as an embalming artifact. *Journal of Forensic Sciences*, 64(3):946–949.

SECTION 2

PRACTICAL FORENSIC TOXICOLOGY

DOI: 10.4324/9781003121060-3

2.1 INTRODUCTION

The very basic question for the toxicology laboratory regarding postmortem investigations is quite straightforward: "what drugs were present, and at what concentration?" Some level of toxicologic analysis on samples collected from decedents is nearly automatic in most medical examiner (ME) offices, certainly for whom an autopsy is performed and often for those for whom only the outside of the body is examined. When there is no expectation or reasonable probability that drugs or alcohol were involved in the death, minimally, perfunctory screening to rule out an unexpected overdose or intoxication will often be performed. In contrast, for cases in which there is a reasonable expectation or concern that a person may have died from a drug overdose or that there may have been some contribution to the death by underlying medications or abused drugs, a more comprehensive screen or panel may be requested. Cases, where either compliance or lack thereof, with a particular prescription regimen may be an important factor (e.g., anti-seizure medications, anti-clotting agents, medication-assisted drug therapy for opioid dependence, etc.) will often receive comprehensive toxicologic analysis, including the quantitative analysis of key target analytes. Finally, the forensic pathologist (FP) may deal with a case in which a particular toxic agent is suspected to have been present, and if it is not part of a regular toxicologic panel, that drug may then become the target for specific analysis (e.g., anti-hypertensives, gamma-hydroxybutyrate (GHB), carfentanyl, etc.). The need for the FP to make a judgment regarding the specific analytical requirements regarding casework emphasizes the need for good communication between the toxicology lab and the autopsy suite. The vast bulk of postmortem toxicologic analyses are relatively straightforward, with no need for input from the toxicology laboratory to the FP, except for the accurate and reliable reporting of the identification and quantitation (as appropriate) of drugs or other compounds, be they many, few, or even absent.

2.2 ANALYTICAL CAPABILITY

The analytical capabilities of toxicology laboratories have consistently expanded and improved over the last several decades, primarily as a function of the increased capabilities of gas-chromatography/mass spectrometry (GC–MS)-based methods; more recently, with the increased utilization of high-performance liquid chromatographic (HPLC)–MS methods; and combined instrumentation, such as triple-quadrupole MS instruments, with either GC or HPLC "front ends." Further, the increased availability of "Time of Flight" instruments, providing "exact mass" capability, also improves the ease with which analytes new to the laboratory may be specifically identified. As such, the reliable detection and quantitative analysis of low-molecular-weight organic molecules (e.g., drugs and toxins), while presenting worthy analytical challenges requiring capable instrumentation, techniques, and analysts, are nevertheless readily available for nearly all the target analytes that would be of interest or concern in the forensic setting. Such capability, coupled with the potential for rapid "screening" of samples, can provide the FP with both a quick idea of what drugs/drug groups might be present in a case; and then, ultimately, a specific identification of what drugs were present; and in what concentration – at least in the sample tested.

The degree to which quantitative values in postmortem samples may be indicative of antemortem values (or not…!) can be critically important for the FP and is discussed further in Section 2.6, below. There will occasionally arise some cases in which a particular analyte is suspected to be present, for which the toxicology laboratory does not have a validated "ready to go" assay. This is not particularly unusual, as several drug/drug groups are easily modified such that new, potentially active species can be introduced into the drug market (e.g., tryptamines, cathinones, methamphetamine, and fentanyl analogueanalogues). Nevertheless, the capability of the field is such that the methodology, in terms of published analytical methods, is readily available as adaptations or modifications of existing methodology for nearly all compounds likely to be encountered in postmortem work. Even as newly synthesized analogueanalogues of current drugs are encountered, analytical methods are quickly promulgated among the forensic toxicology community. Depending on the needs and time considerations of a particular case, samples can either be sent to a reference laboratory, or standard materials can be acquired by the laboratory to facilitate the analysis following validation of methodology. While there are some compounds for which there is no reasonable expectation of postmortem detection, (e.g., succinyl choline), because of rapid disappearance in the body, it is a reasonable expectation for FPs to be able to count on the ability of their toxicology resources to provide valid qualitative and quantitative analysis of nearly every potentially toxic agent that would be routinely encountered in death investigations.

2.2.1 Alcohol Analysis

The analysis of alcohol in blood or other biological samples is quite straightforward and routine in forensic toxicology laboratories, most commonly performed with headspace gas chromatography using flame ionization detectors. Increasingly, laboratories are using mass spectrometers as a detection system, with the advantage that definitive identification of other, perhaps unexpected, analytes (e.g. "huffing" agents, or other inhaled volatiles) can readily be achieved. This capability can also be of particular utility when there are questions regarding the extent to which a decedent may be decomposed or the sample contains fermentation products or even compounds reflecting ketoacidosis. In contrast, most hospital laboratories utilize enzyme-based methods with serum samples which may also be used in some toxicology laboratories as screening methods prior to GC-based analysis. While such serum values require conversion to "whole blood" concentrations for legal purposes, the accuracy of the analysis is only slightly less than provided by GC-based methodologies. This testing is based on a quantitative assay using enzyme-mediated oxidation of alcohol as the basis of the assay and, as such, is significantly more reliable than the immunologically based drug screening commonly also performed in the hospital laboratory environment. Another important point to note regarding alcohol testing is that because of the manner in which alcohol is distributed throughout the body (in body water), there is no antemortem accumulation in any specific tissue, and, as such, postmortem redistribution is not a significant concern [with the exception of unabsorbed material in the stomach/upper gastrointestinal (GI) tract]. The significance and consideration of alcohol findings in the postmortem environment are discussed in Section 4: Alcohol and Related Compounds.

2.2.2 Immunoassay-based Screening

Many laboratories employ the same type of enzymatically based drug screening methodology as is used in hospitals, employment, and other environments where a relatively quick, non-quantitative value can be of use. Such testing is most commonly done on urine in hospitals and, as such, is not necessarily indicative of drugs or concentrations thereof in the blood at the time of collection. Screening procedures can be adapted to whole blood, and a particular type of assay (Enzyme-linked Immunosorbent Assay "ELISA") works particularly well with the whole blood and other fluid samples associated with postmortem samples. Screening testing is based on antibody-mediated binding to the target drug, which then either activates or inactivates an enzyme system with a color-developing end point. Specific components for the immunoassay screen in ME laboratories are usually adjusted to reflect the commonly encountered pharmaceuticals and drugs of abuse in that geographic region. While assays for many drugs or drug groups are available, common components found in screening panels could include:

1. Amphetamine (/methamphetamine).
2. Barbiturates (group).
3. Benzodiazepines (group).
4. Carisoprodol(/meprobamate).
5. Cannabinoids(/THC, cannabidiol, -carboxylic acid).
6. Cocaine(/benzoylecgonine).
7. Fentanyl.
8. Methadone.
9. Opiates (/morphine, codeine, 6-monoacetylmorphine).
10. Oxycodone (/hydrocodone).
11. Phencyclidine (PCP).
12. Tricyclic antidepressants (amitriptyline, etc.).

There are three significant drawbacks to the application of immunologically based screen testing to postmortem work: the potential for false positives, the limitation of screen panels to a defined set of drugs or drug groups, and (when used in a hospital setting) the use of urine as the tested sample. While drug screen results can provide useful information in many settings, both as stand-alone information and as a guide for further confirmation or other testing, it is important to understand the limitations and uncertainties associated with such tests.

Immunologically based screening is based on a reaction to the size and shape of the target molecule, and, as such, "false positive" results can be generated. The likelihood of a positive result being the consequence of the presence of a molecule similar to, but distinct from, the target analyte varies considerably among the various screens. So, as an example, a positive screen result in a cocaine assay is much less likely to be a consequence of an interfering compound than an amphetamine positive result simply because of the complex shape of the cocaine molecule, in contrast to the similarity of amphetamine to a number of other phenylethylamine-related compounds (many of which are neurotransmitters, or analogueanalogues thereof). As such, it is not at all uncommon for screen results to be characterized as "reliable negatives", but "maybe" positives in the absence of confirmation by a more robust method, e.g. GC–MS or HPLC–MS.

While there are a large number of screening assays available, practicality limits the extent to which such testing is applied to casework. The utilization of immunoassays on the common drugs and drug groups does provide a rapid and efficient means of elimination of the need for more complex, time-consuming, and labor-intensive testing in many cases. As long as the FP remains cognizant of the inherent limitations of screen panels and is prepared to request additional testing as may be warranted in specific cases, the combination of immunoassay screen and other analytical methods represents an efficient and adequate approach to postmortem toxicology. Unfortunately, it is not uncommon for "negative" screen results to be interpreted as indicating that no drugs were present in the sample at all. The commonly used screen panel, in both hospital and postmortem laboratory settings, effectively covers many of the commonly encountered pharmaceuticals and abused drugs; however, this approach is by no means comprehensive. In the circumstance of a negative drug screen result in a case where an overdose of some drug is a possibility (or suspected to some extent), generalized drug screening protocols utilizing GC– or HPLC–MS methods, capable of detecting many thousands of drugs, might better be utilized.

A final point worth noting regarding screening assays is that screen testing in the hospital setting is commonly performed on urine samples and is not subjected to the quantitative confirmatory analyses that characterize forensic analyses. Positive results of urine sample screen may be reflective of drug usage within the last 3 days or so for most drugs, (e.g., cocaine, opiates, etc.), with positive results for tetrahydrocannabinol (THC) and related compounds detectable in urine for ~5 days, or even longer in some cases. As such, urine screen results may not be of use in evaluation of the role a particular drug may have played in a fatality.

2.2.3 GC– or HPLC–MS Screening

Preparation and analysis of a sample via GC– or HPLC–MS is considerably more time-consuming and labor-intensive than the batched immunoassay screening methods. However, the trade-off allows a much more comprehensive screen to be employed, with the basis for identification of an unusual, or new drug to the laboratory, being a matching algorithm with one of several libraries covering many thousands of compounds. Based on such identification, a drug suspected to be present in a case can be procured (if not already in the stocks of the laboratory), calibrators and controls can be prepared, and the sample can be re-analyzed and compared to the known material, thereby allowing a definitive identification and accurate quantitation. Modern forensic libraries (e.g., National Institute of Standards and Technology (NIST), Scientific Working Group for Seized Drug Analysis (SWGDRUG)) are consistently updated with information regarding new and developed drugs from around the world, allowing the tentative identification of drugs relatively new to a region to be quickly and reliably identified. Over the last several years, there has been an increased interest in and adaptation of tandem mass-spectropmetric techniques (MS-MS), with either high performance liquid chromatography (HPLC) or –gas chromatography (GCproviding the separation of analytical components for postmortem work. It would not be unreasonable to expect that the capabilities of this type of methodology will continue to expand and improve.

2.2.4 GC– or HPLC–MS Confirmation; Qualitative and Quantitative Analysis

The standard practice for quantitative analysis is based on the use of MS methods, with gas or liquid chromatograph (GC or LC) providing some degree of analyte separation prior to the MS stage, hence "GCMS" or "LCMS". Instruments utilizing multiple MS sections (MS–MS or MS^n techniques) can provide significantly enhanced sensitivity and selectivity.

Regardless of the "front end" of the instrument (GC or LC), analyte-specific procedures can be dedicated to several species (e.g., cocaine and benzoylecgonine, or opiates) and generally result is enhanced sensitivity for the targeted analytes. The combination of instrumental retention time and characteristic mass spectrum (molecular fragmentation pattern and ratios), when compared with reference standards, provides a rigorous basis for qualitative identification (see Figure 2.1). The process then is based on two separate physical properties: the overall size and shape and the electrical configuration of the molecule, leading to interaction with the chromatographic column (reflected as retention time) and the internal bond structure, leading to a characteristic fragmentation pattern and generation of specific ions in a particular ratio. The probability that two different complex molecules (that are not an optical isomeric pair) would generate identical results in such a system is exceedingly small (see Figure 2.2).

Quantitative analysis is a function of the inclusion of appropriate matrix-based calibrators and proper controls of the specific analyte to allow reporting. Certified laboratories will have

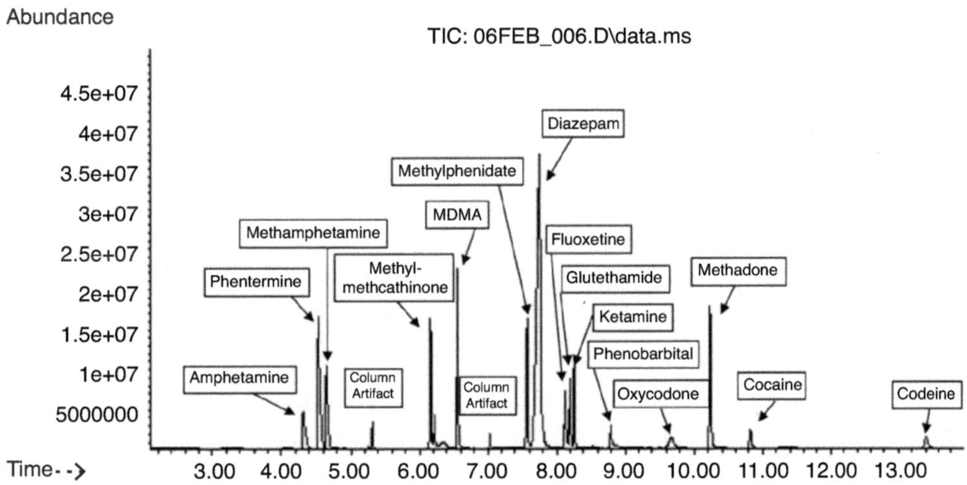

Figure 2.1 Total ion chromatogram (TIC) of a mix of drug standards.

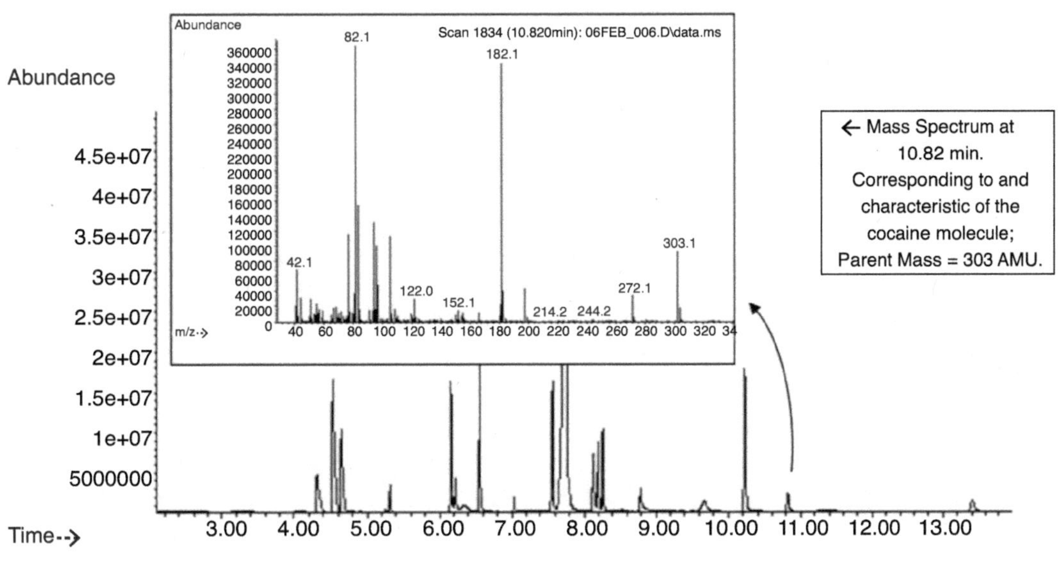

Figure 2.2 Total ion chromatogram (TIC) of a mix of drug standards with the expanded mass spectrum at 10.82 min., corresponding to cocaine.

Table 2.1 Example GC–MS Quantitative Batch

1. Procedure blank calibrator
2. Calibrator 1 (LOQ calibrator; 5 ng/mL cocaine, 25 ng/mL benzoylecgonine)
3. Calibrator 2 (10 ng/mL cocaine, 50 ng/mL benzoylecgonine)
4. Calibrator 3 (25 ng/mL cocaine, 100 ng/mL benzoylecgonine)
5. Calibrator 4 (50 ng/mL cocaine, 250 ng/mL benzoylecgonine)
6. Calibrator 5 (100 ng/mL cocaine, 500 ng/mL benzoylecgonine)
7. Calibrator 6 (250 ng/mL cocaine, 1000 ng/mL benzoylecgonine)
8. Solvent blank
9. Control 1 (target: 40 ng/mL cocaine, 200 ng/mL benzoyllecgonine)
10. Control 2 (target: 200 ng/mL cocaine, 800 ng/mL benzoyllecgonine)
11. Solvent blank
12. Sample 1 (Dilution: 1:1 (each sample dilution determined by screen result))

13–21. Sample 2–10, (with appropriate dilution)

22. Solvent blank
23. Control 1 (40/200)
24. Procedure blank

extensively validated procedures for the analysis of any reportable analytes and should be able to clearly explain both the basis for any qualitative and quantitative finding, as well as the quality control (QC) results obtained during the analysis, providing the basis for acceptance of the analytical results. An example batch for the analysis of 10 suspected cocaine samples, with associated QC criteria, is detailed in Table 2.1:

Quality control considerations for GC–MS or HPLC–MS quantitative analyses are extensive and rigorous. Any method utilized in an accredited laboratory will have been subjected to extensive validation, including the determination of the limit of detection (LOD; the lowest level at which the drug may be identified), the limit of quantitation (LOQ; the lowest level at which the drug may be consistently and reliably quantitated) (further validated by the lowest calibrator, often considered to functionally define the LOQ for a particular batch), the upper limit of linearity (ULOL), and the upper limit of quantitation (ULOQ; again, usually, functionally defined as the value of the highest calibrator). Quality control for the batch includes linearity of the standard curve, the degree of correspondence of each calibrator with the theoretical value calculated at that point, and the agreement of each control with its theoretical value (and defined acceptable range, usually ±20%). Correct qualitative identification of target analytes is evaluated by GC retention time (usually ±5%) and the correct spectra for the analyte, with either multiple characteristic peaks and peak ratios being utilized in a "full spectrum" mode, or one quantitative ion, and two qualitative ions necessarily being present, and in the correct ratios (as established by the batch calibrators). GC–MS batches, with their quality control parameters, are evaluated by the instrument operator and also reviewed by an additional analyst, the "Technical Reviewer", prior to being considered reportable.

2.2.5 Metals Analysis

While metals have played significant roles in forensic toxicology cases historically, most of the species encountered in forensic toxicology laboratories are organic in nature. The analytical capability for the analysis of metals at physiologically significant levels antedated the MS-based methodologies so commonly utilized currently; nevertheless, it is extremely unusual for a laboratory to have modern instrumentation for metal analysis, e.g. atomic absorption (AA) or ion-coupled plasma-based (ICP) instruments. There is of course the potential for metals to be significant in postmortem analyses, and metal-screening procedures are readily available at environmental or forensic reference laboratories. Modern screening procedures are usually based on ICP–MS techniques and are able to readily identify and provide quantitative information regarding all the metal species that might be of interest to the FP in a particular case.

2.2.6 Macromolecules

The methodologies routinely employed in forensic laboratories are generally focused and are the most efficient with target analytes of relatively small molecular weights. However, with the increased appearance of HPLC–MS triple quadrupole units, as well as "Time-of-Flight" mass spectrometers, the upper mass limitation of routine laboratory instrumentation has increased considerably. As such, the capability for forensic laboratories to engage in the analysis of molecules of >~600 amu is enhanced, and the analysis of relatively large toxic species will increasingly continue to be a regular process in forensic laboratories.

2.3 ROUTINE PANELS

Many ME offices utilize standard "routine" immunologically based drug screen testing panels for postmortem cases, as noted in Section 2.2.2, depending on the expectation of the investigating FP. A full, comprehensive search for drugs in all cases may not be the best use of limited laboratory and personnel resources and may not even be warranted, depending on case circumstances.

In cases where there is a concern that there may be a drug or pharmaceutical agent of significant concentration present, the presence of which may not be suggested by the screening process, there will be the expectation that the sample will be subjected to a "General Drug Screen" in addition to any specific confirmatory procedures. This instrumental approach is designed to detect as many drugs as possible such that those not detected in screening procedures may be at least identified as being present in a sample. Subsequent quantitative analysis can then be undertaken if, in the opinion of the FP, such an analysis would be of benefit in their determination of COD and MOD. For most pharmaceutical agents, the general drug screen, containing appropriate standards and controls, will be adequate to detect and provide a reliable quantitative value.

Many laboratories will perform initial screening on "heart" blood, collected from either the heart or associated large vessels. Heart blood, or samples collected in the vicinity thereof, may reflect artificially elevated drug levels due to postmortem redistribution (see Section 2.7) and while useful for screening, should not in most circumstances, be considered as providing an accurate reflection of antemortem drug concentrations. Historically, multiple tissue samples were routinely collected for toxicologic analysis, e.g., vitreous fluid, liver, kidney, heart, brain, bile, and urine, particularly in cases of suspected overdose or poisoning. In some cases, toxicologic analysis of such samples can provide useful insights regarding the nature of drug use or toxic exposure. However, because of the extensive tabulation of drug levels in blood, corresponding tissue level determinations are often deemed unnecessary and are not particularly commonly done. As noted in Section 1, vitreous fluid samples can be of value as "lagging" indicators of drug concentration or confirmation of the validity of otherwise questioned blood values. Urine samples are instructive of drugs/toxins to which the decedent had been exposed or used in the relatively recent past (as much as several days) but may not necessarily accurately reflect or even be indicative of drugs present at the time of death.

Questions are occasionally raised regarding the validity of results generated from samples that have been stored for some period of time. Not uncommonly, the "expiration date" of the tube will be cited as a notation which is actually with reference to expected patency of the vacuum seal itself (failure of which, of course, would simply result in the lack of sample draw into the tube). The contents of the tube, sodium fluoride, and oxalate would not be expected to be subject to any appreciable degradation reason to be suspect of analytical results or the lack of expected findings. Most samples for postmortem toxicologic analysis are collected in a "grey-top" vacuum tubes, containing sodium-fluoride and -oxalate, neither of which are expected to be subject to any appreciable degradation. Samples collected in "grey top" tubes with adequate vacuum to result in fluid flow into the tube may reasonably be expected to have been properly preserved. L

2.4 TOXICOKINETICS

"Toxicokinetics" simply reflects attempts to describe the processes affecting the levels of drugs in the body and may be thought of as a combination of pharmacokinetics – the biochemical fate of drugs in the body, the biochemical processes affecting that fate, and pharmacodynamics – the impact of the drug on the physiologic and biochemical processes in the body. The toxic consequences with which we are concerned result as a drug or poison interacts with the normal biochemical processes of the body and are in both pathologic and physiologic responses. Toxic mechanisms, then, are essentially reflective of biochemical reactions and interactions between exogenous substances and the normal processes of the body.

2.4.1 Fate of Drugs and Poisons in the Body

The processes of absorption, distribution, metabolism, and elimination for nearly all the drugs and toxins we deal with are well understood both in a general sense and for many drugs in great detail (e.g., metabolic pathways, half-lives, etc.). On the other hand, the primary concern for the FP in a case is what were the actual concentrations of potentially toxic agents in the body; what were the reasonable physiologic consequences of those concentrations; and, in conjunction with consideration of underlying pathology and disease processes, what role would those drugs have played, if any, in causing the death. Clearly, consideration of mechanisms underlying the manner in which those drug levels were achieved will be significant factors in many cases, differentiating homicides from accidental overdoses, suicides, etc., but are nevertheless somewhat secondary to the issue of concentration and effects.

2.4.2 ADME (D-ADME)

The basic processes by which drugs and toxins enter the body and are subsequently distributed, potentially subjected to metabolic transformation, and ultimately eliminated are quite well characterized and understood (often described with the acronym "ADME" for absorption, distribution, metabolism, and elimination). From a toxicologic perspective, focused on gaining an understanding of how the drug levels determined postmortem could have been achieved, and their meaning in the larger context of the case, adding "Delivery" to the acronym makes sense; in that, the mechanism by which a drug is introduced to the body can also affect the actual amount of drug ultimately in the system. The delivery process will impact the amount of drug and the speed with which that drug enters the blood stream (thereby affecting the maximal blood concentration).

2.4.3 Blood as a Key Matrix

From a toxicologic perspective, blood has become the standard focus of analysis, with the underlying assumption that postmortem blood levels generally reflect the status of drugs or toxins in the body at the time of death, and with the understanding that in many cases and circumstances, that assumption is not valid. In cases of suspected overdose, it was historically standard practice to collect multiple tissue samples and utilize the quantitative analysis thereof as the basis for the determination of COD. However, while in some cases such analysis can be informative and help resolve difficult issues, the recognition of blood levels as a central common factor between cases (and extensive tabulation of drug level data) has coincided with increasingly limited sample collection and analysis for toxicologic purposes.

Postmortem toxicologic analysis is based on the assumption that the blood samples collected reflect drug(s) present at the time of death, and in some cases, depending on time, manner, collection site, and the conditions of the decedent, may reasonably reflect antemortem concentrations. Perhaps most importantly, there is also the underlying assumption that blood drug/toxin levels are directly proportionate to tissue levels and as such may be used as the basis for evaluation of the magnitude of drug effects, including toxicity and death. The validity of that assumption has been validated by the large volume of literature establishing therapeutic, toxic, and potentially lethal levels of thousands of drugs. A notable exception to this relationship is the neutral (at physiologic pH) and highly lipophilic tetrahydrocannabinol (THC), with well-documented partition following exposure into lipophilic tissues, e.g., brain and central nervous system (CNS), yielding the apparently paradoxical situation of dropping blood levels in the face of rising drug effects. THC, then, is the archetypal drug for which blood levels cannot routinely be utilized to infer any degree of psychotropic or physiologic effect.

2.4.4 Drug/Toxin Delivery

From a toxicologic (either clinical or forensic) perspective, the mechanism by which a drug has been delivered to the body can be of great significance. Direct injection of drugs (either arterial or venous) results essentially in 100% of the dose being "bioavailable," as the drug is distributed around the body. Similarly, insufflation or inhalation results in significant, effective transfer of drug/toxin (depending on the chemical structure and charge, if any, of the compound) into the bloodstream. In contrast, while popular for ease of delivery, oral administration of drugs results in a less complete delivery of drugs to the body. While many pills/tablets can survive transit through the stomach, and essentially release the drug into the small intestine, that process is clearly not 100% efficient and can be variable as a function of pH, the biochemical composition of the GI tract, and the ability of the drug and mechanisms in the body to transport the drug across the intestinal membrane into the blood. Also important is the subsequent delivery of drugs absorbed in the GI tract to the liver, with rapid and facile uptake by hepatocytes, often as a function of active transport due to the action of a wide variety of specific uptake proteins. This incorporation of drugs into the hepatocytes as the first stage of metabolism for many drugs is the basis of "first-pass metabolism." This process can be so effective as to neutralize as much as 50% or more of a particular drug dose. [One could argue that the efficient de-acetylation of heroin and de-esterification of cocaine by the liver is the basis for the primary use of more direct drug introduction mechanisms (insufflation and intravenous) for the recreational use of these compounds.]

Transdermal drug delivery systems are increasingly popular and serve as an effective way of providing long-term administration of a drug with a relatively short half-life, reducing the need for frequent oral or intravenous administration. From a postmortem toxicologic standpoint, the location and condition of drug-containing patches can be critical information, particularly when attempting to assess the potential that drug levels may be reflective of postmortem redistribution. Lipophilic drugs may continue to be absorbed transdermally after death, potentially artifactually increasing the localized postmortem blood level. Documentation of the drug-containing patches left on the body prior to autopsy can provide important information for considering whether or not the drug caused or contributed to the death.

In-dwelling drug delivery systems extend the concept of long-term steady-state drug administration. Clearly, recovery and documentation of such devices can be important in cases, and recognition that death of the patient does not interrupt the delivery of the drug. Drug levels in samples collected at autopsy even at some distance from a drug delivery device can be artificially elevated in concentration as a function of continued operation.

2.5 BIOTRANSFORMATION

The process of biotransformation or metabolism of drugs can often play a role in the considerations an FP may bring to bear in a particular case, in an effort to understand why specific drug levels may have been achieved with a particular dosing regimen. The speed with which the body is able to inactivate or eliminate an active molecule will affect both the maximal blood levels and time course achieved following exposure but will also determine what range of concentrations the body will experience in circumstances of multiple use or a drug treatment plan. Changes in the rate of biotransformation can explain the transition of a dose plan from generating therapeutic levels to either subtherapeutic levels or, alternatively, toxic or fatal levels. Metabolic effects can be elicited by dietary alterations, drug interactions, or pathologic/physiologic changes in the body. As such, a significant change in drug levels, despite stability in a treatment regimen, can result from enzyme induction, inhibition, changes in intestinal microbial constituents, renal clearance, etc. Further, the presence and pattern of metabolic products can be instructive, particularly in cases in which an inactive metabolite is present at a concentration significantly higher than the potentially toxic, parent compound. Depending on information regarding the pattern of consumption, one might be able to discount a toxic contribution of the drug, since the maximal blood concentration (and maximal physiologic effect) would occur well prior to the terminal event.

2.5.1 Phase I and Phase II Reactions

The two basic types of biotransformation are "phase I" and "phase II" (Table 2.2). In short, phase I reactions activate an otherwise unreactive or inactive site on a molecule, and phase II reactions conjugate a highly hydrophilic group (e.g., an acidic sugar molecule) to that site. The net result is the formation of a new molecule with significantly higher aqueous solubility than the parent species, with a corresponding increase in the rate of filtration/elimination. Any enzymatic reaction for which the product species contains a reactive center subject to a subsequent phase two reaction can be considered a phase I reaction. There are a number of enzyme systems that function extensively on xenobiotic metabolism. The major enzymes with phase I reactions are the "Cytochrome P450 (CYP)" superfamily. This ubiquitous group of isozymes plays an important role in the metabolism and elimination of many of the common pharmaceutical and abused drugs which are routinely encountered in postmortem analyses. In addition to the CYP isozymes, there are a multiplicity of enzymes that can generate or activate sites on target molecules (e.g. flavin monooxygenases, alcohol dehydrogenases, amino acyl transferases, etc.)

The phase II reaction system most commonly dealt with in forensic toxicology is a family of transferases that conjugate glucuronic acid onto the active site of the target molecule. The unreacted species is the "aglycone" and the activated transitional molecule is "UDP-glucuronic acid." This family of "UDP-glucuronosyl transferases" is ubiquitous, and "glucuronide" metabolites often comprise a significant fraction of the excreted form of a specific drug. Other phase two, or

Table 2.2 Example Phase I and Phase II Reactions

Phase I	Phase II
Oxidation	Glucuronidation
Reduction	Sulfation
Hydrosis	Acetylation
Hydration	Methylation
Dehalogenation	Amino acid conjugation
	Glutathione conjugation

conjugation, reactions may acetylate, or sulfate, substrates, or may add amino acids or peptides, such as glutathione. Methylation, while technically a phase II reaction, does generally not add to the lipophilicity of a substrate molecule.

2.5.2 Induction/Inhibition

The potential for the CYP-450 and other biotransformation enzymes to be subject to induction and inhibition can play a significant role in the considerations associated with the dosing regimens for an individual. Like many enzyme systems in the body (perhaps most notably, alcohol dehydrogenase), persistent or regular exposure to many CYP isozyme substrates can induce considerable enzyme synthesis to the point of actually affecting the rate of metabolism of some drugs. While this is not "tolerance" in the sense of an altered physiological response to a specific drug concentration, it can result in lowered blood levels (and hence diminished response) to a specific dose, thereby appearing as if some degree of tolerance has been achieved. The induction of alcohol dehydrogenase in regular drinkers provides the basis for understanding the prevalent belief of "tolerance" to alcohol in some individuals. (Naturally, the processes of receptor downregulation and generation of a true tolerance can coincide with enzyme reduction, requiring in some case, a medication adjustment to maintain a particular level of response.)

While the process of enzyme induction can occur over many days, the converse process, that of inhibition of the enzyme, can occur simply as a function of the presence of specific inhibitor. Clearly, inhibition of a metabolic pathway can result in an increase in blood levels of a particular drug, with a concomitant increase in area under the curve (AUC). The classic example of this phenomenon is the inhibition of CYPCA4 by some compounds present in grapefruit juice. Some common drugs that can be affected by this process include the tricyclic antidepressants, a number of selective serotonin reuptake inhibitors (SSRIs), serotonin and norepinephrine reuptake inhibitors (SNRIs), and antipsychotics.

2.5.3 Toxic Species Formation

The CYP enzymes are generally thought of as being protective in the sense that they facilitate the removal of otherwise potentially toxic species. However, it is worth noting that because of the nature of the underlying reaction (usually one-electron reduction), both free radicals and other potentially toxic intermediates can be formed. As an example, the toxic acetaminophen metabolite, N-acetyl-para-quinonimine (NAPQI), is primarily generated by CYP2E1, which in turn is inducible by a wide variety of drugs, including the archetypal cytochrome P-450 inducer, phenobarbital.

2.5.4 Practical Considerations

We recognize that the role of inducers/inhibitors on the eventual levels of drugs in the body does not impact the physiological effects elicited by those levels and, as such, would not necessarily impact the determination of the cause of death. However, the potential for such effects to have impacted drug levels might impact determinations with regard to the manner of death, particularly in clarifying an apparent overdose as either deliberate or accidental.

2.6 INTERPRETIVE CHALLENGES AND UNCERTAINTY IN POSTMORTEM TESTING

The challenges that can arise with the analysis of biological samples for postmortem testing are categorized as either analytical or interpretive in nature. The ability to detect and quantitatedrugs from postmortem material is necessary to be able to provide information for the determination of the cause and manner of death. Interpreting the values obtained can be complex, given the uncertainty of the quality of the specimen received. The most accurate interpretation may be that the drug "was present", even if quantitation could not be performed.

2.6.1 Analytical Challenges

The analytical challenges faced by the forensic toxicologist are a function of the nature and/or the amount of sample available for analysis. For most postmortem cases, the sample volume is more than adequate, especially if an autopsy has been performed. Hospital-derived samples and those obtained in the early postmortem period are in excellent condition. They are neither contaminated nor hemolyzed and are received in properly labeled tubes. Samples degrade as the postmortem interval increases. Cells break down, fluids evaporate, and samples become smaller in volume as time progresses.

People of small stature, pediatric patients, and patients who sustained hemorrhagic or neurogenic shock may have very little obtainable intravascular blood. Samples can be contaminated by nonbiological materials. Sometimes the only samples available are tissue samples that are degraded or desiccated. These samples are very difficult for the laboratory to handle and may not yield the results expected, even if a result is able to be obtained. While "less-than-optimal" samples can be analyzed, there may be questions regarding the degree to which target analytes are extracted from compromised sample materials. It is the responsibility of the testing facility to clearly communicate to the pathologist any unusual level of uncertainty in the analytical process due to the sample conditions.

2.6.2 Interpretive Challenges

One of the main issues in the field of forensic toxicology is the potential for inaccurate conclusions to have been drawn regarding antemortem drug levels based on postmortem drug level analysis. Perhaps the main issue that has been accepted over the last several decades is postmortem redistribution (PMR). When PMR has occurred, drugs concentrated in tissues during life diffuse away from those depots after death, resulting in levels in blood samples drawn close to the organs that are artifactually high and not reflective of true antemortem concentrations. The potential for erroneous conclusions to be drawn regarding cause of death (COD) and manner of death (MOD) are obvious.

Secondly, compounding the problem with PMR is the attempt to apply toxicokinetic calculations to postmortem values. These calculations generally take two forms: the first being a "back extrapolation" from postmortem values to antemortem levels and the second being a determination of the "amount of drug" administered that serves to explain either the postmortem levels or the levels expected to have been present at the time of death. While the calculations and kinetic parameters underlying these processes are clearly well established and relied upon in the realm of clinical toxicology, uncertainty or variability in key underlying assumptions affects the magnitude and overall applicability of the calculations. In short, while the calculations may be quite good and accurate, the uncertainty of the results may be of such magnitude as to render them useless. On the other hand, there may be cases in which PM toxicokinetic calculations can provide reasonably reliable values with which to assist the FP with the determination of COD and MOD. Neither blanket acceptance nor outright rejection of toxicokinetic calculations reflects a reasoned scientific evaluation of the data. What is called for on the part of the forensic toxicologist is a reasoned, justified consideration of the variables and assumptions underlying a particular case and an equally reasoned evaluation of the uncertainty associated with any final value, or range thereof, to be communicated to the case FP.

2.6.3 Postmortem Redistribution

Perhaps one of the biggest challenges that forensic toxicologists deal with is the expectation that a quantitative drug value derived from a postmortem sample is necessarily reflective of antemortem levels of the drug. Depending on the source of the sample, and the circumstances surrounding the collection thereof, they may indeed accurately reflect ante-mortem levels of the drug. However, because the drugs diffuse from high concentration areas to low, the assumption may not be correct at all and may be significantly misleading. Many cases have been labeled as overdose deaths in which the elevated levels are clearly the result of PMR. Unfortunately, the lay public and even many medically trained personnel accept the apparently common-sense assumption that drug levels do not change in the postmortem period (See Sidebar 2.1). In short, PMR is reflective of the transition from a dynamic equilibrium of a drug during life, wherein the active uptake and concentration processes active in organs (primarily liver), resulting in differences in concentration between core organs and peripheral tissues and blood, and the ending of those processes, followed by concentration-driven diffusion, leading to a true equilibrium eventually reached after death, when drug levels are essentially uniform throughout the body.

Sidebar 2.1: Postmortem Redistribution: How and Why

Historically, it was assumed that the distribution of drugs throughout the body during life, albeit with some tissue-based differences, remained static after death and that blood collected from any source provided a valid indication of antemortem drug levels. That view has changed and evolved considerably as an increasing body of evidence has demonstrated significant differences in drug concentrations between blood collected from the heart from within the chambers of the heart and blood collected from a peripheral source, such as the femoral vein. Results obtained from peripheral blood are usually lower than the results obtained from central blood, often markedly so. Central:peripheral drug concentration ratios as high as 10 and 12 have been noted in many cases. However, the differences between "heart blood" and "peripheral blood" drug concentrations are not predictable, sometimes varying considerably between otherwise apparently similar cases.

There has been, understandably, some reluctance to accept the concept that there could be a redistribution process occurring after death that may effectively invalidate the concentrations of drugs determined in many postmortem samples. However, with increasing experimental documentation of the differences between central and peripheral blood, and as the identification of specific transport proteins and systems provided a mechanistic basis for understanding the difference between postmortem blood and drug levels in organs, the process of PMR has become well recognized and accepted in the forensic medical and toxicology community. In short, drugs become concentrated in tissues and organs due to specific uptake mechanisms in the cells that facilitate their concentration during life. Shortly after death, the drugs can (and do) redistribute or equilibrate throughout the body because the biochemical basis for creating and maintaining that intra-organ concentration has stopped.

Most drugs are ionized at physiologic pH. During life, simple diffusion of ionized drugs from blood into tissues is limited by the electrostatic charge on the cell membrane. However, drugs can become concentrated in specific tissues by the action of membrane transport proteins. The concentration of drugs in the liver facilitates enzyme-based metabolic processes, and hepatocyte membranes are extensively populated with drug-transporting proteins. The hepatocellular concentration of drugs well in excess of blood levels is well recognized as a routine physiologic process. After death, the adenosine triphosphate (ATP)-dependent membrane charge on cells disappears, and the membrane becomes increasingly compromised as autolysis proceeds. Cellular structures fail as degradation enzymes catalyze membrane molecular breakdown. In essence, the cell membranes become more porous. As the energy barrier to diffusion of ionized species weakens, and membrane structures become increasingly degraded, drugs that have been concentrated inside the cell are able to transit the degrading cell membrane and enter the blood, approaching a new equilibrium as a function of gradient-driven diffusion. Given a long enough interval after death, adequate to allow equilibration of drugs throughout the body based on diffusion, one would also expect no difference between peripheral and central blood drug levels. Postmortem redistribution represents a dynamic transitional state between equilibria and is not, even on a case-specific basis, amenable to description by statistical parameters. Some drugs (e.g., THC) are not ionized at physiologic pH and are not precluded from distribution (in or out of tissues) via simple diffusion and, as such, do not exhibit PMR. Ethanol and methanol are also able to transit membrane water channels (aquaporins) and, as such, distribute relatively uniformly throughout the body and also are not subject to PMR.

Average PMR or central:peripheral ratios, while potentially instructive, can also be grossly misleading. The concentration of drugs in a sample collected postmortem will depend on the extent to which a particular analyte had been concentrated antemortem, the location of the diffusion front (the leading edge of a diffusion process) of the drug in the region around the tissue in which it had been concentrated, and the location from which the particular sample had been drawn. Obviously, if the sample had been collected beyond the diffusion front, the drug level would not have been affected by PMR. It is important to note that PMR may be a major factor in cases where drugs present had only been used at therapeutic levels. Failure to consider PMR in a case could cause one to inappropriately "blame" a medication taken therapeutically for causing to contributing to death based on artifactually elevated concentrations in a postmortem heart blood sample. Tricyclic antidepressants and SSRIs are particularly vulnerable to PMR.

In contrast, it can be equally problematic to assume that elevated blood levels, even from heart or central blood samples, must necessarily be reflective of PMR. In cases where exposure to the drug has occurred in a drug-naïve individual, and the person dies shortly after exposure, there may simply not have been adequate time for the drug to accumulate in tissues. In such cases, there may be no antemortem gradient and no basis for PMR. There are, of course, cases in which a properly collected femoral (or other peripheral) sample would not be expected to have been artifactually elevated and, as such, provides a reasonable estimate of antemortem values. Particularly, when such elevated levels are consistent with either antemortem clinical or behavioral observations, and/or postmortem pathology, consistent levels observed in PM samples may be given appropriate credence.

The key point for the toxicologist is that because of all the variables potentially impacting the magnitude of PMR in a particular case, it can be nearly impossible to predict the magnitude of redistribution that will be reflected in a given sample. Therefore, it is also nearly impossible to reliably predict an antemortem level of a drug, based on a postmortem sample drawn from a region subject to PMR (e.g., the central cavity). While peripheral blood sources (e.g., femoral vein) may provide a much-reduced expectation for PMR elevation, the practical toxicologist will take great care in attempting to infer an antemortem level from a drug level determined in a sample that may reflect some degree of PMR. Providing a reasonable explanation of the process and its consequences to forensic pathologists who must use toxicologic analytical findings (and on occasion to the legal community) can represent an important task and challenge but can provide considerable value to the FPs in their efforts toward reaching an understanding of COD and MOD.

In short, this complex process is essentially chaotic in nature, meaning that the degree of PMR in a specific case is unpredictable. In the antemortem state, before the heart stops beating and blood stops circulating, there is no expectation of a difference in drug values between peripheral and central blood samples because blood continues to circulate and cellular membranes and membrane potentials are maintained. Blood obtained shortly before death (e.g. in the hospital setting) or very shortly after death before significant PMR has occurred are therefore preferred over blood taken at a later time, with results much more likely to reflect drug levels at the time of death.

2.6.4 Postmortem Toxicologic Calculations

There are two main calculations that may be of value to the FP: basically, how much drug would have been ingested to produce the eventually determined PM value and secondly, what would have the concentration of a drug been at some time prior to death, given a known or hypothetical scenario. While the mathematical basis for both questions is well established, the degree of variability or uncertainty that can be associated with the application of such calculations to real cases is quite significant and should be carefully evaluated and considered.

Some of the more common questions posed to the forensic toxicologist relate to attempts to provide an estimate of drug concentration via simple "back-extrapolation" to a drug level at some time prior to death. This question is most commonly raised regarding alcohol and may be of significance in legal proceedings. Back-extrapolation of alcohol is based on linear elimination (zero-order kinetics) and is therefore relatively straightforward. Further simplifying the process is the fact that because of the nature of alcohol distribution, the issue of postmortem redistribution is generally not a confounder in the extrapolation process. In contrast, however, for nearly all other drugs for which a back-extrapolation calculation may be of interest, the process can become considerably more complex and uncertain. Elimination of drugs is nearly always best described as a first-order kinetic process, and, as such, concentrations increase exponentially further back in time one carries out the extrapolation calculation. Importantly, the magnitude of any inaccurate assumption (be it the half-life, time and amount of dosing/usage, or the accuracy of the estimation of drug level at the time of death inferred by the toxicologic findings), will also increase exponentially with the extent to which the back-extrapolation is carried.

Perhaps the second most common question is "how much drug" would have been necessary to produce this level? The calculation is relatively straightforward for alcohol, but less so for other drugs. Again, the FP and forensic toxicologist must be cognizant of the potential that the postmortem drug level may not accurately reflect the true antemortem level.

The basis for answering the "amount of drug" question is the "Volume of Distribution (Vd)" – a useful, but artificial concept. Basically, the Vd relates the amount of a particular drug ingested to the subsequent peak blood value by considering blood volume as the only space into which the drug is "diluted" or distributed and further considering the blood volume is variable. So, if 6 mg of drug X is delivered intravenously and results in a 0.06 mg/L (60 ug/L) concentration, the Vd would be equal to 100 L in that particular individual. Expressed in terms of body weight, (assuming 180 lbs), we would have a Vd for drug X of ~1.2 L/kg. Working in reverse with an observed 60 ug/L in a 180 lb individual,

$$60 \text{ ug/L} \times 0.001 \text{ mg/ug} \times 180 \text{ lbs} \times 0.4594 \text{ kg/lb} \times 1.2 \text{ L/kg} = 6 \text{ mg}.$$

There is, however, the potential for significant error in the application of this principle to the postmortem situation. First, the underlying assumptions for the Vd relationship are: there has been a single dosing event (no underlying level of the drug), the blood level reflects a maximum following the dose, there is no significant potential difference in drug distribution between individuals, and the administered dose reflects the bioavailable amount. Second is the assumption that the postmortem level of the target drug is an accurate reflection of antemortem values and that there was no underlying level of the drug. [Note that one could apply the Vd calculation to the difference between an observed and an expected level, but such a process would also involve the introduction of considerable uncertainty.]

Vd calculations, particularly when critically evaluated in light of potential uncertainty, can nevertheless be of value in many cases as FPs gain further insight and understanding of fatal cases (see Sidebar 2.2). However, we cannot overstate the need for both FP's and toxicologists to be cautious and conservative with regard to the inferences they may draw from such calculations.

Sidebar 2.2: Hospital Death & Kinetics Run Amok!

A number of years ago, we dealt with the case of a 180 lb., 45-year-old male, who had presented to an emergency department at ~8:00 AM, complaining of a ~3-day history of left flank pain. This gentleman had a medical history of a cardiac dysrhythmia, ischemic heart disease, paraneoplastic syndrome, and myelodysplasia for which he had received a bone marrow transplant. He was subsequently admitted to a medical floor, with a diagnosis of acute herpes zoster (shingles). His hospital stay was unremarkable, and he received treatment with oxycodone, meperidine, and gabapentin over a 4-day period and was considered as "responding to treatment." On the morning of his expected discharge, he was discovered dead at ~4:00 AM on a routine check. An autopsy (non-forensic) was performed at the hospital, with no clear COD identified; however, "cardiac arrhythmia" was suggested, consistent with his past medical history.

Postmortem toxicology testing returned results indicating a blood oxycodone level of 1.2 mg/L from a "heart blood" sample. At this point, considering the apparent high level of the opiate, the ME became involved, re-opened the case, and changed the COD to oxycodone overdose. Interestingly, the patient's last opiate dose would have occurred at ~10:00 PM the night prior to his death, and significantly, the patient was noted to have been engaged in conversation with nursing staff at around midnight. A 2:00 AM check by an experienced nurse indicated that the patient was sleeping normally.

Legal action ensued, suggesting that there had been an inadvertent overdose of oxycodone provided to the patient in the 10:00 PM dose, despite the acceptance of the probability that the blood level was artifactually elevated due to postmortem redistribution. (Central:peripheral ratios as high as 8:1 have been noted with the semi-synthetic opiates.) Interestingly, it was argued, based on an "average" value of central:peripheral ratios selected from literature, that a "corrected" postmortem oxycodone level could be determined and, further, based on that value, that an exponential (first-order) back-extrapolation could be performed, suggesting the degree of "overdose" provided at the 10:00 PM dose.

It was, of course, notable that the patient's behavior at ~midnight, coupled with the 2:00 AM observation, is inconsistent with a significant, potentially lethal level of oxycodone having been administered at 10:00. However, the assumption that there was a statistically definable (albeit with selected values) "average" central:peripheral ratio in cases of PMR fails to recognize that in a dynamic equilibrium process, the concept of "average" fails to adequately reflect the underlying reality. During life, the central:peripheral ratio is essentially 1:1, and at the end of the PMR process, that ratio would also be 1:1 as drugs remaining in the body reach the final equilibrium as a function of diffusion. In short, PMR is a chaotic and unpredictable transitional process between two equilibrium states [active and dynamic in life, static and relatively stable (eventually) after death], not readily describable by simplistic statistical models.

Bibliography

Baselt R. (2017). *Disposition of Toxic Drugs and Chemical in Man*. 11th ed. Seal Beach, CA: Biomedical Publications.

Brunton L., Knollman B. (2022). *Goodman and Gilman's The Pharmacological Basis of Therapeutics*. 14th ed. London: McGraw Hill.

Ellenhorn M.J., Barceloux D.G. (1988). *Medical Toxicology: Diagnosis and Treatment of Human Poisonings*. Amsterdam: Elsevier.

Levine B.S., Kerrigan S. (eds). (2020). *Principles of Forensic Toxicology*. 5th ed. New York: Springer.

Powers R.H., Dean D.E. (2016). *Forensic Toxicology: Mechanisms and Pathology*. Boca Raton, FL: Taylor and Francis.

Schulz M., Schmoldt A., Andresen-Streichert H., Iwersen-Bergmann S. (2020). Revisited: Therapeutic and toxic blood concentrations of more than 1,100 drugs and other xenobiotics. *Critical Care*, 24(1):195.

Winek C.L., Wahba W.W., Winek C.L. Jr, Balzer T.W. (2001). Drug and chemical blood-level data 2001. *Forensic Science International*, 122(2–3):107–123.

SECTION 3

SYSTEMIC TOXINS

DOI: 10.4324/9781003121060-4

3.1 INTRODUCTION

The focus of this section is to discuss drugs and toxins that affect the whole body. From a postmortem perspective, this section could encompass essentially all drugs and toxins, in the sense that lethal end points affect the entire body. We have chosen, however, to include selected topics with effects expressed on either the whole body or generally more than a single organ or organ system. However, we have chosen to include chemical asphyxiants (carbon monoxide, cyanide, hydrogen sulfide, and nitrites) in Section 5.

3.2 ANTICOAGULANTS

Poisoning by or the accidental overuse of anticoagulants is not infrequently encountered in forensic medicine. Anticoagulants, specifically warfarin, and related compounds are commonly referred to as "blood thinners" by nonmedical personnel, due to their effect on slowing the rate of clot formation. In the forensic setting, nonmedically trained family members may understand the question, "Was he taking any blood thinners?" better than "Was he taking any vitamin K antagonists?"

The process of blood clotting is the body's response to bleeding. The initial step after a break in a blood vessel is an unstable clump of cells, formed by platelets. This platelet plug initiates the "coagulation cascade" (see Sidebars 3.1 and 3.2), leading to a more structurally stable clot allowing healing processes to initiate. Eventually, the clot is broken up and dissolved by the action of the fibrinolytic system, with restoration of blood flow through the vessel. Anticoagulants act to limit the magnitude of the clotting response. Toxicity with anticoagulants presents, as bleeding from multiple sites including venipuncture sites, mucus membranes and the GI tract.

The pharmaceutical uses of anticoagulant therapeutics, such as warfarin, are primarily focused on clotting disorders directly (e.g., fFactor V Leiden deficiency) or conditions that may lead to inappropriate clotting, such as atrial fibrillation, dilated cardiomyopathy, or patients who are at risk of thromboemboli. An anticoagulant regimen can limit and prolong the clotting process and allow the body's own mechanisms to prevent inappropriate clot formation, which might then break free and migrate to the brain, causing an intracerebral hemorrhage and stroke. Warfarin is also used to treat acute intravascular thrombi (e.g., venous thromboses, pulmonary thromboemboli, and embolic cerebral infarctions).

3.2.1 Warfarin and Related Compounds

Warfarin is an anticoagulant originally developed as a rodenticide and is still widely used for that purpose. Warfarin and related compounds (e.g., brodifacoum, dicoumarol, and bromadiolone) have a similar mechanism and potential for toxicity. In essence, all these compounds interfere with vitamin K-dependent clot formation (as detailed in Sidebars 3.1 and 3.2) and exhibit a similar potential for mammalian toxicity. In the 1950s, it was recognized that nontoxic levels of the drug could potentially provide an effective means for the prevention of undesired clot formation and may therefore be of value as medicinals, rather than solely as poisons. Warfarin has since become commonly prescribed as an oral anticoagulant.

Currently, newer available rodenticides ("superwarfarins") may contain anticoagulants with a longer elimination half-life than warfarin (e.g., brodifacoum and difenacoum). As of this writing, while the original brand name, Coumadin®, has been discontinued, the generic drug is still available and extensively prescribed. Warfarin is marketed as a pill with a relatively long half-life (15–70h), is easily absorbed by the GI tract, and is highly protein-bound. It is metabolized by the liver into inactive hydroxy derivatives, which are then excreted by the kidney. Compounds related to warfarin are marketed as anticoagulant-containing rodenticides, sold as pellets or granules, also meant to be ingested.

Mechanistically, clot formation is initiated by the action of a number of "clotting factors" which are activated during the enzymatic oxidation of vitamin K from a hydroquinone to an epoxide form. Subsequent enzymatic reduction steps yield vitamin K quinone and then regenerate the hydroquinone, allowing the cycle to repeat. Warfarin and the superwarfarin analogues inhibit the reduction steps, thereby limiting the amount of vitamin K available to form activated clotting factors, in a dose-dependent fashion.

Sidebar 3.1: Vitamin K

Vitamin K (as phylloquinone) is a naturally occurring fat-soluble vitamin produced by plants and contained in leafy vegetables. It is also produced by bacteria in the colon (menaquinone). Pharmacologically, it is used to treat warfarin and warfarin-related compound toxicity. Lack of or a reduced amount of vitamin K can result in hemorrhaging even without exposure to anticoagulant agents. Patients whose diets are deficient in leafy greens likely are not vitamin K deficient because of the production by colonic bacteria. However, patients treated with prolonged courses of antibiotics are at risk of colonic sterilization. These patients are at risk of hemorrhages because vitamin K is required as a cofactor for some enzymes and for some coagulation factors. Parenteral vitamin K replacement usually corrects the deficit.

The reasoning for vitamin K administration just after birth is that neonates without intestinal bacteria may also be at risk of vitamin K deficiency.

The clinical assessment of patients with vitamin K deficiency includes coagulation studies, typically prothrombin time (PT), partial prothrombin time (PTT), thrombin time (TT), and international normalized ratio (INR). PT/INR is commonly also reported to allow patients to obtain consistent laboratory results regardless of which laboratory is used and what analytical methods are employed; the INR is utilized.

The therapeutic range for INR is < 1.3. Patients with high INR values are at risk of clotting issues. INR values > 9 are considered as representing a critically high level, with a high risk for spontaneous hemorrhaging. These patients require fresh frozen plasma infusions in addition to discontinuation of anticoagulant administration and adding vitamin K. Replacing vitamin K and withholding anticoagulant therapy alone did not correct the INR fast enough to prevent hemorrhage. Coagulation studies are not reliable from plasma from a deceased person, but the medical history and antemortem results reported in medical records can yield invaluable clues to an appropriate diagnosis.

Sidebar 3.2: Coagulation Cascade

The coagulation cascade *in vivo* is orderly and complex and refers to the series of steps in the formation of clots by activating proteins called coagulation factors. The cascade has been classically divided into three segments: the extrinsic pathway, the intrinsic pathway, and the final common pathway. The extrinsic pathway refers to the portion of the series of steps activated when there is tissue damage, exposing factor III (AKA tissue factor) to blood. Factor VII in the blood requires vitamin K to become activated (to become factor VIIa, the "a" stands for "activated"). Factor III binds to calcium and factor VIIa in the blood to activate factor X. The extrinsic pathway forms part of the basis for the PT test.

The intrinsic pathway begins in the blood when factor XII (Hageman factor) is exposed to and activated by collagen, kallikrein, and high-molecular-weight kininogen. Factor XIIa activates factor XI. Factor VIII is activated by thrombin (AKA factor II) in blood. Factor XIa activates factor IX. Factor IXa and factor VIIIa, together with calcium, form a complex that activates factor X. This series is the basis for the PTT assay.

Both pathways activate factor X which starts the final common pathway in which fibrinogen is converted to fibrin which cross-links platelets to form a stable clot. Factors Va and Xa form an activated enzyme complex with calcium (called prothrombinase) converting prothrombin (factor II) to thrombin (factor IIa). Thrombin cleaves fibrinogen into monomers that will cross-link with platelets forming a stable clot.

The factors that require vitamin K are factors II (prothrombin, involved in the PT and PTT tests), VII (extrinsic pathway, PT test), IX (intrinsic pathway, PTT test), and X (made by extrinsic and intrinsic pathways and used in final common pathway). In vitamin K deficiency, PT and PTT will be prolonged, but TT will be normal. The TT test uses exogenous thrombin, not native thrombin. Fibrinogen activation does not require vitamin K.

3.2.2 Poisoning, Treatment, and Autopsy Findings

Deliberate and accidental poisoning by anticoagulants, either therapeutics or rodenticides, is characterized by uncontrolled bleeding and internal hemorrhaging. Bleeding will occur initially from small vessels and then progressively from larger vessels. Patients will commonly have numerous petechiae on the face and other areas where skin is thin. When provided with medical therapy, patients may bleed from intravascular catheter insertion sites and venipuncture sites. Death can occur from an intracerebral hemorrhage, hemorrhages in other vital organs, and/or hemorrhagic shock. At autopsy, intravascular blood is in the liquid form. The appearance of the body mimics disseminated intravascular coagulopathy (DIC). The autopsy findings are similar to those caused by a hemorrhagic virus. (If the latter is suspected, other people in the community would also be affected. Postmortem diagnosis of hemorrhagic viruses requires serologic testing for IgG and IgM).

Treatment of a patient with a warfarin overdose includes withholding the drug and initiating vitamin K replacement along with coagulation factors in fresh frozen plasma. The half-life of warfarin is fairly long (15–70 h), so therapy is monitored using PT/INR rather than dosage. The elimination half-lives of the superwarfarins are much longer than those of warfarin and may be in the range of days to a week or more, meaning that patients poisoned by rodenticides must be monitored and treated for a longer period of time than would be appropriate for a patient who had taken an overdose of warfarin.

In the case of suspected poisoning by warfarin or an analogue, the autopsy findings will be as noted above. Coagulation studies for inherited clotting disorders are not valid in PM blood. While warfarin is readily detectable in postmortem samples, analysis for one or more of the superwarfarins is not part of the routine testing protocols in many forensic laboratories but may be available at reference laboratories particularly if a specific rodenticide is suspected.

Because of the time to acquire therapeutic levels of warfarin, some patients requiring immediate anticoagulation may be treated with heparin for 4–5 days during the initiation of warfarin therapy. However, some patients requiring anticoagulation therapy for the prevention of clots in, for example, atrial fibrillation may be started on warfarin as an outpatient without needing subcutaneous or intravenous heparin. Patients with an underlying disease, such as any liver disease, may fare worse than otherwise healthy patients due to their already compromised state of natural coagulation.

3.3 FLUID AND ELECTROLYTE DISTURBANCES

It is difficult to overstate the importance of the ionic constituents ("electrolytes") in the body with regard to providing the intra- and extracellular environments within which the biochemical processes of life can function. While "cardiac or pulmonary failure" is often cited by treating physicians as the end point of chronic disease or organ failure, the immediate cause of death might just as reasonably be characterized as "electrolyte imbalance," fatally diminishing oxygen utilization, nerve conduction, or muscle contraction. Electrolyte constituents function to facilitate and regulate heart, brain, nerve, and muscle actions and activities. Concentration differentials between the intracellular and extracellular compartments provide energy for a multitude of cellular functions, including transmembrane transport of molecules and transmission of oxidizing or reducing equivalents into or out of cells and cellular organelles, and can serve to signal cellular activities, such as hormone secretion. Additionally, electrolyte levels are key in the maintenance of pH and water balance in the body, and a number serves as essential stabilizing and functional elements in enzymes or other active biomolecules (e.g., heme). The six primary electrolytes are sodium, potassium, chloride, bicarbonate, calcium, and phosphate, with magnesium, copper, zinc, iron, manganese, molybdenum, copper, and chromium also being of biological significance.

3.3.1 Fluid and Electrolyte Balance

Electrolyte levels in the body are a function of dietary intake, the available fluid volume, and the rate of elimination. Localized concentrations (e.g., intravascular, intracellular, and extracellular) may be critical with regard to a particular compound, element, or function. The body attempts to maintain fluid volume and electrolyte concentrations within functional ranges, despite variations in oral intake, physiologic fluid loss, GI system, insensible fluid loss (sweating and exhalation), physical activity (changes in metabolic rate), and changes in ambient temperature and humidity. While extracellular electrolyte composition can vary somewhat as a function of changes in body water, uptake, and excretions, the body attempts to maintain intracellular electrolyte composition within narrow parameters, allowing for the function of physiologic processes.

Electrolyte concentration as a function of total body water (TBW) is primarily regulated by the kidney with a small contribution by the lungs and skin. TBW ranges from about 50%–70% of body weight depending on gender and body mass. Men generally have a lower percentage of TBW than women, and lean people generally less than full-figured. About two-thirds of body fluid is found intracellularly, and about 25% of the remaining one-third of body fluid is intravascular, leaving the rest in the interstitium. The pH of the extracellular fluid is influenced by the lungs, more specifically, by the rate of CO_2 elimination (affecting pH via bicarbonate concentration and PO_2 and PCO_2). Lowered rates of respiration or air exchange result in diminished elimination of CO_2, resulting in lower blood pH, and higher respiratory rates increase the blood pH toward the more basic. The kidneys play a major role in the maintenance of electrolyte balance as well, functioning to regulate the internal fluid tonicity (effective osmolality), blood volume, acid–base balance, and the chemical composition of body fluid by impacting the retention or release of ions. Intracellular electrolyte composition is controlled at the level of the cell membrane which, as a function of the membrane charge, presents a barrier to simple diffusion of both anions and cations from the extracellular fluid. Ionic transit is therefore, a tightly controlled process, connected to specific biochemical functions, and in many cases, requiring energy to move ionic species either into or out of cells.

The anion gap (calculated as the difference between ($[Na^+]+[K^+]$) and ($[Cl^-]+[HCO_3^-]$) is extensively utilized by clinicians and can be a useful calculation to help identify the underlying cause of a metabolic or respiratory acidosis. Anion gap is often calculated without consideration of the typically low potassium concentration, hence [sodium − (chloride + bicarbonate)] with a normal range of ~6–12 meq/L.

In living people, blood electrolyte concentrations are routinely measured in serum. After death, however, transmembrane diffusion of electrolytes can rapidly occur as the membrane charge dissipates. As such, serum levels can quickly become unrepresentative of true antemortem electrolyte concentration. However, vitreous humor (VH) samples can remain viable for electrolyte concentration for some time after death, although interpretation is somewhat different than it is for living patients, as addressed below.

3.3.2 Interpretation of Postmortem Electrolyte Levels

It is not uncommon that the cause of death is not immediately obvious at the autopsy table. The deceased person may appear anatomically normal (no penetrating injury, no congenital malformation, etc.) Such "negative autopsies" require additional consideration and perhaps additional laboratory analysis. The use of postmortem chemistry can be invaluable in assessing for medical conditions that were not readily noted upon gross or microscopic examination. There are no specific markers at autopsy to diagnose diabetic ketoacidosis, hypernatremia, water intoxication, or hyperglycemia. However, all of these conditions may be reasonably inferred based on postmortem electrolyte findings. As noted above though, neither postmortem serum nor whole blood provides reliable electrolyte results, primarily due to the rapid postmortem equilibration of potassium and sodium out of and into cells, respectively, after death. Interestingly, negatively charged chloride ions tend to remain in equilibrium between the intracellular and the extracellular spaces, and the overall net charge remains electrically neutral. The progressive compromise and loss of structural integrity of cellular membranes in the postmortem interval result in the mixing of extracellular and intracellular fluid components in an unpredictable fashion. In short, the absolute concentration of a number of analytes changes in the blood postmortem, as does the ratio between analytes. However, in many cases, the analyses of VH, cerebrospinal fluid, or urine can provide significant and useful information for evaluating the underlying COD.

3.3.3 VH as a Postmortem Sample

In 1993, Coe documented the postmortem "behavior" of many serum components in VH. This matrix does not contain blood vessels but does contain phagocytes to remove debris. Collagen fibrils connect the gel-like humor to the ora serrata, the retina, and the lens capsule, and it may contain "stringy" material with age as collagen fibrils detach. Almost all (about 99%) of VH is water, containingminor components such as salts, sugars, collagen, and some protein. VH is essentially an ultrafiltrate of blood, and the inorganic components are reflective of serum levels (although with some "time lag" for diffusion-based equilibria to be reached between blood and vitreous fluid concentrations). VH is commonly utilized for testing for electrolytes, glucose, drugs, and toxins, in the absence of red blood cells (RBCs; that autolyze shortly after death) or other contaminants. Even if significantly contaminated by RBCs, toxicologic findings may still be useful, although other determinations may be compromised. VH is easily collected from the central portion of the globe, using a narrow bore needle (a 20-guage needle and a 5-mL plastic syringe work well; see Figure 3.1).

Vitreous samples may sometimes contain tiny air bubbles, which will not affect analytical results. Occasionally, the sample may have a yellow tinge if the decedent is jaundiced and a red tinge in the event of trauma to the globe that has cause hemorrhage into the vitreous fluid. Electrolyte results from samples contaminated with blood may be unreliable, but the results are not affected by jaundice. Each eye generally contains between 1 and 5 mL of VH, depending on the age of the person and the size of the globe. Vitreous fluid is routinely removed during the process of corneal extraction for tissue donation, but tissue banks will normally reserve and provide the fluid to the ME office upon request. VH components may not be distributed homogeneously; therefore, it is recommended to extract all obtainable vitreous. We recommend obtaining VH from both eyes and combining the samples, unless one is clearly contaminated, with the goal of minimizing any effect of possible inhomogeneity in the samples.

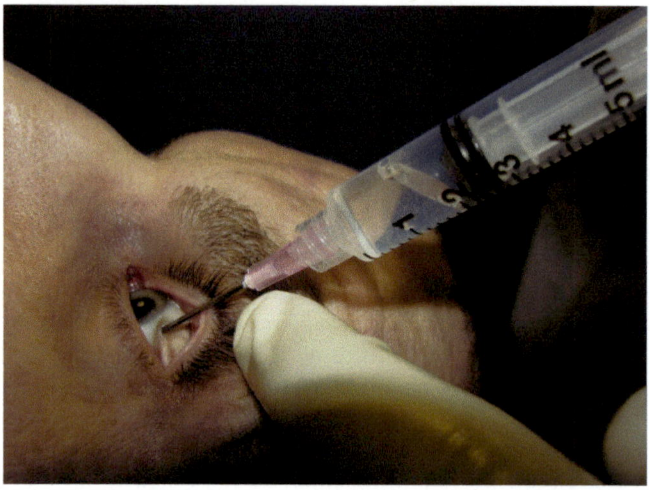

Figure 3.1 VH sampling. The sample is clear and colorless, without debris. The globe of the eye is contracting with the procedure and may be refilled with water, saline, or formalin to restore its shape. Sample collection without cosmetic alteration to the eye can be achieved by insertion of the needle through the lateral aspect near the outer canthus (anterior facing bevel) until the tip of the needle is visualized through the pupil. If either the needle or the syringe is too large in diameter, there is some danger in pulling too hard on the viscous VH and disturbing the retina or blood vessels.

Sodium and chloride levels within the VH remain relatively consistent with and are reasonably reflective of antemortem levels within the "early postmortem period" (considered to be the time during which rigor mortis is still appreciated). The value of sodium in the VH sample does decrease as the time since death increases, and a low sodium value in a decomposed person would not necessarily indicate hyponatremia during life. After death, the levels of sodium and chloride decrease and potassium levels rise in the vitreous fluid; however, the rate of decrease of sodium and chloride is much slower than the rate of rise of potassium. Efforts to link this phenomenon to postmortem interval have been suggested, but the degree of uncertainty and variation in the process has limited any practical application. The relatively rapid rise in potassium levels in the vitreous fluid after death can be problematic, and values of greater that 9 mmol/L are commonly reported. As such, any postmortem diagnosis of hyperkalemia based on VH electrolyte levels might be inaccurate.

Postmortem glucose levels in the VH can decrease very rapidly, with levels of <20 mg/dL reported routinely, even in the very early postmortem period. Low glucose levels in vitreous fluid should not be considered as necessarily reflective of the antemortem levels. Interestingly, urea nitrogen levels are apparently stable in VH for several days, rising by 20%–25% after about 3–4 days postmortem. Creatinine concentration is also generally stable and may provide a reasonable indication of antemortem levels. The combination of these results can be used to form some interpretations and diagnoses of clinical renal function status in some cases. Renal insufficiency can be suggested when the urea and creatinine in VH are both elevated.

As the postmortem interval increases, and with associated decomposition, VH becomes increasingly red-tinged after a few days (or more rapidly in elevated temperatures; see Figure 3.2) and eventually is resorbed. While vitreous fluid from a decomposed person will not be a useful specimen for electrolyte interpretation, it may be used to provide information for other medical considerations and facilitate the determination of cause of death. For example, while glucose levels drop rapidly after death, and neither blood nor vitreous levels can be reliably used to diagnose hypoglycemia, if the VH glucose level is elevated (e.g., greater than 50 mg/dL), hyperglycemia can reasonably be inferred. Further testing of VH for ketones could indicate diabetic ketoacidosis. Dehydration can be confirmed when the sodium and the chloride levels are elevated accompanied

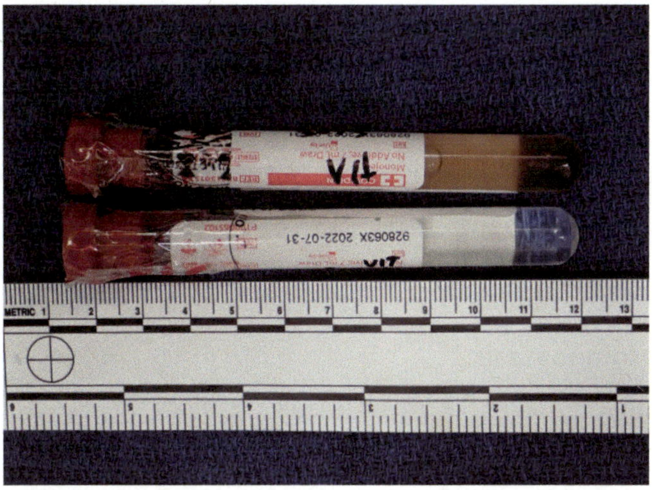

Figure 3.2 VH from the body of a decomposed person (top) and some from a decedent in the early postmortem period (bottom). Note that the sample in the top of the photograph is clear, colorless, and free of debris. The sample at the bottom is red-tinged and slightly cloudy and has some particulate matter in it.

by a moderate increase in urea nitrogen. Similar to the clinical setting, kidney disease can be considered when the urea nitrogen and creatinine are elevated. Reference ranges in the early postmortem period are the same or very close to the serum values in living people: Urea nitrogen: 8–20 mg/dL and creatinine: 0.7–1.4 mg/dL. Similarly, toxicologic analyses of vitreous can provide considerable information regarding the nature of drugs that may have been in the blood of the decedent at the time of death, albeit not with quantitative reliability.

In the case of embalmed bodies, the autopsy procedure can be tedious, as tissues can be very firm and difficult to dissect. Histologic samples, however, can often be very good as the tissues have been to some extent, already been preserved somewhat, prior to sampling. Few RBCs will be present in the vascular lumina as during the embalming process, the blood is entirely or almost entirely replaced by embalming fluid. Commercial products usually contain some mixture of formaldehyde, glutaraldehyde, methanol, and other organic solvents acting as effective tissue preservative and fixative agents, slowing the rate of decomposition, and rendering the tissue very firm. Occasionally embalming solutions that contain pigment or perfume are added to restore a natural appearance and fragrance to the skin. The VH–blood barrier often remains at least somewhat.

VH that has become contaminated by embalming fluid may have some degree of a pink tint. Embalming fluid solvents can be easily detected and are readily recognized as such by toxicology laboratory personnel during their volatile screen analyses. Where there may be an expectation that VH would represent an "undiluted" specimen, its use for diagnostic testing should be approached with caution. Post-embalming levels for both sodium and chloride in the vitreous fluid are lower than prior to the process, but not uniformly so, and the magnitude of decrease is not predictable. As such, post-embalming vitreous sodium and chloride values are not reliable and should not be used for diagnosis. However, urea nitrogen and glucose results appear to be more reliable, at least in the early postmortem period, although may be slightly lower than corresponding values obtained from pre-embalmed vitreous fluid samples.

3.3.4 Sodium

Sodium is the major extracellular cation (positive ion) in the body. It is the primary cationic contributor to the osmolality of the blood and plays a major role in control of blood volume, generation and maintenance of cellular membrane potentials, neural transmission, and muscle contraction. Normally, extracellular sodium is considerably greater than intracellular levels (~ 140 mEq/L).

The large gradient between the extracellular and intracellular spaces is maintained by specific cationic active transport molecules (the Na^+-K^+ATPase). The resulting sodium–potassium differential ("intracellular potassium, extracellular sodium") is the basis for the formation and maintenance of the cellular membrane potential, which is the driving force for numerous important biochemical reactions.

Either an excess of sodium in blood (hypernatremia) or too little (hyponatremia) can reflect a critically dangerous condition for the body. While fatal cases associated with either condition are relatively uncommon, the effective hypernatremia associated with dehydration can play a significant role in a death resulting from that condition. Hyponatremia is occasionally seen with athletes who attempt to rehydrate with water rather than with electrolyte solutions.

3.3.4.1 Sodium Homeostasis

A typical Western diet is relatively high in sodium, and levels in the body are primarily controlled by the kidney by the regulation of body water and the ability to drink water in response to perception of thirst. The kidneys regulate body water by adjusting the overall concentration of the urine. Dilute urine is generated when blood volume is large and/or the sodium level is low. Concentrated urine is made when the blood volume is low and/or the sodium level is high. In response to low blood volume due to dehydration, the body's hormonal response from the kidneys and the pituitary gland stimulates thirst in an attempt to replace the lost fluid. If the kidneys are damaged and unable to respond or the patient is not able or willing to drink water, a dangerous level of sodium can accumulate in the blood.

Hyponatremia can result from excessive diuretic activity; diarrhea; cardiac, hepatic, or renal disease; or organ failure. While correction is in essence, simply electrolyte replacement, and restoration of appropriate blood volume, correction of hyponatremia too rapidly in the clinical setting can cause osmotic-related demyelination in the brain stem in susceptible patients. Hyponatremia is the major cause of seizures in infants younger than 6 months old.

3.3.4.2 Postmortem Interval Considerations

After death, the activity of the Na-K-ATPase cationic transport protein ceases as energy is depleted in the body. Serum sodium levels begin to decrease after death as sodium ions diffuse into cells, consequential to the loss of membrane potential. Because of the unpredictable nature of the postmortem decline, serum sodium levels cannot be reliably used to infer antemortem values after the early postmortem period. While the decline in sodium and the rise in serum potassium levels had been of considerable interest as a basis for inference of the postmortem interval, the apparent variation and uncertainty in interpretation have made these parameters unreliable for such inference to date. As noted above, VH levels may provide useful information in the absence of reliable PM serum electrolyte levels. Coe documented that some decedents studied who demonstrated abnormal vitreous sodium values also had corresponding antemortem hypo- or hypernatremia.

3.3.4.3 Hypernatremia

Hypernatremia can be thought of as an excess of total body sodium compared to TBW. As such, the clinical condition of hypernatremia can be divided into the three possible causes of this imbalance: loss of both TBW and sodium, but a greater loss of TBW than sodium (hypovolemic hypernatremia), decreased TBW with a normal or near-normal amount of total body sodium (euvolemic hypernatremia), and normal or increased TBW with increased total body sodium (hypervolemic hypernatremia). The term "euvolemic hypernatremia" to indicate decreased TBW with a normal or near-normal serum sodium, while sounding inconsistent, indicates that the water loss is from intracellular and interstitial spaces, not intravascular water loss. Generally, however, the underlying natural disease process will be of greater concern to the pathologist than the characterization of the specific nature of the hypernatremia.

Death due to, or partially due to, hypernatremia is not uncommon. Natural disease processes that can result in hypernatremia include both renal and extrarenal causes. Renal water loss can occur from urinary solute excretions such as hyperglycemia causing osmotic diuresis. Insensible water loss occurs in excessive sweating with exercise, fever, heat exposure, and from severe burns. Hypernatremia can also occur due to water diuresis from diabetes insipidus following a head injury. Renal failure leading to impaired sodium excretion may also lead to hypernatremia.

There are numerous literature reports of cases of exogenous salt intake as accidental ingestions by people with psychiatric illness, the elderly, and children. Salt has also been used as an emetic, with the occasional unintended consequence of hypernatremia with inadequate emesis, with some cases being fatal (see Sidebar 3.3). Accidental hypernatremia has been reported in errors in intravascular infusion preparations and with specific drug treatments. Force-feeding of salt as a form of punishment has also been reported. The estimated fatal amount of ingested sodium is 1 g sodium chloride per kg body weight. For a 70-kg (154 lb) person, this is about 70 g, or about 12–13 tsp. of salt. (Recommended daily intake per CDC is less than 2.3 g per day in an adult.)

Sidebar 3.3: Fatal Hypernatremia from Folk Medicine Treatment

In 2001, we reported a case of fatal hypernatremia as a consequence of a "folk medicine" treatment for ethyl alcohol intoxication. The case involved a 14-year-old boy who had reportedly been drinking ethanol with a friend. Upon his return home, his parents thought he was intoxicated, and he was given salt water to help him recover by vomiting any remaining ethanol in his gastric lumen. He subsequently experienced diarrhea, a common side effect of hypernatremia, followed by a seizure. He was taken to a local hospital and continued to seize during transport. Upon hospital admission, his blood alcohol level was 35.7 mg/dL and serum sodium was 195 mmol/L. He was transferred to a children's hospital with a core temperature of 105°F.

Communication between the first hospital and the children's hospital was oral (by telephone), and the blood ethanol concentration was misinterpreted by the receiving hospital as 0.350 g/dL, not the correct value of 0.035 g/dL. Initially, the working diagnosis was ethanol intoxication with hypernatremia. At the children's hospital, he was given anticonvulsants, replacement fluids (normal saline!), and assisted ventilation. Despite aggressive measures, he expired approximately 36 h after the folk medicine therapy. An autopsy with toxicologic analysis for ethanol and drugs of abuse did not reveal any other additional information. His death was certified as seizure-induced hypoxic encephalopathy due to hypernatremia as a consequence of acute salt ingestion. The manner of death was classified as "accident."

Conservation of water by the kidney and stimulation of the thirst response are the mechanisms by which the body normalizes serum sodium. In response to low blood volume, juxtaglomerular (JG) cells of the afferent arterioles of the nephron convert pro-renin to renin, an enzyme that converts angiotensinogen to angiotensin I, a mild vasoconstrictor. Circulating angiotensin I is then converted to angiotensin II by angiotensin-converting enzyme (ACE) from the endothelium of pulmonary capillaries. Angiotensin II is a strong vasoconstrictor, which acts on arterioles and veins, increasing blood pressure immediately. Angiotensin II also acts on the kidney, stimulating aldosterone production, which then increases sodium and water retention in the renal tubules over time facilitating recovery of blood volume and pressure. Antidiuretic hormone (ADH), also known as vasopressin, is also released from the posterior lobe of the pituitary gland in response to low blood volume, low blood pressure, or high serum osmolality. The kidney responds to the serum ADH level by increasing the number of water channels (aquaporins) in the tubules, facilitating solute-free water reabsorption, with a corresponding increase in blood volume and blood pressure and decreased osmolality. An increase in extracellular sodium activates the thirst mechanism via osmoreceptor cells located just outside the blood–brain barrier in the periventricular areas of the brain and the brain stem. These cells also respond to the presence of angiotensin II in blood. In response to low water volume, thus low blood pressure, the level of angiotensin II is increased, also stimulating the thirst response in the hypothalamus. This initiates a feeling of sticky mucus in the mouth (dry mouth) which encourages a person to drink water. Brain damage, especially to the hypothalamus, can lead to loss of desire to drink water, even when the serum sodium level is very high.

The disorders of ion transport and osmolality consequential to hypernatremia can directly impact neuronal function. Patients can experience an altered mental status which can progress to seizure activity, coma, and death (see Sidebar 3.4). The response to hypernatremia at the level of the neuron is a continued transport of sodium out of the cell, albeit against an ever-increasing concentration gradient. Intracellular water is also reduced, in response to osmotic pressure, and to some extent, the extracellular fluid is removed by the kidney. Ultimately, the sodium–potassium pump fails against the increased extracellular concentration gradient, and potassium levels increase extracellularly, and sodium levels increase intracellularly.

Sidebar 3.4: Electrolyte Disturbance

In 2019, we evaluated a case of a 59-year-old woman with a 20-year history of multiple sclerosis (MS). She was significantly disabled from this condition and dependent upon her family for all of her needs. Her family reported that she had become increasingly mentally labile and eventually lost her will to live. She was unable or unwilling to eat or drink for at least a few days prior to being found dead in her bed at home. She was very clean, had no pressure-related injuries, and appeared to have been well-cared for. However, homicidal neglect was considered because she was exceptionally thin at 58 pounds, with a body mass index of 11.3 kg/m^2 (a body mass index of <18.5 kg/m^2 is considered underweight).

According to available medical records, she had been unwilling to receive treatment for her MS, preferring to allow the condition to take its natural course. About 14 months prior to her death, she had been treated in a local emergency room for possible smoke inhalation following a cigarette smoking incident at home. At that time, she was evaluated and sent home with a diagnosis of smoke exposure. Her laboratory values for electrolytes were all within normal limits. The only significant laboratory abnormality was a slightly elevated carboxyhemoglobin at 7.7%; however, she was a tobacco smoker and this level was not considered to be clinically significant. She was discharged in good condition from the emergency department without requiring treatment. There was no mention in either the report from emergency medical services or the hospital medical record at that time that she appeared ill or undernourished.

Fourteen months later at autopsy, she was cachectic and very dry. Her skin tented with gentle retraction and remained in that position (see Figure 3.3). Her internal organs and tissues were sticky. Her vitreous electrolyte panel revealed elevated sodium at 169 mmol/L (ref range 135–145); urea nitrogen, 86 mg/dL (ref range 8–20); creatinine, 0.8 mg/dL (ref range 0.7–1.4); and potassium, greater than 9 mmol/L (ref range 3.5–5.3). These data indicate

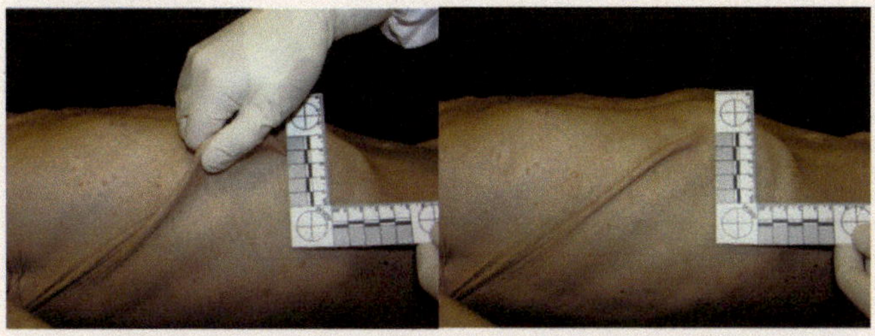

Figure 3.3 Skin tents with gentle pressure and remains in that position for some time.

severe dehydration, thought to be due to an unwillingness or an inability to drink water. The elevated potassium level also is consistent with at least a several-hour postmortem interval. The death was certified as "complications of multiple sclerosis, manner – natural."

Acute and/or severe hypernatremia may cause seizures independently from other causes (e.g., epileptiform, post-traumatic) and can occur in people with no seizure history. Serum electrolyte disturbances are generalized, and the clinical effects resulting from such disturbances are also generalized. While hypernatremic seizures are usually generalized tonic-clonic in nature, partial seizures may also occur. Information that a particular patient had and subsequently died from a seizure may be the only presenting symptom, and there may or may not be any documented seizure history. A VH assay for sodium would be helpful to support the diagnosis of a fatal seizure. Postmortem diagnosis of a seizure can be challenging as there are no definitive pathological consequences. At autopsy, the brain may be edematous; however, cerebral edema is not specific for a seizure. Microscopically, there may be an increased amount of perivascular and pericellular clear space in the gray and in the white matter. Occasionally, a person will bite the tongue during a seizure, but this is neither a constant finding nor necessarily diagnostic, although, when present, would support the diagnosis. The tongue must be removed and bivalved or serially sectioned to properly document bite marks. The tongue and neck block can be removed at the same time, or separately. There is no medical advantage to one approach over the other, and personal preference dictates technique.

3.3.4.4 Hyponatremia

Cases of hyponatremia encountered in the forensic setting may include manifestations of natural diseases (e.g., alcohol withdrawal, accidental trauma, and abuse; see Sidebars 3.5 and 3.6). Hyponatremia can be categorized as either acute or with a gradual onset, with the former being more amenable to clinical treatment. In the living patient, hyponatremia is diagnosed when serum sodium is less than 135 mEq/L.

As noted above, vitreous sodium and chloride values can often be reliably used to diagnose hyponatremia just prior to death, as both analytes are reasonably stable in the early postmortem period. Postmortem vitreous levels of sodium lower than 120 mmol/L are considered indicative of hyponatremia. The differential diagnosis in cases of apparent hyponatremia is salt wasting due to kidney disease, a syndrome of ADH, and adrenal gland insufficiency.

The fatal mechanisms in hyponatremia are presumed to be related to effects on neuronal cellular function and energy generation and related specifically to lowered sodium concentration and more generally to the associated osmotic changes. Acute, dilution-related hyponatremia occurs with the replacement of body water with fluids containing an inadequate amount of electrolytes.

Sidebar 3.5: Sodium and the Long-Distance Runner

Athletes who train or compete for hours, especially in hot conditions, can be at risk of lowered serum sodium and fatal electrolyte loss if they drink only water without added electrolytes, or otherwise fail to maintain sodium levels. Endurance athletes can experience a similar situation, even if training in perfect weather. The diagnosis is termed "exercise-induced hyponatremia," and athletes suffering such hyponatremic episodes may be otherwise healthy. Athletes who develop hyponatremia during training for or during the event itself report feeling similar to when they are dehydrated. They feel confused, lose their ability to concentrate on the race and the clues around them, and have a feeling of "heavy legs." They may collapse during or shortly after they complete the event. Hyponatremia is one of the most common medical emergencies suffered by marathon and ultramarathon runners that require medical attention at the race. The risk of hyponatremia is higher in warmer and more humid conditions.

Race directors are aware of this problem, and a supply of electrolyte-rich tablets, gels, and fluids during and after the race is often available for the competitors. Some races have a weigh station, utilized during the competition at various intervals, and require competitors to maintain their prerace weight within a certain percentage (usually 10%) before they are allowed out of the weigh station area.

Most athletes who train for long-distance races have already experimented with electrolyte-rich products before race day to determine which one(s) they can tolerate and are most effective for them. There are numerous products available for purchase. They come in a variety of flavors and are marketed as gel, liquids, and soft chews. In addition to these products, pure electrolytes are available as tablets and capsules for those people who prefer those formulations.

Individuals with psychiatric illnesses, in particular schizophrenia, may develop "psychogenic polydipsia" – ingestion of so much water that their electrolyte levels become dangerously depressed as a function of dilution. These patients may have the sensation of a dry mouth and continue to drink water to quench their perceived thirst. When severe, serum sodium levels can drop below 100 mEq/L, putting the patients at risk of seizures, cerebral edema, coma, and death. Treatment may be difficult, as the sensation of dry mouth in these patients is unrelated to their hydration status. Pathologists should consider requesting a vitreous electrolyte panel for their patients with a significant psychiatric history, especially if there is no other compelling cause of death detected at autopsy. However, as noted above, the result may be difficult to reliably interpret with increasing postmortem interval.

Forced water ingestion has been documented as an abusive punishment for children. In a reported circumstance, a number of children were forced to drink a large amount of water, in the range of many liters. All of the children presented with vomiting, had seizures, became comatose, and died. The serum sodium levels upon hospital admission were about 112 mEq/mL, corresponding to significant hyponatremia. At autopsy, in addition to their findings of physical abuse, all had cerebral edema. The rapid reduction of serum sodium caused by dilution of blood from excess free water ingestion causes an influx of free water into cells driven by the osmotic gradient across the cell membrane. The rate of sodium dilution is too fast for the compensatory mechanisms of cells to accommodate the change and maintain homeostasis. The brain is encased in the unyielding skull. Cerebral edema can lead to fatal cerebral herniation if hyponatremia is not corrected. Accidental hyponatremia can result when infants are given water to drink, rather than a solution specifically designed to contain the proper concentration of electrolytes, for example, infant formula. Infants rely solely on solute containing liquid for nutrition and hydration, and plain water, or diluted formula may not be an adequate electrolyte source.

The above are clear examples of when evaluation of medical records is essential. If a child dies with no obvious signs of physical abuse, forced water ingestion could be considered with the support of the clinical documentation of hyponatremia upon hospital admission. Often, children are kept on life-support measures for days until the family and the medical team agree that additional therapy is futile. Postmortem VH chemistry would not be helpful in these patients as serum electrolyte imbalances are usually corrected, or nearly so, in the hospitalized patient. The prolonged inhospital survival period negates the need to request VH analysis. Additionally, the eyes may need to be examined pathologically in cases of suspected child abuse. Obtaining VH from them could introduce an artifactual hemorrhage or artifactual retinoschisis.

Chronic alcohol abuse is a complex, total body disease affecting many organs and tissues, involving bone marrow suppression, toxic effects on the myocardium and hepatocytes, and enzyme induction in the liver, etc., and may include hyponatremia. Some patients with chronic alcoholism can become malnourished and hyponatremic as a greater percentage of their caloric intake is via their drinking. The term "beer potomania" was coined in 1972 to describe the syndrome of an excessive intake of alcohol (beer) over the course of several days with very little solute intake. These individuals may suffer fatigue, dizziness, and muscular weakness. Overconsumption of beer is especially risky because beer has a low solute content relative to the amount of water present. Drinking too much beer can, therefore, lead to dilutional hyponatremia. Individuals who are already nutritionally compromised may be especially vulnerable in the absence of a normal physiological reserve. People with severe chronic alcohol use disorder also can have low levels of other important ions (magnesium, calcium) as well as low levels of serum protein. This clinical picture is in marked contrast to otherwise healthy athletes and patients with acute water ingestion who develop dilutional hyponatremia.

Sidebar 3.6: Alcohol Withdrawal-Based Electrolyte Disturbance

The office of one of the authors (Dean) investigated the sudden death of an otherwise healthy man in his mid-30s who attempted to detoxify himself from ethanol. He recognized that he had a problem with alcohol and wanted to become sober. He did not want to reveal his condition to others, except his close relatives, so he did not request the help of a medical professional. Rather, he attempted to stop drinking on his own. On the day he died, he told his roommate that he was not feeling well. He went to take a nap and was found dead a short time later. He had no significant documented medical conditions, so an autopsy was performed. At autopsy, his heart was enlarged, 530 g, with left ventricular hypertrophy at 1.9 cm, but no atherosclerosis of the coronary arteries or elsewhere. A VH profile was requested after the information was revealed regarding his desire to stop drinking. VH sodium was 125 mEq/mL, glucose was < 20 mg/dL, and ethanol was negative in VH and blood. There were no drugs of abuse detected. Based on the history given, the autopsy findings, and the laboratory results, we concluded that this man died from acute ethanol withdrawal based on the electrolyte disturbance and the manner of death was classified as "natural."

3.3.5 Potassium

Potassium is the major intracellular cation, with relatively low levels extracellularly, and in blood. As such, variations in serum potassium levels have very little effect on osmotic pressure. The sodium–potassium balance across the cellular membrane functions in neuronal transmission, muscular contraction, and multiple transmembrane transport processes. Potassium excretion occurs in the renal tubules and is increased by the action of aldosterone, as sodium is retained. The reference range for serum potassium in living adults is 3.5–5.0 mEq/L and is tightly controlled, primarily by the kidney.

3.3.5.1 Potassium Homeostasis

Regulation of total body potassium as well as the proper distribution of potassium between the cytoplasm and the extracellular space is a dynamic process with two major prongs: concentration of potassium in organs and tissues and excretion by the kidney. Potassium is sequestered into cells when insulin is released from the pancreas. When insulin binds to cell surface receptors, glucose enters the cell. Glucose entering the cytoplasm stimulates an intracellular signal to activate the Na^+-K^+ATPase pump, bringing potassium from blood into the cytoplasm. Patients with type 2 diabetes mellitus have adequate insulin, but the cellular membrane response (glucose uptake) is diminished or absent. However, these patients do not seem to have an increased risk of hyperkalemia, presumably because of adequate activity of the Na^+-K^+ pump to maintain potassium homeostasis.

In the normal adult, physical exertion results in movement of intramuscular potassium from the cytoplasm into the interstitium. This leads to a higher-than-normal concentration of extracellular potassium, thereby changing the cell membrane resting potential. The rise in extracellular potassium inhibits the cell membrane from repolarizing. The effect is to limit cell excitability and contractile force. Patients experience fatigue and local soreness of the muscle group affected. To compound the problem, vasodilation is stimulated, in part, by the intracellular concentration of potassium. When cytoplasmic potassium is depleted, as in physical exertion, vasodilation is reduced, further reducing blood flow to the affected muscle group. Sequestration of potassium, primarily in skeletal muscle and liver, appears to be important for the regulation of local as well as total body potassium. Potassium is also stored in cardiac muscle, but the movement across the cardiac myocyte membrane is under tighter control than it is in skeletal muscle. This may explain why healthy patients without underlying cardiac conditions can exercise hard, developing skeletal muscle fatigue without developing cardiac muscle "fatigue."

Serum potassium is freely filtered from the glomerular capillaries into Bowman's space. Most of the potassium is reabsorbed into the cells of the proximal collecting tubule and the loop of Henle, returning it to blood. In the proximal tubule, potassium absorption is primarily passive and proportional to sodium and water. In the ascending limb of the loop of Henle, potassium resorption is by an active Na^+-K^+-$2Cl^-$ cotransporter transmembrane pump and by simple diffusion between tubular cells.

Serum potassium is also controlled by the adrenal gland. In response to elevated serum potassium and high angiotensin II levels, the adrenal cortex synthesizes aldosterone. Aldosterone acts in the distal nephron to increase the activity of the transmembrane Na^+-K^+ATPase pump as well as other transmembrane pumps to promote renal excretion. Potassium excretion begins in the early distal convoluted tubule and progressively increases along the distal nephron into the cortical collecting duct and, finally, out into the urine.

3.3.5.2 Hyperkalemia

Hyperkalemia, usually considered as a serum potassium level above 5 mEq/L, occurs in renal insufficiency and excessive oral intake. With either reduced glomerular filtration rate or tubular dysfunction, renal potassium excretion reduced. Major risk factors for hyperkalemia are renal failure; diabetes mellitus; adrenal gland insufficiency; and the use of ACE inhibitors, angiotensin receptor blockers, or potassium-sparing diuretics. Excessive oral intake is not usually accidental in nature. It is difficult to consume more potassium than the kidney can regulate, even if a patient is using a potassium chloride "salt substitute." Excessive intake is usually suicidal in nature (see Sidebar 3.7).

Sidebar 3.7: Suicidal Ingestion of Potassium

A 62-year-old woman (5′2″, 128 pounds) with a past medical history of hypertension and depression presented to the emergency department several times within a week for chest pain radiating to her left arm. Blood pressure was 163/85, and she reported feeling anxious. A cardiac workup was initiated with negative results for acute coronary syndrome. On those visits, laboratory values were all within the reference range, including troponin and potassium at 3.6 meq/L two days prior to her intentional ingestion. An electrocardiogram (EKG) showed sinus rhythm with ST depression and T-wave inversion in leads V3 to V5. The medical team recommended hospital admission for further evaluation including a nuclear medicine cardiac stress test, but she left the hospital against medical advice. On the day of her suicide, her husband had called emergency medical services twice. The first time she refused transport; the second time he found her unresponsive in bed and had attempted CPR.

When emergency medical services responded, her initial rhythm was asystole, but return of spontaneous circulation was achieved after approximately 25 min of cardiopulmonary resuscitation, six doses of epinephrine 0.1 mg IV, five 50 mEq IV injections of bicarbonate, two doses of 1,000 mg calcium chloride IV, and multiple shocks for ventricular tachycardia. Her cardiac rhythm degenerated to pulseless electrical activity while in the emergency department. Her blood pressure was variable, but she was never normotensive, reaching 96/61. Her EKG was significantly different from two days prior. At this admission, she had wide complex tachycardia to 107 beat per minute, left axis deviation, prolonged QTc, and changing rhythms from left bundle branch block to right bundle branch block and back to left bundle branch block. Her pulse and blood pressure were improved after aggressive treatment, and she was transferred to the intensive care unit in guarded condition. She started bleeding from her intravenous catheter sites and developed a gastrointestinal hemorrhage, indicating that she developed DIC, and she died about 5 h after admission.

Final laboratory values upon ICU admission were as follows:

Chemistry:
- Sodium: 147 (136–145 mmol/L)
- Potassium: >10 (3.5–5.1 mmol/L)
- Chloride: 119 (99–110 mmol/L)
- Glucose: 428 (70–99 mg/dL)
- Creatinine: 1.4 (0.6–1.2 mg/dL)
- Calcium: >100 (8.3–10.6 mg/dL)
- Lactic acid: 15.3

Liver enzymes:
- Alt: 217 (10–40 IU/L)
- AST: 220 (15–37 IU/L)
- Blood gases:
- pH: 6.985 (7.35–7.45)
- pCO2, venous: 73.6
- pO2, venous: 41.3
- HCO3, venous: 17.1
- Base excess, venous: –15.2

Hematology:
- PT: 14.4
- INR: 1.26
- Fibrinogen: 164 (200–397 mg/dL)
- d-Dimer: 5 250 (0–229 ng/mL)

Elevated potassium blood levels can affect neuronal signaling by causing cell membrane hypopolarization and also affect all cells including skeletal muscle and the heart. At lower, nonfatal concentrations, symptoms of central nervous system (CNS) impairment may be exhibited. Hyperkalemic hypopolarization of myocytes can be seen on the EKG as a prolongation of the P wave and a decrease in amplitude (corresponding to sinoatrial (SA) nodal hypopolarization). Hyperpolarization of the atrioventricular (AV) node and the bundles of His are seen as alterations in the T wave, causing them to be taller and sharper. With a progressive increase in serum potassium, hypopolarization of the conduction system worsens and the amplitude of the T wave continues to increase, remaining above the isoelectric line. With severe hyperkalemia, the QRS complex widens to incorporate the P wave, and the EKG signal then mimics a sine wave. This cardiac rhythm is not sustainable and can degenerate into ventricular fibrillation. Depending on concentration, repolarization can also be affected to the point of cardiac failure and death.

The treatment for hyperkalemia includes correction of acidosis, if present, and administration of insulin to facilitate transfer of potassium from the serum to the cytoplasm concurrent to the regulation of serum glucose. Hemodialysis may be required in patients with renal failure as the kidneys in those patients do not have an adequate glomerular filtration to remove potassium from blood and move it to the urine.

3.3.5.3 Hypokalemia

Hypokalemia, as reflected in a serum level below 3.5 mEq/L in living adults, could cause a cardiac arrhythmia and become a medical emergency. If the patient lives long enough to have blood drawn in the hospital, the antemortem serum chemistry results are essential to review. Due to the rapid rise of potassium levels in VH after death, hypokalemia is a very difficult diagnosis to make postmortem. In the living patient, low blood potassium occurs as a consequence of four possible abnormalities: inadequate dietary intake, overconcentration of potassium inside cells, loss of extracellular (total body) potassium, and urinary loss. Inadequate dietary intake alone usually cannot cause severe hypokalemia if renal regulation is intact. However, kidney disease in addition to starvation may cause a clinically significant hypokalemia. In some cases of type 1 diabetes, potassium can be taken into the cells with glucose, causing a shift from the extracellular to the intracellular space. Total body potassium can be lost through fluid loss with vomiting, diarrhea, and an ileostomy stoma, as well as fluid loss from major burns and major trauma. Profuse sweating can contribute. Overuse of diuretics can also cause urinary depletion. Patients treated with a loop diuretic for congestive heart failure or hypertension are at risk of hypokalemia and often require potassium supplementation.

The EKG tracing of a patient in a hypokalemic state reflects hyperpolarization of myocytes. There is ST segment depression, sometimes below the isoelectric line and the appearance of a U wave. Normally, the U wave is a very small deflection in the EKG (if visible at all) following and in the same direction as the T wave. It represents delayed or prolonged repolarization. The appearance of large U waves, greater than 25% of the height of the T wave, could indicate hypokalemia or intoxication by digitalis or any drug that inhibits the Na^+-K^+ATPase transmembrane pump.

3.3.6 Chloride

Chloride is the major extracellular anion, and with sodium are the primary determinants of tonicity. Functionally, chloride balances the cationic electrolytes, thereby maintaining system neutrality. In the kidney, secretion and reabsorption of chloride occur along with sodium ions. Hypochloremia, abnormally low blood chloride levels, can be caused by electrolyte loss, for example, by vomiting or diarrhea. Insufficient renal reabsorption can also be a cause, as can acidosis. Hyperchloremia can be caused, similar to hypernatremia, by excessive salt intake, dehydration, and seawater ingestion. The absolute value of serum or VH chloride is evaluated along with the absolute value of sodium in the corresponding matrix to aid in diagnosis.

3.4 INSULIN

Diabetes mellitus is a condition affecting millions of patients in the United States and worldwide. Patients with diabetes mellitus have either abnormal insulin production, release, or cellular resistance to insulin uptake. Insulin is a peptide hormone produced by the pancreas and plays a major role in the regulation of metabolism, glucose absorption and utilization, and energy production in the body. Insulin is synthesized and stored in the beta cells of the islets of Langerhans in the pancreas until it is needed (as signaled by elevated serum glucose, etc.). Preproinsulin is the first precursor protein of insulin and consists of alternating segments of proinsulin and signal peptides. At this stage, the proinsulin molecule is insulin wrapped by a C-peptide (so named for its shape) protein chain and becomes proinsulin as it is cleaved to leave the two insulin subunits, A and B, joined by disulfide bonds, as well as the linking C-peptide. Insulin is a peptide hormone only composed of the two peptide chains, A and B, linked by disulfide bonds. Diagnosis of an overdose of exogenous insulin requires laboratory analysis for insulin and C-peptide. The ratio of insulin to C-peptide should be ~1:1 for endogenous insulin; exogenous insulin does not have the C-peptide and, to the extent present, distorts the normal ratio. While possible, this analysis is not routine.

Forensic concerns involving patients with diabetes mellitus and, specifically, the magnitude of contribution of the disease and its consequences to COD and MOD are usually related to severity of disease, associated drug use, or trauma. However, elevated glucose accompanied by ketone production may be the first sign of diabetes mellitus in a patient with no documented medical history. Undiagnosed diabetes may be the cause of death in patients with an otherwise negative autopsy and may contribute to death in combination with other natural diseases. The history of physical symptoms in deceased patients can often only be obtained from friends or relatives. Occasionally, people who keep a diary or journal will chronicle how poorly they are feeling. Forensic investigators can interview people who knew the now-deceased as well as look for diaries in the person's residence. This level of investigation is critical for the pathologist, especially if the now-deceased person does not have documented medical history. For this reason, some pathologists routinely request testing of VH for glucose, electrolytes, and ketones of their decedents. Some laboratories report ketone production as acetone and others as β-hydroxybutyrate. Diabetic ketoacidosis can be readily diagnosed by analysis of ketone bodies and glucose in VH.

In the setting of inadequate insulin, most cells in the body cannot take up adequate levels of glucose, blood glucose level rises, often to greater than 300 mg/dL, but intracellular glucose remains low. Patients may report a variety of symptoms including lethargy, gait instability, trouble concentrating, and a feeling of dehydration. Onset of symptoms can be gradual. Patients are sometimes not aware that they are becoming hyperglycemic. In contrast, glucose is readily transported (across the blood/brain barrier) into neurons. Brain cells survive for a while in acute hypoglycemia, because the transport proteins for glucose are efficient even when blood glucose levels are low.

Metabolic derangements caused by inadequate insulin in the setting of excess glucose are metabolic acidosis, osmotic diuresis, and electrolyte disturbance, all of which can be fatal. When somatic cells cannot accept glucose, there can be a biochemical call for more by triggering the release of glucagon from the pancreas. Glucagon then causes:

- Hepatic release of glucose from the polysaccharide glycogen into the blood.
- Induction of gluconeogenesis in the liver.
- Lipolysis of adipose tissue causing an increase in free fatty acids in the blood from stored fat.
- Diversion of free fatty acids in the liver toward beta-oxidation rather than triglyceride production.
- Inhibition of renal tubular sodium resorption.

As blood glucose increases, in the absence of adequate insulin, the somatic cells still cannot effectively take it in, and the cycle continues. Free fatty acids accumulate in blood and are converted into the ketone bodies (ketones), acetoacetic acid, and beta-hydroxybutyrate. Acetoacetic acid is further converted to acetone in the blood. Ketone bodies, when present, can easily be detected in blood, urine, and VH. The accumulation of ketone bodies in the blood lowers the blood pH, resulting in some degree of metabolic acidosis or "diabetic ketoacidosis" in patients with diabetes. Living patients may have a sweet scent to the breath, a "fruity odor" as acetone is expired during by respiration. Clinically, "keto strips" are used to detect the presence of ketone bodies in the urine of living patients with diabetes mellitus and those on a ketogenic diet checking for. In the deceased person, ketone bodies can be detected in urine and vitreous, with vitreous being the preferred specimen. These authors have not seen reports of or had personal experience with a "fruity odor" on or from a deceased person.

Glucose can be detected in urine when the (antemortem) serum value is greater than approximately 225 mg/dL and can be a good screening method for hyperglycemia. Vitreous glucose can be detected in the early postmortem period when the serum value is high but declines with a prolonged postmortem interval.

In the forensic setting, insulin overdose can occur in patients requiring insulin. These patients with type 1 diabetes or advanced type 2 diabetes (those requiring insulin supplementation) occasionally use too much and develop hypoglycemia. Treatment is the administration of glucose which will be reflected in the medical record if they are hospitalized.

Suicidal administration of insulin is marked by profound and intractable hypoglycemia. Analysis for insulin is not a routine test in most laboratories because it is an infrequently requested assay. Additionally, postmortem blood samples are frequently at least partially hemolyzed. Hemolysis interferes with most immunoassays. Serum samples are preferred, especially samples obtained upon hospital admission. Refrigeration helps to preserve insulin in the sample.

The interpretation of the absolute insulin value is complicated. Serum insulin is not static and rises with a glucose-containing meal and drops as glucose enters the cells. Insulin levels tend to be higher in overweight or obese patients. If an insulin overdose is suspected in patients with profound hypoglycemia and is not prescribed insulin, the insulin:C-peptide ratio should be evaluated. If the insulin:C-peptide ratio is about 1, there is an organic (endogenous) source for the insulin. The differential diagnosis is an insulin-producing tumor.

The elimination half-lives of insulin and C-peptide are in the range of 5–8 min and 10–20 min, respectively. This short window complicates the interpretation of results from postmortem blood. Profound hypoglycemia is not immediately fatal. The overdosed patient can linger in a coma for hours, all the while metabolizing the evidence. Investigative information is critical. Helpful information can be found at the patient's residence. For example, if the patient has insulin vials not prescribed for him or has evidence of overuse, this information can be used to collaborate the diagnosis, even if the insulin levels are low.

Insulin is subject to postmortem degradation by enzymes in blood and is almost completely degraded in less than a week if left at room temperature. Postmortem whole blood is not a good specimen to use for insulin analysis. For optimum results, hospital admission plasma or serum that has been stored at 4° C should be used. The next best specimens to use would be cerebral spinal fluid or VH stored at 4° C. Insulin in serum or plasma is stable for about 6 days if the specimens are refrigerated.

3.5 NON-OPIOID ANALGESICS

Aspirin and other nonsteroidal analgesics are over-the-counter medications used to treat low-grade fever, inflammation, and minor pain. This class of drugs is not usually associated with fatal overdoses; however, their overuse in combination with significant medical disease and the use of other medications can contribute to death. Toxicity results from either renal or hepatic failure. Overuse alone can cause fatal hemorrhages.

Aspirin and other NSAIDS are rapidly absorbed from the stomach and the small intestine. Low-dose aspirin, 81 mg/day, is prescribed prophylactically for the prevention of arterial and venous thromboses based upon its inhibition of cyclooxygenase (COX)-1. Low-dose aspirin is used to prevent clots in patients with atrial fibrillation, acute coronary syndrome with or without a myocardial infarction, and venous thromboses due to platelet aggregation in patients with malignancies. Inhibition is irreversible.

Aspirin also promotes fibrinolysis by the acetylation of coagulation factors and fibrinogen. This is the theory for prescribing aspirin to patients who have some venous thrombi already formed. Continuous, regular use of low-dose aspirin maintains the appropriate anticoagulation effect. Patients at risk of clotting events who use aspirin as prescribed are usually not at risk of hemorrhage. However, if taken to excess, the risk of bleeding increases. Bleeding is the most common adverse effect. Patients who administer too much aspirin are at risk of hemorrhagic cerebral infarctions and bleeding ulcers of the stomach and duodenum.

Aspirin has been associated with Reye's syndrome in children following or in close temporal proximity to a viral infection. Aspirin appears to cause a metabolic disturbance in some vulnerable patients at the level of the mitochondria in liver causing hepatic failure followed by hepatic encephalopathy. The clinical presentation is that of typical liver failure, with or without jaundice. At autopsy, the liver will be grossly enlarged, pale, and soft. The brain will be edematous.

Nonsteroidal anti-inflammatory drugs (NSAIDs) other than aspirin are used to treat or prevent thromboses as well as to treat inflammation and fever. The mechanism of action is similar, although NSAIDs inhibit COX-2 as well as COX-1 enzymes. The enzyme inhibition is reversible. The inhibition of COX-2 is the basis for the anti-inflammatory properties of NSAIDs. NSAIDs also inhibit prostanoids, such as PGE2. Prostanoids cause vasodilation and excitation of peripheral pain neurons. Inhibition of prostanoids reduces the blood flow to affected areas, reducing edema. Chronic overuse of NSAIDs can cause kidney damage based on reduced blood flow due to inhibition of prostanoids. Patients can develop acute renal tubular necrosis and interstitial nephritis. These conditions are reversible with the cessation of the drugs. NSAIDs are metabolized by hepatic CYP450 enzymes and are contraindicated in patients with hepatic failure. The metabolism of acetaminophen (APAP) produces a toxic intermediate, N-acetyl-p-quinone amine, which can serve as a source of oxygen radical toxicity. At normal levels of APAP, the body is able to adequately detoxify the level of NAPQI generated. However, at elevated, or overdose levels, hepatic toxicity, event to the point of fatal hepatic failure can be caused (see Section 7).

Bibliography

Agency for Toxic Substances and Disease Registry (ATSDR). (2023). *Toxicologic Profiles*. Atlanta, GA: U.S. Department of Health and Human Services, Public Health Services.

Castilla-Guerra L., del Carmen Fernández-Moreno M., López-Chozas J.M., Fernández-Bolaños R. (2006). Electrolytes disturbances and seizures. *Epilepsia*, 47(12):1990–1998. https://doi.org/10.1111/j.1528-1167.2006.00861.x

Chemical Suicide – The growing phenomenon. *Riverview Health*. https://www.riverview.org/downloads/pdfs/rvh-ems-chemical-suicide-presentation.pdf. Accessed 20 December 2021.

Coe J.I. (1993). Postmortem chemistry update. Emphasis on forensic application. *The American Journal of Forensic Medicine and Pathology*, 14(2):91–117. https://doi.org/10.1097/00000433-199306000-00001.

DiMaio V.J., DiMaio D. (2001). *Forensic Pathology*. 2nd ed. BocaRaton, FL: CRC Press.

Gidlow D. (2017). Hydrogen cyanide-an update. *Occupational Medicine*, 67:662–663. https://doi.org/10.1093/occmed/kqx121.

Labay L.M., Bitting C.P., Legg K.M., Logan B.K. (2016). The determination of insulin overdose in postmortem investigations. *Academic Forensic Pathology*, 6(2):174–183. https://doi.org/10.23907/2016.019.

Levin M., Pizon A., Padilla O., Jones A., Ruha A.M. (2014). Warfarin overdose: A 25-year prospective. *Journal of Medical Toxicology*, 10:156–164.

Liamis G., Milionis H., Elisaf M. (2008). A review of drug-induced hyponatremia. *American Journal of Kidney Diseases: The Official Journal of the National Kidney Foundation*, 52(1):144–153. https://doi.org/10.1053/j.ajkd.2008.03.004.

Lieberman M., Marks A. (eds) (2009). Liver metabolism. In: *Mark's Basic Medical Biochemistry: A Clinical Approach* (pp. 910–929). 3rd rev. ed. Philadelphia, PA: Wolters Kluwer Health/Lippincott Williams & Wilkins, 910-929.

McGuire L.C., Cruickshank A.M., Munro P.T. (2006). Alcoholic ketoacidosis. *Emergency Medicine Journal*, 23(6):417–420. https://doi.org/10.1136/emj.2004.017590.

Reichl F.X., Ritter L. (eds). (2011). *Illustrated Handbook of Toxicology*. Stuttgart: Thieme.

Sangalli B.C., Bidanset J.H. (1990). A review of carboxymyoglobin formation: A major mechanism of carbon monoxide toxicity. *Veterinary and Human Toxicology*, 32(5):449–453.

Sterner W.Q. (2006). *Spitz and Fisher's Medicolegal Investigation of Death*. 4th ed. Springfield, IL: Charles C. Thomas.

Umbreit J. (2007). Methemoglobin: it's not just blue: A concise review. *American Journal of Hematology*, 82(2):134–144. https://doi.org/10.1002/ajh.20738.

Wilcox G. (2005). Insulin and insulin resistance. *The Clinical Biochemist Reviews*, 26(2):19–39.

SECTION 4

ALCOHOLS AND RELATED COMPOUNDS

DOI: 10.4324/9781003121060-5

4.1 INTRODUCTION

Ethyl alcohol (ethanol, "drinking alcohol") is probably the most commonly encountered drug within forensic settings, as evidenced by its status as a standard analyte for both emergency and routine medical situations, law enforcement issues (e.g., driving under the influence (DUI)testing), and within postmortem toxicology panels. Other related alcohol species (e.g., methanol, isopropanol, and ethylene glycol) are less often encountered but, because of comparably greater toxic potential than ethanol, may be of greater forensic significance in a particular case, depending on circumstances.

Alcohols are organic molecules containing a hydroxyl functional group (–OH). The single carbon form, CH_3OH, is methanol, also known as "wood alcohol." The two-carbon ethyl alcohol, also known as grain alcohol, is the "alcohol" present in beverages. The (arguably) low toxic potential, euphorigenic effects elicited at low doses, and ease of preparation/acquisition provide underlying reasons for the extensive recreational use of ethanol, worldwide. Other alcohols that may be encountered in forensic settings are propyl (iso- and n-; a three-carbon alcohol), butyl (iso, n-, and tert-; a four-carbon alcohol), and ethylene glycol (the two-hydroxy analogue of ethanol). While each has its own toxic potential, methanol, isopropanol, and ethylene glycol are the most commonly observed in forensic casework. Generally, the CNS depressive effects and, hence, the toxicity of alcohols parallel the molecular weight, with the lone exception of methanol which has a paradoxically high toxic potential (discussed in Section 4.3, below). Alcohols are readily eliminated from the body because of their aqueous solubility, following oxidation primarily in the liver, by the actions of alcohol and aldehyde dehydrogenases (alcohol dehydrogenase and aldehyde dehydrogenase, respectively) producing even more hydrophilic species. Alcohols are also eliminated unchanged in breath, sweat, and urine to a small extent (with such elimination being the basis for forensic testing of specimens other than blood).

4.2 ETHANOL

Consumption of ethyl alcohol as a socially acceptable recreational drug is extensive in most modern societies, and certainly pervasive in the United States. Alcohol can be purchased legally and consumed freely by those "of age," with some limitations, for example, "legal drinking age" and restrictions based on a definition of "DUI" being established by the States. Laboratory analysis of ethanol in biological fluids (e.g., blood, urine, and vitreous humor (VH)) is relatively straightforward; however, interpretation of results can be challenging for both the pathologist and forensic toxicologist. Evaluation of the meaning of a result in a specific case setting may require an understanding of the nuances of the specific samples utilized, analytical techniques employed, and the metabolic processes that ethanol undergoes in the body, as well as the possible contribution by the effects of decomposition.

4.2.1 Pharmacokinetics

Ethanol is rapidly absorbed and distributed in total body water and, hence, throughout the body. Because of the extensive distribution, and lack of concentration in any particular tissue, ethanol does not exhibit postmortem redistribution (with the exception that antemortem unabsorbed concentrations in the stomach or small intestine may serve as a reservoir and thereby provide a localized high concentration from which diffusion can proceed). Ethanol consumption is often considered in terms of number of drinks ingested in a given time period. A "standard" drink is considered to contain ~14 g ethyl alcohol (hence, ~12 oz. beer, 5 oz. wine, 1.5 oz distilled spirits). Consumption of a single standard drink will raise the blood alcohol content (BAC) of an ~180-lb individual by ~0.02 g/dL, with that value inversely proportional to weight.

4.2.1.1 Absorption

Following ingestion, ethanol is relatively rapidly absorbed from the stomach and small intestine. Depending on the means of exposure, alcohol can be absorbed through the skin (particularly if damaged—denuded, abraded, burned), mucus membranes, and the large intestine. As much as 20% can be absorbed through the stomach, but by far the bulk of absorption occurs in the small intestine. The rate of absorption is a function of the concentration of alcohol, with the maximal rate occurring when the alcohol ingested is in the range of ~25% alcohol, or 50 proof. (Proof=2×% alcohol; 40% alcohol is 80 proof.) Absorption of ingested alcohol will generally be essentially complete in 15–40 min on an empty stomach. Fats, protein, and carbohydrates limit absorption from the gastric mucosa. Food in the stomach delays gastric emptying and slows the transit of ingested alcohol to the small intestine, delaying the time for maximal BAC to be achieved. The maximum blood level in a person who drinks alcohol concurrently with eating food or with food in the stomach will be lower and the time to achieve that maximum BAC will be extended.

4.2.1.2 Distribution

Ethanol rapidly distributes and equilibrates throughout the body, as a function of an ability of the molecule to transit "aquaporin" water channels, present in all cell membranes. Ethanol is also able to easily cross the blood–brain barrier, and the blood:CNS ratio for ethanol is generally close to 1:1. Because of the relatively rapid and extensive distribution and the lack of specific tissue concentration, the ethanol level in a heart blood sample is expected to be about the same as that in femoral blood or any other peripherally sourced blood sample. In short, postmortem redistribution is not a concern with alcohol sampling and testing. However, there can be a relatively minor differential between arterial and venous blood levels when collected during active processes of absorption and distribution (or from a decedent who died while those processes were still ongoing). Victims with extensive chest/abdominal trauma may have variable ethanol levels (if collected from within the chest/abdominal cavity because of rupture and leakage from the stomach and small intestine into the surrounding vasculature). Testing of VH or femoral blood samples in such cases may provide a more reliable indication of true antemortem alcohol concentration, bearing in mind that vitreous alcohol levels tend to lag somewhat behind blood levels.

4.2.1.3 Metabolism and Elimination

Metabolism of ethanol consists primarily of two sequential oxidation steps: first to acetaldehyde and then to acetate catalyzed by ADH and acetaldehyde dehydrogenase (AADH), respectively. The primary metabolic site for alcohol is the liver, and extensive hepatic disease can affect alcohol metabolism. Unlike most enzyme systems engaged in metabolism of drugs, ADH is "saturated" by its substrate at physiologically significant concentrations (e.g., ~0.02 g/dL and higher). As such, the oxidation of ethanol proceeds as a function of amount of enzyme, rather than amount of substrate (hence "zero-order" kinetics). For most casual or social drinkers, this rate tends to be ~0.02 g/dL/h. ADH is an inducible enzyme, and so experienced/frequent drinkers and patients with alcohol use disorder can exhibit significantly higher elimination rates, even exceeding 0.03 g/dL/h. Conversely, individuals who rarely drink can have elimination rates somewhat lower than 0.02 g/dL/h. Alcohol in the blood is filtered and eliminated via the kidneys, although this represents a relatively small percentage of the total amount ingested. Alcohol is also lost in expired air (the basis for forensic breath alcohol testing) and volatilizes off the skin, albeit in small amounts. Ethanol can be conjugated, with both ethyl sulfate and ethyl glucuronide formed, and appeared in the urine. Both of these conjugates have been utilized as "markers" of prior ethanol usage but are not generally of use in postmortem analysis.

4.2.2 Physiologic Effects

Ethanol functions as a CNS depressant, with euphorigenic effects being perceptible in some users at concentrations as low as 0.01 g/dL. Alcohol effects are proportional to blood concentration, and as those levels increase, the magnitude of CNS depression-related effects become more obvious as diminished cognitive and motor skills, increased reaction time, and such specifically observable effects as slurred speech. Muscular paralysis, coma, and death are the effects of very high concentrations. While a specific mechanism of action of ethanol has not been identified, the ability of ethanol to affect functional neurotransmission resulting in the slowing or limiting signal conduction is well recognized. Ethanol effects are markedly similar to the action of elevated or overdose levels of gamma-aminobutyric acid (GABA)-nergic CNS depressant drugs (e.g., barbiturates and benzodiazepines), prompting an expectation that ethanol may function to some extent in a manner similar to the inhibitory neurotransmitter GABA. While no activity of ethanol on the $GABA_A$ receptor (a ligand-gated postsynaptic chloride channel) has been demonstrable, some researchers have postulated that ethanol enhances $GABA_B$ receptor (a metabotropic potassium channel activator) activity and may also function to inhibit NMDA receptors (excitatory glutamate receptors). It should be noted that because (at least to date) a receptor-mediated function for ethanol has not been identified, "tolerance" to the drug is presumed to reflect an enhanced rate of metabolism and, to some extent, learned behavior rather than an effect on cell membrane receptor expression or function.

4.2.3 Correlation of BAC with Physiologic Effects

The dose-dependent effects of ethanol and their clear correlation with BAC have been recognized for many decades. A table, originally published by Dr. Kurt Dubowski in 1970, reflected those relations, and while appearing in various revised forms, it has become a standard for the evaluation of the impact of ethanol on an individual. In a simplified format, a correlation table between blood alcohol concentration and effects can be presented as follows.

Table 4.1 Adapted/Modified "Dubowski Table"

0.01–0.05 g/dL	Slight impairment, perceptual and emotional effects
0.03–0.12 g/dL	Euphoria, decreased social inhibition, decreased emotional control, decreased judgment and cognitive function, decreased fine motor skills start of sensorimotor impairment
0.09–0.25 g/dL	Emotional instability, impaired perception, decreased memory, impaired coordination, impaired cognitive function
0.18–0.30 g/dL	Dizziness; blurred vision; slurred speech; significant impairment of cognitive, perceptual, and related functions
0.35–0.50+ g/dL	Anesthesia, coma, possible death

4.2.4 Alcohol Calculations and Inferences

Most calculations regarding alcohol ingestion in forensic cases tend to focus on the amount of alcohol required to have produced the particular BAC determined in postmortem specimens. Such questions, generally relating to legal questions or issues, are often not relevant to cause of death (COD) and manner of death (MOD) determination. However, understanding the methodology with which such issues can be addressed may be of some use in either facilitating a legal investigation or helping resolve questions for the family or friends of the deceased. The basic or most common question is, of course, how many drinks would have been required to produce the specific BAC determined? Recognizing that this question must usually be answered in terms of "standard drinks" (Section 4.2.1) providing a reasonably accurate estimate is not particularly challenging. The first step is simply determining the expected BAC rise that would be associated with one standard drink. Calculation of the elevation of BAC that would reasonably be associated with a single drink can be accomplished by one of several ways, although for most purposes, a simple "rule of thumb" is that one standard drink will raise the BAC of an ~180-lb. individual 0.02 g/dL inversely proportional to weight, ((180 lb/BW)*0.02 g/dL)). Hence, a 220-lb. individual would be expected to gain ~0.016 g/dL per (standard) drink. Secondly, metabolism during the time period of drinking can be simply calculated, and for most circumstances, ~0.02 g/dL/h will generally be useful (somewhat lower, e.g., 0.015–0.018 g/dL/h for naïve drinkers; higher, e.g., 0.022–0.028 g/dL/h for heavy drinkers or patients with alcohol use disorder).

4.2.4.1 Example Calculation

For a 160-lb man who has been in a bar drinking for ~4 h, and when tested ~1 h after leaving the bar, indicated a 0.12 g/dL would be as follows (using 0.02 g/dL/h as an elimination rate): 0.0225 g/dL/drink ((180/160) * 0.02 g/dL). Five hours of metabolism at 0.02 g/dL/h = 0.1 g/dL. Total BAC to be accounted for is then 0.22 g/dL. At 0.0225 g/dL/drink = ~10 standard drinks.

4.2.4.2 Volume of Distribution-based Calculation

The volume of distribution (Vd) calculation commonly employed by physicians and clinical toxicologists can of course be applied to questions related to alcohol. Similarly, a specific alcohol-based adaptation, the "Widmark" formula, relating a number of specific drinks to an expected BAC is also commonly used by forensic toxicologists.

4.2.4.3 Back-Extrapolation of Alcohol Cases

While it is quite unusual for a forensic pathologist (FP) to be asked to "back-extrapolate" a postmortem BAC to an earlier time, the process is commonly undertaken by forensic toxicologists. However, such estimates may be subject to considerable error and uncertainty, depending on the validity of the assumptions underlying the particular case circumstance. The key assumptions of course are rate of elimination, time when drinking stopped, and the overall pattern of drinking and eating. A responsible effort of "back-extrapolation" will include clear identification of the assumptions made, the basis for those assumptions, and incorporation into the overall estimate of the impact of uncertainties in the variables utilized in those calculations. With such caveats, back-extrapolation can, in some cases, provide valuable and reliable information regarding BAC in a decedent in the antemortem period.

4.2.5 Toxicology Considerations

In many fatal cases, the role of alcohol may reasonably have been limited to the CNS depressive effects, ultimately leading to a fatal motor vehicle crash, or some other fatal circumstance not a function of systemic alcohol toxicity. However, alcohol can of course be an adequate explanation for death by itself, as a consequence of direct toxicity to the body. Such deaths are not normally associated with levels much below ~0.5 g/dL. However, high levels of alcohol may play a contributory factor in cases of sudden cardiac death, as a function of depression of respiratory and cardiac activity, due to overall CNS depression. Clearly then, alcohol would be expected to play a contributory role with other CNS depressant drugs, most notably opiates, but certainly including GABA-nergic and other relatively mild antidepressant medications. Similarly, the long-term deleterious changes seen in the liver as cirrhosis progresses will add to the susceptibility of the body to other toxic or physiologic insults and may, therefore, play a significant role in a seemingly unrelated death.

4.2.5.1 Alcohol and Diabetes Mellitus

The ingestion of alcohol by patients with diabetes may cause a significant medical problem. The primary biomedical challenge with diabetes is the constant effort to achieve and maintain normal blood glucose levels. Excessive alcohol use can worsen blood glucose control by affecting the intracellular NAD^+/NADH ratio, impacting the gluconeogenic pathway. However, for many patients, occasional alcohol consumption while eating or just having eaten may have little to no effect on blood glucose. However, the effect is different for patients with diabetes and who are also chronic alcohol consumers. These patients may experience some degree of hyperglycemia. The mechanism for the increase in blood glucose is not characterized, but may be related to increased insulin resistance, or the increase may simply be a result of less compliance with the diabetic regimen already established for the patient. Patients with diabetes who also consume alcohol increase their risk of adverse health effects and sudden death, and a history of alcohol abuse or the presence of ethanol in PM samples may inform the FP's determination of contributory factors in the COD.

In the fasting state, or several hours after a meal, alcohol consumption can cause dangerously low blood glucose and may therefore have played a role in fatal hypoglycemia. Alcohol ingestion in a patient with diabetes can exacerbate hypoglycemia, by at least four mechanisms. The primary impact is a direct reduction in gluconeogenesis as oxidation of alcohol and acetaldehyde produces NADH, increasing the NADH:NAD^+ ratio and thereby providing negative feedback to gluconeogenesis. Secondly, alcohol may cause some degree of enhanced insulin release from the pancreas (in patients with type 2 diabetes mellitus), although the specific mechanism underlying the chemical triggers for this response remains unclear. Depending on individual circumstances, some patients with alcohol use disorder may be significantly deficient in the nutritional basis for maintaining glycogen stores, and in such individuals, hypoglycemia may also be coupled to an underlying nutritional deficiency, particularly of complex carbohydrates. Because of the effects of ethanol on cognitive capability, patients may become less aware of their symptoms of hypoglycemia and fail to react appropriately as symptoms develop.

4.2.5.2 Health Effects of Chronic Ethanol Use

Alcohol dependence (also known as alcohol use disorder) is defined by the American Medical Association as a "primary chronic disease with genetic psychosocial and environmental factors influencing its development and manifestations." Patients with alcohol use disorder drink frequently and/or heavily and lose their ability to stop drinking. They may also develop physical dependence on ethanol and can experience life-threatening withdrawal symptoms. Consideration of the extent to which such an underlying medical condition may have caused or contributed to death can present a challenge to an investigating FP.

Chronic ethyl alcohol abuse affects every organ and tissue in the body, with the liver being the primary target of disease. Alcoholic liver disease is progressive, although not necessarily in a temporally linear manner. In the early stages, the liver becomes steatotic. While initially only evident microscopically, with progression, the liver becomes grossly enlarged, pale, greasy, and soft. With continued ethanol use, periportal inflammation is evident microscopically, progressing to hepatocyte damage and fibrosis. Until the organ becomes fibrotic, these changes are reversible. However, once fibrosis begins, the liver can structurally remodel, but the underlying fibrotic changes do not resolve. Eventually, many chronic alcohol users progress to cirrhosis (globally nodular hepatic parenchyma due to clusters of hepatocytes entrapped in scar tissue), liver failure, and death.

Mechanistically, chronic alcohol consumption induces the synthesis of lipogenic enzymes and inhibits triglyceride metabolism and correlated release of low-density lipoprotein (LDL) from hepatocytes. The net result is microvesicular steatosis, beginning centrilobularly and progressing to the more metabolically active periportal zone. Hepatocytes may balloon with accumulated lipids, water, and other intracellular products. Necrotic hepatocytes lose their typical cytologic characteristics. Cell membranes become indistinct, the cytoplasm becomes pale and foamy, and the nuclei become pale before, eventually, disappearing. Neutrophils marginate in response to necrosis, at first in the centrilobular areas and progressing to the periportal areas. Senescent hepatocytes collapse, and fibrosis is initiated (see Figures 4.1–4.4). Patients with chronic alcohol abuse

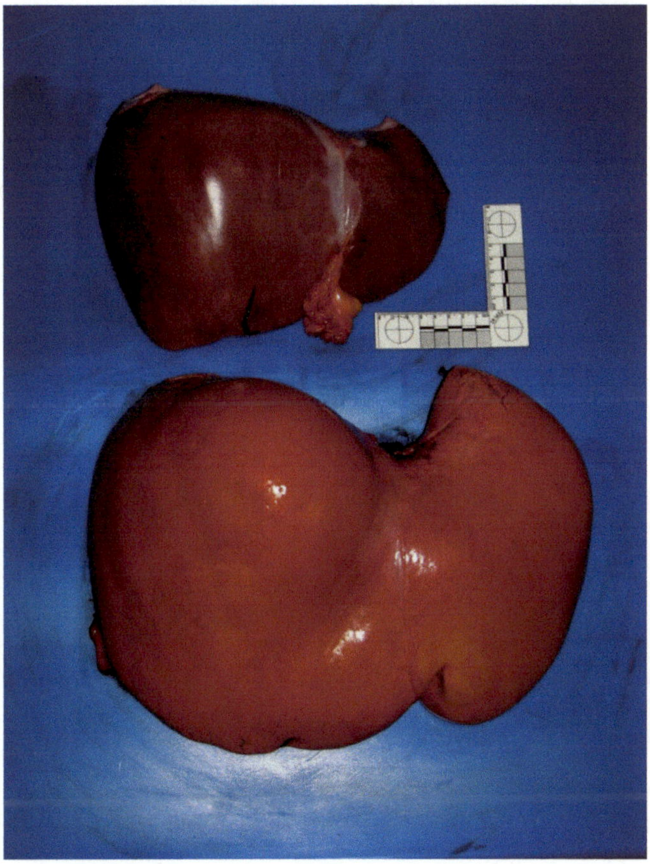

Figure 4.1 Normal liver (top) and steatotic liver (bottom). Note the red-brown color of the normal organ. The fatty liver is enlarged, pale, with some very pale areas, and greasy.

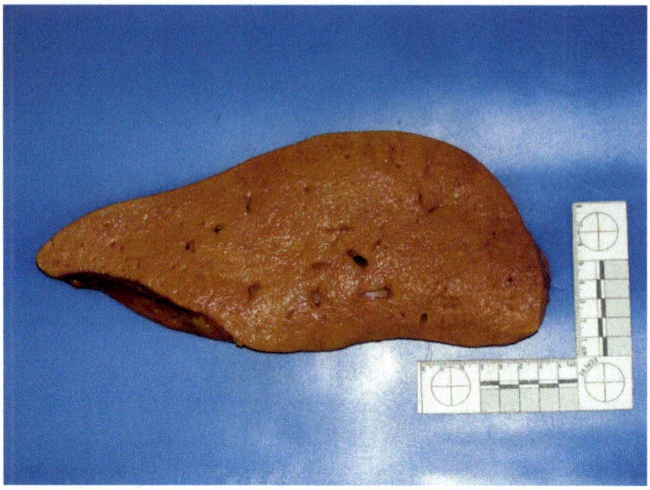

Figure 4.2 Pale, greasy liver, cut section

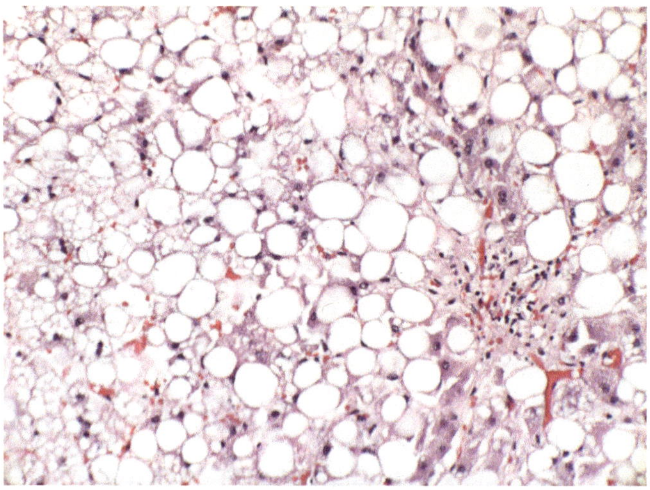

Figure 4.3 Hepatic steatosis, 20×, H&E stain. Most hepatocytes contain droplets of fat, pushing the nucleus to the periphery.

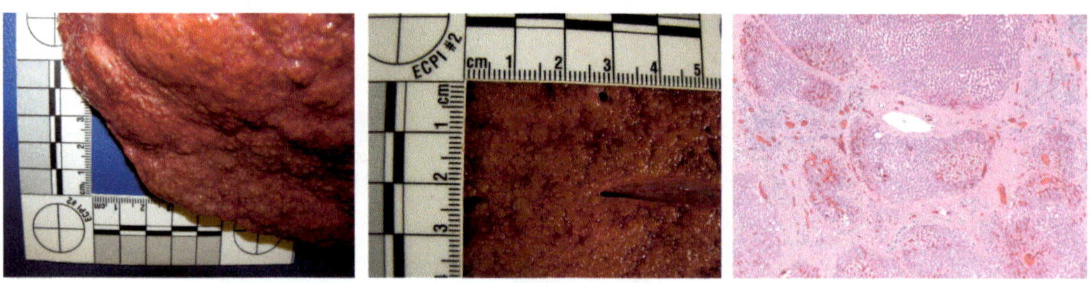

(a) (b) (c)

Figure 4.4 Cirrhosis of the liver. (a) Nodular surface of alcoholic cirrhosis. Nodules are somewhat variable in size, but all are under 5 mm in this case. (b) The cut section of that liver. The entire liver parenchyma is nodular; the nodules are not all the same size. This is the common appearance of end-stage liver disease. There is no longer any significance to the size of the nodules. (c) Nodules of hepatocytes surrounded by fibrous tissue bridging between portal triads. A mononuclear inflammatory cell infiltrate is present in the fibrous tissue. H&E 4× magnification.

can develop jaundice as bile flow is blocked consequential to fibrosis. Bilirubin is normally conjugated in hepatocytes and released across the hepatobiliary membrane into the bile. In the case of bile duct blockage, bilirubin transits into blood from hepatocytes and can then impart a yellow tinge to the skin and sclerae. Clinical indicators of biliary blockage will be elevated serum bilirubin, alkaline phosphatase, and aminotransaminases levels. The yellow discoloration of jaundice remains after death. The skin, the sclera, and the VH are tinted some shade of yellow due to the accumulation of bilirubin. This discoloration indicates to the pathologist that the patient, now deceased, had some degree of liver failure. Chemical analysis for glucose and electrolytes in VH should not be affected by jaundice.

4.2.5.3 Ethyl Alcohol Withdrawal Syndrome

Ethyl alcohol dependence is a common problem facing physicians. Withdrawal from chronic or habitual alcohol use may cause CNS excitability and even manifest as seizure activity, hallucinations, and delirium, as the body attempts to accommodate to functioning in the absence of a depressant drug. Treatment can often be gained in an outpatient setting, but some patients will require hospitalization. Individuals with alcohol dependence may attempt to keep their blood alcohol concentration at or above a level adequate for them to avoid unpleasant symptoms. In some cases, ethanol abusers will ingest another liquid intoxicant (e.g., ethylene glycol) in an effort to relieve withdrawal symptoms without actually drinking ethanol. Similarly, some patients may attempt to "detoxify" themselves, occasionally with fatal results depending on the composition of the particular detoxification remedy. In the forensic setting, historical information about a patient's ethanol use or attempts to limit or control that addiction may provide helpful information for the interpretation of toxicologic and pathologic findings.

Alcohol withdrawal syndrome can reflect a continuum of signs and symptoms, potentially ranging from mild to debilitating to fatal. The earliest signs can be observed after about 8 h after the last drink and may appear as hyperactivity and rebound drinking (drinking to mitigate). With sudden alcohol cessation, in a habitual drinker, the body may "overreact" with a catecholamine surge leading to the defining signs and symptoms of withdrawal, including irritability, tremors, disorientation, hypertension, tachycardia, fever, and, perhaps most relevant from the postmortem perspective, seizure activity. If a person abruptly stops drinking, especially after a binge period, they can experience severe, potentially fatal "delirium tremens" (DTs) which may include tachycardia and seizures. Seizures consequential to alcohol withdrawal can be readily detected by EEG and are more likely to occur in patients with preexisting epilepsy or seizure disorders. Alcohol withdrawal-associated seizures generally occur between 8 and 24 h of abstinence and are characterized by tonic-clonic movements.

Potentially fatal arrhythmias may develop in patients with chronic ethanol abuse, and those who suddenly stop drinking have the additional risk of atrial fibrillation because of activation of the sympathetic nervous system. Patients with alcohol use disorder are at risk of infection and malnutrition, making the diagnosis of withdrawal even more complicated. Vitreous sodium will likely be low, either because of fluid and electrolyte loss (sweating, vomiting, and diarrhea), overhydration, low dietary intake of solutes, or overproduction of antidiuretic hormone due to volume depletion. Total body potassium is usually low in patients with chronic alcohol abuse due to malnutrition, vomiting, and diarrhea. Postmortem serum potassium may also be artifactually low, however, because of the rapid postmortem rise in vitreous potassium, so that analytical parameter cannot be reliably used to support the diagnosis.

Depending on the pattern of drinking, amount of alcohol ingested, and the time between drinking and death, blood alcohol levels at autopsy may be zero or low, reflective of ongoing metabolism prior to the terminal event. Metabolism of even a high level of alcohol (e.g., a blood alcohol level of 0.3 g/dL) with chronic alcohol overuse could be essentially complete within as short as 10 h.

4.2.5.4 Alcoholic Ketoacidosis

Patients with chronic alcoholism are also at risk of other metabolic derangements. In alcoholic ketoacidosis, hepatic glycogen stores become low as a consequence of the ethanol-metabolism-based inhibition of gluconeogenesis (shift of the NAD:NADH ratio). As the body shifts to fatty acid metabolism, characteristic ketones are formed (acetone, acetoacetate, and b-hydroxybutyrate). As with diabetic ketoacidosis, alcoholic ketoacidosis can be fatal. Serum and vitreous alcohol may be low or not detected. In the postmortem setting, ketones are easily detected in VH. The differential diagnosis for the presence of ketones is small: diabetes mellitus, starvation, and alcohol-induced. All three conditions stem from the same biochemical problem: not enough glucose available in the body for the cells to use as an energy source. The clinical presentation is a combination of nausea with intractable vomiting and abdominal pain. Patients may be hypotensive, tachycardic, and tachypneic following fluid loss. Clinical testing would show metabolic acidosis, a widened anion gap, and the presence of ketone bodies. In the postmortem setting, ketones are routinely detected in blood.

4.2.6 Ethanol–Drug Combinations

Clearly, with the routine presence of alcohol in many cases, a frequent challenge facing the FP will involve a determination as to if and to what degree ethanol, or the consequences of chronic alcohol use, may have contributed to death. For many trauma victims, the impact of the drug on decision-making, reaction and response, and perception of hazard or risk may have played a role in leading to the circumstances resulting in injury and death. However, such determinations fall somewhat outside the traditional scope of "Cause and Manner." More challenging is the scenario when alcohol is present, and the death is a consequence to some extent of a contribution, via physiologic effects, of alcohol to the effects of another pharmaceutical or recreational drug also present. In such situations, the capability of ethanol to act as an additive factor to other CNS depressants should be considered, and "combined effects of" might well be a reasonable conclusion in a case of even a relatively low level of alcohol in the presence of a CNS depressant agent. The classic example of such a role would be the combination of a barbiturate and alcohol, to which a number of people succumbed during the years when barbiturates were not uncommonly utilized as sleeping aids.

Many patients administer drugs in combination with ethanol or, perhaps more accurately, utilize alcohol while taking either routine medications, such as antidepressants or sleep-facilitating drugs, or short-term analgesic medications such as opiates or NSAIDS. The interpretation of the effects of a combination of alcohol and drugs can be challenging, particularly in light of the relatively innocuous view that most lay people have with regard to the potential for alcohol to affect the body beyond simply inducing intoxication effects. It may be helpful for a pathologist to consider the mechanism of action of the drugs reported in the deceased person to be able to determine whether the combination of CNS depression caused by the drug and the presence of alcohol may reasonably be contributory to the cause of death.

4.3 METHANOL

Methanol, also known as wood alcohol, is the "single carbon" alcohol (CH_3OH). It is a colorless liquid that smells and tastes like ethanol. Methanol is well recognized for its potential toxicity, with ingesting as little as 70 mL of methanol being potentially fatal. Unlike ethanol, it is the metabolic products of methanol (not methanol itself) that elicit the toxic effect. Like ethanol, it is quickly absorbed by the stomach and small intestine and is completely water soluble, transits aquaporin proteins, and equilibrates quickly throughout the body. It is a forensically important substance in that poisoning may occur following accidental or purposeful ingestion of methanol-containing liquids that are inexpensive and easily obtained. Methanol-containing products include solvents and cleaning solutions, such as windshield washing liquid and liquid fuels. Methanol can also be a contaminant in alcohol brewed in nonregulated distilleries, or "home brew" scenarios. Methanol exposures are usually consequential to deliberate or accidental ingestion, as absorption through the skin or inhalation of vapors is not efficient methods of achieving toxic blood levels. While low levels of methanol can be endogenous in normal, healthy people by the anaerobic production by intestinal bacteria, methanol is not normally detected in forensic samples in the absence of specific ingestion or other factors (e.g., production by decomposition of tissues). Levels of methanol in blood considered potentially fatal are in the range of ~0.09 g/dL and up, considerably less than the corresponding potentially lethal levels of ethanol (>0.4 g/dL).

4.3.1 Pharmacokinetics

Methanol is metabolized in the liver by ADH, yielding formaldehyde and then formic acid by the action of formaldehyde dehydrogenase. The initial oxidation occurs at a rate somewhat slower than the corresponding oxidation of ethanol, reflecting a lower binding affinity for the enzyme. The slow initial step results in an elimination rate longer than that of ethanol and can explain the delay in the development of symptoms. Like ethanol, peak serum concentration following ingestion is roughly 30 min after the first dose. Unmetabolized methanol is not efficiently cleared by the kidney, and the elimination half-life is longer for methanol than it is for ethanol, with a corresponding increase in the time in which the drug may be detected in the blood and urine. In contrast, formaldehyde is rapidly metabolized, and the resulting formate is ultimately oxidized to carbon dioxide.

4.3.2 Toxicity

Methanol toxicity is multifaceted. The methanol-related CNS depression is similar to that of ethanol, although methanol seems to be somewhat more potent on a molar basis. Metabolism of the drug, producing formaldehyde, and subsequently formate contributes to metabolic acidosis. A major toxic potential of methanol is related to the ability of formate to affect the mitochondrial electron transport chain by inhibiting cytochrome oxidase.

The potential consequence of damage to the retina or optic nerves as a function of methanol exposure leading to visual impairment or even blindness is well known and appears to be due to the effect of formate on cellular energy production. Demyelination of optic nerves has been observed radiologically and at autopsy. Demyelination is only a possible marker and not considered specific for methanol exposure. Demyelination can also be seen in natural diseases, such as multiple sclerosis. Medical records of a decedent may facilitate identification of methanol poisoning, based on patient reports of some visual disturbance, for example, blurring of the visual field analogueous to looking into a snowstorm. Antemortem physical examination and imaging findings may include retinal edema, optic disc atrophy, and/or focal necrosis in the brain. Clinical chemistry observations in methanol poisoning would be expected to confirm a wide anion gap and the presence of ethanol (the enzymatic assays commonly utilized in hospital testing does not distinguish between ethanol and methanol).

Co-ingestion of methanol with ethanol may be especially toxic because ethanol effectively "inhibits" the metabolism of methanol by more effectively binding to ADH, thereby slowing the rate of methanol metabolism. Ethanol has been utilized historically as a treatment for suspected methanol poisonings, reducing the rate of production of formaldehyde and formate and thereby keeping the levels of toxic metabolites low enough to avoid cellular damage. One downside of this approach is the need for prolonged treatment since the half-life of methanol is longer than ethanol. Such treatment has been utilized in combination with hemodialysis which can shorten the time required for the overall treatment process. Neither methanol nor formate are protein-bound molecules and are readily dialyzed from blood. Currently, fomepizole is utilized instead of ethanol as an ADH inhibitor, because of its ability to inhibit ADH without causing CNS depression.

There may be no definitive or diagnostic findings at autopsy. In a decedent for which there has been no medical intervention, or corresponding history, toxicological findings may be the primary basis upon which to consider the potential for methanol toxicity to have caused the death. Focal white matter necrosis has been reported but may be subtle, especially in decomposed patients. After a period of survival, optic nerves may be thin, and there may be demyelination in the centrum semiovale and in the putamen. Demyelination of the visual cortex may be a late finding. In the absence of any physical changes, the diagnosis is only made after the toxicology results are reported.

4.4 ISOPROPANOL

This three-carbon alcohol is inexpensive and readily available to the public but is only rarely encountered in toxicology laboratories (albeit readily detected in routing alcohol testing). It is sold as "rubbing alcohol" and is commonly utilized as an antiseptic and disinfectant. Isopropanol is usually available as a 70% formulation in water. Isopropanol has a very strong, characteristic odor and an unpleasant taste, so poisonings by oral ingestion are not common. However, it is easily absorbed through skin, especially when the keratin layer is thin or has been disrupted (e.g., abraded or burned). Toxic exposures in children (who have thin skin) have resulted from "sponging" with isopropanol (e.g., in an effort to reduce a fever). Like the other low-molecular-weight alcohols, the mechanism of action producing CNS depression remains somewhat unclear, and the toxicity of isopropanol, unlike methanol, is linked to the magnitude of that CNS depression as opposed to the formation of toxic metabolites. The primary metabolite of isopropanol is acetone and, while able to also function to some extent as a CNS depressant, does not contribute to acidosis.

4.4.1 Pharmacokinetics

Isopropanol is water-soluble and is as easily absorbed as ethanol. It is equilibrated in body water, just like the other alcohols, and similarly, it is not subject to postmortem redistribution. It is metabolized to acetone by isopropyl dehydrogenase. Detection of acetone in postmortem samples may indicate isopropanol administration; however, acetone is also produced endogenously from acetoacetate and β-hydroxybutyrate (ketone bodies) and detection of it may represent ketoacidosis instead of isopropanol oxidation (see Section 4.5., below). Elimination of isopropanol is predominantly by renal clearance and metabolism to acetone. Evaluation of clinical history or other information may be required to distinguish between naturally produced acetone in ketoacidosis and ingested isopropanol. However, in cases of significant isopropanol ingestion, such that some degree of toxicity may be associated with the exposure, blood levels of both isopropanol and acetone would be expected to be markedly elevated. Acetone is readily eliminated in the urine. While acetone can be converted to isopropanol by ADH, that reaction is generally energetically unfavorable. However, in certain disease states (diabetes mellitus, starvation, occasionally ethyl alcohol abuse), patients with high serum acetone may also have some isopropanol in blood.

4.4.2 Toxicity

Toxicity is based on respiratory depression with subsequent respiratory acidosis, albeit without a metabolic contribution, in that isopropanol cannot be oxidized to an acidic species. Isopropanol is more effective as a CNS depressant and is therefore somewhat more toxic than ethanol. The lethal dose, regardless of the route of administration, is about 2 mL/kg, corresponding to a blood level of ~0.26 g/dL. In a 22-pound (10 kg) child, such a lethal dose is only 20 mL of isopropanol, or ~30 mL of a 70% solution.

Toxicity as a function of inhalation or dermal exposure of isopropanol has been well recognized. Toxic consequences, including CNS depression, were noted in a woman with hepatic cirrhosis and renal failure due to type 2 diabetes mellitus and hypertension, receiving once-weekly hemodialysis. This patient was using isopropanol as a self-prescribed therapy followed by a heating pad for muscle cramps for several months. She was discovered at home, lethargic, and confused. Upon hospital presentation, she was hypothermic, hypoglycemic, and encephalopathic, with elevated isopropanol and acetone levels. The patient had applied isopropanol frequently and over large areas of her body for a prolonged time period, illustrating the potential for toxicologically significant levels of isopropanol to be reached in a patient via a transdermal exposure route.

4.5 ACETONE

Acetone is an inexpensive, commonly utilized industrial solvent, readily available from various retail locations. Acetone is formed endogenously (Section 4.5.1) and as a metabolite of isopropanol (Section 4.4). Acetone may be detected in postmortem specimens generally as a consequence of either actual exposure, as a consequence of ketone production, or as a product of decomposition. Acetone is generally considered to be relatively nontoxic, although CNS effects are noted with significant exposures. Acetone, a volatile, small molecule that is easily inhaled, absorbed through the skin, and absorbed from the gastrointestinal tract after ingestion. Acetone is excreted unchanged in urine and breath. Acetone is neither neurotoxic, cardiotoxic, nor hallucinogenic, but can be an irritant to skin and mucus membranes. While frank toxicity associated with an exposure to acetone is unusual, the presence of the compound in toxicologicsamples may provide the investigating FP with useful information regarding the underlying medical condition of the decedent and, as such, can be a significant finding. Most commonly, the presence of acetone in a postmortem sample will suggest that the decedent had diabetes mellitus or was inadequately nourished.

4.5.1 Pharmacokinetics

Ketone bodies (acetone, acetoacetate, and b-hydroxybutyrate) are produced in the setting of inadequate *intracellular* glucose, regardless of the amount of serum glucose, as the body utilizes free fatty acids (FFAs). Metabolism of FFAs in hepatocytes results in the formation of acetoacetate and b-hydroxybutyrate. Acetoacetate non-enzymatically decarboxylates to acetone, which can then be detected in blood, urine, VH, or other aqueous samples.

Endogenous acetone levels are generally negligible or non-detectable in most patients; however, patients with diabetes may become ketogenic as a consequence of fluctuations in glucose availability and utilization. The presence of some serum insulin distinguishes the patient with type 1 diabetes mellitus (having no detectible insulin) from those who have alcohol use disorder or are starving. All three will have high levels of ketones, but only the latter two patient groups will have detectable insulin. Some patients with type 2 diabetes mellitus also develop diabetic ketoacidosis. High glucose in blood and VH will support the diagnosis of diabetes-related ketoacidosis.

4.5.1.1 Alcohol-Related Ketoacidosis

People who consume large amounts of alcohol over a prolonged period of time without taking proper nutrition are at risk of ketoacidosis, primarily as a function of depletion of glycogen stores, and distortion of the NAD+/NADH ratio as alcohol is metabolized. The biochemistry of alcohol-related ketoacidosis is similar to diabetic ketoacidosis, except that the former's poor nutritional status provides the biochemical signal to utilize FFAs as an energy source, rather than the intracellular lack of glucose. Ketosis can also develop in patients with prolonged, heavy alcohol misuse followed by sudden abstinence. Patients with this condition may stop drinking because they are feeling ill from gastritis or pancreatitis. In such cases, serum and VH alcohol level may be low or non-detectable.

4.5.1.2 Starvation

In the early period of starvation (about 12 h), the hepatocyte shifts from storing glucose as glycogen to mobilizing glucose from glycogen in an effort to ensure that there is enough fuel for the brain and CNS. As dietary glucose becomes increasingly restricted or unavailable, fatty acids are released from adipose tissue and are taken up by the liver to be used to provide usable energy molecules. Ketogenic diets (high fat, low carbohydrate) utilize this pathway for weight loss. Individuals on such diets may therefore have significant acetone levels present in toxicological testing results, which may not represent either alcoholic or diabetic ketoacidosis.

4.5.1.3 Decomposition

The presence of acetone in VH and other body fluids may be the result of loss of cell membrane integrity during decomposition. The distinguishing features between otherwise healthy, but decomposing remains and a person who did not have diabetes during life or who did not die from alcohol-related ketoacidosis can only be made with clinical and social history combined with scene investigation. Ethanol can be produced in decomposing remains by bacterial activity; therefore, it is not possible to use the presence of low levels of ethanol in the blood to diagnose alcohol-related ketoacidosis.

4.6 ETHYLENE GLYCOL

Ethylene glycol is a two-carbon di-alcohol that is the active ingredient in antifreeze solutions for vehicles. It is also used industrially. As it is manufactured, it is a slightly viscous, slightly sweet, colorless, and odorless liquid. When sold as a commercial product, the appearance is altered, generally to an iridescent green. The alteration in color does not alter the taste. Its sweet taste is the basis for accidental poisonings of pets and children. As a mode of suicide, ethylene glycol can be ingested straight or mixed with other beverages. The lethal dose is about 1.5 mL/kg (e.g., a 180-pound (81 kg) individual need only to ingest about 120mL for a potentially fatal result). Ethylene glycol is similar to methanol, in that the basis for toxicity is the effect of the metabolic products, not the parent compound.

4.6.1 Pharmacokinetics

Ethylene glycol is water-soluble and hence is readily absorbed from the stomach and the small intestine and equilibrates in total body water. It is not readily absorbed through the skin. It is not subject to postmortem redistribution. Ethylene glycol is metabolized by ADH, producing glycolaldehyde, which is oxidized to glycolic acid by aldehyde dehydrogenase. The remaining C–OH moiety may be oxidized to glyoxalic acid and oxalic acid. Approximately 80% of ingested ethylene glycol is oxidized, with the remainder eliminated in the urine.

4.6.2 Toxicity

Ethylene glycol can cause CNS depression caused by the parent compound. Metabolites cause metabolic acidosis. Additionally, oxalic acid binds to calcium forming oxalic acid crystals that can become lodged in tissues. Crystals form preferentially in the kidneys because oxalate is taken up by the proximal renal tubules and is concentrated there. Calcium oxalate can become deposited in other tissues as well. The formation of calcium oxalate also removes some calcium from serum, potentially causing or contributing to cardiac arrhythmia. Laboratory findings in the emergency department include a widened anion gap, metabolic acidosis, and hyperosmolality.

Many forensic toxicology laboratories do not routinely analyze blood or urine for ethylene glycol but will do so upon request. There are no characteristic findings at autopsy of a person with either acute or chronic ethylene glycol poisoning. It is possible to see the fluorescent green color in gastric contents, but the fluid may have already passed beyond the stomach and been absorbed. Calcium oxalate crystals are too small to see without a microscope. Grossly, the kidneys do not appear unusual, except if they are affected by another disease process with grossly observable findings. The presence of polarizable crystals in the renal tubules is a characteristic pathologic finding. They may take on any shape but are characteristically octahedral or dumbbell shaped. They are visible by the H&E stain and blue-green when polarized (see Figure 4.5).

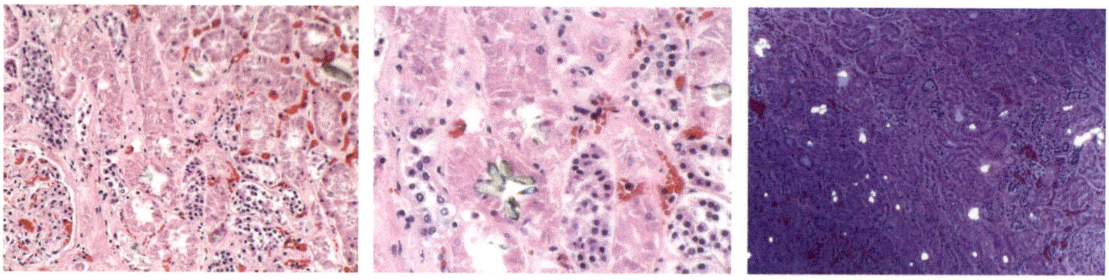

(a) (b) (c)

Figure 4.5 Calcium oxalate crystals in the kidney from ethylene glycol ingestion, (a) H&E 20×, (b)H&E 40×, and (c) H&E 10× with polarization.

4.7 ALCOHOL TESTING

Blood, urine, and VH are used as forensic specimens for alcohol, with blood samples providing the most reliable indication of the effective concentration of ethanol in the body (BAC) at the time of sample collection. Whole blood preserved in sodium- or potassium-fluoride-containing tubes (e.g., "gray tops") obtained at autopsy is the preferred specimens. Fluoride inhibits any production of alcohol by microorganisms (bacteria and fungi). It is important for the FP to know that the blood obtained from a deceased person contained ethanol at the time of collection, (albeit) not necessarily the time of death. In the early postmortem period, the ethanol contained in blood (BAC) is likely to reflect a true antemortem value. If, however, the deceased person is decomposed, the BAC will more likely be a combined value of any antemortem level plus that produced postmortem. Blood from decedents recovered from water is especially vulnerable to postmortem alcohol production because of the shortened time frame for decomposition once on dry land.

Urine alcohol levels, however, are particularly unreliable indicators of BAC, in that, as a concentrated ultrafiltrate of blood retained in the bladder, there may be a significant difference between blood alcohol concentration and that in the urine. The degree of difference will depend on the type and volume of beverages consumed, the time period between ingestion(s) and sample, absorption and metabolic rate, and the voiding pattern. Unfortunately, there is a common expectation that urine alcohol levels do or at least should reflect or be directly relatable to blood levels, and further, that BAC can be inferred from a urine concentration via a "ratio," reflecting the relationship between blood and urine alcohol levels. Commonly, a value of roughly 1.3 or 1.4:1 [urine]:[blood] is utilized, and indeed, such a ratio will be accurate at some point in the time period following drinking as that ratio moves from 0 (alcohol appearing in the blood, but not yet in appreciable or detectable concentrations in the urine) to infinity, as levels of alcohol remain in the urine, while undetectable in the blood. In many cases, that ~1.3:1 ratio will be a (very) roughly accurate estimate ~2 h or so following cessations of drinking, but the large uncertainty associated with an estimate relying on that ratio and assumptions regarding metabolism and elimination will render most such calculations forensically unreliable. In short, beyond validating the process of alcohol ingestion antemortem, a urine alcohol concentration (UAC) in the postmortem setting will generally have limited utility, and significant inferences based on such numbers should be very carefully and critically considered. Similarly, in the postmortem situation, urine alcohol concentrations cannot be used to reliably estimate antemortem levels.

In contrast to urine, VH can be a very useful specimen for alcohol analysis in the postmortem setting. VH is somewhat protected from microorganisms, and as such, postmortem alcohol production is minimal. The vitreous fluid concentration of ethanol tends to lag somewhat behind the blood level, but can provide a very useful BAC estimate, and may provide information regarding the more-or-less immediate drinking history (e.g., within hours) of an individual. For this reason, many advocate obtaining all available such fluid from a decedent. Interpretation can be somewhat complicated. Because VH is an ultrafiltrate of blood there can be a time lag as analytes diffuse or are transported from blood into the VH compartment. The time lag for ethanol is generally thought to be about 30 min to 1 h or so. As such, one would expect a vitreous alcohol result lower than blood during the absorption phase, and for some time thereafter. Conversely, during the elimination phase, with BAC declining, vitreous alcohol content (VAC) would reasonably be somewhat higher than BAC. Drawing any quantitative inference from the difference between BAC and VAC would involve a considerable degree of uncertainty (see Sidebar 4.1: Alcohol concentrations over time in VH and blood).

Sidebar 4.1: Alcohol Concentrations over Time in VH and Blood

Sampling of postmortem blood provides only a single value, presumably representing BAC at the time of death. However, vitreous alcohol levels tend to lag blood levels by ~30 min to 1 h or so, and as such, comparison of the results with blood levels can provide both a measure of the relative reliability of the BAC and an indication as to whether the blood level was rising or falling at the time of death (in the early postmortem period). A typical example of expected BAC/VAC levels versus time in a 180-lb individual, having ingested the equivalent of four "standard drinks" (e.g., two "double shots"), is illustrated in Figure 4.6. Several points are worth noting: The maximal BAC value is achieved between ~30 and 40 min. After the maximal BAC has been achieved, the elimination rate reflects both distribution and metabolism, until distributional equilibrium has been achieved (~70 min.). A linear elimination rate of ~0.02 G/DL/H is demonstrated until BAC approaches ~0.02 g/dL, at which point enzyme saturation no longer occurs, and the kinetics of elimination move from zero to first order. Vitreous alcohol, representing a relatively slow diffusion process, lags BAC and does not exactly mirror BAC, but nevertheless tracks relatively closely to such levels.

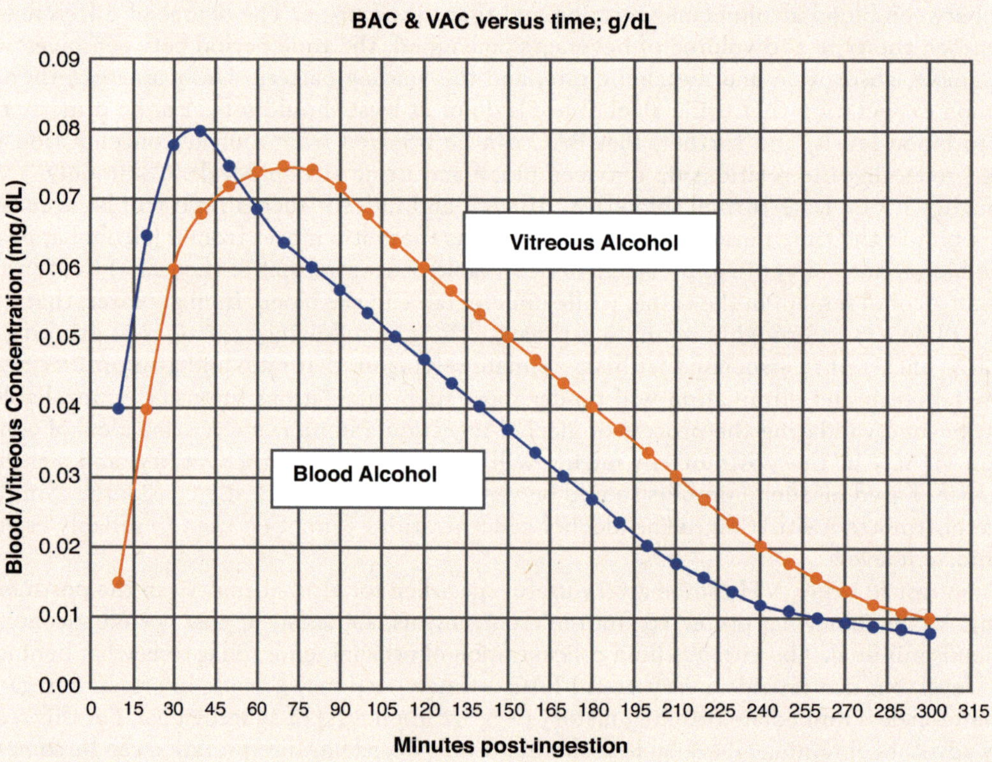

Figure 4.6 Typical example of expected BAC/VAC levels versus time in a 180-lb individual, having ingested the equivalent of four "standard drinks."

Breath alcohol testing is a commonly used forensic process that can provide a reliable measure of alcohol in the blood. Breath alcohol concentration is typically used in suspected "DUI" cases and provides an accurate indication of the concentration of alcohol in the expired breath sample. The equilibrium ratio between alcohol in the blood and the air in the lungs is ~1:2400, and based on this principle, a BAC can be calculated from the expired breath. While clearly not applicable in the postmortem situation, breath alcohol testing is not uncommonly utilized in a hospital setting, and breath testing results may be incorporated into the medial records of patients eventually becoming ME cases. Analysis for ethanol and related volatile compounds is a relatively straightforward analytical procedure and is almost universally performed by headspace gas chromatography. This procedure is fast, accurate, and reliable and also detects other volatile compounds in the sample. Blood, urine, and VH are acceptable samples for analysis.

4.7.1 Biomarkers for Chronic Ethanol Use

The direct determination of BAC provides only an indication of current alcohol status and does not provide any information about a decedent's status or history of use. Considerable efforts have been expended in attempting to discern a clear parameter that would correlate to chronic alcohol abuse, and to this end, two markers reflecting relatively long-lasting ethanol metabolites, ethyl glucuronide and ethyl sulfate, can provide an indication of alcohol use by an individual for approximately one week prior to the collection of the sample. While clearly not of value in the postmortem setting, such testing and the results thereof may be present in antemortem medical records. Testing for the disease state "chronic ethanolism" is a clinical assessment on live people and is different from testing for acute ethanol use. The clinical assessment is beyond the scope of this book. While interesting and potentially significant in some clinical settings, making such a diagnosis on the autopsy protocol cannot be done. Currently, there are no definitive biochemical markers for chronic ethanol abuse available in postmortem samples.

Bibliography

Coe J.I. (1976). Comparative postmortem chemistries of vitreous humor before and after embalming. *Journal of Forensic Sciences*, 21(3):583–586.

Emanuele N.V., Swade T.F., Emanuele M.A. (1998). Consequences of alcohol use in diabetics. *Alcohol Health and Research World*, 22(3):211–219.

Kugelberg F.C., Jones A.W. (2007). Interpreting results of ethanol analysis in postmortem specimens: A review of the literature. *Forensic Science International*, 165:10–29.

McGuire L.C., Cruickshank A.M., Munro P.T. (2006). Alcoholic ketoacidosis. *Emergency Medicine Journal*, 23(6):417–420. https://doi.org/10.1136/emj.2004.017590.

McKeon A., Frye M.A., Delanty N. (2008). The alcohol withdrawal syndrome. *Journal of Neurology, Neurosurgery, and Psychiatry*, 79(8):854–862. https://doi.org/10.1136/jnnp.2007.128322.

Palmiere C.A. (2014) The postmortem diagnosis of alcoholic ketoacidosis. *Alcohol and Alcoholism*, 49:271–281.

Savini F., Tartaglia A., Coccia L., Palestini D., D'Ovidio C., de Grazia U., Merone G.M., Bassotti E., Locatelli M. (2020). Ethanol determination in *post-mortem* samples: Correlation between blood and vitreous humor concentration. Molecules. 25(12):2724. https://doi.org/10.3390/molecules25122724.

Slaughter R.J., Mason R.W., Beasley D.M., Vale J.A., Schep L.J. (2014). Isopropanol poisoning. *Clinical Toxicology*, 52(5):470–478. https://doi.org/10.3109/15563650.2014.914527.

Widmark E.M.P. (1981). *Principles and Application of Medicolegal Alcohol Determination*. (Translation of 1932 edition). Davis, CA: Biomedical Publications.

van de Wiel A. (2004). Diabetes mellitus and alcohol. *Diabetes/Metabolism Research and Reviews*, 20(4):263–267. https://doi.org/10.1002/dmrr.492.

SECTION 5

RESPIRATORY TOXINS AND CHEMICAL ASPHYXIANTS

DOI: 10.4324/9781003121060-6

5.1 INTRODUCTION

There are very few toxins that mechanistically affect only or primarily the lung. However, there are numerous chemicals and materials that are irritants or, otherwise, can directly damage tissues. Additionally, inert gases and vapors can be fatal if inhaled in an enclosed space or other circumstances such that fatal oxygen deprivation is caused.

Inhalation of caustic material, such as strong acids or agents that form acids when combined with body water, will damage mucus membranes and respiratory epithelium. Caustic chemical dusts and aerosols can be similarly hazardous. Inhalation of strong bases will have a similar effect. Injury may be mild but could be so severe as to cause significant edema and necrosis. The extent of tissue injury depends upon the type of material and the extent to which tissues are exposed to the material. The longer the exposure to harsher materials, the more tissue is damaged. Additionally, much like any other insult, patients with significant comorbid conditions will generally fare worse than otherwise healthy people. The resulting injury to the patient is a combination of direct tissue injury and asphyxia from a narrowed airway due to mucosal edema.

Smoke from a burning structure is a complex mixture capable of causing direct tissue injury, tissue edema, and asphyxia on a cellular level. Dust and other small particles, even if composed of inert material, pose an additional hazard. Examples of these are silica, asbestos, tobacco smoke, and filler material in drugs not meant to be inhaled.

Much of pulmonary-related toxicity is associated with oxygen absorption, transport, and subsequent delivery to tissues. Most of the oxygen in the blood is bound to hemoglobin (Hb), but a small percentage remains dissolved in the blood, unbound. This small amount is reflected in the oxygen tension (PaO_2), or the partial pressure of the dissolved oxygen gas (units are mmHg). With normal breathing room air at sea level, the arterial PaO_2 ranges from 70 to 100 mmHg. This number is commonly measured in blood taken from a small artery in the wrist (ABG or arterial blood gas test) and can be used, along with the $PaCO_2$ (partial pressure of carbon dioxide) to determine the effectiveness of gas exchange at the alveolar level. The percentage of Hb saturation (or arterial oxygen saturation, $\%O_2$ sat) is measured non-invasively by pulse oximetry. The oxyhemoglobin dissociation curve is a graphical representation of the mathematical relationship between PaO_2 on the *X*-axis and $\%O_2$ sat on the *Y*-axis. The shape is sigmoidal, not linear, because the affinity for oxygen increases with each successive molecule bound to it. The position of the sigmoidal curve on the axes (left, right, or center) is affected by the strength with which Hb binds to oxygen. A leftward shift indicates an increased affinity of Hb for oxygen, as is the case with methemoglobin (metHb).

The binding of one oxygen molecule to one heme iron atom causes a change in the physical shape of that portion of the molecule. That one change in shape subsequently changes the shape of the rest of the Hb molecule, exposing the iron ion more than it had been exposed before. This change in shape allows for faster binding of subsequent oxygen molecules to the available iron. In other words, the second, third, and fourth iron ions are bound faster than the first one was bound. In chemistry, the property of the enhanced ability to bind more oxygen molecules is called "cooperative binding".

5.2 INHALATION OF PRODUCTS OF COMBUSTION

Smoke inhalation is commonly reported as a cause of death, but a more accurate expression may be "inhalation of products of combustion" because this phrase better characterizes the entire process. Smoke is a mixture of hot gases, soot, and particulate matter. Inhalation of products of burning material can quickly become fatal due to chemical asphyxiants (e.g., CO or CN), by anoxia in an oxygen-depleted environment, or by direct tissue damage caused by thermal injury from inhaled hot gas.

At autopsy, patients who die from smoke inhalation will usually have black, finely granular, or dusty material on and inside the nasal ala, on the tongue, and coatingthe mucosa of the hypopharynx and trachea. This material will also be mixed with mucus and look like either a dry deposition of soot or a mucoid mixture. Decedents who had received oxygen therapy may not have as much soot remaining after therapy, which after a structural fire may include airway management and supplemental oxygen. Hyperbaric oxygen may be also used to drive carbon monoxide off the Hb faster than treatment with atmospheric oxygen. Analysis of hospital admission samples may give a more accurate result of carbon monoxide exposure than if blood from autopsy were used if the patient had oxygen therapy before death (see Figure 5.1).

Livor mortis in cases of "smoke inhalation" will be "cherry red" in light-skinned or lightly pigmented decedents, but this color change might not be obvious in darkly pigmented people (see Figure 5.2). The blood will usually all be in liquid form and will have a bright red color. Decedents who are deeply charred may not have apparent livor mortis on the skin because the skin is either charred or burned away. However, organs and tissues may look brighter than usual. Even after formalin fixation, blood and tissues retain the bright red color. The color change may or may not be obvious in decedents who are markedly decomposed.

Carboxyhemoglobin formation is a marker of smoke inhalation and can be measured in the laboratory. It is only a *marker* of inhaled smoke. Patients who have succumbed to injuries sustained in a structural fire may have lower levels of carboxyhemoglobin (COHb) than those who die from inhaling vehicle exhaust fumes because of the combined effect of hot gas and toxins in smoke. Also, people who have significant comorbidities, especially cardiac and pulmonary conditions, will succumb to the physiological stress of smoke inhalation faster than healthy people. Patients who

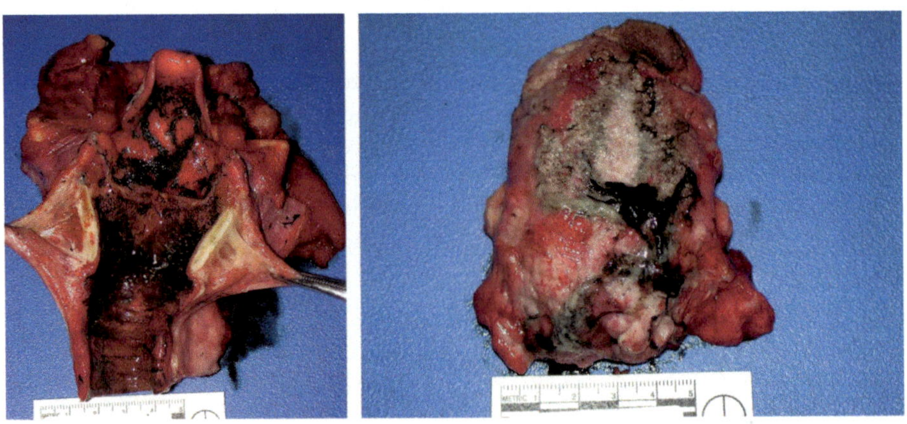

(a) (b)

Figure 5.1 Soot in the airway (a) and on the tongue (b) following a death during a house fire. Note also that the mucosa of the trachea is reddened, caused by carboxyhemoglobin (COHb) in the blood and by irritation of the mucosa by the hot gases in the fire. The soot is admixed with mucus.

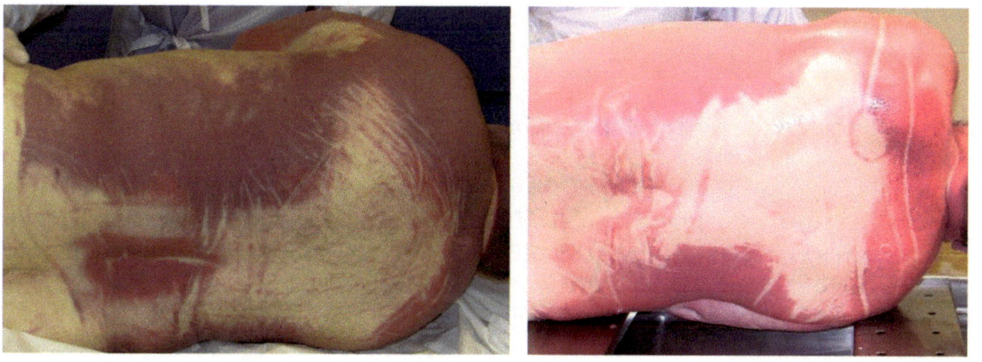

(a) (b)

Figure 5.2 (a) Normal red-purple livor mortis in a patient who died from cardiovascular disease (b) Cherry red livor mortis in a patient who died from carbon monoxide intoxication, COHb 47%.

also have burn injuries to the face, the oral mucosa, or circumferentially around the neck or torso fare much worse than those without burns. Their COHb may be lower than expected, even if they have a large "soot burden".

Pathologists routinely request a COHb determination on deceased people who have been rescued or recovered from a structural fire, even if there is no evidence of smoke inhalation at autopsy. A low or negligible level of COHb may indicate that the patient died before the fire started. If COHb is low, some pathologists will request a cyanide level in the blood because the patient might have died primarily of cyanide before carbon monoxide level built up. Livor mortis in patients with cyanide intoxication is also cherry red.

Cardiac and skeletal muscle contain myoglobin, which can also react with carbon monoxide to form carboxymyoglobin and may, therefore, elicit cardiotoxic as well as an asphyxiant effect. While analysis of muscle tissue is not routinely performed in most forensic laboratories, some reference laboratories can analyze muscle carboxymyoglobin. As such, muscle may be a good specimen to obtain for analysis in the absence of obtainable blood. Because of the single heme molecule in myoglobin, the carboxymyoglobin result is multiplied by four to provide an estimate of the COHb value. With that in mind, analysis of any skeletal muscle or cardiac muscle would be expected to work, but sampling a large muscle group, such as the psoas or quadriceps muscle, will provide the laboratory with more samples with which to work.

5.3 ASPHYXIA AND HYPOXIC AGENTS

Humans require a minimum level of oxygen in inspired air to maintain cerebral and cardiac function. Hypoxic environments are those in which the oxygen level is below that which is necessary to maintain life. The usual concentration of atmospheric oxygen is approximately 21%. When the concentration falls between approximately 10%–15%, judgment and coordination are impaired; loss of consciousness occurs at about 8%–10%. Levels below 8% are almost uniformly fatal. Because the symptoms that develop often overlap with those with a toxic exposure or ingestion, investigators might not realize that the altered mental status, nausea, ataxia, and coma are due to oxygen deprivation and not due to a toxin.

Asphyxia refers to the physiologic effects of hypoxia. Fatalities of this nature are mechanistically different from deaths by strangulation and hanging. The latter two involve compression of blood vessels, thereby limiting venous return from the head. Petechial hemorrhages can be seen above the level of constriction: on the facial skin; on the conjunctivae; on the oral mucosa; and occasionally, on the mucosa of the trachea and oropharynx. Petechial hemorrhages are not a feature of chemical asphyxia or oxygen displacement. In contrast, chemical asphyxia is the blockage of the chemical reactions generating energy for the body by the reduction of molecular oxygen to water, including blocking or interfering with oxygen transport and delivery.

Hypoxia can also be the result of respiratory depression due to CNS depressants, such as opiates, barbiturates, benzodiazepines, and ethanol. Opiate-based respiratory depression is well-recognized as a specific consequence of overdose, but the phenomenon can occur with any central nervous system (CNS) depressant. In many cases, a combination of several CNS depressant drugs may act in a synergistic or additive manner with other asphyxiants. Toxicologic analysis may reveal a mixture that provides an adequate explanation for a death related to respiratory depression.

Virtually, any inhalable gaseous mixture can cause a lethal asphyxia as a function of simple displacement of oxygen from the breathable air supply. Many different gases have been associated with accidents and suicides. Scene investigation can be crucial in these types of cases because the collection and analysis of potential asphyxiant gas mixtures from decedents is not a routine aspect of forensic toxicology. With few exceptions, gas mixtures are not visible, and few crime scene or death investigators are equipped to evaluate "breathable" air. In the toxicology laboratory, the detection and quantitation of most gases in blood is straightforward, although certainly not a routine analysis. If forensic pathologists (FPs) encounter a case for which an analysis of this type may be required, direct communication with the forensic toxicology laboratory may be of benefit.

5.3.1 Carbon Monoxide

5.3.1.1 Introduction

Carbon monoxide (CO), well recognized as a potential poison, is a colorless, odorless gas that is not an irritant to mucus membranes. Because of these features, it is known as the "silent killer". CO is a product of the incomplete combustion of hydrocarbons and is a normal component of air, although only comprising less than 0.001% of atmospheric gas. There are many possible sources of carbon monoxide exposure, including structural fires, motor vehicle exhaust, simple combustion in either an unvented or enclosed space or in vehicles with leaky or faulty exhaust systems. Damaged or obstructed furnace exhaust flues can cause an accumulation of carbon monoxide in an otherwise well-vented home. A less common, but increasingly recognized source is an improperly vented space heater that uses natural gas or kerosene as the fuel source. CO poisoning is, therefore, not uncommon in wintertime when supplemental heating devices are used in inadequately ventilated rooms. One of the more well-recognized means of toxic CO exposure is combustion fumes and smoke. As above, CO can represent a significant component in smoke from structural fires and is often the cause of death in such events, even in the absence of thermal injuries. Fortunately, carboxyhemoglobin can readily be detected in embalmed remains (See Sidebar 5.1).

Sidebar 5.1: Carbon Monoxide Intoxication from an Obstructed Furnace Exhaust

A 53-year-old woman was discovered deceased in her home. She had lived alone, and her medical record documented significant cardiovascular disease as well as diabetes mellitus. When she failed to show up for work, police were called for a welfare check. Police and emergency medical services (EMS) found her home to be secure, with no evidence of foul play. No comment regarding odor, if any, was documented. The decedent was found in her bed, appearing to have died in her sleep. Her primary care physician was willing to sign her death certificate based on her natural disease. In the absence of forensic concerns, her body was released from the scene directly to the funeral home, and routine preservation procedures were initiated. The next day, however, family members contacted local law enforcement to report an odor of natural gas. Representatives of the gas company tested the air for the presence of natural gas and determined an initial reading was 500 ppm (reference range 0.5–5 ppm). After turning off the gas supply to the house and ventilating the home, inspectors were able to enter the residence and reported a strong odor coming from the area of the furnace that was also noticeable throughout the house. Based on this new information, her body was taken to the coroner's Office for an autopsy.

Officers also noticed a "red liquid" dripping from the flu vent at the top of the furnace. A heating and air conditioning company checked the chimney vent leading from the furnace and water heater to the roof and discovered that a raccoon had gotten into the system from the open top and had died in the duct work, blocking gasses from escaping (Figure 5.3).

The autopsy procedure revealed a previously embalmed body with a faint chemical odor. Cherry-red livor mortis that still blanched with firm pressure was present on the posterior aspect of the body. However, the musculature did not have a pink tint. Hypertensive cardiovascular disease was documented with cardiomegaly (heart weight 510 g and left ventricular wall thickness of 2.0 cm.) Vitreous humor glucose was 169 mg/dL, sodium 101 mmol/L, methanol (clearly from the embalming fluid) was >400 mg%; however, the COHb was 33%. (The embalming process does not produce COHb. Diabetes mellitus was re confirmed via vitreous glucose, even though the sample had a pink tinge and was clearly contaminated with embalming fluid. The cause of death was determined to be carbon monoxide intoxication

(a) (b) (c) (d)

Figures 5.3 (a) Furnace and water heater (b) Furnace with "red liquid" (c) raccoon revealed after the flu was removed (d) cherry red livor mortis, visible even after embalming.

with hypertensive cardiovascular disease as a contributory cause. The manner of death was classified as "accidental" as she had remained inside her home which had an obstruction of the ventilation pipes from the furnace, presumably leading to a build-up of carbon monoxide inside the residence.

5.3.1.2 Mechanism

Carbon monoxide is a small molecule and easily diffuses across the alveolar capillary membrane into the blood. CO is an example of a chemical asphyxiant in that it blocks the ability of the body to utilize molecular oxygen, although the mechanism by which it does is very different from cyanide or hydrogen sulfide. CO has an ~210- times higher affinity for Hb, than does oxygen itself, effectively precluding oxygen binding at CO-occupied sites. When present in a significant concentration, CO preferentially binds to Hb, forming COHb, limiting Hb availability for oxygen transport. Adding to the effect, the binding of CO to one of the subunits of the Hb molecule causes a conformational change in the molecule affecting the other three oxygen-binding sites, increasing their affinity for molecular oxygen. This tighter O_2 binding results in a less facile release of O_2 to tissues in the low-oxygen regions of the body. CO binding to Hb shifts the Hb-O_2 dissociation curve to the left. Because of the high affinity, CO is only slowly displaced by O_2 and eliminated by exhalation. Other hemeproteins that can bind CO are a number of cytochromes and some enzymes. However, the greatest impact of CO poisoning is elicited on Hb and myoglobin molecules. The hypoxic effect on cardiac muscle due to the formation of carboxymyoglobin can further compound tissue hypoxia and compromise cardiac function.

5.3.1.3 Clinical Presentation

Family members, or other associates, of a decedent who may have succumbed to CO poisoning may have survived but exhibited symptoms of such exposure. Clinical presentation of these individuals may help inform the investigation of the death and the death scene. The symptoms of carbon monoxide poisoning are the same as those for other types of asphyxiation, although symptoms can be insidious. There are no symptoms that are diagnostic of CO inhalation. However, the exposed patient may also complain of gastrointestinal disturbances and muscular cramping. Some people experience nonspecific symptoms of fatigue and headache that persist for months. Consequences of exposure are related to dose, which is a function of the concentration of CO in the air mixture at the time of exposure. There are charts in multiple reference sources that show the relationship between the concentration of CO in the air, time of exposure, and physical results (See Sidebar 5.2).

Sidebar 5.2: Carbon Monoxide Intoxication by Vehicle Exhaust

In the authors' experience, CO intoxication by vehicle exhaust is primarily suicidal in nature. Auto exhaust has often been used as a means of this purpose, and various arrangements for directing the flow of gas into the vehicle cabin have been used, such as a hose from a clothes dryer, etc. The following case, in contrast, is somewhat unusual in that this person's death was preventable if only he had taken his usual careful precautions.

This middle-aged man kept two sports cars in a detached garage. His routine of caring for them was to test the engines, one at a time, with both the overhead door and the pedestrian door open. He kept careful notes on the vehicles' performance. On the day of his death, he ran the engines as usual, but kept the garage door closed because of the wind and cold air. He

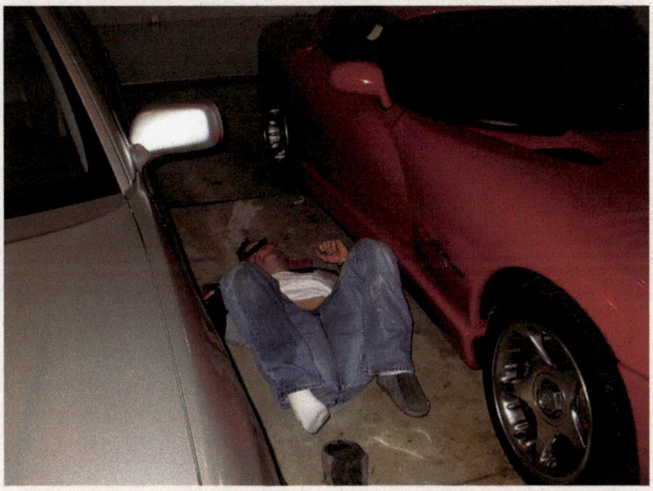

Figure 5.4 Victim overcome by exhaust fumes while tending to his vehicle. Note the narrow space between the vehicles, the left upper extremity flexed in rigor at the elbow with the hand directed upward, and the flexion of the right lower extremity with the right foot off the floor. These features are consistent with the history given by the decedent's girlfriend finding him kneeling between the two cars.

was discovered on a welfare check because he missed a meeting. When his girlfriend went to his home, she found him in the garage unresponsive in a kneeling position between the two cars. Both engines were off, but she thought she noticed an odor of vehicle exhaust, and further, she thought that she could wake him up if she could get him outside. As he was too heavy for her to lift and the space between the cars was small, she rolled him over, and put a pillow under his head, thinking he was merely passed out (Figure 5.4). At that moment, she realized he was dead, so she immediately called EMS. EMS personnel pronounced the victim dead and notified the medical examiner (ME)'s office.

The medical examiner's investigator found the decedent in the position (as in the Sidebar 5.2 figure) with strong rigor mortis with elbows and knees flexed, compatible with the position in which his girlfriend had found him. At autopsy, he had barely blanching, cherry-red livor mortis anteriorly. The autopsy procedure revealed hypertensive cardiovascular disease (heart weight 490 g, left ventricular hypertrophy, wall thickness 1.8 cm), but no coronary atherosclerosis. The toxicologic evaluation revealed a COHb level of 75.8%, but no other intoxicants. The cause of death was determined to be carbon monoxide intoxication and the manner of death was classified as accidental.

In this case, had it not been for the meticulously detailed log of the vehicle and an interview with his girlfriend, the manner of death might have been inappropriately classified as "suicide". As noted above, simply running vehicles in a closed space can generate levels of CO adequate to be toxic or fatal.

The clinical or postmortem diagnosis of carbon monoxide intoxication can be made by determination of the percentage of COHb in venous blood. Typical COHb concentration in nonsmokers is ~1%–3%, whereas smokers tend to have a higher average value that can reach as high as 9%. The level of COHb varies with the source and duration of exposure and the medical condition of the victim. People who are otherwise healthy and inhale smoke from a structural fire may die with COHb levels around 40%–60%, while those who inhale the exhaust from an improperly vented vehicle may have COHb levels much higher, around 80%. The explanation for the apparent discrepancy is simple in that smoke from a structural fire contains toxins other than carbon

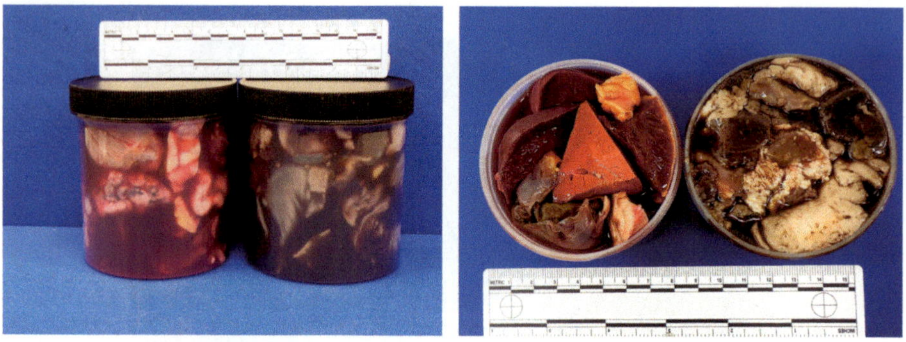

(a) (b)

Figure 5.5 (a) and (b) show the stock tissue (retained tissue) from the victim of carbon monoxide intoxication (left side) and from a person who died from blunt trauma (right side). The tissues had been fixing in formalin for the same number of days. Note that the tissue on the left side of the photograph is still cherry red, while the tissue on the right side has the usual brown color of tissue after formalin fixation.

monoxide, as well as particulate matter and hot gases, with the added potential for toxicity and tissue damage. People can succumb to the toxic effects of smoke inhalation (e.g., cyanide, thermal burns) before their blood becomes rich in carbon monoxide. While vehicle exhaust is hot and may elevate the ambient temperature in an enclosed space, gasoline vehicle exhaust contains relatively few other toxins, allowing for a higher COHb to be generated.

5.3.1.4 Autopsy Findings

Autopsy findings in cases of carbon monoxide asphyxiation are pronounced. Livor mortis will be a cherry-red color well appreciated in patients with fair skin, but in patients with darkly pigmented skin can be difficult to see. The blood of patients with carbon monoxide intoxication will also be cherry red. Carboxyhemoglobin does not dissipate with fixation. Stored blood and tissues will retain the bright color (see Figure 5.5a and b, retained tissue).

Carbon monoxide exposure represents some degree of metabolic stress on patients, and lower levels of CO exposure may have worse consequences in some medically challenged people than would normally be expected. Patients who are particularly at risk are those with compromised respiration and those with an increased demand for oxygen. As such, patients with asthma, chronic obstructive pulmonary disease, and occupational lung disease, or those with reduced lung volume may succumb to CO faster than if they had been otherwise healthy. Similarly, people with increased oxygen demand, such as those in heart failure, pregnant women, and infants, are also more vulnerable. Developing fetuses are also considered in the high-risk category toxicity as CO easily crosses the placenta. Effects are those of hypoxia and include brain damage and may be serious enough to result in intrauterine fetal demise. Because the skin of fetuses can be translucent and appear red, the cherry-red color of COHb may not be as apparent in these victims.

When elevated COHb levels are obtained in cases in which opioids or other drugs causing CNS depression are also detected, developing a clear opinion on the combined role of drugs and CO effects can present a significant challenge (see Sidebar 5.3).

Sidebar 5.3: Carbon Monoxide with Other Intoxicants

A 56-year-old man was found deceased by his brother on a welfare check. The decedent had been restoring a home and was using a portable generator for heat, Figure 5.6a. At autopsy, barely perceptible pink–purple, virtually fixed livor mortis was present over the posterior

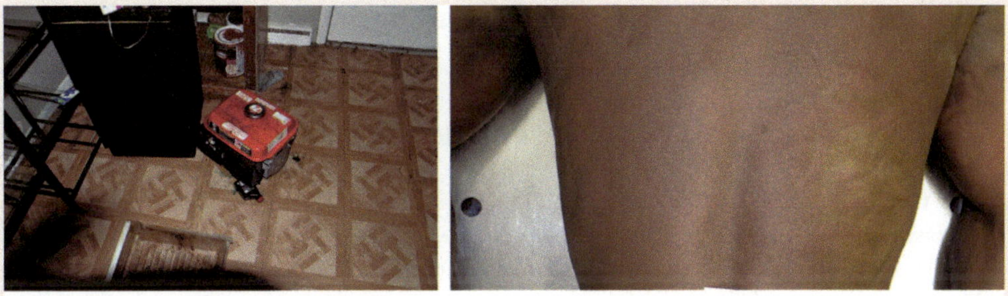

(a) (b)

Figure 5.6 (a) Portable generator near the body (the body is just out of frame). (b) Barely perceptible pink-purple livor mortis. Note that this decedent had moderately darkly pigmented skin, making the "cherry red" color of the livor mortis less noticeable than it would be in pale skin.

aspect of the body, Figure 5.6b, compatible with the position in which he had been discovered. The musculature and blood had a cherry red tinge. There was no anatomic cause of death identified at autopsy, but CO intoxication was suspected. The toxicologic analysis of peripheral blood revealed COHb 46%, cocaine 0.061 mg/L, benzoylecgonine 0.942 mg/L, ecgonine methyl ester 0.225 mg/L, cocaethylene 0.017 mg/L, and ethanol 0.019 g/100 mL. Vitreous humor ethanol was 0.011 g/100 mL. The cause of death was carbon monoxide intoxication with cocaine use and cocaethylene exposure as contributory factors (see Section 8 regarding implications based on cocaine and metabolite determined in PM samples). The manner of death was classified as "accidental". It was suspected that he used the generator for heat and/or electricity without realizing the potential for the generation of carbon monoxide gas. There was no indication that this man intended to harm himself with the device.

The treatment of serious CO exposure is to remove the patient from the contaminated atmosphere and provide supplemental oxygen as necessary. Breathing atmospheric air without oxygen supplementation may not be adequate in potentially lethal exposures, because the greater affinity for CO to Hb than for O_2 to Hb causes the elimination half-life of COHb to be greater than 5 h. As such, the patient may be at high risk for permanent brain and other organ damage unless supplemental oxygen is provided. Breathing 100% oxygen reduces the half-life of COHb to less than 1 h. Hyperbaric oxygen therapy involves breathing 100% oxygen under pressure, (2 to 3 times atmospheric pressure.) With hyperbaric oxygen therapy, the time to reduce COHb by half is reduced to about 15 min.

5.3.1.5 Chronic Effects

If the toxic exposure is not immediately fatal and the patient survives for a time, the brain may have anatomically evident changes. Hypoxia causes the release of nitric oxide from endothelial cells and platelets initiating vasodilation. However, nitric oxide can also combine with oxygen to form free radicals, with the potential for membrane damage, causing capillary leakage, leukocyte margination, and cell death. If the patient had lived long enough for reperfusion, perivascular hemorrhages may be observed. Later, the white matter can become permanently demyelinated. The neurons of the basal ganglia are metabolically very active and have a greater demand for oxygen than the surrounding tissue, and so small vacuoles in the gray matter can be seen at autopsy. These changes are not specific to carbon monoxide poisoning and can be seen after survival following any prolonged hypoxic event. Patients who survive can have permanent sequelae, including cognitive and motor deficits and succumb to complications thereof (see Sidebar 5.4).

Sidebar 5.4: Delayed Death Following Carbon Monoxide Exposure

We were asked to investigate the death of a 60-year-old woman who had died at home, found by her caregiver who had last seen her alive minutes before her death. A coroner's investigator responded to the home, finding it to be extremely neat, orderly, and clean. The body of the deceased woman was in a hospital bed clad in a pullover shirt and an adult incontinence pad. She was clean, well groomed, and without pressure injuries.

The reason for the coroner's Office involvement was that this woman had been exposed to high levels of carbon monoxide from a faulty furnace as a teenager. Other people in the home at that time died several days afterward. Prior to that accident, the woman had been fully functioning and active, ready to start college in a few months. She had survived the accident, albeit barely. Initially, she had been in a coma but was able to regain some physical and cognitive function. She had very little spontaneous movement but was thought to interact with her brother and her caregivers to a limited extent. She had remained severely disabled with spastic quadriplegia, requiring almost constant help with her daily needs. She developed a seizure disorder, limb contractures, and dysphagia, despite aggressive medical attention. Thanks to the care and attention of her family as well as excellent medical care and on-going therapy, she was able to live in her own home until she died at age 60 from complications of remote carbon monoxide poisoning. The manner of death was classified as "accidental".

At autopsy, she was 60 inches tall and 154 pounds (BMI 30.1 kg/m^2). Other than the effects of quadriplegia, she looked well and appeared younger than her given age. She had no evidence of chronic pressure on bony prominences. She had no evidence of chemical cellulitis from prolonged skin exposure to urine or stool. Her skin was moist and supple; her

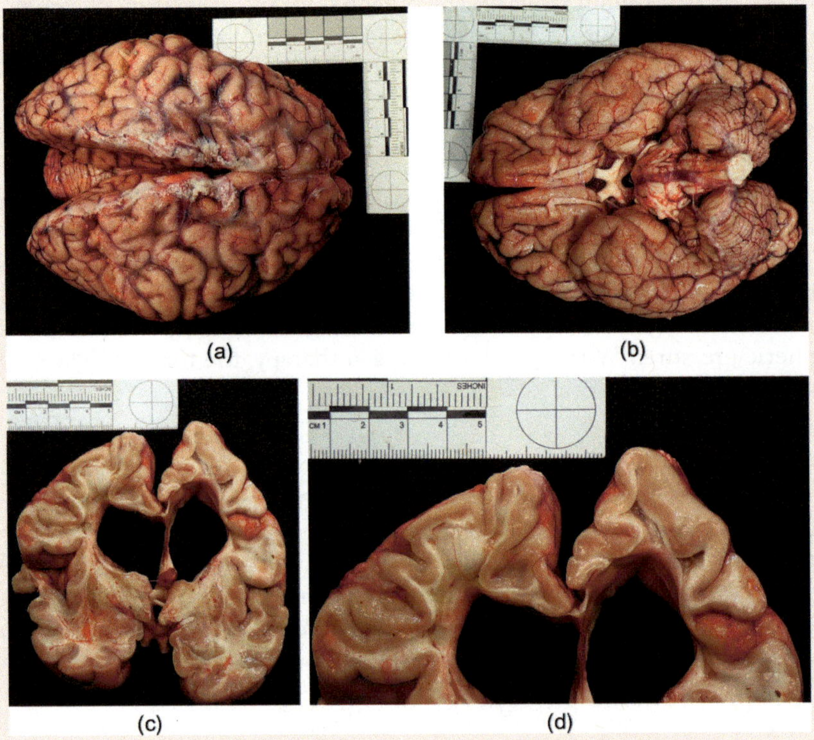

Figures 5.7 (a) Superior view of the brain from this woman. (b) Inferior view of the brain. (c) and (d) Coronal sections from the brain of the woman described above.

nails were neatly groomed. Her teeth were in good condition. Her lower extremities were atrophic, and her feet were down-going with smooth soles. She had several surgical scars on her extremities from the release of contractures as well as an indwelling gastrostomy tube. Her COHb level at the time of the accident was no longer available at the time of autopsy.

Her internal organs and tissues had no evidence of natural disease except for nonobstructive cholelithiasis. The brain looked grossly normal from the outside but was only 920g. Serial coronal sections revealed significant white matter atrophy with subsequent dilation of the ventricular system. The corpus callosum, septum pellucidum, and centrum semiovale were barely perceptible because of extensive demyelination. There was atrophy of the gray matter, particularly the thalamus and the putamen portions of the basal ganglia. The cortical ribbon was also atrophic, more prominent in the parietal lobes than elsewhere. The cerebellum was grossly intact (Figure 5.7a–d).

5.3.2 Oxygen Displacement

In cases of apparent asphyxia due to oxygen displacement, scene investigation, including identification of a gas source, may suggest the nature of the asphyxiant. Depending on the circumstances of the death, the asphyxial gas may no longer be present. Emergency response personnel are often equipped with instrumentation for measurement of carbon monoxide and the oxygen percentage available in "breathing air." The measured level of oxygen may have eventual legal as well as medical implications. Employees working in, or accidentally exposed to "air" that has, a low level of oxygen may be eligible for some monetary compensation if they suffer any injury because of the hypoxic environment. Industrial accidents resulting in hypoxic injury or death can result from an individual unknowingly entering an enclosed space with limited or no oxygen, such as a large reaction vessel, tank or tank car, storage area, or work room (see Sidebar 5.5: Nitrogen in a Tank Truck.)

Sidebar 5.5: Nitrogen in a Tank Truck

In late 2010, we were asked to investigate the death of a middle-aged man who had been "overcome by toxic nitrogen gas." The initial investigative information revealed that a man was washing out an emptied, semi-tanker trailer that had been used to transport a mildly caustic (but non-volatile) aqueous solution. To facilitate emptying the tank, the unit has been slightly pressurized (< 20 PSI) with nitrogen. After venting the tank, the operator opened the access port at the top of the tank and was observed to lean into the tank while using a hose for the washing process. He was not wearing a supplied air mask. His body was bent at the waist. In this position, his head and upper torso were inside the tank while his lower torso and lower extremities were outside, making him somewhat "top heavy". He was later observed to be inside the tank. It was concluded that the venting process had been incomplete, and he was breathing almost pure nitrogen, lost consciousness, fell into the tank, and suffered some mild caustic burns. He died from asphyxia due to oxygen displacement by nitrogen. The "Toxic Nitrogen" characterization was presented during civil actions in the case and became somewhat moot as the court was made aware of the high percentage of nitrogen in atmospheric air and the actual nature of the death. (Atmospheric air is composed of approximately 78% nitrogen and 21% oxygen, with a small contribution of other gases.)

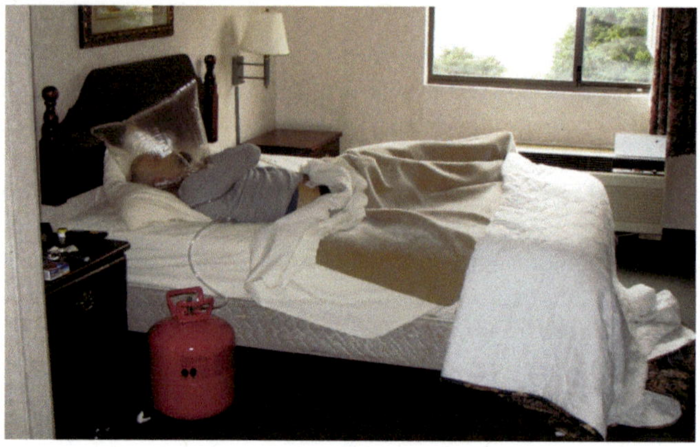

Figure 5.8 The helium tank with attached tubing running into the plastic bag. Note that the bag is still inflated, indicating the continued presence of the gas.

Suicide by hypoxia is not uncommon, frequently encountered in the form of a plastic bag with or without an inert gas supply, thereby either restricting air exchange or displacing breathable air. Helium, nitrogen, carbon dioxide, and propane are readily available, and all have been used in this fashion (Figure 5.8).

Some people use anti-anxiety medication or drugs capable of inducing respiratory depression in combination with a plastic bag over the head. The medication is thought to reduce the panic and discomfort induced by hypoxia. There may be droplets of exhaled (humidified) air inside the bag, indicating the person was breathing after the bag was secured around the head (see Sidebar 5.6).

Sidebar 5.6: Oxygen Displacement

A 45-year-old woman, with multiple medical problems, was discovered lying in her bed with a plastic bag securely tied around her neck. Her residence had been locked from the inside. There was a tank of nitrogen next to her bed with a tube going from the nozzle to the space between her head and the plastic bag. Small vapor droplets were noted on the inside of the bag just over her slightly opened mouth. Upon the arrival of the coroner's investigator, the valve of the tank was in the "Refill" position, indicating that the tank was now empty. Her medical record documented spinal stenosis associated with severe pain, polyneuropathy, and a neurogenic bladder. She had apparently been depressed because of these medical problems and already had a "Do Not Resuscitate" order in place. She had attempted suicide by overdose about a year before this event. The autopsy procedure revealed hypertensive cardiovascular disease (heart weight 630g). The toxicologic analysis confirmed the presence of fentanyl (7.3ng/mL), norfentanyl (1.1ng/mL), sertraline (0.589 mg/L), oxymorphone (0.228mg/mL), and cyclobenzaprine (0.275 mg/L). All these medications had been prescribed for her. The death was classified as a suicide by asphyxia due to oxygen displacement by nitrogen gas in an enclosed space with hypertension and CNS depressant drugs contributing. The presence of the droplets indicates that she was alive and breathing, at least for a short while, after the bag was secured around her head (Figure 5.9).

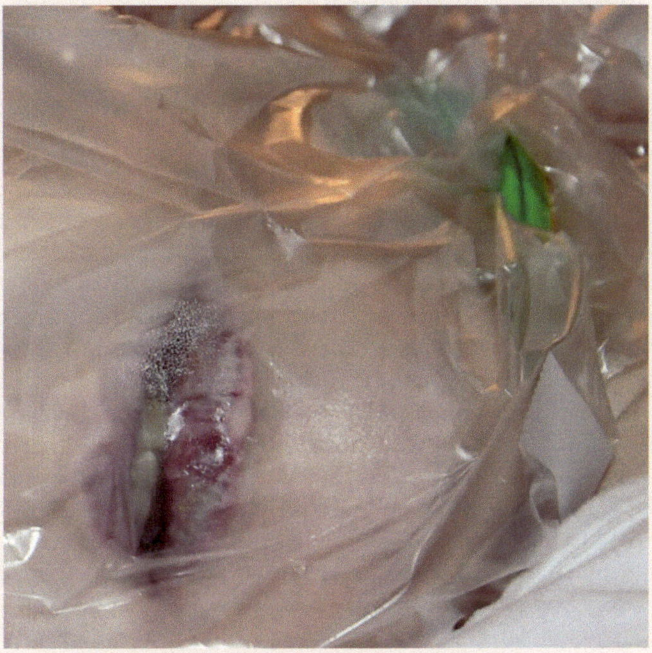

Figure 5.9 Water vapor droplets inside the plastic bag.

5.3.3 Recreational Inhalation of Toxic Fumes: Huffing

"Huffing" is the purposeful inhalation of volatile compounds (most commonly aerosol propellants) to induce euphoria. While recreational huffing may be popular in various age groups, the practice is mostly observed with teenagers. Some people huff to get "high", thinking that their drug use will not be detected. A variety of agents can be used, especially those easily obtained or purchased. The containers are often household products. The aerosol propellants do not trigger a positive result on drug screens, so the offender is generally at a low risk of discovery. Unless there is a large volume of such containers, or they are out of their usual place, family and friends might not be suspicious of someone's drug use.

One of the more popular sources of huffing materials is compressed air canisters ("dusters") containing the halogenated hydrocarbon 1,1-difluoroethane (DFE) have become popular with huffers. These small aerosol cans are often available at stores that sell electronic products, at hardware stores, and some all-purpose ("big box") stores. The products are designed to blow dust from sensitive electronics and may be misused recreationally for a "quick high". Some users inhale the product as it is sprayed into a cupped hand; some use a rag or other clothing item; and some use a bag over the head to contain and concentrate the product. Some abusers may exhibit frostbite-type burns on their hands, mouth, and tongue, (a function of the DFE cooling as it volatilizes (this happens with any compressed gas, refrigerant or not...). Inhaled DFE rapidly diffuses across the alveolar capillary membrane, resulting in a rapid onset of euphoria. The half-life in blood is approximately 30 min. When the exposure is fatal, death is due to CNS depression combined with hypoxia from inhalation of an oxygen-deficient gaseous mixture. DFE-related CNS depression is due to its effect on neurotransmitters in the brain, particularly the glutamate and gamma-aminobutyric acid (GABA) receptors.

There is currently no pharmaceutical purpose for DFE; therefore, a medical reference range has not been established. The toxicologist will often report DFE qualitatively as "present" rather than quantitatively as there should be no DFE in blood. Detecting DFE (or a related species) in a deceased person in association with investigative information may be sufficient to establish the correct diagnosis. Because of the volatile nature of the analyte, samples must be sealed to prevent evaporation. Blood is a good specimen, but DFE may be detected in other tissues as well as vitreous humor. DFE can be detected in blood, even after several days postmortem. DFE is lipophilic and concentrates in adipose tissue. As such, a sample of body fat may be useful, especially if the body is decomposed and liquid specimens are no longer available. DFE can also be detected in brain tissue, lung tissue, and tracheal "air."

DFE toxicity is not limited to acute asphyxia; there can be an effect on other organs. Acute kidney injury and chronic renal damage have been reported. DFE apparently can sensitize the myocardium to catecholamines. As such, scenarios in which the decedent may not have been actively huffing may still represent DFE-based toxicity albeit not via oxygen displacement. A fatal case of DFE exposure has been reported in a man who was found deceased in his vehicle with no evidence of airway obstruction or other means of oxygen displacement. The decedent in that case had a history of DFE use and significant cardiovascular disease, including an acute myocardial infarction, which was diagnosed at autopsy. DFE was detected in multiple tissue samples as well as blood and vitreous humor. It was concluded that the mechanism of death was other than oxygen displacement and a fatal arrhythmia was suggested. Electrolyte imbalance and cardiac myocyte damage have been demonstrated in rats exposed to DFE.

Huffing may also be associated with aerosol paints, solvents, and glues. The active components in many paint mixtures are toluene, xylene, and related small substituted aromatic compounds. The fumes from solvents, paint thinners, and related materials may be inhaled from a rag, directly from the container, or some other open-top vessel. Scene investigation in a potential huffing case is critical for the proper classification of cause and manner of death. When spray paints are used in huffing, evidence of recent use may be quite obvious with paper or plastic bags spattered with paint residue, paint around the mouth and nose, etc. Sometimes glue residue may be stuck to the decedent's fingers. The volatile agent may not be obvious at the scene. The cause of death may not be identifiable in the absence of evidence of huffing. Many of these volatiles cannot be identified during routine toxicology screening; however, with the increasing use of headspace-mass spectrometry for the determination of alcohol and other volatiles, the potential for their detection and quantitation is considerably increased. In the absence of such methodology, analysis of these volatiles requires special testing and, unless suspected, the pathologist may not know to request the appropriate testing.

The most commonly encountered volatile liquids used in huffing that have effects on multiple organs are toluene and the related xylenes. The symptoms of overexposure to these aromatic compounds are CNS and respiratory depression as well as electrolyte disturbance and cardiac arrhythmia. Toluene specifically increases the sensitivity of the myocyte to epinephrine which may cause a fatal arrhythmia. Toluene also appears to have a direct effect on myelin, and chronic toluene abusers can have irreversible damage to the brain. Demyelination and gliosis of white matter leading to atrophy manifest as lesions detectable by magnetic resonance imaging (MRI). Demyelination appears to start in the periventricular white matter and progresses outward toward the cortical gray-white junction and to the brain stem. If extensive, demyelination can be seen histologically on hematoxylin and eosin (H&E)-stained material. Periodic acid-Schiff (PAS) positive granules can be seen in macrophages in the white matter, even before demyelination is evident. Unlike the demyelination that occurs with multiple sclerosis, there is no inflammatory reaction. The term "toluene leukoencephalopathy" has been given to the dementia caused by chronic toluene abuse (see Sidebar 5.7).

Sidebar 5.7: Chronic Glue Huffing

A few years ago, a middle-aged man was found deceased in the wintertime. Investigative information revealed that he had been outside in low environmental temperatures for at least 8 h before having been found. His body was cold and with apparently fully fixed and strong rigor mortis. Livor mortis was pink, blanching, and consistent with the position in which he had been found. The autopsy revealed no significant traumatic injuries, but there was some debris on his hands consisting of hard, dry, white-gray material (see Figure 5.10a). Investigative information revealed that he had been taken to the emergency department several weeks before this incident after he had been found unresponsive while trespassing. At the time of that incident, he had a plastic bag next to his face; however, there had been nothing of evidentiary value in or on the bag noticeable to investigators. Police and emergency medical technicians had noted a strong odor of glue coming from his body. Based on this observation and the findings at autopsy, we suspected that this man was a chronic "huffer". A toxicologic analysis performed on postmortem peripheral blood yielded only the following results: ethanol; 0.09 g/dL, acetaldehyde; 1.5 mg/dL, and toluene; 9.3 ug/mL (reporting limit 0.30 ug/mL). The other significant autopsy findings were hypertensive cardiovascular disease (heart weight 475 g, left ventricular hypertrophy, wall thickness 1.9 cm) and pulmonary emphysema. He did not have cerebral edema or any other abnormality of the brain. Histologic examination of H&E-stained brain sections contained ill-defined, patchy demyelination with apparent preservation of neurons and glial cells. Staining with PAS highlighted rare PAS-positive granules in macrophages highlighting myelin debris (see Figure 5.10b–d). These features are similar to those of other demyelinating diseases and conditions, such as multiple sclerosis, except without inflammation.

The cause of death was certified as asphyxia due to toluene inhalation in combination with hypertensive cardiovascular disease and hypothermia. Levels of toluene in the blood above 2.5 ug/mL are considered toxic, and the manner of death, in this case, was classified as "accidental".

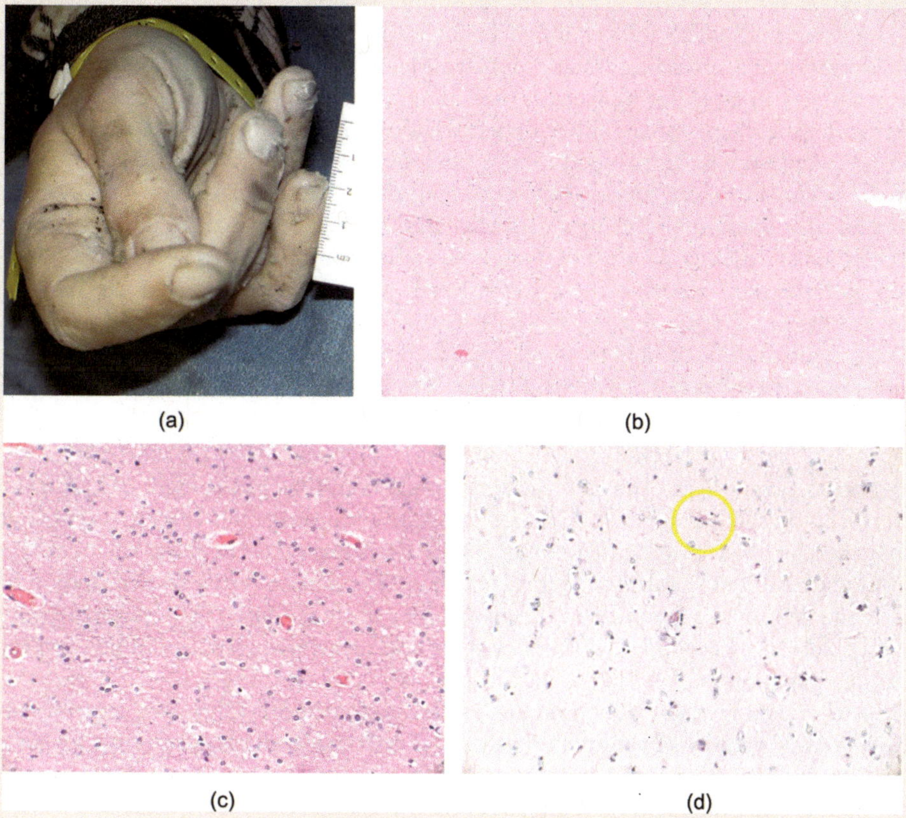

(a) (b) (c) (d)

Figure 5.10 (a) Decedent with glue residue on his hands, (b) Ill-defined, patchy demyelination H&E stain 4×, (c) H&E stain 20×, (d) PAS stain 20× PAS positive (pink) granule in a macrophage.

5.3.4 Cyanide

"Cyanide" is one of the most commonly known poisons among the general public, although not one often encountered in forensic practice at this time. Historically, hydrogen cyanide gas has been used as a homicidal poison; an agent of chemical warfare; a means of suicide; and, of course, as an agent of mass execution in concentration camps during World War II. Hydrogen cyanide is a colorless gas whose odor may be detected by some people as the smell of "bitter almonds" (The ability to recognize cyanide is an X-linked recessive characteristic, and only about 25% of the general population exhibits this trait).

Inhalation of gaseous cyanide can cause death within minutes; ingestion of a salt form can take considerably longer. Cyanide salts have long been utilized as an effective agent for suicides and homicides. Perhaps the largest mass ingestion occurred in Jonestown, Guyana in South America in 1978 in which hundreds of people died when a cyanide salt was added to beverages.

Analysis of cyanide in forensic samples can be accomplished by colorimetric methods, or instrumental analysis (GC– or HPLC–MS), although it is not a routine component in most standard forensic toxicology panels. Often, suspicious circumstances, or pathologic findings (e.g., "cherry red" livor mortis and internal organs, or the odor of almonds noted during autopsy may reasonably suggest a request for a cyanide analysis (see Sidebar 5.8.)

Sidebar 5.8: Homicide by a Medical Professional

Donald Harvey (1952–2017) worked as an orderly in hospitals in the Cincinnati, Ohio area. He killed dozens of terminally ill patients, claiming to have been acting as an "angel of death." He used several methods to achieve his goals, including physical asphyxiation and administration of various toxins, including arsenic and cyanide. For the most part, Harvey's victims were already critically ill or suffering from severe injury. Until one particular case was identified as a homicide, the deaths of the other patients had not raised suspicions. Routine toxicology at the time would not have included metals analysis or a test for cyanide. However, in 1987, Dr. Lee Lehman, a forensic pathologist at the Hamilton County Coroner's office, believed he detected an odor of almonds during an autopsy and requested an analysis for cyanide. While a bit of "collegial convincing" was needed to get the laboratory to set up the rarely requested test (a "Conway Diffusion"-based method was utilized), the laboratory did perform the test, with positive results. This discovery led to the eventual confession of multiple other homicides. Had Dr. Lehman not been able to smell cyanide or if he had ignored the finding, this serial killer may never have been caught. Mr. Harvey was killed in prison in Toledo, Ohio in 2017.

Cyanide exists primarily as the neutral hydrogen cyanide at physiologic pH; and, as such, is fat-soluble; easily absorbed through skin and mucus membranes; and readily diffuses across cell membranes and alveolar capillaries leading to a rapid distribution throughout the body. It is metabolized to thiocyanate by the sulfotransferase enzyme "Rhodenase" with an elimination half-life of between 20 and 60 min as a function of the availability of thiosulfate. Thiocyanate is water soluble and is readily cleared by the kidney. Blood cyanide and urine thiocyanate can be used to diagnose acute cyanide exposure.

Cyanide, either as a free ion (CN^-) or as a substituent group (–CN), is a component of many organic molecules. Cyanide is contained in some plants in the form of "cyanogenic glycosides" (e.g., cassava, apricot and peach pits, and apple seeds). While many plants contain trace amounts of cyanide, those containing cyanogenic glycosides represent poisonous species, and their toxic potential is well known. Consumption of parts of these plants containing cyanogenic glycosides can result in the release of cyanide during digestion. (Ingestion of peach pits was used as a method of execution and "ordeal trials" in Roman times and into the Middle Ages). Some plants containing cyanogenic glycosides are prepared and eaten as food (e.g., cassava) after multiple washings to remove the water-soluble glycosides and leave the edible starch behind.

At the molecular level, cyanide ion readily combines with the ferric form of iron (Fe^{+3}) in heme-containing molecules, e.g., Hb in the red blood cell (but only as the oxidized, metHb form) and cytochrome c oxidase, an important enzyme in the mitochondrial electron-transport chain. Unlike carbon monoxide, cyanide does not inhibit oxygen binding to Hb nor does it limit the transfer of oxygen from Hb to tissues. However, cyanide is an effective chemical asphyxiant, acting to block the utilization of oxygen at the cellular level. Specifically, cyanide binds to (ferric) iron in mitochondrial cytochrome c oxidase, blocking the reduction of the molecule and thereby limiting the ability of the enzyme to reduce oxygen, the final reaction in the energy-capturing "electron transport chain." This "uncoupling" of the electron transport chain essentially shuts down oxidative phosphorylation and the generation of energy within the cell as effectively as if oxygen were not available at all. Therefore, anaerobic respiration proceeds with the accumulation of lactic acid, leading to metabolic acidosis.

The lethality of hydrogen cyanide gas is dependent on dose and time of exposure, but even relatively small amounts for a short duration of time can be fatal. A concentration of 270 ppm hydrogen cyanide gas in the air can cause immediate death; 50–100 mg ingestion of the solid form causes a rapid collapse and death. The average lethal dose of cyanide is about 1.5 mg/kg body weight Center for Disease Control (CDC) (blood level ~3 mg/L), but much lower doses can be fatal, especially if the exposure is concomitant with other toxic exposures or in the setting of significant natural disease. Survivors of cyanide poisoning can have permanent neurological impairments due to hypoxic damage to the CNS.

Cyanide can be released from organic compounds during combustion and may, depending on the materials being burned, comprise a significant toxic component to the smoke formed. Cyanide gas may be produced from the burning of cyano-group-containing materials, such as some types of foam rubber and other manmade material as well as some animal fibers. Cyanide has therefore been responsible for countless deaths as a component of the "smoke inhalation" gas mixtures in both residential and commercial building fires. In addition to carbon monoxide, cyanide represents an inhalation exposure risk for firefighters not utilizing breathing apparatus.

In a house fire, inhaled cyanide may actually cause death before inhalation of carbon monoxide can form a substantial amount of COHb. Because hydrogen cyanide is lighter than air, residents on the upper floors of a burning building may be exposed and succumb to lethal levels of the compound before they actually inhale a significant amount of soot and hot gas (see Sidebar 5.9). Because victims of smoke inhalation from house fires may have inhaled some amount of hydrogen cyanide as well as carbon monoxide, these authors advocate the phrasing of the cause of death statement for victims of structural fires encompass the toxic effects of multiple gasses as well as the thermal effect: "inhalation of products of combustion" rather than carbon monoxide intoxication. If a deceased person has the features of inhalation of products of combustion (e.g., soot on the tongue and in the airway along with cherry-red livor mortis) but the COHb levels are inconsistent with CO toxicity, testing for cyanide might be reasonably considered, especially if the patient does not have significant demonstrable natural disease. Because cyanide-containing substances occur naturally, some people will have a detectable level of cyanide in their blood. Blood plasma levels can be as high as 14 microgram/dL (0.14 mg/L). Cyanide levels in blood from smokers can be on the high end of the reference range.

Sidebar 5.9: Cyanide on the Second Floor

In a case of a house fire with multiple fatalities, questions arose regarding response time for Fire Department personnel to respond to the scene. Because of language-based confusion at the time of the initial 911 call, police were the first responders dispatched to the residence. The criticism was that a quicker response by fire personnel would have resulted in fewer, if any, fatalities. The initial cause of death in the second-story victims was indicated to be "Smoke Inhalation" with the implication of hot gases and possible carbon monoxide. However, there was little appreciable soot in the airways, and COHb levels were low. The pathologist requested an analysis of cyanide in blood. The fire in this case had started on the first floor of the home in furniture with a considerable amount of foam padding. Apparently, combustion of the couch cushions resulted in a significant liberation of cyanide, which wafted into the upstairs area, causing the fatalities. The toxicologic analysis of cyanide in the blood of the decedents supported this conclusion. Cyanide fumes would have risen to the second floor before the subsequent smoke and other products of combustion. Even if fire personnel had been called initially and responded immediately, these patients would have already been dead from the cyanide, explaining the low COHb and lack of evidence of smoke inhalation.

The consequences of cyanide exposure at toxic, but nonfatal doses can result in coma, seizures, apnea, and cardiac arrhythmias, depending on the dose. Absorption of ingested salts of cyanide takes some time, increasing the opportunity to attempt treatment conversion of cyanide to thiocyanate (described below).

5.3.4.1 Signs and Symptoms

Cyanide poisoning has the features of hypoxia without cyanosis. Survivors are initially dyspneic, tachypneic, and hypotensive. Venous PaO_2 will be high because of the lack of utilization of oxygen to tissues. A potentially fatal acute respiratory distress syndrome (ARDS) may occur following exposure.

5.3.4.2 Treatment

The basis for treatment of cyanide-exposed patients is multi-pronged. Therapy is aimed at providing more oxygen to the patient as well as enhancing metabolism and elimination. Treatment of inhaled cyanide poisoning is generally supportive only because of time constraints: often the patient will die before antidotes can be administered. Supportive treatment for cases of ingestion may include supplemental oxygen and gastric lavage. An effective treatment regimen for ingested cyanide, or cyanogenic glycosides, utilizes nitrite (e.g., amyl- or sodium-) compounds, which oxidize a portion of the Hb molecules to metHb (Fe^{+3}), which then binds cyanide more effectively than does cytochrome oxidase. Cyanomethemoglobin (CNmetHb) is biochemically inactive. The net result is a decreased amount of cyano-cytochrome oxidase while CNmetHb is formed. Obviously, the iatrogenically formed metHb would further reduce the overall oxygen-carrying capacity of blood; therefore, such treatment is carefully monitored. Subsequent treatment with thiosulfate facilitates the formation of thiocyanate by the enzyme rhodanese. The highly water-soluble thiocyanate is readily eliminated by the kidney. Similarly, the cobalt-containing metalloprotein hydroxocobalamin will more effectively bind cyanide ions than does cytochrome c oxidase, thereby effectively removing the toxin from the target molecule. Hydroxycobalamin is also currently approved as a standalone cyanide antidote.

5.3.4.3 Autopsy Findings

Cyanide-poisoned patients often have "cherry-red" livor mortis, but cyanide poisoning may not be recognizable at autopsy, particularly in victims with significant natural diseases. Because some people can detect the presence of cyanide in a deceased person at levels as low as 1 ppm, a suspicion of cyanide poisoning, even if otherwise unsuspected, may be raised in the autopsy suite. However, because not everyone can smell cyanide, if cyanide poisoning is suspected at autopsy, appropriate care, precautions, and labeling should be utilized regarding the body and the clothing, as well as materials recovered from the scene. However, "outgassing" of cyanide gas from a decedent would not be expected to represent a toxic risk.

Cyanide can be detected in all body tissues, and decomposition should not prohibit testing if there is adequate soft tissue remaining. Cyanide does not accumulate in blood, so significant levels would be expected to be representative of recent exposure. The plasma half-life is between 20 min and 1 h. The natural mechanism of elimination of cyanide is via the urine as thiocyanate. Interpretation of blood cyanide levels can be difficult because many people have a detectable baseline level of cyanide in their blood (as noted above). The amount of cyanide and thiocyanate (SCN–) found in serum, saliva, and urine is dependent on personal habits and genetic traits, with smokers having two to three times the levels detected in nonsmokers.

5.3.5 Hydrogen Sulfide

Hydrogen sulfide (H_2S) is a relatively common industrial intermediate and byproduct in the petroleum and gas industry. It is a chemical irritant; a potent CNS depressant; and, like cyanide, potentially fatal, even in low concentrations. At concentrations of greater than 1,000 ppm hydrogen sulfide, victims reportedly became unconscious with one breath and die shortly thereafter. The mechanism by which hydrogen sulfide is toxic is similar to the cyanide mechanism in that it also forms a complex with the iron ion in cytochrome c oxidase, inhibiting cellular respiration at the level of mitochondria. Hydrogen sulfide gas has a strong smell of "rotten eggs", readily detected at concentrations well below any toxic threshold. However, with prolonged exposure, the olfactory nerve can become overwhelmed such that the victim is less aware of the potential danger. In contrast to cyanide, H_2S is heavier than air, and testing of exposure scene routinely is performed at or near floor level.

Hydrogen sulfide is not commonly encountered in forensic cases perhaps because the odor of the toxin serves as an effective warning well below potentially toxic concentrations. However, hydrogen sulfide has been used as a means of suicide, a trend that was reported in Japan in the early-2000's. Social media was blamed for the rapid dissemination of the method in which sulfur-containing compound is mixed with an acidic solution, releasing H_2S gas. Because the result of the mixture is gaseous, first responders and others at the death scene may also be at risk of exposure, although with the readily detectable odor, responding personnel would be expected to recognize the exposure risk.

"Detergent suicide" or "chemical suicide" has been documented in the US in several jurisdictions across the country. The chemical mixture is the same, albeit with different products: a sulfurated lime-based cleaning product mixed with a product containing hydrochloric acid. Only about one cup of each chemical is needed to produce enough toxic gas to quickly fill a small, enclosed space with hydrogen sulfide at potentially lethal concentrations. Because the reaction is gas producing, people tend to close themselves up in a small space to concentrate the gas faster, such as a vehicle or closet. In some cases, the victim may have put out warning notes to warn or protect first responders.

Based on the nature of the exposure and the potential for contamination, the chemical reaction source may require neutralization and proper cleanup. Calling upon the services of the local "HazMat" Team may be required before the medicolegal team attempts to remove the body. Additionally, the clothing of the victim may require careful packaging to limit off-gassing and secondary exposure to investigatory or morgue personnel. Depending on the amount of H_2S generation, the gas may have penetrated the soft materials inside the space utilized by the victim, which may then "off gas" over time. In the absence of air exchange, this off-gassing may be a hazard to anyone near the scene for many hours, although with the odor of the gas would not represent an insidious danger. The rate of decay of the gas is between 12 and 37 h and is temperature dependent. Patients exposed to, or surviving exposures, to hydrogen sulfide gas may be treated with a nitrite salt. The mechanism is the same as for the treatment of cyanide poisoning.

5.3.6 Nitrates and Nitrites

5.3.6.1 Introduction

Nitrates and nitrites are extensively utilized industrially and are also used as preservatives for meat and as antimicrobial agents. As such, they are commonly encountered in household products such a "cold packs" for food storage and in some pharmaceuticals. Common exposure to small amounts is harmless. Volatile products containing nitrites, such as amyl nitrite, have been used recreationally, presumably for the euphoric effect during a state of mild hypoxia.

5.3.6.2 Mechanism of Action

The active component of these drugs and chemicals causing toxicity is nitrite. Bacteria that naturally live in the intestine convert nitrates to nitrites. Nitrites convert normal Hb to metHb. Normal Hb (hemoglobin A, Hb A) is composed of two polypeptide (amino acid) chains (the "globin" portion) and four heme groups each containing an iron in the ferrous (+2) state. The heme portion reversibly binds oxygen and carbon monoxide (although, as noted above, the dissociation constant for CO is much lower than for O_2).

MetHb is formed when the ferrous iron (Fe^{+2}) in Hb is oxidized to ferric iron (Fe^{+3}). Normal oxygenation of Hb causes a partial transfer of an electron from the ferrous iron to the oxygen, binding them together but loosely. The oxygen-bound iron is now partially in the ferric state (Fe^{+3}) and the oxygen resembles superoxide ($O_2^{-\cdot}$). When oxygen dissociates as a function of low PO_2 in the tissue capillaries, the electron returns to the iron as the oxygen is released, effectively reducing the iron back to the ferrous (+2) state. The oxygen binding and subsequent release cycle leave about 1% of Hb as the oxidized, ferric iron form, metHb inside the red blood cell. MetHb is quickly reduced back to the ferrous state by cytochrome b5 reductase. Ascorbic acid and metHb reductase also can reduce metHb to Hb. The metHb reductases require a cofactor, as an electron donor, usually nicotinamide adenine dinucleotide hydrogen (NADH) or nicotinamide adenine dinucleotide phosphate hydrogen (NADPH). Interestingly, both ascorbic acid and methylene blue are used as such cofactors for the treatment of acquired methemoglobinemia. Even severe methemoglobinemia due to sodium nitrite can be successfully treated in this manner. In one case, the patient reportedly ingested 15 g of sodium nitrite and was seen at the hospital for cyanosis and loss of consciousness, with a metHb level was 92.5%. Treatment with an intravenous infusion of 2 mg/kg body weight of methylene blue reduced his metHb level to about 1% in about 5 h. As red cells lyse, during decomposition, the newly free (no longer contained in a red blood cell) Hb A is quickly oxidized to metHb. However, prior to frank decomposition, postmortem measurements of metHb percentage can still be useful.

In the presence of a large amount of nitrite, metHb forms as the shared electron from the heme iron–oxygen complex is abstracted by a nitrite molecule, releasing O_2, and an oxidized heme group (Fe^{3+}; MetHb). This oxidation of one of the Hb heme subunits increases the affinity for the remaining three heme for oxygen. As such, a metHb molecule is unable to bind oxygen at one heme site and less able to release oxygen from the remaining heme subunits in regions of low PO_2, further limiting the functional effectiveness of the molecule. The oxygen dissociation curve is shifted to the left, reflecting the increased heme–oxygen affinity. This enhanced oxygen affinity makes this Hb molecule essentially physiologically useless. The result is tissue hypoxia despite a normal blood oxygen saturation level.

5.3.6.3 Clinical Presentation

Patients with methemoglobinemia are cyanotic as a function of some degree of tissue oxygen deprivation, but their blood oxygenation (oxygen saturation) level is normal. These patients do not respond to supplemental oxygen because their Hb is already saturated with oxygen. Clinically, these patients may have a blue-gray discoloration of their skin, especially of their facial skin, and nail beds will be deeply cyanotic. Depending on the degree of methemoglobinemia, the blood will be a dark brown color.

Congenital methemoglobinemia is seen in patients with genetic mutations in the globin molecule that stabilizes iron in the ferric state (Fe^{3+}). These patients usually do not need therapy but should be cautioned about the use of nitrite-containing medications, such as nitroglycerin. MetHb concentration in these patients is usually about 1%. With chronic tissue hypoxia, these patients may compensate for the condition by an elevated production of red blood cells to increase their oxygen-carrying capacity. If the hematocrit becomes too high, therapeutic phlebotomy may be the only treatment necessary (see Sidebar 5.10).

Sidebar 5.10: Blue People of Kentucky

There is a small rural area in Kentucky in which an extended family affected by congenital methemoglobinemia, an autosomal recessive condition, lived. The family was concentrated in a region near the town of Hazard, Kentucky. In the early 1800s, Martin and Elizabeth Fugate married and eventually had seven children. Both Martin and Elizabeth were heterozygous for met-H, the gene responsible for the condition. Because each partner had only one copy, neither expressed the condition, but both were able to pass on a copy of the gene. Four of their children were born with blue skin as these four had inherited one copy of met-H from each parent and were therefore homozygous for the trait. The skin of these individuals was not actually blue but did appear to be blue because blood with a high level of metHb is brown and when viewed through pale skin, gives the skin a bluish appearance.

This area of Kentucky in the Appalachian mountains was very much isolated from the rest of the state; at the time, there were no real roads, and there was very little interaction between the Fugates and other people except for their extended family. The blue skin color caused the family to be ridiculed by outsiders, making them further isolate themselves. At that time in history, little was understood about genetic transmission, much less about genetic testing. Because there was no scientific information about this condition that would cause people to reconsider childbearing and there were few eligible marriage partners, some members married within the family and had children of their own. Intermarriage perpetuated the gene. People with this condition were otherwise healthy, the only effect was the blue color of their skin.

As time went on and more of the science of genetics became understood, two members of the Fugate family approached Dr. Madison Cawein (a hematologist). He and nurse Ruth Pendergrass studied the ancestry of the Fugate family and found a cure for methemoglobinemia. Aptly (ironically?) named, the "cure" is methylene blue (MB), which converts metHb to Hb A, reducing the oxidized heme iron to the normal Hb Fe^{2+} state. Blood with normal levels of Hb is red, showing through pale skin as pink. MB is a dye and easily absorbed through the GI tract and may also be given intravenously. Methylene blue does not cure the condition but is used to manage the resultant tissue hypoxia by increasing the percentage of normal Hb.

The last known descendent of the Fugate family was born in 1975. He had a blue tint to his skin in infancy. Because there were no homozygotes for metHb in at least two previous generations, the medical team was unaware of the condition and thought the hue was due to heart and/or lung pathology until his father revealed that his paternal grandmother was a "blue Fugate", saying: "it was real bad in her". This little boy, Benji, outgrew his hue by about age 7, presumably because he was heterozygous for met-H. The genetics of metHb is more complex than simple Mendelian inheritance and symptoms vary from patient to patient. The inconsistent phenotypic expression can cause confusion among both patients and medical personnel.

MetHb [autosomal *r*ecessive *c*ongenital *m*ethemoglobinemia(RCM)] is a rare hemoglobinopathy classified by phenotype into RCM type 1 (mild) and RCM type 2 (more severe).

Patients with RCM type 1 have cyanosis at birth, headache, fatigue, and dyspnea on exertion. Patients with RCM type 2 can also have neurological dysfunction that is not reversible. RCM type 1 is caused by mutations in the cytochrome b5 reductase 3 (CYB5R3) gene on chromosome 22 encoding NADH-cytochrome b5 reductase in red blood cells. RCM type 2 is caused by other mutations in CYB5R3 leading to total loss of NADH-cytochrome b5 reductase.

5.3.6.4 Intoxication

Acquired methemoglobinemia results from ingestion of oxidizing agents, e.g., nitrate- or nitrite-containing medications or the chemical itself and the subsequent formation of metHb. Cyanosis becomes detectable at metHb levels above 10%, and the blood becomes chocolate brown at about 15%–20%. Symptoms of serious hypoxia begin at levels of about 35%, with patients experiencing fatigue and muscle weakness. Myoglobin is a muscle protein that contains a single heme subunit, which is susceptible to the same electron abstraction and oxidation as the Hb tetramer, and results in the formation of metmyoglobin. The oxidized metmyoglobin is unable to bind oxygen, leading to muscle hypoxia and patients may feel weak, lethargic, and crampy. Symptoms and signs of slightly elevated methemoglobinemia are non-specific and include fatigue, headache, tachycardia, and vertigo. Serious complications from the formation of metHb related to tissue hypoxia include cerebral ischemia that can eventually lead to coma and death. Symptoms of cerebral ischemia can be demonstrated at metHb levels of 20%–50%. Levels above about 50% can be fatal and over 70% are expected to be so; however, these levels are variable and patients with levels greater than 94% have survived.

Accidental poisoning by sodium nitrite is uncommon. Sometimes patients do not know from where they ingested the intoxicant. Sodium nitrite is a common preservative agent as an antioxidant and antibacterial, which looks and tastes like table salt and has been mistakenly consumed as such. The material is easily purchased from grocery stores and from internet markets. It is relatively inexpensive, available in small quantities (5 ounces) for household use and in larger quantities (2 lb.) as a laboratory reagent. The lethal dose in an adult is about 2.5 g; however, patients who have ingested larger amounts have survived.

Suicidal ingestions are extremely uncommon; however, based on literature reports, the incidence of suicidal ingestions appears to be increasing. The authors of this text have investigated four cases within a several-month period of fatal ingestions of sodium nitrite (two of which are discussed in Sidebar 5.11) When mixed with water, nitrite salts become a watery, white, turbid solution. In suspected cases of poisoning, investigators should look for white powder; chemical containers, the actual product container; a cloudy solution, or white residue. Livor mortis is gunmetal gray in light-skinned decedents, but this abnormal color may not be apparent in darkly pigmented people. Fingernail beds and lips will be cyanotic, but these are common features of deceased persons, even without sodium nitrite.

Sidebar 5.11: Suicidal Ingestion of Sodium Nitrite

We have investigated several cases of suicidal ingestion of the pure chemical sodium nitrite. Two of them are briefly presented here.

Case #1 is a 24-year-old woman found deceased in her apartment. She lived alone in a small house. Investigators were called to her home for a welfare check as she had not been to her college classes in about a week. It appears that she had died suddenly. She was found partially slumped in the supine position off her bed onto the floor. Her legs rested on the bed and her torso, head, and her left upper extremity were on the floor. Her right upper extremity was resting on a blanket that appeared to have been partially dragged to the floor as she slumped off the bed. Her body was in the early stage of decomposition when discovered. Her body was cool and rigor mortis had passed. Fixed, red-purple livor mortis was present on the posterior aspect of the body and on the right side of her face and head, compatible with the position in which she was found. Her body temperature taken in the axilla was 58.4°F, slightly lower than the ambient temperature of 61.7°F. Her lips were dry and dark. Her fingertips were moderately dry and darkened; her nail beds were dark. Two reagent-grade bottles of sodium nitrite were on her kitchen table. Other medications in plain view were Pepcid, Tagamet, IP-6, Inositol, and Tylenol Extra Strength.

At autopsy, she was 60 inches long, 142 pounds, and appeared to be of Asian heritage. Because she was slightly decomposed, her nails and lips were dry. Her skin was somewhat dark with yellow undertones. The usual blue-gray or gray color of methemoglobinemia was not apparent. The autopsy procedure, including histopathology, did not reveal the cause of death. The toxicologic analysis of peripheral blood was negative for ethyl alcohol, other volatiles, and drugs of abuse. The presence of sodium nitrite at the scene prompted an analysis for metHb, which was eventually determined to be 62% in this decomposing woman. It is, however, likely that at least some of the metHb was formed after death as the red blood cells lysed.

Case #2 is a 22-year-old Caucasian man who was reportedly well until his brother found him vomiting. He suddenly became unresponsive, so his brother called the emergency services and attempted cardiopulmonary resuscitation (CPR). Upon paramedics' arrival, he was "discolored", had agonal breathing, and a pulse in the 40s/min. Resuscitative efforts, including administration of naloxone, were unsuccessful and he expired at home.

During the subsequent scene investigation, suicide notes and a warning note were discovered in plain view. A bottle of chemical-grade sodium nitrite and a glass with white residue was also collected. The autopsy of this 71-inch, 171-pound man revealed the following. The skin of the face and some of the skin on the fingers had a blue-gray discoloration. The nailbeds were dusky gray. The pad of the left thumb was discolored light brown. All available blood was brown, thin, and in liquid form. There were linear hemorrhages in the mucosa of the body of the stomach on the ridges of the rugae. There were similar hemorrhages in the distal portion of the small intestine and the proximal portion of the large intestine. The gastric contents were composed only of thin, brown liquid with no identifiable pills, tablets, or fragments thereof. The kidneys, especially the medulla, were brown. There were multiple purpural hemorrhages beneath the scalp

The gray discoloration of the skin and the brown color of the blood along with the scene investigation prompted an analysis for metHb in addition to the routine toxicologic evaluation. The toxicologic analysis revealed a metHb level of 33%. Neither ethanol nor drugs of abuse were detected. A vitreous electrolyte panel showed sodium 148 mmol/L and chloride 124 mmol/L, both elevated.

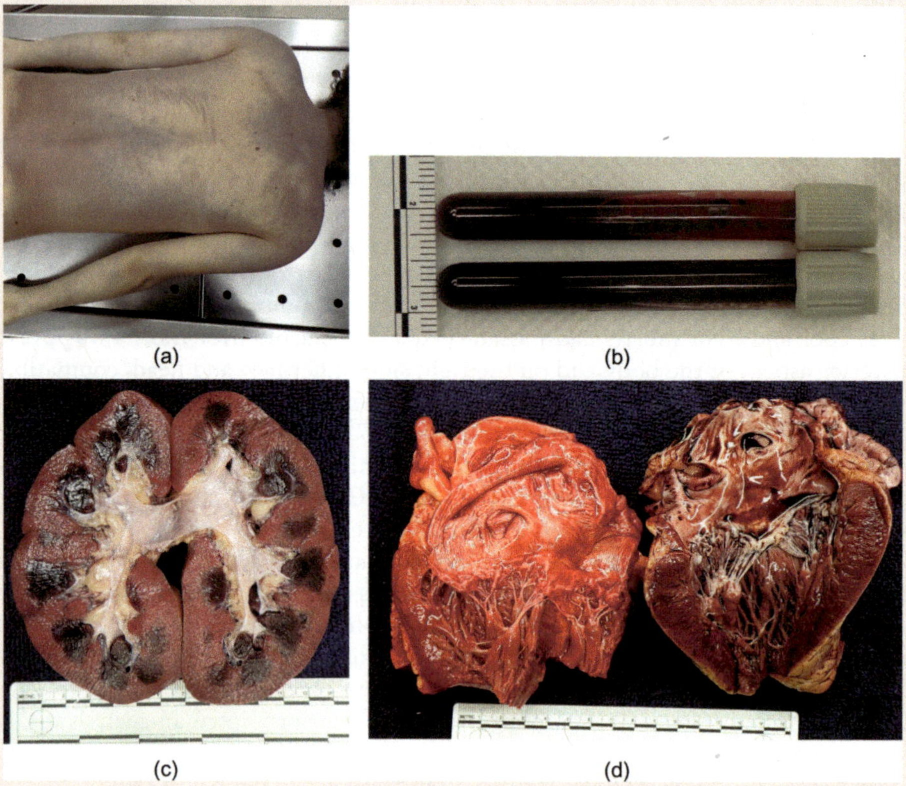

Figure 5.11 (a) The back of the torso of a man. Livor mortis is blanching and gunmetal gray as opposed to the usual red-purple hue. (b) Two sodium fluoride (gray top) blood tubes. The tube on the top of the photo is from a person who died of a natural disease. The tube on the bottom is from the index case. Note that the blood in the index case is deep brown. (c) A bivalved kidney from the index case. The cortex is of the usual red-brown color, but the medulla is deep brown. (d) Two different heart specimens opened along the line of blood flow. Both are opened to show the endocardium and myocardium of the left atrium and left ventricle. The heart on the left is from a person who died from trauma. The heart on the right is from this patient who died from methemoglobinemia. Note that the muscle and the blood are both brown in the index case.

Laboratory testing for metHb is appropriate for living patients for diagnosis and to monitor therapy. In deceased people, metHb can be measured; however, interpretation may be difficult. Postmortem values may differ from antemortem levels as the blood metHb increases with increasing postmortem interval. Fresh blood stored in ethylenediaminetetraacetatic acid (EDTA)-containing tubes (lavender top) and tested soon after collection may be the best specimen to use, if available. If testing is to be delayed for longer than two weeks, freezing the sample at –80°C may provide some degree of preservation. An alternative test for sodium nitrite poisoning is to test for nitrate in the blood as nitrite is oxidized. Nitrate values in postmortem blood are stable in the early postmortem period.

5.3.6.5 Therapeutic Use

As noted above, nitrites, (e.g., Na- or amyl-), are used as therapy for cyanide poisoning by producing metHB. The preferential binding of cyanide to metHb precludes the binding of those CN- ions to and inhibits key enzymes in the cellular electron transport system (see Section 5.3.4).

5.4 OTHER COMMON TOXINS

5.4.1 Ozone

Ozone (O_3) is a gaseous trioxygen species related to but more reactive than the more stable dioxygen, O_2. Ozone is used for purifying air and drinking water, in wastewater treatment, and in the manufacture of some petrochemical products. It is also detected in vehicle exhaust. Exposure to ozone gas is usually employment related. It has a sharp odor, similar to, but less disagreeable than chlorine. Ozone may be considered a true pulmonary toxin in that it has direct toxic effects on the pulmonary system, in addition to producing the effects of irritation with its sequelae. It is a powerful oxidizing agent that can damage the mucosa of the tracheobronchial tree as well as the pulmonary parenchyma. The ciliated columnar epithelium of the trachea and bronchi and type I alveolar pneumocytes of the pulmonary parenchyma are the most vulnerable cells to ozone toxicity. Type I pneumocytes are the thin, flat cells that form the gas exchange region of alveoli. Type II pneumocytes (the cuboidal-surfactant-producing cells) proliferate in the alveoli in response because these type II cells can differentiate into type I cells and replace those that are damaged. Type II cell proliferation and pulmonary edema are characteristic of ozone poisoning. The effect is the destruction of the mucociliary elevator and the site of oxygen–carbon dioxide exchange.

Unlike the agents that combine with body water to form acidic or basic species in the lungs, ozone is capable of reacting directly with organic double bonds and generates species for oxygen free radicals, leading to lipid peroxidation and oxygen radical toxicity. Thus, the clinical presentation of patients experiencing ozone toxicity is non-specific. Diagnosis is dependent on scene investigation.

5.4.2 Nicotine

Nicotine is an agonist of cholinergic receptors, which are located in the brain, the adrenal medulla, and at neuromuscular junctions. As a cholinergic drug, it is not, therefore, a direct pulmonary toxin; however, because the major route of exposure is tobacco smoking and because of its effect on the bronchi and bronchioles, nicotine is included in this section. Nicotine, particularly in combination with cigarette smoke, is an irritant and pro-inflammatory agent, particularly in the respiratory system. Nicotine-related vasoconstriction can reduce gas exchange and exacerbate asthma. Prolonged use of tobacco products can lead to emphysema and chronic bronchitis, as well as accelerate cardiovascular disease. The smoke from tobacco products is directly toxic to ciliated epithelial cells in the respiratory tree. Direct effects on the lungs are primarily a function of nicotine-based toxicity to the mucociliary elevator, thereby limiting the ability of the lungs to remove such environmental workplace or environmental toxins, such as coal dust, asbestos, smoke, or related aerosolized or particulate matter.

Means of exposure other than smoking are also possible. Accidental ingestions of nicotine-tainted saliva ("spit") have been reported, most often in children. Nicotine is a bitter-tasting material, so a child might only ingest a small amount. Currently, patches and gum containing nicotine are readily available as smoking cessation agents. Children could become nicotine-toxic if they eat or chew on these products. A suicide has been reported which utilized an application of multiple transdermal patches by a patient who also asphyxiated herself with a plastic bag.

Nicotine poisoning can be suspected clinically. Symptoms are constitutional: nausea, vomiting, abdominal pain, somnolence and/or agitation followed by coma. The onset of action of the drug is relatively rapid, although the dose and time to peak concentration in blood will be dependent upon the delivery system. The peak concentration of nicotine by smoking is achieved much faster than from absorption from the patch. There are no characteristic signs of nicotine toxicity at autopsy. Laboratory testing of blood or serum for nicotine and its metabolite cotinine is straightforward, and both species are regular constituents of routine broad-spectrum mass-spectrometer-based drug screening protocols. Vitreous humor, urine, brain, and liver tissue can also be evaluated in cases of suspected poisoning.

Nicotine is readily metabolized in the liver (CYP2A6) to cotinine and other metabolites, but some is eliminated unchanged in the urine. Cotinine is considered a biomarker for the use of tobacco products, e.g., smoking, chewing, gum, or absorption from dermal patches. It also can be a biomarker for passive inhalation of smoke from burning tobacco, depending on the duration and intensity of exposure. The elimination half-lives for nicotine and cotinine are about 2 and 16h, respectively, but they vary somewhat with age, gender, smoking habits, ethnicity, other drug use, as well as diet and meals. Generally, nicotine metabolism is faster after meals, presumably due to increased hepatic blood flow. Nicotine clearance is faster in younger people than in the elderly, except for neonates for whom it is slower. Nicotine clearance is somewhat faster in females, especially pregnant and menstruating women CYP2A6-inducing drugs will also increase the rate of nicotine metabolism.

If a deceased person is suspected of having been poisoned with nicotine, the pathologist may be asked to determine which product was used. Unfortunately, there is no way to differentiate between tobacco-containing products in a deceased person other than scene investigation (although identification of co-constituents may provide some information in this regard). However, if the patient was administered or was poisoned with a nicotine-containing product not derived from tobacco, e.g., smoking cessation aids, the tobacco alkaloids anabasine, and anatabine will not be present as they would have been, in a tobacco product-related poisoning.

5.4.3 Ammonia Gas

Ammonia (NH_3) is a colorless gas with a strongly pungent odor. It is primarily used in agriculture and industry as a part of fertilizers and animal feeds and as an important synthetic intermediate and reactant. Ammonia gas readily forms the caustic compound ammonium hydroxide with any available water molecules as an exothermic reaction. Direct skin contact with or inhalation of ammonia gas can cause a chemical burn of skin, mucus membranes, or alveoli leading to inflammation, edema, and water loss. If the initial exposure is prolonged, the patient may die of non-cardiogenic pulmonary edema and liquefactive necrosis of the exposed tissues. At autopsy, the deceased person will have extensive caustic burns on the exposed skin and mucus membranes and opacified corneas. They will not have singed body, scalp, or facial hair. This feature differentiates these patients from those having died in a fire.

At autopsy, the mucosa will be hyperemic or sloughed. Microscopic examination of the tracheobronchial tree can reveal sloughed epithelium and necrosis of the submucosa. The pulmonary parenchyma will be congested and edematous with cellular debris in the alveolar ducts and alveoli. If the patient has survived the initial exposure, the pulmonary parenchyma and the tracheobronchial tree may be scarred. Serum ammonia level will be high; COHb and cyanide will be low or negligible.

5.4.4 Chlorine Gas

Chlorine gas is yellowish-green and can be highly irritating to the respiratory tree and mucus membranes, including the eyes. In low concentrations, it causes a burning sensation of skin and eyes, but can also cause coughing and bronchospasm. Chlorine is commonly used as an industrial cleaner; a pool water conditioner; and, in the diluted form, as a household cleaner. Exposure to large quantities of chlorine gas is usually accidental in nature, resulting from a "chemical spill" from a large transport vessel, as chlorine is a significant industrial chemical. However, significant exposures to chlorine gas have also occurred when household bleach (sodium hypochlorite) is mixed with another cleaning agent that contains an acid or ammonia. Chlorine gas is denser than air and can travel along the ground as it dissipates. When inhaled, chlorine gas combines with water to form hydrochloric and hypochlorous acid, causing irritation, inflammation, and delayed pulmonary edema. Chlorine gas was used extensively in World War I as an agent of chemical warfare and had been reportedly used in later civil conflicts as well.

There are very few reported cases of sulfur dioxide poisoning. If the patient dies soon after exposure, tracheobronchial erythema and pulmonary edema will likely be the only autopsy findings. Cases of poisoning by inhalation of chorine fumes in a paper pulp mill resulted in one fatality; one exposed patient lived, but with restrictive lung disease. Following a chlorine gas spill from a freight train derailment; the health effects on employees inside a factory were detailed. Eight patients died at the scene; one died the day after the accident. Seventy other patients required some hospitalization, including intensive care. All affected patients had pulmonary edema and mucosal erythema. The diagnosis of chlorine gas exposure is commonly made by investigation; however, both dissolved Cl_2 gas and consequential HCl solutions can be readily detected.

5.4.5 Sulfur Dioxide

Sulfur dioxide can be released in the burning of oil, coal, and other petrochemicals. It is also used as an intermediate component for the production of sulfuric acid, as a fruit preservative, as a preservative for other foods to be served following drying, and to bleach pulp in making paper. When inhaled, it reacts with water to form sulfuric acid which is a strong pulmonary corrosive or irritant. Prolonged, or extensive exposure, can cause bronchospasm and pulmonary edema. Exposure can exacerbate emphysema, asthma, and other respiratory conditions.

There are very few reported cases of sulfur dioxide poisoning. If the patient dies soon after exposure, tracheobronchial erythema and pulmonary edema will likely be the only autopsy findings. Cases of poisoning by inhalation of toxic fumes in a paper pulp mill have been reported, with a consequent fatality. One exposed patient died after 17 days, and at autopsy, the lungs were not edematous, rather they appeared to be overinflated as in pulmonary emphysema. Microscopically, there was acute inflammation and ulceration with pseudomembrane formation of the mucosa of the trachea and bronchi. The pseudomembrane was composed of necrotic debris and neutrophils. The trachea and bronchi also had proliferation of goblet cells and an overproduction of mucus. Peripheral airways showed destruction of alveolar septa and an inflammatory cell infiltrate composed primarily of neutrophils with an admixture of foamy macrophages. The lamia propria of bronchioles was focally fibrotic with fibrosis extending to the pleura appearing like bronchiolitis obliterans. Sulfur dioxide can be readily detected in blood and urine, as it quickly crosses the alveolar–capillary membrane and is transported to body tissues.

5.5 UNCOMMON TOXINS

5.5.1 Phosgene

Phosgene ($COCl_2$) is a liquid used as an intermediate component in the production of some plastics and pesticides. It was first used as an agent of chemical warfare in World War I and was found to be more effective than chlorine gas alone. It is a gas that is denser than air at room temperature, with an odor similar to that of newly mown grass or hay. Because the odor is not unpleasant, people may be exposed to phosgene for some time before succumbing to its effects. It is a potent respiratory irritant that is extremely toxic if inhaled, hydrolyzing upon contact with water to form hydrochloric acid, with subsequent tissue damage and causing massive pulmonary edema.

5.5.2 Silicon

Elemental silicon is inert and non-toxic, but silica dust can cause irritation and scar tissue after prolonged exposure. The condition is called silicosis. Inhalation of silicon dioxide over time has also been linked to lung cancer. The usual mechanism for exposure is occupation related, for those individuals who work in the mining industry, quarries, and foundries. Acute silicosis can cause shortness of breath, cough, fever, and even cyanosis. Silica particles can be small enough so as to reach the alveoli to be phagocytized by macrophages. Grossly, the well-demarcated, firm-to-hard nodules resemble any other granuloma. They may be white, gray, or gray-black, depending on the color of the contaminants also trapped in the histiocytes forming the granulomata. Histologically, the nodules are eosinophilic whorls of paucicellular fibrous tissue that may be rimmed by fibroblasts. Sometime, silica particles can be seen near the center of the granuloma as polarizable, birefringent needle-like foreign bodies.

5.5.3 Asbestos

Asbestos is a special type of fibrous silicate material that had been used as thermal insulation for piping and ceiling tiles. It is fireproof and moldable, so in that sense, it is a near-perfect product. However, it is a noxious substance that causes extensive, permanent lung damage and is now strictly regulated. Asbestos toxicity lies in the potential for inhaled small, pointed fibers that can become trapped in alveoli causing inflammation and fibrosis. Grossly, the entire lung is affected with the lower lobes and the periphery preferentially. At autopsy, in the early stages, the lungs may look and feel normal. In advanced disease, the lungs will be diffusely fibrotic, sometimes gray, with a honeycomb appearance. The differential diagnosis is idiopathic pulmonary fibrosis and other interstitial lung diseases. A history of prolonged exposure and the histologic findings should be enough to separate these entities. Histologically, asbestos particles are brown-beaded rods with a pale core associated with or embedded within mononuclear inflammatory cells that can be seen with H&E staining. The asbestos fiber itself is colorless, but becomes coated with an iron mucopolysaccharide material, giving it the characteristic "brown dumbbell" appearance. Although they are obvious with the H&E stain, they may be trapped in an area of other pigment-laden macrophages and may need to be highlighted with a stain for iron (e.g., Prussian blue reaction). Fibrosis is also a necessary feature for the diagnosis and begins at the level of the alveoli around bronchioles, progressing outward from there. There are multiple forms of the silicate with one in particular, "crocidolite" being associated with mesothelioma and other lung cancers which can be a fatal condition in persons exposed.

5.5.4 Paraquat

Paraquat is a highly toxic nonselective herbicide widely used throughout the world as a weed killer. It is inactivated by environmental exposure in soil; therefore, it is useful for immediate weed control just prior to crop planting. Seeds are not affected by paraquat. However, it is not effective as a long-term solution to weed infestation. Currently, it is not available for personal use because of its toxic nature. However, it is still available requiring a license for its use and, therefore, still has human toxic potential. Overall, the risk of damage is greatest by inhalation, followed by ingestion, then dermal absorption. Paraquat crosses alveolar cell membranes by active transport and is concentrated in lung tissue. It readily participates in redox cycling of electrons from NADH or NADPH to iron or oxygen, thereby forming free radicals in tissue causing direct damage with eventual fibrosis of the lung. Other organs are similarly affected, but the lung appears to be the primary target.

Bibliography

Agency for Toxic Substances and Disease Registry (ATSDR). (2006). *Toxicologic Profile for Cyanide (Update)*. Atlanta, GA: U.S. Department of Health and Human Services, Public Health Services.

Avella J., Wilson J.C., Lehrer M. (2006). Fatal cardiac arrhythmia after repeated exposure to 1,1-difluoroethane (DFE). *The American Journal of Forensic Medicine and Pathology*, 27(1):58–60. https://doi.org/10.1097/01.paf.0000202715.71009.0e.

Batchelor T. (Sept 29, 2020). Kindergarten teacher sentenced to death for poisoning 25 children, killing one. https://www.newsweek.com/kindergarten-teacher-sentenced-death-poisoning-children-oatmeal-china-1534890. Accessed 15 December 2020.

Blumenthal I. (2001). Carbon monoxide poisoning. *Journal of the Royal Society of Medicine*, 94(6):270–272. https://doi.org/10.1177/014107680109400604.

Boron W.F., Boulais E.L. (eds). (2012). *Medical Physiology*. 2nd rev. ed., updated. Philadelphia, PA: Saunders-Elsevier.

CDC. (2002). Methemoglobinemia following unintentional ingestion of sodium nitrite – New York 2002. *MMWR Weekly Report*, 51(29):639–642.

Cvetković D., Živković V., Lukić V., Nikolić S. (2019). Sodium nitrite food poisoning in one family. *Forensic Science, Medicine, and Pathology*, 15(1):102–105. https://doi.org/10.1007/s12024-018-0036-1.

Dean D.E., Looman K.B., Topmiller R.G. (2021). Fatal methemoglobinemia in three suicidal sodium nitrite poisonings. *Journal of Forensic Sciences*, 66(4):1570–1576. https://doi.org/10.1111/1556-4029.14689.

Filley C.M., Halliday W., Kleinschmidt-DeMasters B.K. (2004). The effects of toluene on the central nervous system. *Journal of Neuropathology and Experimental Neurology*, 63(1):1–12. https://doi.org/10.1093/jnen/63.1.1.

Joshi K., Barletta M., Wurpel J. (2017). Cardiotoxic (arrhythmogenic) effects of 1,1-difluoroethane due to electrolyte imbalance and cardiomyocyte damage. *The American Journal of Forensic Medicine and Pathology*, 38(2):115–125. https://doi.org/10.1097/PAF.0000000000000262.

Galea M. (1964). Fatal sulfur dioxide inhalation. *Canadian Medical Association Journal*, 91(7):345–347.

Gidlow D. (2017) Hydrogen cyanide – An update. *Occupational Medicine*, 67:662–663. https://doi.org/10.1093/occmed/kqx121.

Lawson-Smith P., Jansen E.C., Hyldegaard O. (2011). Cyanide intoxication as part of smoke inhalation: A review on diagnosis and treatment from the emergency perspective. *Scandinavian Journal of Trauma, Resuscitation and Emergency Medicine*, 19:14. https://doi.org/10.1186/1757-7241-19-14.

Leikauf G.D. (2013). Toxic responses of the respiratory system. In: Klassen C.D. (eds). *Casarett and Doull's. Toxicology: The Basic Science of Poisons*. 8th rev. ed. New York: McGraw-Hill. 691–745.

Morris M., Davey F. (1996). *Clinical Diagnosis and Management by Laboratory Methods*. 19th ed. Philadelphia, PA: WB Saunders.

Physiology of the respiratory system. In: Patton K.T., Thibodeau, GA. (eds). *Anatomy and Physiology*. 7th rev. ed. St. Louis, MO: Mosby-Elsevier, 2010.

Pulmonary Toxicology. In: Powers R.H., Dean D.E. (eds). *Forensic Toxicology: Mechanisms and Pathology* (pp. 147–164). Boca Raton, FL: Taylor and Francis, CRC Press, 2016.

Roggli V.L., Gibbs A.R., Attanoos R., Churg A., Popper H., Cagle P., Corrin B., Franks T.J., Galateau-Salle F., Galvin J., Hasleton P.S., Henderson D.W., Honma K. (2010). Pathology of asbestosis: An update of the diagnostic criteria: Report of the asbestosis committee of the College of American Pathologists and Pulmonary Pathology Society. *Archives of Pathology & Laboratory Medicine*, 134(3):462–480. https://doi.org/10.5858/134.3.462.

Sagar G.R. (1987). Uses and usefulness of paraquat. *Human Toxicology*, 6(1):7–11. https://doi.org/10.1177/096032718700600102.

Sangalli B.C., Bidanset J.H. (1990). A review of carboxymyoglobin formation: A major mechanism of carbon monoxide toxicity. *Veterinary and Human Toxicology*, 32(5):449–453.

Smith L.L. (1987). Mechanism of paraquat toxicity in lung and its relevance to treatment. *Human toxicology*, 6(1):31–36. https://doi.org/10.1177/096032718700600105.

Smith L.L. (1985). Paraquat toxicity. *Philosophical Transactions of the Royal Society of London. Series B. Biological Sciences*, 311(1152):647–657. https://doi.org/10.1098/rstb.1985.0170.

Wyatt J.P., Allister C.A. (1995). Occupational phosgene poisoning: a case report and review. *Journal of Accident & Emergency Medicine*, 12(3):212–213. https://doi.org/10.1136/emj.12.3.212.

SECTION 6

CARDIOTOXINS

DOI: 10.4324/9781003121060-7

6.1 INTRODUCTION

Cardiac pathology that can cause or play a contributory role in a death can be caused by drugs, toxins, inflammatory reactions to foreign material, as well as structural abnormalities from natural diseases. This section focuses on the effects drugs and toxins may have on the cardiovascular system. There are almost innumerable drugs and toxins that have adverse effects on the heart. Only some of them are discussed here, with a focus on the commonly encountered ones. A short section on less-commonly encountered poisons is included for interest as an illustration of some of the toxic mechanisms that may lead to a fatality or may exacerbate an underlying disease state with lethal consequences.

Some cardiovascular conditions are mentioned, as these conditions are treated with medications with a high potential for toxicity. Other conditions such as inflammation of the myocardium (myocarditis) and cardiomyopathies are not specifically discussed, although we recognize that patients with these conditions may die from a combination of their native disease and the toxic effects of drugs. The key question that is posed to the FP is: "Was the death of a particular person caused by a cardiac (or other) disease alone, or was there some degree of contribution by the effects of drugs or toxins?" The answer to this question can be more challenging for fatalities involving cardiac medications and underlying cardiac conditions than for other drug mechanisms.

One of the complicating factors surrounding cardiac-based causation or contribution to death is that in many cases, a sudden, ultimately fatal cardiac event may not be readily detectable at autopsy. This can be especially troubling to members of the general public who expect that such a traumatic event as a terminal "heart attack" would, of course, be readily identified by the Forensic Pathologist. For this reason, tissues (which may include the conduction system) may be submitted for histologic examination at this stage or may be reserved until the medical records and the toxicology results are available for review. Also, unexpected toxicology findings may include the presence of a drug not prescribed for that patient, the absence of a drug that would reasonably be expected to be present, unexpectedly high or low levels of an expected drug, or a toxin/poison known to have the potential for significant adverse effects. Results such as these would prompt an in-depth review of the medical records of the deceased and potentially a discussion between the FP and the toxicologist.

Inferences based on quantitative results from PM toxicologic analysis can play a significant role in the eventual decisions that an FP may make regarding the determination of COD and MOD. In cases of sudden cardiac death, reliable PM levels (e.g., from peripheral sources) can suggest the potential for a toxic effect of a particular drug or toxin to have occurred at the time of death. Quantitative considerations may be significant when drug action is being inferred regarding cardiac activity. In many cases, the mere presence of a potentially cardiotoxic drug would not be an adequate explanation for a cardiac effect or impact, making the availability of reliable quantitative levels of considerable value. Further, toxic or overdose levels of some drugs may have impacts on cardiac function to a degree that may cause a cardiac event or exacerbate an underlying condition, leading to a significant and potentially fatal result. As discussed below, in many cardiac deaths, there may be a dearth of concomitant pathological findings, increasing the emphasis on the interpretation of the significance of any exogenous drug or toxin that may be present. It is important to bear in mind that such results may, in some cases, not accurately represent true antemortem levels (see PMR in Section 2), and further, that any inference regarding antemortem drug levels or consumption pattern/amount based on PM analysis should clearly identify and address the magnitude of uncertainty and underlying assumptions accompanying any such inferences.

6.2 ANATOMY AND PHYSIOLOGY

All lethal, rapidly acting toxins inhibit cardiac function by having direct effects on the myocardium, the signals controlling contraction, or by affecting the availability or utilization of oxygen. Longer-acting agents can modify cellular chemistry, affecting all somatic cells in addition to myocytes and associated nervous tissues. Familiarity with the cardiac conduction cycle facilitates understanding the actions of some drugs and toxins directly affecting the heart.

The normal anatomy, electrophysiology, and overall function of the heart will doubtless be more than familiar territory for most of our readers. We have included brief overviews as sidebars 6.1 and 6.2 for those who might be interested. More detailed descriptions and details for specific aspects and processes are addressed in several references iterated in the section bibliography. The routine evaluations and assessments performed during the autopsy process and subsequent evaluation of tissues (including toxicologic analysis) are detailed in Section 1.

Sidebar 6.1: Cardiac Anatomy and Electrophysiology

By convention, the start of the heartbeat cycle occurs as venous blood, received into the right atrium from the vena cava, and oxygenated blood, received in the left atrium from the pulmonary veins, are pumped into the right and left ventricles, respectively, during atrial contraction. Ventricular contraction follows, with deoxygenated blood being delivered to the lungs from the right ventricle via the pulmonary arteries and oxygen-enriched blood delivered to the rest of the body via the aorta. The left ventricular contraction represents the most energetic effort of the heart, generating the pressure required to deliver blood throughout the body and ultimately returning to the right atrium.

The heart is partially controlled by the vagus nerve (cranial nerve X), but it also has its own internal electrical system, allowing it to beat on its own for a few minutes after a person is brain dead or the spinal cord has been severed at the neck. The contraction of the heart is caused by rhythmic, coordinated signals originating in the sinoatrial node (SA node) and propagated to both atria and then to both ventricles. The SA node, an ovoid bundle of conduction myocardial cells, is in the right atrial appendage near its junction with the superior vena cava within the crista terminalis. In most people, it is a branch of the right coronary artery. In the remainder, the SA nodal artery branches off the left circumflex artery.

Neuronal stimulation of the SA node causes contraction of both atria by sending a signal to the myocytes as a wave of depolarization. In healthy persons, the SA node rhythmically, regularly, and continuously produces electrical impulses. The SA node is located deep to the epicardial adipose tissue and surrounds the SA nodal artery, associated with and sometimes surrounded by contraction myocardium. The SA nodal conduction myocardium is composed of small cells without intercalated discs that stain slightly less eosinophilic with H&E stain than contraction myocardial cells (Figure 6.1). Neuronal fibers run parallel to the epicardium and the SA node. The myocardium, including the conduction myocardium, should have no inflammatory cells in it. Occasional inflammatory cells may be present in the epicardial adipose tissue, but they should not be among the myocytes. If there are inflammatory cells within the myocardium associated with myocytolysis, myocarditis should be considered in the differential diagnosis for the COD.

Like neurons, depolarization of myocytes results in an influx of calcium and sodium ions through voltage-gated channels. The cationic influx facilitates depolarization, and calcium specifically facilitates further calcium release from within the sarcoplasmic reticulum into

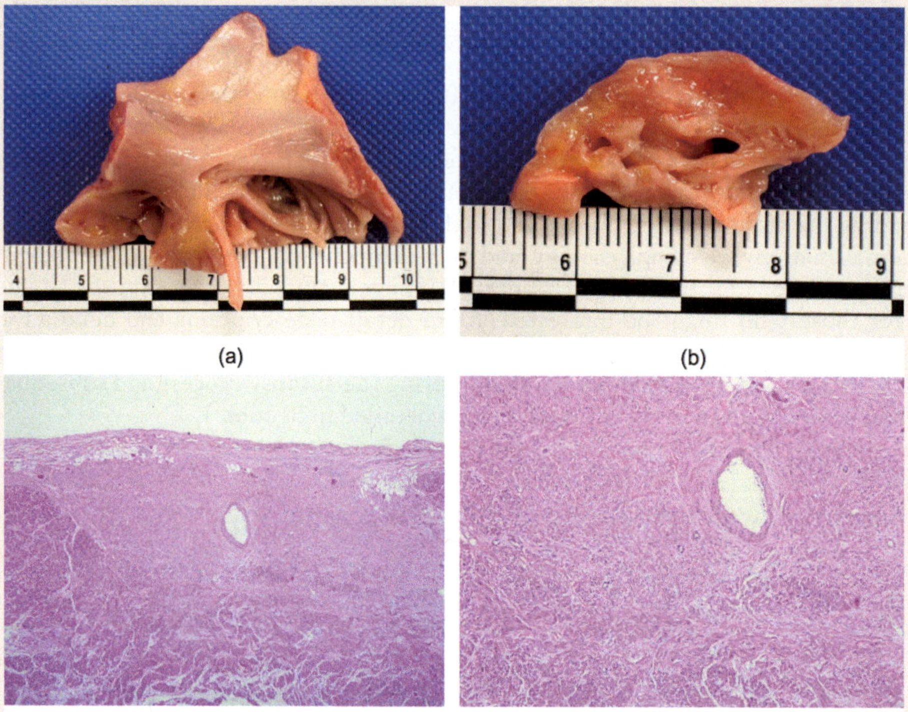

(a) (b) (c) (d)

Figures 6.1 Gross and histologic sections of the SA node, H&E stain, (c) 2×, and (d) 10×. Note that the nodal myocardium is the group of paler cells surrounding the SA nodal artery. The other myocytes are contraction myocardium. (a) and (b) show a section containing the SA node taken from an anatomically normal heart. In (a), the endocardial side of the section shows the area of the crista terminalis. In (b), the cross-section shows what would be used for histologic examination. (c) and (d) show the histologic appearance of normal SA nodal tissue with the H&E stain. This section is from a 20-year-old man who died in a traffic collision and donated his heart for valves. After the valves were procured, the residual heart tissue was examined by a cardiac pathologist. There were no cardiac abnormalities diagnosed.

the cytoplasm, resulting in the contractile response. Contraction of the atria then stimulates the atrioventricular (AV) node, which is situated on the interatrial septum between two anatomic landmarks: the coronary sinus and the membranous septum, when viewed from the opened right side of the heart. It is a small, generally ovoid structure supplied by a branch of the right coronary artery. The AV node delays the signal and then stimulates contraction of the ventricles, transmitting the signal through the bundle of His and Purkinje fibers. The delay between atrial and ventricular contraction allows for blood to flow into the relaxed ventricles during atrial contraction. Cardiac arrythmias can be caused by a disturbance in the normal progression of depolarization. If the SA node is unable to initiate or conduct an electrical impulse, the AV node can do so at a rate between 40 and 60 beats per minute.

CARDIAC ACTION POTENTIAL

Cardiac myocytes contract as a result of a depolarizing electrical impulse, normally in a rhythmic manner defined by the heart rate. The action cycle of a contraction myocyte may be visualized in terms of membrane potential. The voltage—time sequence representing the contraction of a single ventricular myocyte is the "Action Potential Cycle" (See Figure 6.2).

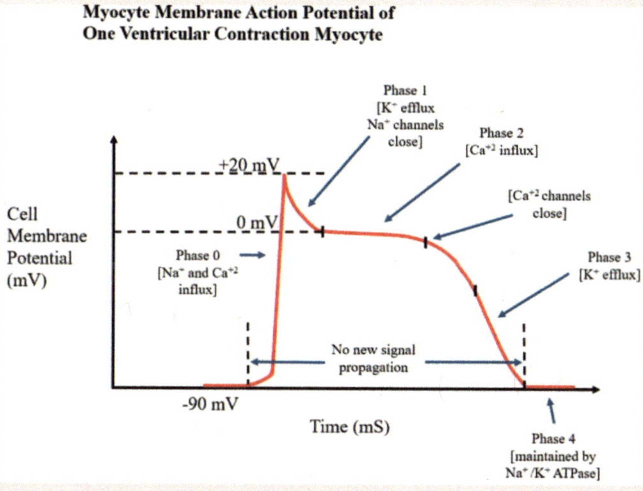

Figure 6.2 Cardiac action potential of a contraction myocyte.

The action potential cycle of the contractile cells of the atria is similar; however, the cells of the SA and AV nodes, as well as Purkinje cells in the ventricles, have a different wave form.

- While the contractile myocytes are at rest, voltage-gated sodium and calcium channels are closed, while "inwardly rectifying" potassium channels are open, and the cellular membrane is at its resting potential ~−90 mV. Action of the sodium-potassium ATPase pump functions to maintain the resting potential.
- This stage represents phase 4 of the cardiac action cycle. A new cycle, phase 0, begins with SA nodal cells triggering an action potential in the contraction myocardiam, and, propagated to the AV nodal cells, which then continues through the bundles of His and Purkinje fibers to the contraction myocardium of the ventricles.
- The phase 0 excitation of the cardiomyocyte begins with the rapid influx of sodium into the cell through voltage-gated sodium channels, driven by the concentration gradient for sodium, resulting in a sharp reversal of membrane potential. At the end of phase 0, the action potential across the membrane is above 0, approximately +20 mV.
- At the end of phase 0, sodium channels close and voltage-gated potassium channels open. The resulting cationic efflux initiates the repolarization of the cell. This is represented by a short, relatively steep downstroke in phase 1. At the end of phase 1, the action potential approaches 0 mV. Throughout the repolarization process, the sodium-potassium ATPase functions to remove intracellular sodium.
- At this point, (phase 2) voltage-gated calcium channels open, allowing an influx of calcium ions, roughly negating the cationic loss due to continued sodium efflux. The relatively small amount of calcium entering the cell triggers a significant release of calcium from the sarcoplasmic reticulum, facilitating contraction. During this plateau, when ion exchange across the cell membrane is in electrical equilibrium, the action potential remains ~0 mV. Phase 2 ends as voltage-gated calcium channels close.
- The final step, phase 3, happens as potassium channels stay open, allowing repolarization of the cell and returning the cell membrane to its resting state. Internally rectifying potassium flow is eventually limited by the extracellular positive potential. The re-establishment of it is represented by a slow downstroke back to the resting potential of ~−90 mV. The sodium-potassium ATPase remains functional during the process and is the mechanism by which the sodium ions, entering phase 0, are eventually removed from the cell.

Ventricular myocardial cells are refractory to additional signals between phase 0 and the middle of phase 3. Beyond the middle of phase 3, and prior to the re-establishment of the resting potential, the cell may be triggered by an abnormally strong depolarization signal (Figure 6.2).

Calcium is essential for myocyte contraction and, hence, cardiac contractility. However, the calcium influx to the cell in phase 2 is not adequate to support contraction and serves (in addition to prolonging phase 2 of the cardiac cycle) as a trigger for the release of significant quantities of stored calcium from within the sarcoplasmic reticulum. Calcium from the sarcoplasmic reticulum diffuses into the cytoplasm, where it binds to troponin on the actin protein, allowing that protein to bind to myosin, resulting in the shortening of the myosin filaments and causing myocyte contraction. Upon relaxation, intracytoplasmic calcium is re-sequestrated into the sarcoplasmic reticulum by an active, transmembrane ATP-dependent calcium pump, releasing action from myosin. The total intracellular myocyte calcium concentration remains almost static over time and is equal to the sum of the intracytoplasmic concentration plus the calcium within the sarcoplasmic reticulum.

Sidebar 6.2: The Electrocardiogram and the Ionic Basis for the EKG Wave Form

Myocyte and neuronal membranes maintain a charge difference (negative intracellular and positive extracellular) across the cellular membrane, commonly called the resting potential. This charge differential is maintained by the action of a sodium-potassium ATPase and potassium channels.

Changes in membrane potential in the myocardium occur as a consequence of the successive depolarization and repolarization caused by the activation of voltage-gated ion channels. The propagation of electrical depolarization along the myocardium from cell-to-cell is amplified by the number of myocytes contracting in a coordinated fashion and can be recorded through the skin as minute variations in electrical potential, by monitoring pads, and recorded as an electrocardiogram (EKG). By convention, each 1 mm square in the horizontal direction (X-axis) represents 0.04 seconds (5 squares equal 0.2 seconds). Each 1 mm square in the vertical direction (Y-axis) represents 0.1 mV. As in Figure 6.3a, at least two electrodes are required to acquire an EKG, but tracings are often made from multiple leads, generating more detailed information about the electrical conduction in different sections of the heart. The waveform may be muted in very obese patients because of the thickness of the intervening tissue.

Beginning at the SA node, depolarization of the myocardium causes atrial contraction and forms the P wave on the EKG. As depolarization reaches the AV node, the signal is slowed down. This delay forms the horizontal portion of the wave after the P wave. At this time, blood fills the ventricles. Repolarization of the atria is not usually represented on the EKG because the wave is very small due to the relatively thin nature of the myocardium there. The electrical signal passes through the left and right bundle branches of His through Purkinje cells into the contraction myocardium of the left and right ventricles. Depolarization and contraction of the ventricles form the QRS complex on the EKG. The Q wave represents the initial signal from the AV node, ventricular depolarization forms the R and S waves, and ventricular repolarization forms the T wave. The ST segment is the horizontal portion between the S wave of the QRS complex and the T wave. Any vertical deviation of the ST segment away from the horizontal may indicate myocardial ischemia or infarction. See Figure 6.3b: EKG annotated.

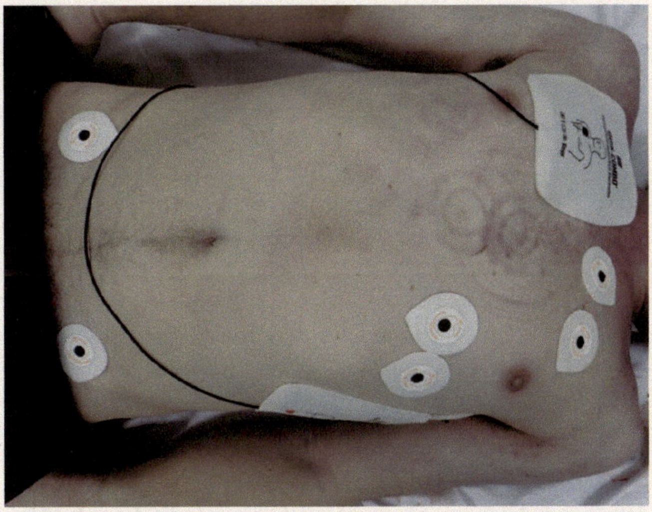

Figure 6.3a Six-lead EKG monitoring and defibrillation pads on the torso. The targetoid impressions in the skin of the chest were formed by an automated compression device for cardiopulmonary resuscitation.

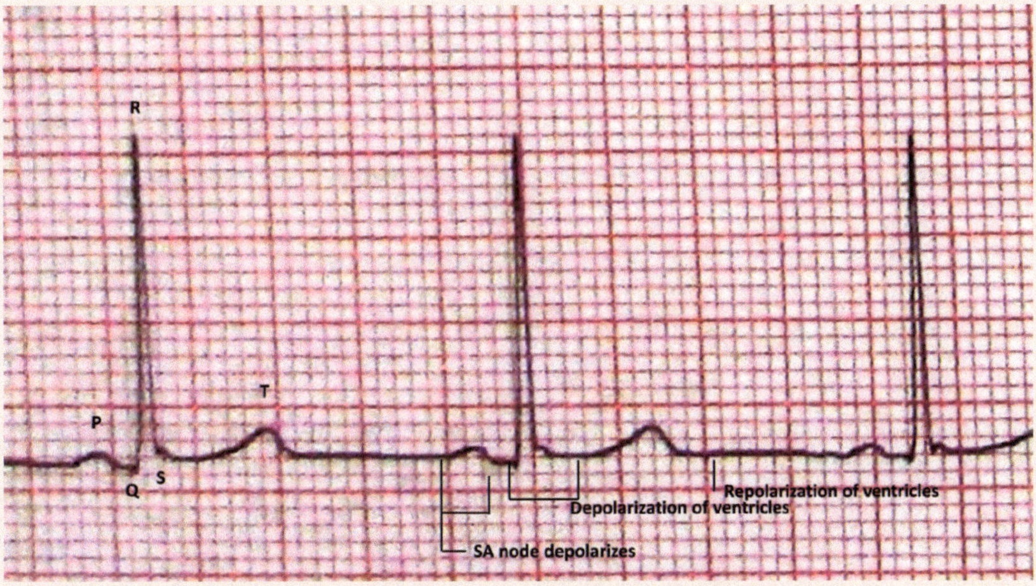

Figure 6.3b The EKG annotated, labeling the waves and the signal that forms them.

THE IONIC BASIS FOR THE ELECTROCARDIOGRAM WAVE FORM

In addition to a difference in charge across the membrane, there is a difference in the concentration of several ions, all positively charged ions. Sodium is more concentrated extracellularly, and potassium is at a higher concentration intracellularly.

At rest, each contracting myocyte is in phase 4 of the cardiac action potential. (Traditionally, the cardiac action cycle graph is described as beginning with phase 4 and resting.) With depolarization, the influx of sodium reverses the localized membrane potential (phase 0). At the maximum depolarization, sodium channels close and voltage-gated potassium channels open. Potassium efflux initiates a repolarization of the membrane reflected in the QRS segment of the EKG (phase 1). Phase 1 ends with the opening of calcium channels, and the influx of calcium ions is roughly equivalent to the efflux of potassium ions, with a resulting "plateau" of membrane potential and a neutral EKG signal. At the end of phase 3, as calcium efflux ends, the continued function of the sodium-potassium ATPase, coupled with the inwardly rectifying potassium channels, restores the resting potential with a net outflow of cations, and the restoration of membrane potential appears as the T wave. Any drug or toxin that affects the influx of either potassium or calcium can prolong the QT interval, which may then be reflected in the EKG.

The EKG is not the same entity as the cardiac action cycle. The cardiac action cycle is a graphical representation of the membrane potential across one cell membrane. It is measured and recorded only experimentally, not clinically. The EKG is a graphical representation of all the conducting and contracting myocytes cumulatively. It is measured by electrodes on the skin and recorded in real time (Figure 6.3c).

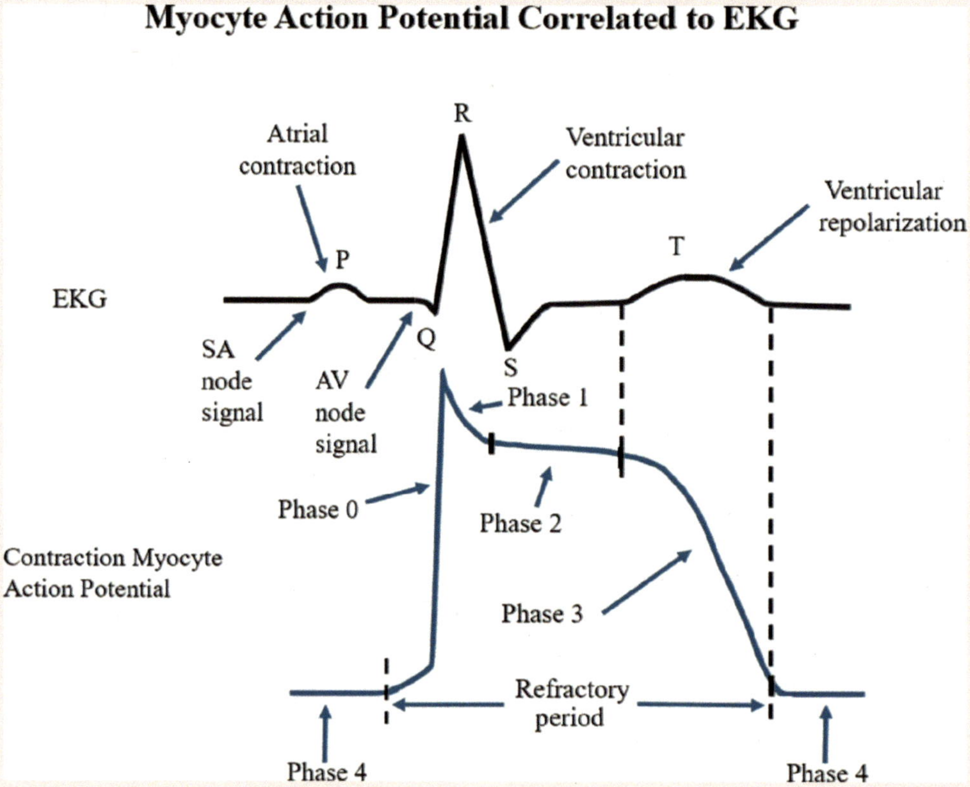

Figure 6.3c Cardiac myocyte action potential compared to the EKG wave form.

6.3 CLINICAL AND POSTMORTEM ASSESSMENTS OF CARDIAC CONDITIONS

Evaluation of the state of the heart itself and the associated vasculature is a basic and essential part of the autopsy process. In many cases, the FP will be able to quickly determine if there is a potential that the underlying condition of the heart may have played a major role in causing the death (e.g., an ischemic-based event) or, similarly, if any underlying condition or pathology may have made the heart more susceptible to other stressors (e.g., opiate-based hypoxia or stimulant-based hypertension). Some conditions are not detectable by the autopsy procedure as they are functional in nature, such as a native cardiac dysrhythmia (e.g., atrial fibrillation), a native rate disturbance (e.g., supraventricular tachycardia), and coronary artery spasms. These conditions may have caused or significantly contributed to the death. Such conditions may also have made patients more susceptible to drugs and toxins, which may not of themselves have proven fatal but may, in combination with underlying pathology, be causative or contributory to the death.

Clearly, in such cases, toxicology findings or drug abuse histories will then play a significant role in considerations regarding the overall COD and MOD. A review of the medical records and history of the deceased person can yield valuable information about any clinical condition that may, alone, be the cause of death. For example, some patients have a clinical diagnosis of hypertension without cardiomegaly at autopsy. These patients are at risk for sudden death. Their risk is increased with the use of some drugs. The detection of a drug that was unexpected, not prescribed, or not expected to have been available to the patient could lead the pathologist to consider its contribution to the cause of death. However, as suggested throughout this text, care needs to be taken to ensure that the levels of drug are both truly reflective of antemortem concentrations and that the uncertainty with which such estimations are made is understood and factored into any subsequent COD/MOD determination.

There are many decedents that will have been examined prior to the receipt of any medical history or clinical information, and some people will not have any documented medical history. In many such cases, the underlying disease will be readily apparent to the examining pathologist and may be appropriately evaluated and incorporated into the consideration of COD and MOD, in association with whatever toxicologic findings might also be considered relevant. Naturally, to the extent that some knowledge regarding the underlying medical state of the decedent prior to death can be ascertained during the evaluation of associated medical records, the task of correctly ascertaining the true COD and MOD will be facilitated.

6.3.1 Hypertrophy

Heart weight is a key measurement taken at autopsy, and cardiomegaly is a well-recognized independent risk factor for sudden death. However, a clearly defined and accepted definition of what would constitute "hypertrophy" in a particular decedent has not become standard, although comparisons of heart weight as compared to body height, body weight, and ideal body weight have been explored with no real consensus as to what would be considered hypertrophic. Multiple studies have been presented on the topic, and while there can be variation among pathologists in individual offices regarding the tables or standards utilized from which to define the presence and characterize the magnitude of hypertrophy, several references addressing this issue are included in the section bibliography.

Preparation of the heart for weighing includes ensuring that the organ is free of blood clots and trimmed of any extraneous tissue. The aorta and the pulmonary artery should be trimmed 1 cm from the valves, but the epicardial adipose tissue should not be removed. Hearts should be weighed before formalin fixation, as this process causes unpredictable changes in organ weight.

Cardiac hypertrophy, as determined by an echocardiogram during life, correlates with but does not adequately substitute for assessment at an autopsy. Left ventricular hypertrophy alone is a well-recognized risk factor for sudden death because of its arrhythmogenic potential, especially if there is an increase in intramyocardial fibrosis.

Cardiac hypertrophy is commonly a consequence of hypertension associated with the aging process as the vasculature becomes less compliant. Significant cardiac hypertrophy can be caused by chronic stimulant abuse, e.g., cocaine, methamphetamine, etc. Hypertrophic cardiomyopathy is a commonly occurring inherited heart condition affecting the intracytoplasmic contractile protein myosin, increasing myocyte contractility, and eventually leading to compensatory hypertrophy, disarray, and eventual fibrosis. The condition may only be exhibited as left ventricular hypertrophy and is characterized by microscopic evidence of myocyte disarray, including Y-branching of myocytes and myocardial fibrosis. This distinction would differentiate (or be suggestive of a differentiation) from an SMA-induced hypertension-based hypertrophy. These are just two of the numerous other diseases states that can cause cardiomegaly with or without left ventricular hypertrophy.

6.3.2 Ischemia and Infarction

The disruption in blood flow from coronary artery spasm or atherosclerotic luminal narrowing, causing tissue ischemia leading to infarction, is one of the more common causes of sudden cardiac death. The risk of ischemia worsens with decreasing luminal diameter due to a reduction in blood flow, even if the myocardium can develop collateral circulation.

Atherosclerotic plaques are composed of a central core of lipid-laden macrophages covered by a fibrous cap composed of fibroblasts and smooth muscle cells that have migrated from the media into the intima. Some plaque may develop dystrophic calcification with time. The thin fibrous cap over the core can erode or rupture, exposing the pro-inflammatory elements of the lipid core and increasing the risk for thrombosis. The presence of unstable atherosclerotic plaque, even if it does not significantly narrow the lumen, is a risk factor for sudden death based on plaque rupture and plaque hemorrhage, essentially rapidly decreasing the luminal diameter at that segment. Calcification within the plaque increases the risk for plaque rupture.

Estimation of the percentage of coronary artery luminal stenosis by gross examination can be somewhat variable from pathologist to pathologist but usually provides a reasonable approximation, consistent with previous clinical measurement. The estimation of calcium deposition within coronary artery plaques by computed tomography (CT) coronary angiogram performed in the clinical setting appears to correlate well with that detected at autopsy, especially when the calcification is advanced. Reduction of the cross-sectional area by more than 75%–80% can lead to clinically significant angina, stunned myocardium, myocyte necrosis, and eventual fibrosis and can be fatal. Significant stenosis makes a patient more vulnerable to the effects of cardiotoxic drugs and those causing coronary artery spasm.

One clinical assessment tool that has gained increasing popularity is the coronary artery calcium score. Using CT scanning, the amount, density, and extent of calcium contained in coronary arteries correlate to a risk assessment for coronary artery events. The extent of calcium deposition is directly related to the amount and extent of atheromatous plaque in the arteries. This assessment is a noninvasive tool that can aid in prophylactically treating patients at risk for ischemia, even when they are asymptomatic.

6.3.3 Rate Abnormalities

Adult resting pulse rate is considered to be between 60 and 100 beats per minute (bpm); readings outside this range are usually considered abnormal. The rate is controlled by a signal sent from the SA node to the AV node, followed by appropriate myocyte depolarization in the ventricular myocardium.

Appropriate depolarization, but slower than 60 beats per minute, is termed "sinus bradycardia." The EKG reading has a normal-shaped pattern but is slower than 60 beats per minute. Endurance athletes may have a normal resting heart rate below 60 bpm. A wide variety of conditions that affect the blood supply to or structural disorganization of the SA node can cause bradycardia. These include trauma to the area (e.g., chest trauma and surgically induced trauma during the repair of a cardiac abnormality), diseases that cause reduced blood flow to the artery (e.g., atherosclerosis and vasculitis), and conditions that cause deposition of material (e.g., amyloidosis) or cause an inflammatory cell reaction (e.g., myocarditis and radiation therapy). Fibrous tissue may destroy the SA node completely by replacing the specialized myocytic cells comprising the node with non-conductive fibrotic cells. There are also a number of drugs and toxins that affect signal propagation without necessarily altering the anatomic structure. These include benzodiazepines, anti-arrythmics, narcotics, and other CNS depressants. Hypothermia (a core temperature below 95° F or 35° C) can also cause sinus bradycardia. Rewarming the patient should normalize the heart rate. Patients experiencing hypothermia may be sensitive to drugs or toxins affecting cardiac conduction. Paradoxically, the hypothermic state can be protective against the effects of hypoxia.

Sinus tachycardia, a normal but fast sinus rhythm induced by physiologic or psychological stress, is usually benign in otherwise healthy people. Some drugs cause or are associated with rate abnormalities. Stimulants such as cocaine and amphetamine/methamphetamine and other sympathomimetic amines can cause tachycardia. Likewise, sudden discontinuation of drugs that reduce heart rate can cause rebound tachycardia (e.g., beta blockers, calcium channel blockers, alpha-2 agonists, and opioids). Obviously, heart rate is not detectable at autopsy. However, heart rate can be ascertained from implanted pacemakers and/or defibrillators for patients with those devices. Evaluation of medical and/or prescription information may provide an indication of treatment of the decedent for underlying rate abnormalities.

6.3.4 Rhythm Disturbance

Variation in the progression of the electrical impulse from the SA node through the atria, the AV node, and the ventricles can result in a rhythm disturbance reflected in the EKG and can be fatal. Rhythm disturbance can be classified into three general groups: abnormal signal timing from the SA node, abnormal origin of the initiating signal outside the SA node, and retrograde or re-entry pathways of the electrical impulse anywhere in the heart. Rhythm disturbances can cause disordered myocardial contraction, leading to fibrillation of either the atria or the ventricles and inadequate chamber filling or emptying. Prolonged fibrillation can induce clot formation, leading to thrombi in the chamber and emboli to other vessels.

Anti-arrhythmic drug therapy is prescribed to correct these conditions (discussed below) and, as such, can be present in PM samples. These medications can often have serious, even fatal consequences in overdose, and careful consideration must be given to the validity of PM results, such as whether an overdose is missed or a therapeutic level is misinterpreted. In some cases, medication-based therapy is not enough to control the rhythm disturbance, and a cardiac ablation is required to remove the aberrant electrical pathway. Surgical ablation results in a visible scar in the myocardium.

6.3.4.1 Atrial Fibrillation

Atrial fibrillation (AF) is the most common cardiac arrythmia, particularly in the elderly population, and causes uncoordinated contraction of the atria. It arises when the originating contractile signal does not arise from or propagate from the SA node. The abnormal depolarization may arise from anywhere in either atrium, may arise at multiple points, and may cause multiple re-entry pathways. The atrial contractions are fast and irregular, impeding adequate filling of the ventricles, and are observable by EKG as abnormal P waves, irregular in shape, height, width, and timing.

AF can begin spontaneously without an underlying condition (paroxysmal AF) and can resolve spontaneously, even without treatment. When AF results from an underlying heart or lung condition, most often hypertension, congestive heart failure (CHF), cardiomyopathies, or pulmonary hypertension, it is termed continuous or persistent AF. With disease progression, AF can progress from paroxysmal to persistent due to myocyte remodeling of cardiac ion channels.

AF is not usually life-threatening, and some patients may not be aware of an episode. However, some patients report a feeling of a pounding or racing heart. Some patients may experience dyspnea that resolves with rest, and some patients just feel tired and sluggish. AF may be treated, even if the patient is unaware of the condition because AF can cause eddy currents in the chamber and thrombi to form on the endocardium that could become dislodged and embolize to the brain, causing an embolic ischemic infarction. Patients with AF are often prescribed anti-coagulation therapy to minimize the formation of thrombi. Chronic AF sometimes progresses to ventricular fibrillation (VF), which can be a terminal rhythm.

6.3.4.2 Ventricular Fibrillation

VF or V-fib is caused by a chaotic progression of the electrical signal through the ventricular myocardium and is usually associated with ischemic heart disease. Other causes include hypoxic events (e.g., drug overdoses, drowning, and suffocation), cardiomyopathy, infection, and direct trauma to the chest. Signal propagation within the ventricle is irregular because the myocardium has been structurally altered (e.g., by fibrosis) or electrically altered by remodeling of the myocyte cell membrane. Fibrotic tissue is unable to propagate depolarization, and a contractile signal has to bypass the area of fibrosis. Such alternate pathways can cause multiple electrical impulses and irregular signals, causing the ventricular walls to contract in an uncoordinated way. Both systole and diastole are affected; chamber filling as well as pumping are incomplete. The abnormal signal appears as a rapid, erratic pulse, eventually degenerating into pulseless electrical activity. The EKG shows no identifiable P waves and poorly formed QRS complexes at a rapid rate. Without immediate attention, including cardiac defibrillation, VF is usually a rapidly terminal rhythm. VF is, of course, not recognizable at autopsy. However, the EKG reading done by the pre-hospital or hospital clinical team would document this rhythm. At autopsy, myocardial fibrosis, even focal fibrosis, can be seen grossly.

6.3.4.3 Long QT Syndrome

Long QT syndrome (LQTS) reflects the condition when the process of repolarization of the myocardium is abnormally prolonged, resulting in a lengthened QT interval. In this condition, the atria contract before the ventricles are ready to receive the signal and are unable to contract at the proper time. LQTS is caused by a retardation of the progression of the electrical signal through the myocardium or delay in repolarization; the time between the start of ventricular contraction and the completion of ventricular repolarization is abnormally long. LQTS is reflected on an EKG by an extended amount of time between the beginning of the Q wave (initiation of ventricular contraction) until the beginning of the T wave (repolarization of the ventricular myocardium). Repolarization of the myocyte occurs as sodium is removed from the cell, as an influx of potassium and calcium into the cell occurs and as the cellular membrane potential is restored to ~–85 mV. Biochemically, the QT interval becomes prolonged when repolarization of the myocardium is mechanistically impeded.

LQTS can be either acquired or congenital but it reflects a serious condition that should be managed medically. Persons with LQTS are at an increased risk of sudden death. Some patients are unaware of this abnormality but may become hypotensive and faint during an episode. Syncope can be transient as the heart spontaneously returns to normal sinus rhythm. Female gender is also a risk factor, as the QT interval in women is, on average, slightly longer than it is for men.

Some patients have genetic mutations in one or more of the genes for potassium ion channels, increasing the risk for LQTS. Congenital LQTS can be detected in children and adolescents after a syncopal episode and can be treated so that the patients can have a normal, active life. The autosomal dominant form, Roman-Ward syndrome, is more common than the autosomal recessive type, Jervell and Lange-Neilsen syndrome. In the latter type, children are also hearing-impaired. Genetic studies are available and may provide useful information to family members.

A prolonged QT interval of a transitory nature can also be caused or exacerbated by a number of prescribed medications. A number of drugs and drug classes are associated with the potential for causing this condition, including some antibiotics, some antiarrhythmics, some psychotropic drugs, some antihistamines, methadone, and some dietary supplements.

LQTS can degenerate into a more complex dysrhythmia, "Torsades de Pointes." Torsades is caused by an electrical signal that begins in the ventricle but not in the SA node, causing ventricular tachycardia (200–250 bpm). The ventricles can neither fill nor empty completely. Torsades can be self-correcting and transient; may be corrected medically, but may also be fatal as a function of degeneration to VF. Serious symptoms of cerebral hypoxia; seizures or seizure-like activity, and syncope may also be exhibited.

Torsades de pointes can be perceived by the patient ("my heart is going too fast") based on pulse rate and may then be confirmed by EKG. The EKG wave form is seen as a gradual cyclic rise and fall in the amplitude of the QRS complexes, and with few if any identifiable P waves. The QRS complex goes above *and* below the isoelectric line, and the QT interval is prolonged.

6.4 MECHANISMS OF THERAPY

There are multiple classes of drugs designed to treat specific biochemical derangements in the rate and/or rhythm of myocardial contraction. While most patients utilizing such medications are able to lead relatively normal lives, there can be toxic events associated with their medications, particularly in overdose. Naturally, there may be terminal events occurring in patients, despite the presence of therapeutic agents. Many cardiac medications are readily detected and reported in forensic toxicology testing (albeit not in immunologically based screening procedures). Most anti-coagulants and beta-blockers will be detected and reported in "general drug screens," although "cardiac glycosides" (e.g., digoxin) do not. When a pathologist finds medical records listing prescribed medication, a focused toxicology analysis can be performed.

Sidebar 6.3: Sodium-Potassium ATPase

The sodium-potassium ATPase is a protein on cell membranes of virtually all human cells. Its function is to maintain the action potential across the cell membrane by exchanging three intracellular sodium ions for two extracellular potassium ions, driven by the hydrolysis of one ATP molecule.

Cation exchange occurs in a series of steps. Three intracellular sodium ions bind to the protein. A molecule of ATP is hydrolyzed, phosphorylating the enzyme and causing conformational change, which rotates the sodium ion binding site to the outside of the cell and changing the affinity of the protein for sodium ions, such that they are then released into circulation. The pump then binds extracellular potassium ions and is dephosphorylated, with a resulting conformational change that rotates the potassium ions to the inside of the cell, where they are released into the cytoplasm. The number and activity of sodium-potassium ATPase pumps on cellular membranes are fluid. A number of conditions and metabolic states can influence how many of them are active at any one time.

6.4.1 Cardiac Glycosides, Na-K ATPase Inhibitors

Digitalis is considered the prototypical "cardiac glycoside" with a long history as an effective herbal-based folk medicine remedy for CHF, derived from the Foxglove plant. The current commercial formulation of the drug, "digoxin," and related cardiac glycosides (indicating one or more sugar (glyco-) molecules attached to the basic structure) are commonly utilized in the treatment of CHF and supraventricular tachycardia. These drugs functionally decrease the rate of contraction but increase the contractile volume, resulting in an inotropic effect. Mechanistically, these drugs bind to and inactivate the sodium-potassium ATPase pump, thereby extending the time required for re-establishment of the localized membrane resting potential. The net effect is to slow the rate of progression of depolarization throughout the neurons and myocytes, thereby slowing the rate of contraction.

As a consequence of the depressed level of activity of the Na/K ATPase, the intracellular concentration of sodium increases, inhibiting the function of a sodium-calcium antiport transporter, which normally functions to rapidly remove calcium from the cell (transporting three sodium ions inside the cell for each calcium ion moved out). The resulting increase in the intracellular sodium concentration. Calcium (normally released intracellularly from the sarcoplasmic reticulum) is required for cross-bridging during myocyte contraction. The elevated calcium concentration increases the degree of contraction resulting from a single excitatory event. Thus, the overall effect of digitalis or related drugs is a slower but stronger heartbeat.

Cardiac glycosides have a somewhat narrow therapeutic window, and there is a high potential for toxicity, even from chronic therapeutic use. The plasma half-life is relatively long at about 40 h, and as such, small changes in elimination rate can have significant consequences with regard to blood levels. The glycosidic drugs are primarily cleared by the kidney, and patients with CHF may develop an associated renal insufficiency, prolonging the half-life and AUC for a particular dose regimen and consequentially building up a potentially toxic level of drug.

Like other drugs, impacting the Na-K ATPase glycosides decreases electrical conduction through the SA and AV nodes, thereby modulating heart rate. Patients with acute toxic ingestions may exhibit any abnormal cardiac rhythm, from complete AV block to junctional escape rhythms to ventricular tachycardia leading to VF. Co-ingestions with other cardiac medications as well as pre-existing myocardial injury worsen glycoside toxicity. The Na-K ATPase is ubiquitous in all cells, functioning to maintain the cellular membrane potential. Other organ systems beyond the heart may be affected by cardiac glycosides, and toxic levels may result in seizures or GI distress.

Digoxin levels are routinely assessed clinically in hospital laboratories; however, they are usually handled as a "send out" assay from postmortem toxicology laboratories. In a living patient, serum potassium levels are also monitored, so information relevant to the FP may be available in medical records. Serum potassium will be very elevated in the acutely poisoned patient, but less so than in a patient with chronic therapeutic use. Unfortunately, as noted in Section 2, serum potassium levels, as measured in postmortem samples, are not at all reliable.

Treatment in suspected digoxin and related glycoside poisonings is supportive, although there is a digoxin-specific antidote available (albeit reportedly expensive and rarely used). The antidote is a digoxin-specific antibody fragment (Fab), binding to and inactivating the digoxin molecule, which is then subsequently renally cleared.

Toxicologic Considerations: Historically, the analysis of cardiac glycosides was not considered within the realm of toxicologic analysis, primarily because of the difficulty in the analysis of such relatively large molecules in general and glycosidic species in particular by gas chromatography/mass spectrometry (MS). However, with the increasing availability and routine utilization of HPLC/MS (and -MSMS) units, quantitative analysis is readily available.

Pathologic Considerations: There are no specific findings associated with digitalis toxicity observable at autopsy. An investigation may be key to resolving such cases.

6.4.2 Antiarrhythmics

Antiarrhythmic agents are classified in general into four categories, as originally described by Vaughan Williams in 1970. This classification scheme (sodium, potassium, calcium channel blockers, and adrenergic receptor agents) remains in use today. The drugs are classified by mechanism of action as they relate to the cardiac action potential cycle and provide a useful overview of most of the cardioactive agents encountered in PM work. Some drugs, although classified in one category, can also overlap, with effects on other receptors that elicit other effects.

Toxicologic Considerations: Most antiarrhythmic cardiac medications are readily detectable on generalized drug screening protocols. However, few, if any, are detected by the common immunoassay-based panel commonly incorporated in hospital "drug screening." As such, there may then be toxicologic confirmation either of the presence or absence of prescribed cardiac medications, as well as quantitative information from which information regarding antemortem level may, in some cases, be inferred.

Pathologic Considerations: The use of antiarrhythmics is quite common in current medical practice, particularly in the older patient population. The implications of the presence of such drugs for the FP start with the indication that, for a specific decedent, there has been a diagnosis of an underlying cardiac condition of sufficient severity as to warrant pharmaceutical intervention. The implications, then, of an overdose of these agents will naturally depend on the actual case circumstances, pathologic findings (or lack thereof), and toxicology results. One might also carefully consider the absence of the expected medication and the potential that such circumstances might have made the decedent somewhat more susceptible to an arrhythmic or other cardiac event than they would have been otherwise.

6.4.2.1 Sodium Channel Blockers (Class I Antiarrhythmics)

Voltage-gated sodium channels are found in the membranes of the contraction myocardium of the atria and ventricles, but not in the SA or AV nodes. Sodium channel blockers inhibit the propagation of signals during phase 0 of the cardiac action potential. This inhibition of the voltage-dependent opening of sodium channels, thereby diminishing or functionally stopping membrane sodium transport, causes a slower transmission of depolarization. At the level of the myocyte, there is a corresponding increase in the magnitude of the neurotransmitter signal required to achieve the excitation potential and initial contraction. The overall effect, as demonstrable on the EKG, is to prolong the QRS interval and reduce its peak height. Drugs in this class are used to interrupt aberrant pathways in the atria and ventricles in patients whose conduction myocardium in the SA and the AV nodes are functioning properly, and to mitigate tachycardia by slowing the propagation of the electrical impulse, which will, in turn, reduce the rate of contraction (reduce pulse rate).

This class of drugs is further divided into classes IA, IB, and IC based on differences in their affinity for the sodium channel as well as their different effects on the duration of the action potential and pharmacokinetic profile. Class I drugs generally have a narrow therapeutic window and can be pro-arrhythmic precisely because they slow the propagation of the electrical signal. If the signal propagation is slowed down too much (e.g., with a toxic ingestion), re-entry arrythmias can develop, which can progress to fatal VF. Patients can develop prolonged QT intervals and complete AV block. Some drugs in this class have other mechanisms of action, such as blockage of voltage-gated potassium channels, thereby extending repolarization and prolonging the recovery period.

Common examples are phenytoin, flecanide, propafenone, disopyramine, lidocaine, procainamide, tocainide, quinidine, and mexiletine. All of these drugs are readily detected in routine PM general drug screening procedures.

6.4.2.2 Beta-1 Adrenergic Receptor Blockers (Class II Antiarrhythmics)

Adrenergic receptors are complex proteins expressed as four different types; α and β, each with two different subtypes, 1 and 2, hence α1, α2, β1, and β2. These receptors are targets for epinephrine and norepinephrine as a function of the sympathetic response. Distribution receptors are tissue- and location-specific. Beta 1 adrenergic receptors are G-coupled proteins expressed primarily on myocyte membranes and act to increase heart rate and contractility by activating adenylyl cyclase and cAMP-dependent functions in the cell. There are some beta blockers that affect the entire cardiac conduction cycle, depressing the speed of signal conduction and prolonging the overall refractory period.

Beta 1 receptors are also present in juxtaglomerular cells, where stimulation increases renin release, with a corresponding increase in blood pressure and volume. Beta 2 receptors are primarily found on the vascular smooth muscle and act to reduce contraction of vessel walls, reducing blood pressure by reducing afterload. Drugs predominately active as agonists at beta 2 receptors (e.g., albuterol) are commonly utilized in the treatment of asthma, with a minimal effect on cardiac function.

Beta blockers inhibit epinephrine/norepinephrine β1 receptor binding, causing slowing of the signal propagation from the SA and the AV nodes to contractile myocytes, thereby extending phase 4 of the cardiac cycle, especially when there are high circulating levels of catecholamines. Examples of drugs in this class are the *-lol drugs*, propranolol, labetalol, and atenolol. The clinical response of beta blockers is a reduction in blood pressure, pulse rate, and contractility. Beta blockers have been known to prohibit an appropriate cardiac response to exercise, tachycardia, and elevated blood pressure. Over time, the reduction in contractile force of the left ventricle can lead to remodeling of the muscle and a reduction in blood pressure. Therapy with beta blockers just after an acute myocardial infarction can be protective of the injured muscle, reducing the chance for rupture and leading to better patient outcomes.

The toxic profile is reflective of which drug has been administered, with some having more extra-cardiac effects than others. All drugs in this class, when taken in toxic amounts, will result in profound hypotension. As such, if the patient has presented to the ER and dies, the FP might consider an anti-hypertensive drug as a causative agent, potentially causing an intractable hypotensive crisis.

6.4.2.3 Potassium Channel Blockers (Class III Antiarrhythmics)

Potassium channel blockers inhibit the efflux of potassium via the voltage-gated channels, causing a prolongation of the repolarization phase (phase 3) in both neurons and myocytes. This results in an increase in the duration of the action potential and an extension of the effective refractory period. The result on the EKG is a prolonged QT interval. Drugs in this class are used to treat aberrant electrical pathways (e.g., Wolf Parkinson White (WPW) syndrome) because myocytes are less able to propagate an electrical signal during repolarization. The common clinical condition often requiring potassium channel blockers is ventricular tachycardia. Similarly, VF may also be halted with a potassium channel blocker. As these drugs do not affect the sodium channel, the overall conduction velocity is not altered. An overdose of a potassium channel blocker can result in a potentially fatal prolongation of the QT interval, possibly degenerating into torsades de pointes.

Amiodarone is an example of a commonly utilized medication in this class, although amiodarone is also a sodium channel blocker that, when taken in overdose quantities, can slow myocardial conduction velocity (phase 0), leading to bradycardia. Amiodarone also blocks calcium ion channels in the SA and AV nodes as well as the Purkinje cells (conduction myocytes). In doing so, it retards the signal propagation from nodal tissue. In toxic ingestions, amiodarone and similarly functioning drugs can cause complete heart block.

6.4.2.4 Calcium Channel Blockers (Class IV Antiarrhythmics)

Calcium channel blockers inhibit calcium from entering the myocyte (and vascular smooth muscle cells of vessels). Repolarization of the myocyte during phase 2 (the plateau) of the cardiac action potential is prolonged by the opening of calcium channels and providing an influx of positive charge, counteracting the efflux of sodium ions. These drugs shorten phase 2 by inhibiting some myocyte calcium channels. The result is decreased conduction through the AV node. The decreased calcium influx diminishes contractility and results in reduced blood pressure and a slower heart rate. Drugs in this class include amlodipine, diltiazem, and verapamil. When taken in overdose quantities, the cardiac effects, hypotension, and bradycardia are exacerbated. Additionally, calcium is required for the release of insulin from the pancreas. An overdose of a calcium channel-blocking drug can present as hyperglycemia and lactic acidosis. Both conditions can be diagnosed clinically (and documented in the medical record) and at autopsy via evaluation of the vitreous chemistry profile.

6.4.3 Nitrates

Nitroglycerine and isosorbide nitrate are commonly utilized arterial vasodilators that may be prescribed to relieve pain from angina and dyspnea associated with CHF. The mechanism of action involves the conversion of the nitro group to the active species, nitric oxide (NO), by an aldehyde dehydrogenase. NO binds to and activates guanylate cyclase, increasing the intracellular concentration of cyclic guanosine monophosphate (cGMP). cGMP acts on the vascular smooth muscle endothelium, lowering intracellular calcium causing reduced contractile magnitude.

Nitrates reduce both pre- and afterload. The reduction of preload is associated with venodilation of peripheral vessels, sending less blood to the heart and reducing work and overall oxygen demand. Afterload reduction is a consequence of arteriole vasodilation, which has a direct effect on vascular smooth muscle, increasing blood flow to target tissues, including the myocardium.

Nitrate medications are available to the consumer as pills for sublingual administration and as transdermal patches, typically used for symptom relief and not meant as definitive therapy. Confusion on the part of the patient regarding the distinction may lead to an unintentional overdose. Nitrates having a rapid onset of action (e.g., nitroglycerine) may also be used via IV solution during surgery to emergently treat myocardial ischemia arising from coronary artery spasm from the use of cocaine or other stimulant abuse.

The side effects of nitrates in overdose are related to hypotension and vasodilatory shock. An overdose can be fatal due to profound hypotension. Another potentially fatal mechanism involves the failure of oxygen delivery from hemoglobin to tissues. If the nitrate-containing drug is taken in large quantities, the normal physiologic mechanisms for maintaining hemoglobin iron in a reduced (Fe^{+2}) state may become overwhelmed, such that some iron becomes oxidized to Fe^{+3}, increasing the percentage of methemoglobin in the blood. This pathologic methemoglobinemia results in cyanosis but is easily reversed with methylene blue. There is a more detailed discussion of nitrate and nitrite poisoning in Section 5.

Toxicologic Considerations: Analysis for nitroglycerin and other NO-generating drugs is not performed routinely in toxicology laboratories, but it is generally available as a specialized, or "send-out" assay for a reference laboratory.

Pathologic Considerations: There are no specific findings associated with nitrate toxicity observable at autopsy. An investigation may be key to resolving such cases.

6.4.4 Angiotensin-Converting Enzyme (ACE) Inhibitors

The renin-angiotensin-aldosterone system is activated when the juxtaglomerular cells in the kidney sense hypoperfusion, in the setting of hypovolemia, heart failure, and shock. Angiotensin II causes vasoconstriction of the arterioles of the nephron, efferent greater than afferent. These drugs reduce the activity of the renin-angiotensin-aldosterone system by preventing the conversion of angiotensin I to angiotensin II. Angiotensin II is a potent vasoconstrictor, so less circulating angiotensin II means less vasoconstriction (relative vasodilation). Aldosterone causes sodium absorption at the level of the distal tubule. This results in increased serum sodium, thereby increasing blood pressure. An increase in serum sodium also increases pulmonary edema, peripheral edema, and third-spacing of fluids in patients with heart failure. ACE inhibitors because they inhibit the conversion of angiotensin I to II, reduce aldosterone levels. These drugs are also used to treat volume overload, heart failure, and hypertension, especially in patients with a high risk for a myocardial infarction or patients who have already had myocardial damage. ACE-inhibitors are the *-pril* drugs lisinopril, captopril, enalapril, benazepril, quinapril, etc. An overdose can be fatal by causing intractable hypotension.

ACE inhibitors can also produce life-threatening angioedema of the soft tissues of the mouth and tongue, as well as in the intestinal mucosa. Angioedema more commonly develops shortly after treatment is initiated but can develop after years of continued therapy. Prescription levels are not necessarily predictive of the potential for the occurrence of angioedema. The mechanism of ACE inhibitor-induced angioedema appears to be related to its effect on bradykinin. Angiotensin II degrades bradykinin. With an ACE inhibitor, the breakdown of bradykinin is inhibited, too. This increase in circulating bradykinin increases vascular permeability by stimulating the release of substance P, a vasodilator. Fluid extravasates from the leaky blood vessels into the surrounding soft tissue, resulting in angioedema. A diagnosis of ACE inhibitor-related angioedema can be made with a clinical history of therapy and autopsy findings.

Toxicology Considerations: Toxicologic testing may not be helpful as an indicator of the presence of ACE inhibitors; however, such drugs may be identified and reported depending on the generalized drug screening protocol utilized by the laboratory.

Pathologic Considerations: Grossly, the tissue appears edematous. At autopsy, the lips and tongue will be pale and enlarged with the usual appearance of edema, although not more firm than pitting edema. Microscopically, the edema is paucicellular. Angioedema is not histamine- or mast-cell-mediated. Serum tryptase will not be elevated, distinguishing it from anaphylaxis.

6.4.5 Alpha Receptor Agonists

The alpha-adrenergic receptors are G-protein-coupled receptors, albeit with very distinct consequences of agonist (or antagonist) binding. Alpha-1 receptors are primarily located in smooth muscle. Activation promotes increased levels of intracellular calcium and muscular contraction, and agonists are therefore vasoconstrictive. In contrast, the alpha-2 receptor acts as an allosteric inhibitor, inhibiting adenylyl cyclase and thereby reducing the amount of intracellular cAMP and calcium (essentially, the reverse of the cAMP activation of protein kinase A) by reducing influx via calcium channels and decreasing calcium release by the sarcoplasmic reticulum.

Alpha adrenergic receptors are located in the heart and vasculature, primarily at pre-synaptic terminals as well as throughout the brain, spinal cord, kidneys, and lungs. Alpha-2 receptor agonists inhibit norepinephrine release from presynaptic neurons as a function of decreased intracellular calcium. The cardiac effects of drugs in this class act on the alpha-2 receptor and reduce blood pressure, reducing cardiac output and afterload. The major effect of toxicity with alpha-2 agonists is the central depletion of catecholamines (epinephrine and norepinephrine), leading to potentially fatal CNS depression, bradycardia, and hypothermia.

A common, typical drug of this class is clonidine. Because alpha-2 receptors are also located in the nervous system, agonists can cause sedation and may provide some degree of pain control. Clonidine may be prescribed as an adjunct to sedation for anesthesia and it appears to ameliorate the delirium that occasionally follows such procedures. As such, it may occasionally be observed in PM tox samples.

Xylazine, an alpha-2 agonist drug similar to clonidine, is a sedative analgesic that has been used in veterinary medicine for large and small animals. However, its use in humans has not been approved by the FDA. Currently, xylazine is found as an adulterant in illicit opioids, presumably having been diverted from legal veterinary use. Xylazine is occasionally used as an adjunct with ketamine in DMSA (drug-mediated sexual assault) cases. Xylazine may be encountered in postmortem cases in combination with other drugs, often opioids, and is assumed to have at least an additive effect on CNS depression.

Xylazine is not included in hospital immunoassay-based screening laboratory analyses but is readily detectable in forensic toxicology laboratories. If xylazine is suspected and the deceased person has been hospitalized for some time after administration, analysis of the blood taken upon admission would be expected to demonstrate the presence of the drug. The onset of action is a few minutes, and the duration of action is several hours. Although the symptoms mimic those of an opioid overdose, the mu-receptor blocker naloxone is not an effective treatment because xylazine does not act on the mu-receptor and naloxone has no effect on the alpha-2 receptor.

6.5 COMMON TOXINS

From both a toxicologic and pathologic perspective, the "common toxins" capable of eliciting some degree of cardiotoxicity would probably lead with the currently popular drugs of abuse, and as such, the opiates and SMAs. However, so many commonly prescribed medications (e.g., benzodiazepines, SSRIs, antiarrhythmics, anti-hypertensives, etc.) have the potential to be cardiotoxic in overdose that one could argue that any potentially fatal agent is at least in part cardiotoxic. We do recognize that many of these ultimately cardiotoxic effects are secondary to the action of the drug, for example, the energy-limiting functions of the chemical asphyxiants, the respiratory depressant action of the opiates, and the hypertensive and potentially hyperthermic actions of the SMAs.

Fortunately, there are very few pharmacologic agents, whether utilized for their intended purpose or recreationally, that are not readily detected in broad-spectrum toxicologic drug screening protocols. Similarly, drugs that are essentially only utilized in a "recreational" sense are also readily detected, identified, and reported. The challenge for the forensic toxicologist is to incorporate a mechanistic understanding of the actions of the drug or drugs present, with consideration to levels, correlate to any expected or observed pathologic findings, and in light of underlying medical history/conditions, in an effort to assist the FP in their determination as to the magnitude of the contribution, if any, of the drug to the death in the case.

6.5.1 Cocaine, Methamphetamine, and Other Sympathetic Amines

In a toxicologic sense, the detection of the SMAs is often relatively trivial, in that when use is concurrent temporally with death, the levels tend to be quite high, and accurate quantitation of both parent drug and metabolite is quite straightforward (however, low levels of cocaine can be toxic, particularly in the case of a catecholamine (or analogue)-sensitized myocardium). With the increasing availability of new and unique structural analogues (e.g., the "Bath Salt" variations of tryptamines and cathinones), there can be analytical challenges; however, with the extensive sharing of information and spectral data regarding new compounds via such organizations as the Drug Enforcement Agency and the Scientific Working Group for Seized Drug Analysis (DEA and SWGDRUG), there are extensive resources available to toxicology laboratories to allow for the ready identification of new or previously unencountered substances.

With the identification of both parent and metabolite, there can be, in some cases, reasonable inferences drawn with regard to time of use and the concentrations of the drug that may reasonably have been experienced by the decedent at that time. While such calculations and inferences must be carefully considered in light of the validity of the underlying assumptions, e.g., metabolic/elimination rate, potential for postmortem redistribution, chronic or multiple usage (as opposed to a single-dose event), such considerations may be of use to the pathologist.

However, interpretations of PM levels of cocaine can be particularly problematic in that the parent drug can, depending on circumstances, be subject to some degree of hydrolysis in the blood during the postmortem interval. Such hydrolysis may distort the ratio between cocaine and its primary metabolite, benzoylecgonine (BE), and may lead to erroneous conclusions regarding the possible use scenarios and timetables.

Care should also be taken with regard to the interpretation of low levels of methamphetamine in cases of chronic therapeutic amphetamine administration. While the "standard assumption" is that while methamphetamine can be readily de-methylated to form amphetamine (and this is the primary elimination pathway), there is a general expectation that the reverse reaction, the methylation of amphetamine, does not occur. However, while the N-demethylase reaction is expected to predominate, an enzyme in the sympathetic neurotransmitter pathway, "pheneylethanolamine N-methyl transferase" (PNMT), has been shown to be able to methylate amphetamine.

The SMAs as a group, while acting on the body in a manner completely distinct from the opiates, nevertheless have pronounced euphorigenic effects and have significant abuse potential. Acute toxic effects are primarily a consequence of acute hypertension (with or without a hemorrhagic cerebral infarction) as well as coronary artery spasm leading to myocardial ischemia followed by a fatal arrhythmia.

The illicit use of stimulants such as cocaine and a wide variety of drugs structurally related to amphetamine (e.g., methamphetamine, MDMA, various tryptamines, and cathinones) underlies the expression of a number of medical conditions, from cardiovascular and pulmonary conditions to infectious diseases to dental decay, in a younger cohort than would otherwise be expected. Cocaine, amphetamine, methamphetamine, and other stimulants in the SMA class cause euphoria, heightened alertness, and physical stimulation by affecting the concentration of monoamine NTs in the synaptic space, primarily by blocking re-uptake of NTs to the pre-synaptic neuron at the level of specific transporters. The SMAs have different affinities for the monoamine transporters, which then equates to differential psychotropic profiles. Cocaine has about the same affinity for the dopamine, serotonin, and norepinephrine transporters. Methamphetamine has about a five- to nine-fold higher affinity for the norepinephrine transporter than it has for the dopamine transporter and virtually no affinity for the serotonin transporter. Dopamine causes pleasurable feelings and an increased ability to concentrate on tasks. The increase in circulating dopamine levels is the mechanism by which drug use and addiction to the euphoric effects are based.

6.5.1.1 Cocaine

Cocaine can be thought of as the quintessential sympathetic amine, has a high abuse potential, and is one of the primary drugs of abuse in all industrialized countries. Cocaine has a long history as both a pharmaceutical and psychotropic agent; however, therapeutic use (primarily as a nasopharyngeal and dental anesthetic) has all but disappeared. Cocaine is a potent peripheral vasoconstrictor, facilitating its local anesthetic utility. Mechanistically, cocaine acts primarily as a norepinephrine and dopaminergic reuptake inhibitor, and the elevated levels of NTs in the excitatory neurons underlie its psychotropic response. Secondarily, cocaine also behaves as a functional antagonist of voltage-gated sodium channels. Because of the potential of the drug to reduce the depolarizing flow of sodium ions into the neuronal cytoplasm at the initiation of depolarization (action potential phase 0), cocaine can cause myocardial conduction abnormalities. In addition to the reuptake inhibition of NTs caused by cocaine, the drug also functions to some extent as an alpha and beta receptor agonist, which may then lead to some cardiac effects, such as vasospasm. The onset of action of the psychotropic effect as well as the vasoconstrictive effect of cocaine can be almost immediate, depending on the mode of exposure. The duration of action is in the time frame of minutes to hours, depending on dose, and the half-life of the drug in the user is usually about one hour. Sudden death due to recreational cocaine use is relatively uncommon. However, chronic cocaine use is associated with multiple cardiovascular diseases, including MI, heart failure, cardiomyopathies, arrhythmias, aortic dissection, and endocarditis.

The challenge with the identification of cocaine in cases where there is some degree of underlying pathology is then the determination of the extent to which the presence of the drug either caused or contributed to the death. The potential for cocaine to exacerbate underlying cardiac conditions by causing significant hypertension is well recognized, but the potential for the initiation of a cardiac event by other, direct actions on the heart should also be considered. Even low levels of cocaine may have been contributory to a person's death, and if parent cocaine is detected in PM blood, the FP may wish to consider the potential magnitude of such a contribution.

At autopsy, the signs of acute cocaine use are not obvious grossly. Cocaine is a potent constrictor of coronary arteries, which can lead to local myocardial ischemia and can lead to a myocardial infarction. Vasospasm appears to be linked to the release of endothelin-1 in the presence of cocaine. Physiologically, endothelin-1 is released by vascular endothelial cells when stimulated by thrombin, epinephrine, tumor necrosis factor, angiotensin II, and local tissue hypoxia. The effect is local vasoconstriction. Coronary artery stenosis and myocardial scarring can also be seen in patients with essential hypertension, and microscopic evaluation does not provide any basis for differentiation. Over time, multiple episodes of coronary artery constriction (spasm) can lead to advanced atherosclerotic plaque formation. Often, but not always, plaque formation is concentric, as opposed to the eccentric plaque formed in hypercholesterolemia. Smoking crack cocaine can lead to advanced anthracotic pigment deposition in the pleura and the parenchyma of the lung, the so-called "crack lung," but this feature is not diagnostic (see Figure 6.4).

Toxicologic analysis performed on postmortem blood can be used to diagnose acute cocaine administration. The elimination half-life of cocaine in blood is about 1–1.5h. Cocaine is primarily metabolized to BE and, via a minor pathway, to ecgonine methyl ester (EME). About 90% of cocaine is metabolized to BE, and about 10% goes to EME; very little (~10%?) leaves the urine unchanged. BE has a much longer half-life (4–6h) in the blood and is therefore often detected in PM samples at levels well in excess of parent cocaine.

Cocaine can be hydrolyzed to some extent in the postmortem interval, although this process is pH- and temperature-dependent. As such, the cocaine:BE ratio may not be a reliable indicator of the degree of metabolism (and hence time since use) of the drug. While BE does not have any psychoactive properties, it may have some vasoconstrictive properties and possibly contribute to cocaine-induced vasoconstriction. The half-life of EME in the blood is quite short, and significant levels are not generally observed in antemortem blood. Furthermore, both BE and EME may be formed from cocaine in the postmortem interval prior to sample collection.

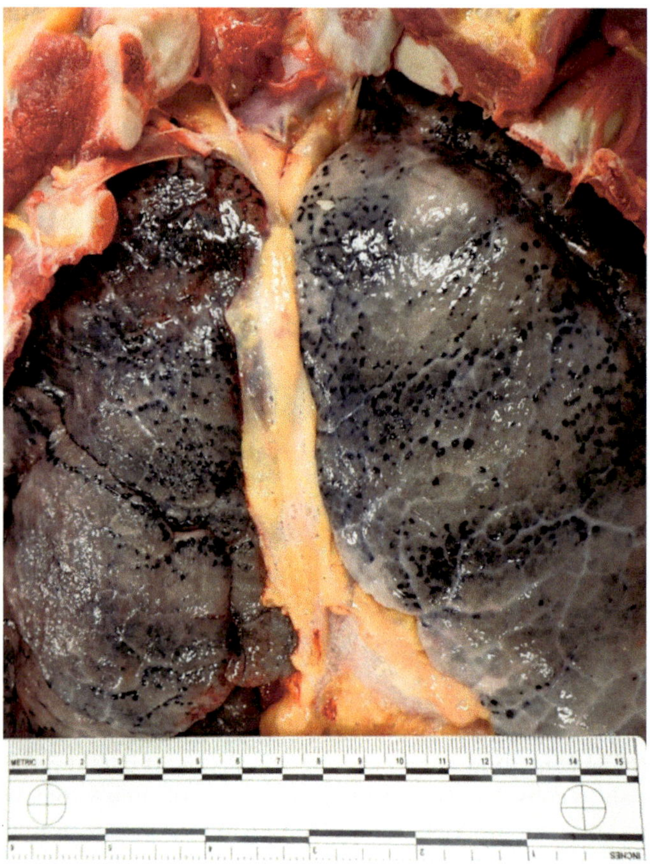

Figure 6.4 Lung with heavy deposition of anthracotic pigment associated with smoking crack cocaine. This appearance can also be seen in patients who have smoked other smokable products (e.g., methamphetamine) and in patients who have inhaled polluted air over a long period of time.

6.5.1.2 Cocaethylene

Cocaethylene is formed in the liver when both ethanol and cocaine are present (e.g., concurrent or proximate use). Cocaethylene (formed by trans-esterification) is a more potent vasoconstrictor than cocaine, and is thought to be perhaps somewhat more effective as a psychotropic agent as well. The half-life of cocaethylene is about five times longer than cocaine, so it may appear alone in postmortem peripheral blood after cocaine and ethanol have been metabolized during life. The presence of cocaethylene is diagnostic of antemortem use of cocaine.

6.5.1.3 Methamphetamine

In recent decades, the illicit synthesis and use of methamphetamine have increased dramatically, running parallel to the increasing rate of opioid use. Methamphetamine is relatively easily synthesized from readily available materials, even by unskilled chemists. (Such sources of the drug may then represent additional toxic issues as a function of synthetic byproducts or contaminants in addition to the synthetic drug.) Methamphetamine can be smoked, inhaled, injected, and ingested, although smoking appears to be the most commonly used method at this time. This highly potent amine has significant psychosocial implications as well as cognitive effects. This drug is known for its ability to sustain wakefulness, increase mental acuity, and induce euphoria, but at a significant cost to the cardiovascular system. It is a highly lipophilic drug, easily crossing the blood–brain barrier. Its toxicologic action on the central nervous system is further described in Section 8.

Somewhat counter-intuitively, methamphetamine use causes accelerated atherosclerosis in chronic users, despite the apparent reduction of some risk factors traditionally associated with heart disease. Specifically, methamphetamine is an appetite suppressant (as are amphetamine and related SMA) and reduces the desire for fatty foods. However, methamphetamine causes transient hypertension and coronary artery vasospasm, which can lead to the early development of atherosclerotic coronary artery stenosis. Vasospasm appears to be linked to the release of endothelin-1 in the presence of methamphetamine in a manner similar to that of cocaine.

Methamphetamine abusers can also have accelerated pulmonary hypertension (cor pulmonale-thickened right ventricular free wall). Microscopically, there can be endothelial and smooth muscle cell proliferation, hypertrophy, and chronic inflammation leading to remodeling of vessel walls. Advanced pulmonary hypertension is characterized by anastomoses between the pulmonary and bronchial circulations. Methamphetamine also stimulates pro-inflammatory responses from macrophages, which contribute to atherosclerosis. This complex series of events may explain the fibrous tissue formation in chronic methamphetamine abusers. In addition to the atherogenic potential in the arteries, methamphetamine also causes electrical and structural changes in the myocardium that may lead to dilated cardiomyopathy. The hearts of chronic users can become heavy, enlarged, and dilated with reduced cardiac output. The pathogenesis of these alterations is not completely understood but appears to be linked to myocardial edema, abnormal mitochondria, and loss of intracellular myofilaments.

The colloquial term "meth mouth" derives from the accelerated and severe tooth decay associated with the chronic use of this drug. Deceased persons who have had a chronic substance abuse condition tend to have had poor hygiene in general and poor dental hygiene as well. The phenomenon is multifactorial, and chronic users tend to have poor nutrition with inadequate essential nutrients but often an excess of simple sugar from sweets and sugary carbonated beverages. The acid in carbonated beverages, combined with any acid in the drug mixture, further erodes enamel. Chronic methamphetamine abusers can become dehydrated, with a resultant decrease in saliva production. Saliva is necessary to mitigate the effect of acids on tooth enamel.

6.5.1.4 MDMA

MDMA, methylene-dioxymethamphetamine, "Ecstasy" is a drug of abuse with stimulant and psychotropic potential and has the same cardiovascular risks as the other sympathetic amines, although thought to be somewhat less addictive and less acutely toxic than methamphetamine because of differential affinities for the various NT transporters. Like other SMAs, it functions to inhibit the function of pre-synaptic NT transport into NT vesicles as well as blocking membrane re-uptake of NT transport, thereby increasing their concentration in the synaptic space. MDMA has a somewhat higher affinity for serotonin transporters, which may then explain the somewhat unusual effect of causing the user to have intense feelings of empathy for other people. MDMA and a number of structurally related species ("synthetic club drugs") are often referred to as "entheogens" or "entactogens" to describe these effects. Overdose symptoms of MDMA are similar to those associated with "Serotonin Syndrome."

While the effect on the nervous system has been well-established, the mechanism of the effect of MDMA on the cardiovascular system is somewhat unclear. Serotonin receptors are located in the myocardium and other cells of the cardiovascular system, and an increase in extracellular serotonin may have long-term deleterious consequences, as excess serotonin has a proliferative effect on myocytes and on the valvular endothelium.

6.5.2 Doxorubicin

Doxorubicin is an antibiotic and chemotherapeutic agent that has a profound toxic effect on cardiac myocytes. Doxorubicin is used in the treatment of a variety of cancers from a variety of cell types, including breast, gastrointestinal, endometrial, sarcomas, and pediatric lymphomas. Cardiotoxicity is a function of free-radical generation and is usually the limiting factor in the dose/duration of use of the drug.

Pathologic findings may not be observed until months or years after the cessation of treatment. The most serious complications may include dilated cardiomyopathy and CHF as a function of direct damage to the myocyte, primarily at the level of the mitochondria. The exact mechanism of toxicity appears to involve the formation of oxygen-free radicals, resulting in tissue damage and iron accumulation. Oxygen-free radical toxicity causes irreversible myofibrillary loss and vacuolization of myocyte cytoplasm, followed by apoptosis.

6.5.3 Tricyclic Antidepressants

Tricyclic antidepressants (TCAs, e.g., amitriptyline, nortriptyline, and doxepine) have been extensively utilized for the treatment of clinically significant depression since the late 1950s. All of the drugs in this class function as serotonin and norepinephrine reuptake inhibitors, with only a weak affinity for dopamine reuptake transporters. While still prescribed, these drugs are less commonly utilized than other antidepressant medications and may be utilized as second-line therapy after more selective serotonin-reuptake inhibitors (SSRIs) have been utilized. TCAs may also be used to treat or manage fibromyalgia, migraine headaches, anxiety, and neuropathic pain. TCAs are not uncommonly encountered in an older patient demographic who has been on the drug for significant portions of their adult lives. As such, both accidental and deliberate overdoses may be encountered.

Tricyclic antidepressant medications function as voltage-gated sodium and calcium channel blockers at high concentrations, causing hypotension and potentially fatal arrhythmias. Like class I antiarrhythmics, blockade of sodium channels increases the duration of the action potential (phase 0). TCAs are also calcium channel blockers, like class IV antiarrhythmics, increasing the length of the refractory period (phase 2). The effect on the EKG is to prolong the PR, QRS, and QT intervals. Similar to the cardiotoxic effects of anti-arrhythmic agents, patients may develop a variety of tachy- or bradycardic arrythmias, which may ultimately prove fatal.

Analysis of TCAs in the postmortem setting is routine. While some hospital (and postmortem) immunoassay-based screening panels include TCAs, this is less common in current configurations. However, the TCAs show up readily in GC- or HPLC-based assays, and concentrations associated with potentially fatal levels are often above the 1 mg/L range. TCAs were the first group of drugs for which postmortem redistribution was recognized, and as such (like essentially all drugs), samples collected from femoral (or other peripheral sources) are much more likely to accurately reflect true antemortem levels than samples collected from within the central areas.

6.6 UNCOMMON TOXINS

The presence of a pharmaceutical or other toxic agent outside the realm of those normally or routinely encountered in forensic practice can present a considerable challenge to both the FP and the toxicologist. Often, there will be a negative autopsy, or at least the absence of pathology, that might provide a compelling or at least reasonable explanation for the death, thereby raising the suspicion that there may be a toxic effect underlying the death. In some cases, there may not be an entirely satisfactory explanation for the observed pathologic findings, leading to suspicions regarding the potential for a toxic agent. In many cases, toxicologic analysis of PM samples will identify a potentially explanatory agent. There is a multiplicity of toxins that will not be identified during routine comprehensive drug screening procedures, and based on the evaluation of such history, scene evidence, and the multiplicity of factors that may accompany the considerations around a particular case, the pathologist and toxicologist may strategize regarding specific target drugs/toxins or broadly-based screening procedures to help identify a toxic substance.

6.6.1 Aconitine

Aconitine, a toxin produced by plants in the Aconitum genus, has been extensively used in the past as a potentially rapid-acting poison, for hunting and as an arrow poison, and also as an effective homicidal agent. It is still in use today as an antipyretic and an analgesic in herbal medicine therapy (albeit with a narrow therapeutic window; preparation must be very accurate). Even if prepared and dispensed properly, patients may inadvertently receive a supratherapeutic dose. Examples of the genus are known by several common names, including the devil's helmet, Wolfsbane, purple poison, and monkshood. The plants are flowering perennials known for their deep blue to purple flowers on a stalk, similar to the snapdragon. All parts of the plant are toxic to humans. Confusing one of these plants for an edible species can have serious or fatal consequences, as the lethal dose is only a few milligrams of the extract.

Aconitine functions by binding to the alpha subunit of the voltage-gated sodium ion channels on the cell membranes of myocytes and neurons, thereby keeping the channels open and delaying or blocking repolarization of the membrane. Poisoned patients are hypotensive, have muscle weakness, and paresthesia (especially perioral paresthesia). They may also have a variety of abnormal cardiac rhythms. There is no specific antidote.

Making a diagnosis of a plant-induced fatal arrythmia can be very difficult unless the history given is supportive. Autopsy findings are those of nonspecific heart failure: cyanosis, pulmonary edema, and congestion of organs and tissues. Family or friends of the poisoned patient may be able to provide a history of using herbal medical treatments, or the remainder of a dose may still be available. The case history, any documentation in the medical record of EKG abnormalities, as well as pertinent negative findings at the autopsy may support the diagnosis.

Testing for aconitine is not part of routine postmortem analysis; however, based on suspicions of a particular toxic agent, directed testing may be able to demonstrate the presence of aconitine or a related species.

6.6.2 Tetrodotoxins

Tetrodotoxin is a neuro- and cardiotoxin produced by some bacterial species found in some fish, frogs, worms, and crabs. The host species do not produce tetrodotoxins; rather, they are accumulated by the ingestion of bacteria that produce the toxin. Farm-raised aquarian life are unlikely to contain any such poisons as they have a prepared diet. Pufferfish raised for sushi are also unlikely to contain the toxin, but wild pufferfish should be assumed to be poisonous.

Poisoning occurs when these animals are not prepared properly prior to consumption. The toxin is heat-stable, so cooking the fish or meat does not make the food safe. Exposure to toxic levels via water, air, or soil is exceedingly unlikely.

Tetrodotoxins are also sodium ion channel blockers, but their mechanism is to keep the channels closed, minimizing the influx of sodium into the cytoplasm, preventing depolarization, and preventing signal propagation. Patients experience paresthesia and flaccid paralysis. The onset and severity of symptoms are dose-dependent, but usually patients experience some abnormality within about 30 min of consumption. Treatment is supportive; there is no known antidote.

The autopsy findings in cases of tetrodotoxin poisoning are nonspecific, and there is no routine toxicology assay available in the postmortem setting. However, a confirmatory analysis is available as a send-out test via HPLC-MS methodology. Diagnosis is generally made by the reported history of having eaten some marine life or meat prior to death.

6.6.3 Grayanotoxins

Grayanotoxins are plant-derived toxins coming from some species of the rhododendron plant. All parts of the plant are potentially poisonous, as is the honey produced by bees from the flowers ("mad honey disease"). Grayanotoxins bind to the alpha subunit of the voltage-gated sodium channel while it is in the open state, causing continuous efflux of sodium, leaving the cell in a hyperpolarized state. Patients develop hypotension, sinus bradycardia, and AV node block. Symptoms are dose-dependent, not generally fatal, and treatment is not usually necessary. However, symptoms may persist or become life-threatening in combination with other medical conditions. Atropine may be used to correct cardiac conduction abnormalities during emergency medical treatment.

6.6.4 The Yew Plant

Nearly all parts of these popular and virtually ubiquitous landscaping plant species in the *Taxus* genus contain toxins ("Taxines") act as potent cardiac sodium and calcium channel blockers, acting thereby in a manner similar to class I and class IV antiarrhythmics. All are evergreens with thin, needle-like leaves. These plants form red berries containing seeds in the autumn, with the highest concentration of toxins found in the seeds. The soft, red part of the berry covering the seed is the only part that is not known to be toxic, as it contains very little taxine. Yew-related poisonings are uncommon and are almost always suicidal in nature, rarely accidental, and rarer still, homicidal. The lethal dose varies by species but is considered between 0.6 and 1.3 g of Yew leaves/kg body mass for humans. The onset of symptoms can be rapid, in the order of minutes, and consist of heart palpitations accompanied by gastrointestinal upset, possibly followed by or including seizure activity. At autopsy, the gastric contents will contain what was ingested: leaves, partial leaves, stems, and/or berries. As death is not immediate, some degree of cerebral and/or pulmonary edema may have developed.

The primary toxins in the Yew plant are alkaloids (taxine A and B), affecting atrio-ventricular conduction as reflected in the EKG as a widening of the QRS complex. Initially, patients develop tachyarrhythmias, a prolonged PR interval, and widened QRS complex, and decreased cardiac contractility. Cardiac rhythms can degenerate into bradyarrhythmia's, cardiogenic shocks, and death. The cytotoxic antineoplastic actions of taxine-related antineoplastic agents ("taxanes," e.g., paclitaxel (Taxol) and docetaxel (Taxotere)) are a function of the inactivation of microtubule function rather than the ion-channel inactivation associated with acute toxicity as described above. Taxine alkaloids A and B can be detected by specialty laboratories using HPLC-MSMS techniques, but this is not a routine analysis offered by most laboratories in the forensic setting.

6.6.5 Lily of the Valley and Oleander

Lily of the Valley, a common ground cover with small, white flowers and broad, pointed, deep green leaves, is deceptively poisonous. These perennials bloom in spring to form short stalks of bell-like flowers that may be attractive to small children. Eating as few as two leaves can be fatal in a small child. The plant contains cardiac glycosides, inhibiting the sodium-potassium ATPase pump in a manner similar to digitalis. Symptoms are referable to bradycardia and cardiac arrythmias. Treatment is supportive, as there is no known antidote. Similarly, oleander, a tropical and subtropical ornamental shrub with white, yellow, or pink flowers, contains the cardiac glycoside oleandrin, another digitalis analogue. All parts of the plant are poisonous. The symptoms of ingestion are dose-dependent. Patients may develop hyperkalemia that may require treatment. Treatment may also be needed for sinus bradycardia.

6.6.6 Loperamide

Loperamide, the active ingredient in over-the-counter anti-diarrheal medications, is a mu-opioid receptor agonist; however, the drug is unable to effectively transit the blood–brain barrier. Loperamide has a negligible CNS effect when taken as prescribed and does not elicit an analgesic or euphorigenic response. The drug has a wide therapeutic index as compared to other opioids and is currently available as a variety of brand-name and generic formulations. It has activity primarily on the myenteric plexus of the intestine, causing reduced intestinal motility and prolonged transit time of the intestinal contents. The extended transit time allows for more water resorption from the intestinal lumen.

There are some people who attempt to abuse loperamide for its euphoric effect (nicknamed "poor man's heroin"), but the dosing needs to be very high to achieve that effect. Also, some people use it to mitigate cravings from chronic opioid dependence. Loperamide is normally restricted to the systemic circulation because it is a substrate for the transmembrane transport protein, P-glycoprotein (permeability glycoprotein). P-glycoprotein is found within the cell membrane on the luminal side of cells of the intestinal mucosa, bile canaliculi in the liver, renal tubules, and capillaries in the brain. This protein aggressively transports drugs and other xenobiotics out of the cytoplasm and into the lumen, which the cells face, preventing them from remaining in the body. P-glycoprotein is heavily expressed on capillaries in the brain and is one of the most robust portions of the blood–brain barrier. Loperamide is almost completely excluded from the central nervous system by its attachment to and removal by P-glycoprotein.

The toxic mechanism of loperamide is associated with cardiac conduction abnormalities, not CNS depression. In toxic doses, patients may experience syncope and survive, or die suddenly. Loperamide can cause a variety of potentially fatal cardiac dysrhythmias, including ventricular tachycardia, bradycardia, prolonged QT interval, as well as VF degenerating to Torsade's de Pointes. Multiple case reports detail transient conduction abnormalities that mimic those observed in the "Brugada Syndrome" during self-prescribed loperamide overuse. At high doses, loperamide appears to block the calcium ion channel on the SA and AV nodes, slowing the progression of the electrical signal from the nodal tissue, with the clinical effect of bradycardia. Brugada syndrome is a very serious condition in which the heart is structurally normal but the patient is at risk for sudden death from conduction abnormalities. The syndrome is characterized by EKG abnormalities of coved ST-elevation and J point elevation of at least 2 mm in at least two of the right precordial leads (V1 – V3) and ventricular arrhythmias, syncope, and sudden death, although some patients are asymptomatic. Several gene mutations have been identified linked to Brugada syndrome. These mutations can be inherited in an autosomal dominant pattern and cause alterations in cardiac sodium and/or calcium channels.

Loperamide is similar to methadone in that it can also prolong the QT interval. Both opioids appear to block the potassium channel that regulates repolarization by allowing potassium efflux from the myocyte (cardiac action potential phase 3). In toxic doses, the potassium channel is blocked, effectively prolonging repolarization and extending the refractory period of the ventricular myocytes. Prolonging the refractory period is reflected in the EKG as a widened QRS complex and a prolonged QT interval. Patients with an opioid use disorder may be prescribed methadone as part of their medication maintenance therapy. Co-ingestion of methadone with a toxic ingestion of loperamide increases the risk for ventricular arrythmia.

6.6.7 Nicotine

Nicotine functions as an acetylcholine receptor agonist at specific neuronal and neuromuscular junctions and in the brain. When inhaled in tobacco smoke, the onset of action is about 30 s, and the half-life in blood is about 2 h. In addition to smoking, nicotine is readily available as a medication in patches and gum formulations, used to reduce cravings by using nicotine in a controlled manner in an effort to provide users with a means of reducing their use.

Nicotine causes a modest release of norepinephrine, serotonin, dopamine, acetylcholine, and vasopressin. This NT release is the basis for the stimulant effect and is responsible for tachycardia and the cardiovascular damage caused by vascular smooth muscle vasoconstriction. The nicotine-induced dopamine release is responsible for the reward and addiction components of nicotine. Similarly, the release of epinephrine and norepinephrine is the basis for the hypertension and tachycardia associated with the drug.

The stimulant effects of nicotine are minimal to modest. However, it can be fatal if ingested in adequate concentrations or in an inappropriately concentrated form. Both nicotine and its primary metabolite, cotinine, are readily detectable in routine laboratory analyses of biological specimens. Nicotine is discussed further in Section 5.

Bibliography

Aaronson P.I., Ward J.P.T., Connolly M.J. (2012). *The Cardiovascular System at a Glance*. 4th rev, ed. Walden, MA: Wiley Blackwell.

Basso C., Michaud K., d'Amati G., Banner J., Lucena J., Cunningham K., Leone O., Vink A., van der Wal A.C., Sheppard M.N., Association for European Cardiovascular Pathology. (2021). Cardiac hypertrophy at autopsy. *Virchows Archiv: International Journal of Pathology*, 479(1):79–94. https://doi.org/10.1007/s00428-021-03038-0.

Bell D.R. (2009). The electrical activity of the heart. In: Rhoades R.A., Bell D.R. (eds). *Medical Physiology: Principles for Clinical Medicine* (pp. 237–259). 3rd rev. ed. New York: Lippincott Williams & Wilkins.

Brown G., Monteleone C. (2017). Angiotensin-converting enzyme inhibitor-induced angioedema: A review of the literature. *Journal of Clinical Hypertension* (Greenwich). 19(12):1377–1382. https://doi.org/:10.1111/jch.13097.

Campbell T.J., Williams K.M. (1998). Therapeutic drug monitoring: Antiarrhythmic drugs. *British Journal of Clinical Pharmacology*, 46(4):307–319. https://doi.org/10.1046/j.1365-2125.1998.t01-1-00768.x.

Cunningham K.S., Spears D.A., Care M. (2019). Evaluation of cardiac hypertrophy in the setting of sudden cardiac death. *Forensic Sciences Research*, 4(3):223–240. https://doi.org/10.1080/20961790.2019.1633761

Dean D.E., Schultz D.L., Powers R.H. (2001). Asphyxia due to angiotensin converting enzyme (ACE) inhibitor mediated angioedema of the tongue during the treatment of hypertensive heart disease. *Journal of Forensic Sciences*, 46(5):1239–1243.

Del Rosario M.E., Weachter R., Flaker G.C. (2010). Drug-induced QT prolongation and sudden death. *Missouri Medicine*, 107(1):53–58.

Fozzard H.A., Sheets M.F. (1985). Cellular mechanism of action of cardiac glycosides. *Journal of the American College of Cardiology*, 5(5 Suppl A):10A–15A. https://doi.org/10.1016/s0735-1097(85)80458-7.

Frumin H., Kerin N.Z., Rubenfire M. (1989). Classification of antiarrhythmic drugs. *Journal of Clinical Pharmacology*, 29(5):387–394. https://doi.org/10.1002/j.1552-4604.1989.tb03350.x.

Jufer R.A., Wstadik A., Walsh S.L., Levine B.S., Cone E.J. (2000). Elimination of cocaine and metabolites in plasma, saliva, and urine following repeated oral administration to human volunteers. *Journal of Analytical Toxicology*, 24(7):467–477. https://doi.org/10.1093/jat/24.7.467.

Karch S.B. (2006). *A Brief History of Cocaine*. 2nd ed. Boca Raton, FL: Taylor and Francis.

Kitzman D.W., Scholz D.G., Hagen P.T., Ilstrup D.M., Edwards W.D. (1988) Age-related changes in normal human hearts during the first 10 decades of life. Part II (maturity): A quantitative anatomic study of 765 specimens from subjects 20 to 99 years old. *Mayo Clinic Proceedings* 63(2):137–146.

Lee V., Byard R.W. (2013). Variation in methods of cardiac dissection: A potential confounder in measuring cardiac weight at autopsy. *Journal of Forensic Sciences*, 58(3):811–812. https//doi.org.10.1111/1556-4029.12117.

McCorry L.K. (2009). *Essential of Human Physiology for Pharmacy*. 2nd ed. Boca Raton, FL: CRC Press.

Molina D.K., DiMaio V.J. (2012). Normal organ weights in men: Part I – The heart. *The American Journal of Forensic Medicine and Pathology*, 33(4):362–367. https://doi.org/10.1097/PAF.0b013e31823d298b.

Molina D.K., DiMaio V.J. (2015). Normal organ weights in women: Part I – The Heart. *The American Journal of Forensic Medicine and Pathology*, 36(3):176–181. https://doi.org/10.1097/PAF.0000000000000174.

Paratz E.D., Cunningham N.J., MacIsaad A.I. (2015). The cardiac complications of methamphetamines. *Heart, Lung and Circulation*, 25(4):325–332. https://doi.org/10.1016/j.hlc.2015.10.019.

Silver M.D., Gotleib A.I., Schoen F.R. (2001). *Cardiovascular Pathology*. 3rd ed. Philadelphia, PA: Churchhill Livingstone.

Thanacoody H.K., Thomas S.H. (2005). Tricyclic antidepressant poisoning: Cardiovascular toxicity. *Toxicological Reviews*, 24(3):205–214. https://doi.org/10.2165/00139709-200524030-00013.

Wu P.E., Juurlink D.N. (2017). Clinical review: Loperamide toxicity. *American College of Emergency Physicians*, 70:245–252. https://doi.org/10.1016/j.annemergmed.2017.04.008.

SECTION 7

HEPATOTOXINS

DOI: 10.4324/9781003121060-8

7.1 INTRODUCTION

The liver is one of the largest and most functionally diverse and important organs in the body. Although the liver is structurally relatively simple, hepatocytes themselves are biochemically complex, serving as the primary location for the synthesis of a wide variety of proteins, glycoproteins, and other biomolecules (e.g., clotting factors and plasma proteins). Hepatocytes play the major role in the processes of energy production and storage, as the primary location for carbohydrate, protein, and fat metabolism. Similarly, the liver is the major site for the metabolism of drugs and xenobiotics and elimination of waste products.

The gross examination and subsequent histologic evaluation and interpretation of the pathology of the liver can be challenging, because a variety of distinct pathologic processes can cause similar patterns of injury, making the scope of differential diagnosis very broad. The forensic pathologist (FP) has an advantage over the surgical pathologist (SP) as the former has the entire organ to examine, while the SP is generally limited to small biopsy specimens. In the postmortem scenario, the liver can be sliced from end to end with as many tissue blocks taken as necessary to look for evidence of disease. The microscopic examination of tissue sections is similar to the microscopic examination of biopsy specimens, and pathologists document the pattern of injury; the extent, type, and location of inflammation; necrosis; and pattern of steatosis. If there are any inclusions, the extent, location, color, and polarizing nature is noted. Special stains may be used to further refine the differential diagnosis list.

Determination of whether the observed pathology reflects acute injury, was the result of a chronic assault, or reflects some combination of the two can often be accomplished by the combination of gross and microscopic examination. Generally, if the liver is already grossly cirrhotic or has extensive fibrosis evident microscopically, the insult, injury, or disease process is not likely to be acute, as the accumulation of fibrous tissue and bile duct proliferation take time. Evidence of a well-established change in microstructural arrangement or content would reflect a chronic process.

Acute liver injury that has become fatal is usually obvious grossly. The liver may be enlarged, pale, and very soft. Microscopically, hepatocytes will have lost their typical cytologic characteristics and may be ballooned and pale. Many may be without recognizable nuclei. Patients who survive an acute hepatic insult may go on to develop chronic liver disease and demonstrate an acute process superimposed upon chronic features. Medical records, reflecting liver function tests over time, medications prescribed, and other underlying medical issues may provide valuable information for the FP.

In contrast to the wide variety of drugs capable of producing an acute CNS or cardiac-based toxicologic illness or fatality, there are relatively few potentially fatal "acute" hepatotoxins. One of the primary challenges the FP faces is the determination of the extent to which underlying disease or impaired hepatic function has played a contributory factor in a death, if indeed, at all. Naturally, this consideration is unique and specific to each case. As an example, one of the more common hepatotoxic pathologic findings evident at autopsy is steatosis, fibrosis, and cirrhosis reflective of extensive or prolonged ethanol use. Alcohol-related cirrhosis may contribute to death simply because the liver can no longer perform its normal functions, leading to hepatic failure. A patient with cirrhosis of the liver who sustains minor trauma may develop an expanded subdural hematoma (SDH) with a mass effect, because the patient has impaired clotting ability. Although the patients who die from an acute SDH in this scenario did not die of liver disease, *per se* cirrhosis of the liver contributed to the death by its inability to make adequate clotting factors.

Other than ethanol-induced damage, perhaps the most common or familiar hepatotoxic finding is the acute necrosis associated with acetaminophen (APAP) and other compounds capable of being metabolically activated to toxic species in the liver. While there is some degree of this type of hepatotoxic potential associated with a number of drugs utilized for a wide variety of conditions, such as some antibiotics and antineoplastics, this potential is usually well characterized in literature, allowing the role such drugs may have played in a hepatotoxic scenario to be considered. Less commonly encountered, but equally potentially deadly are the poisons affecting protein synthesis, such as mushroom toxins and ricin. Because of the essential function of the liver in energy production, systemic toxins affecting those processes are also "hepatotoxic" in a sense, such as the chemical asphyxiants, for example, cyanide, carbon monoxide, and various nitrite species (discussed in Section 5: Respiratory Toxins and Chemical Asphyxiants). Cases involving a wide variety of relatively unusual hepatotoxins, for example, aflatoxins and microcystins, among a wide variety of naturally occurring compounds may still be encountered.

7.2 STRUCTURE AND PATHOLOGY

7.2.1 Functional Units

The most commonly utilized microstructural description of the liver for toxicologic consideration is the "classic hepatic lobule" in which the center of a hexagon is a branch of the central vein (terminal hepatic vein), and the vertices contain the portal triad (branches of the hepatic artery, portal vein and bile duct). This "classic hepatic lobule" is then considered the functional unit in the liver. In terms of toxicology and pathology, this description allows regional identification (e.g., "centrilobular") in terms of the relative oxygen availability, which in turn is linked to the energy available for driving synthetic and catabolic reactions, detoxifying molecules, and supporting overall hepatocellular viability. The structure of the hepatic lobule provides extensive contact between hepatocytes and blood, as blood flow proceeds from the hepatic artery in the portal triad, along the hepatocellular sinusoids, toward the central vein eventually draining into the hepatic vein. As such, extensive cross-membrane transport by target-specific proteins can effectively concentrate molecules from the blood and eliminate metabolic waste from the hepatocyte back into the blood for removal by the kidney, or across the hepatobiliary border into the bile.

An alternate way of describing the histologic structure from the point of view of the portal triad is the acinus. Each portal triad serves the lobules to which it touches, while each central vein drains only one lobule. This representation is useful because it is based on oxygen supply to hepatocytes. Hepatocytes that receive the blood with the highest oxygen content are the ones around the portal triad, proximate to the hepatic artery. Pericentral hepatocytes are exposed to blood with the lowest oxygen concentration. The acinus is loosely divided into zones 1, 2, and 3, reflecting the amount of oxygen available to the surrounding hepatocytes. Zone 1 is periportal, around the portal triad; zone 3 is pericentral, around the central vein; and zone 2 is in the middle.

7.2.2 Hepatic Blood Flow

The liver receives both oxygenated blood and partially deoxygenated blood from two different, but companion systems. The bulk of the blood flow through the liver is partially deoxygenated venous blood from the gastrointestinal system entering via the hepatic portal vein. The main tributaries that join to form the hepatic portal vein are the veins from the lower portion of the esophagus, the stomach, the superior mesenteric vein (small intestine, ascending and a portion of the transverse colon), the splenic vein (spleen and pancreas), and the inferior mesenteric vein (part of the transverse colon and descending colon). This mixture of blood contains nutrients, drugs, toxins, and other materials that had been absorbed in the GI tract. From the hepatic portal vein, the blood flows into the liver parenchyma into portal veins (in zone 1), through sinusoids, traversing zone 2, into the central veins (in zone 3), and finally into the hepatic vein. Central veins in the hepatic lobule are tributaries that join to form the hepatic vein. Blood from the hepatic vein drains into the portion of the inferior vena cava just proximal to the heart.

Blood entering the liver from the portal vein will contain such drugs and toxins as may have been absorbed in the intestine and will be subject to metabolism prior to reaching the systemic circulation. The extent of absorption and metabolism in the liver may be extensive and is referred to as "first-pass metabolism," reflecting the extent of hepatic detoxification/metabolism to which some drugs may be subjected prior to reaching other, potential target organs. This phenomenon explains why some medications (and drugs) are not as effective when taken orally. Nevertheless, quite a number of drugs, although taken orally, are subject to such extensive first-pass metabolism. One of the more notable of these is morphine. The effective dose of morphine following as an intravenous or intranasal administration (thereby going directly into the systemic circulation) is much greater than with the corresponding oral administration. This is why, in part, patients who are struggling with a morphine or heroin addiction rarely ingest the drugs, preferring to inject or "snort" the substance.

The second hepatic blood supply is arterial, fully oxygenated blood. The common hepatic artery is a branch of the celiac trunk that comes off the aorta and branches to form hepatic arterioles that are part of the portal triad (zone 1). The blood in the hepatic arterioles enters the hepatic sinusoids, mixing with the blood from the much larger hepatic portal vein. The hepatocytes surrounding the portal triad (zone 1) are the most oxygenated, proximate to the entry of arterial blood from the hepatic artery; those around the central vein (zone 3) are the least oxygenated. The hepatocytes in zone 3 are arranged in a radiating pattern around the vein. These are the most sensitive to hypoxia and toxicologic insult from drugs and toxins and are dependent upon oxidative metabolism for detoxification.

7.3 CONSIDERATIONS AT AUTOPSY

As noted above, in the absence of medical history, medical records, or other information that may shed light on the case, there may be no basis for any expectation of a significant involvement of the liver in the death. However, from that point of initial observation, through the consideration of microscopic and laboratory results including toxicology findings, there may be indicators regarding the degree of involvement (if any) of the liver. In particular, the extent to which the liver is observed to depart from "normal" size, shape, and color and the presence of jaundice can raise the potential for some degree of expressed hepatotoxicity, which may, in turn, inform considerations of cause of death (COD).

It is relatively unusual to deal with a case in which suspected hepatotoxicity is the working COD but may be encountered in a suspected APAP overdose, drug-related toxicity, advanced cirrhosis, or even exposure to a plant-based toxin. In such cases, the approach at autopsy is similar to the examination a treating physician would perform on a live patient. However, the FP may not always have the advantage of a panel of liver function tests with which to evaluate the patient and may have to rely on toxicologic testing and pathologic findings to assess the magnitude of hepatic injury.

At autopsy, even prior to the direct observation of the liver, evaluation of the color of the skin and sclera can provide important clues as to the nature of a potential hepatic insult or disease state. In hepatic failure, the ability of hepatocytes to convert biliverdin (generated from hemoglobin released by senescent erythrocytes by reticuloendothelial macrophages) to bilirubin and subsequently to conjugate and eliminate bilirubin across the hepatobiliary cell membrane will be compromised, resulting in a characteristic yellow tinge of jaundice to the skin and sclera. However, while jaundice (and by inference, serum bilirubin) is indicative of hyperbilirubinemia, the underlying cause may be cholestasis, or an enzymatic- or transport-based hepatocyte functional issue, and the obvious symptom (and/or serum bilirubin level) may not, of themselves, provide clarification. The patient may have sought medical attention for uncontrolled itching or icterus. They may also have reported pale clay-colored stools and brown urine as excessive bilirubin is excreted into the GI tract and urinary system. A review of medical records may provide clues to the underlying cause of cholestasis.

The definitive determination of the actual cause of jaundice may require evaluation or investigation to a degree not readily available in the postmortem setting. Further, there may be adequate information to provide an accurate COD and MOD without a detailed understanding of that underlying cause. Depending on the degree of investigation a particular case warrants, family members may be able to provide useful information regarding recent illness, long term or familial history, or even potential toxic exposures. Recent medical records from any care provider or facility can also be of value and may provide insight for the differential diagnosis, as an information regarding prescription medications, over-the-counter (OTC) drugs, herbal supplements, and drugs of abuse. The analysis of serum bilirubin is not a routine assay performed on postmortem samples, but if collected in the early postmortem period, it can provide an indication of the antemortem level. Serum bilirubin increases with increasing postmortem interval, but in deceased patients with jaundice, the small incremental increase is insignificant. Figures 7.1–7.4 show the effects of hyperbilirubinemia: jaundice of the skin and eyes as well as the internal tissues. A patient with cirrhosis has yellow-tinged ascites.

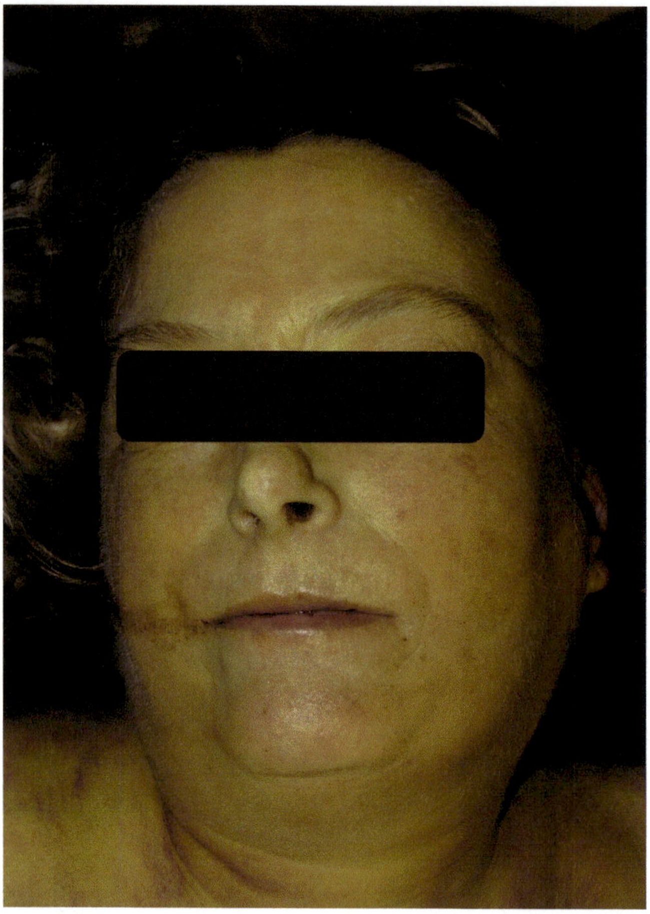

Figure 7.1 The face and part of the shoulders of a Caucasian woman with jaundice. Her eyes are covered to protect her identity. Note that her skin has a deep yellow tinge.

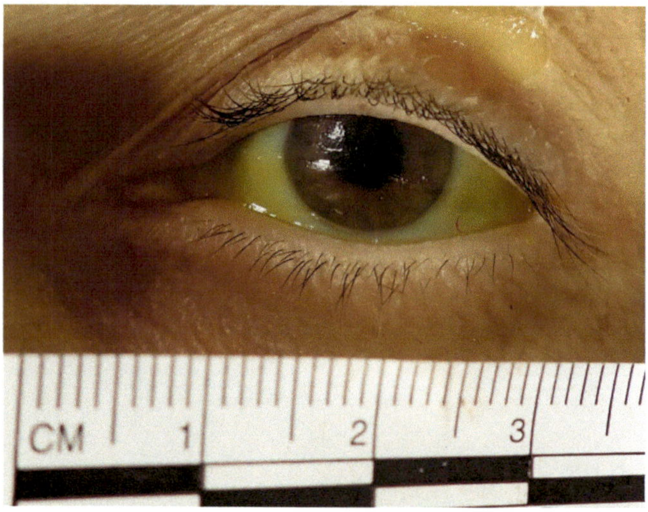

Figure 7.2 The yellow color of scleral icterus.

Figure 7.3 Cirrhotic liver in situ with jaundice of internal tissues in the opened abdominal cavity. Note that the internal tissues are also yellow-tinged.

Figure 7.4 Eight hundred milliliters of yellow-tinged ascites from a patient with cirrhosis.

7.4 HEPATIC TESTING – CLINICAL AND TOXICOLOGY

In addition to the gross and microscopic evaluation of liver during autopsy, consideration of medical history and antemortem medical records including clinical measures can provide potentially significant information regarding the structural integrity and functional capacity of the liver. The status of hepatic function is regularly assessed during medical treatment by a combination of determination of serum levels of intrahepatic enzymes (reflecting issues of hepatocyte structural integrity) as well as a wide variety of metabolic substrates, products, and intermediates reflective of different aspects of hepatocellular function. Records reflecting such antemortem clinical assessment can be extremely useful in the determination of the role that a drug or toxin may have had (if any) on the actual cause of death.

The primary intracellular enzymes utilized as indicators of hepatocellular integrity, measurable in serum, are the "transaminases" – alanine transaminase (ALT) and aspartate aminotransferase (AST). Other enzymes that may reflect hepatotoxicity are alkaline phosphatase (ALP), lactate dehydrogenase (LDH), and gamma-glutamyl transferase (GGT). However, these enzymes are also contained in other body cells, so interpretation should be viewed considering the potential for damage to have occurred in tissues other than the liver. Enzyme isozyme-specific analysis may be particularly useful in the diagnosis of specific disease states and may, therefore, be of value in postmortem considerations. Common products reflecting aspects of hepatic function measurable in the serum are bilirubin, reflective of the process of formation and elimination of bile acids; serum albumin and "total protein," reflective of the synthetic pathways; and prothrombin time (PT), reflective of the synthesis and secretion of vitamin-K-related clotting factors. Unfortunately, serum liver enzymes are also not stable postmortem, and the evaluation of liver function by such assays in postmortem blood does not provide reliable information. Most other serum enzymes increase unpredictably after death. Enzymes do not penetrate the blood–vitreous humor (VH) barrier well, and using VH to predict antemortem enzyme levels is not valid.

ALT and AST from the hepatocyte become elevated in the serum due to direct hepatocellular membrane injury or death. Antemortem serum ALT and AST values provide a sensitive indication of hepatocellular damage. AST is also contained in the heart, skeletal muscle, the kidney, and erythrocytes. ALP is present in hepatocytes and in the cells forming the biliary tree, bone, intestine, and the placenta. Serum ALP levels can provide an indirect marker for cholestasis. While ALT and AST are both intracellular enzymes, ALT is primarily cytoplasmic and is only found in hepatocytes. Elevated serum levels thereof can provide a good indication of acute hepatocyte damage. AST is cytoplasmic in the hepatocyte, but is also present in myocytes, erythrocytes, and renal cells. Elevated serum AST levels may, therefore, indicate injury to tissues other than liver. Interestingly, AST is also contained within mitochondria, so elevated AST may be reflective of toxicologic processes adequate to affect mitochondrial structural integrity as well as the hepatocyte itself.

The alkaline phosphatases (ALPs) represent a group of isozymes catalyzing the hydrolysis of organic phosphate esters. While there are both tissue-specific and nonspecific isozymes, the levels found in serum represent hepatic and bone-derived forms. Within the liver, ALP is cytosolic and associated with the canalicular membrane. As such, elevation of ALP is associated with hepatobiliary disorders, and increased synthesis appears to be a consequence of biliary obstruction, although its appearance may lag the serum aminotransferases in such conditions. Clinically, ALP facilitates diagnosis of cholestasis, but will also be elevated in hepatic injury or trauma, for example, cancer, drug-induced toxicity, alcoholic cirrhosis or steatosis, or hepatitis.

Lactate dehydrogenase (LDH) is a major enzyme of the anaerobic metabolic pathway, catalyzing the reversible conversion between lactate and pyruvate. In conditions of normal oxidative respiration, equilibrium favors pyruvate, but in oxidative stress, for example, hypoxia, the formation of lactate is favored. LDH is present in almost all body tissues, with a varying relative percentage of isozymes, and as such, the distribution of isozymes can be used to help diagnose specific damaged tissues. LDH levels are occasionally utilized in associated with the transaminases as indicators of hepatic damage.

Gamma-glutamyl transferase (GGT) is produced in multiple organs besides the liver and functions in the transfer of gamma-glutamyl moieties from peptides to other amino acids. The enzyme is associated with cells demonstrating high secretory or absorptive functions. GGT levels can be elevated in several disease states and is not necessarily strictly related to hepatic disease. GGT is not found in bone, and therefore may be somewhat more specific for biliary disease than ALP. Chronic alcohol use and other hepatotoxic drugs can result in elevated GGT levels, even in the absence of overt hepatotoxicity. In cases of bile duct obstruction, the GGT levels can be markedly elevated, while ALT levels remain low. In contrast, in cases of hepatitis or hepatotoxicity, ALT levels can be significantly elevated. When coupled with other data (e.g., AST and MCV), elevated GGT levels have been associated with chronic alcohol abuse.

In hepatic failure or severe hepatic injury, the multienzyme process of transformation of waste ammonia from amino acid metabolism to urea becomes compromised, and serum ammonia is correspondingly elevated. While not a component of routine metabolic panels, measurement of serum ammonia in the clinical setting is often performed as a measure of hepatic function and may be of value in the evaluation of the magnitude or severity of liver failure and hepatic encephalopathy.

The consequence of hepatic toxicity on the important synthetic functions of the liver can be demonstrated in a wide variety of compounds. Commonly, serum albumin levels can be evaluated and may provide an indication of some degree of malnutrition or depressed hepatic function. The synthesis of most coagulation factors also occurs in the liver, and coagulopathies, presenting as hemorrhage at intravascular catheter sites, cutaneous purpura, and petechiae can indicate failure or disruption of production or release of these factors (see Figure 7.5).

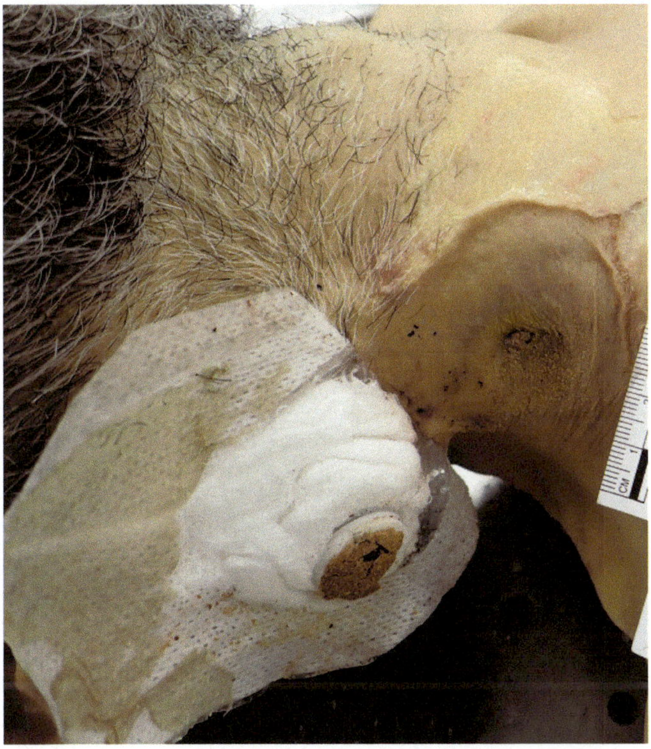

Figure 7.5 A former intravascular catheter site in a patient with hepatic failure. Note the surgical pledget and thick gauze bandage as well as the subcutaneous ecchymosis surrounding the puncture site.

Hepatotoxins

The evaluation of the liver for a toxic reaction can be complicated. Many of the acute toxins normally encountered in postmortem work can be fatal without associated gross or microscopic evidence of liver failure (e.g., opiates, sympathomimetic amines (SMAs), and neurotoxins). The liver can be transiently damaged and repaired before death from antibiotics, antihypertensive agents, or alcohol. Many of the toxins that primarily affect the liver also exhibit effects on other organs (usually the kidney), and the eventual cause of death is essentially a combined renal–hepatic failure. Most commonly, the deceased person will have some evidence of liver failure from hepatomegaly to steatosis, to fibrosis, to cirrhosis. Histologic findings are nonspecific for most toxins, often making the differential diagnosis list very long.

7.5 COMMON HEPATOTOXINS

The most common hepatotoxin is, by far, ethanol (which we discuss in Section 4: Alcohol and Related Compounds) followed by APAP and iron. While the general public has become increasingly aware of the toxic potential of APAP, people still die from the effects of APAP toxicity. The toxicity of APAP is discussed in Section 7.5.2. True acute hepatotoxin-related deaths are a relatively unusual event for the FP.

Evaluation of the clinical history of a patient with a potentially fatal liver toxicity can be extremely useful to the FP because liver failure may be evident within hours to several days of administration of some toxins (e.g., APAP). However, not all drugs affecting the liver will cause signs and symptoms this quickly. Liver damage can develop weeks after a patient starts some antibiotics and chemotherapeutics, and a direct temporal link may be difficult to establish.

Grossly, the toxic liver will usually be pale and soft. Histologically, hepatic damage can be divided into those causing predominantly zone 1 damage (e.g., iron) and those that primarily cause zone 3 damage (e.g., APAP and halothane). In the circumstances of extensive liver damage, there may be disruption of hepatic cytoarchitecture such that the zonal demarcations are no longer appreciable.

7.5.1 Iron

Iron is a key metal in the body, primarily because of its ability to easily gain or lose an electron, alternating between the +2 and +3 ionization state (ferrous and ferric, respectively). This capability is an important part of the electron transport system, which is the basis for cellular respiration, plays a role in the metabolism of many drugs and xenobiotics as a component of the cytochrome P450 (CYP450) enzymes, and is the basis of the affinity of molecular oxygen for the hemoglobin molecule. The facile oxidation and reduction also provide the basis for the toxic potential of the atom. The ability of ferrous iron to directly reduce molecular oxygen (producing superoxide radicals and resulting in the formation of other "active oxygen" species) coupled with the ready reduction of ferric iron by the such molecules at NADH or NADPH or other "redox cycling" molecules (e.g., the quinone-type metabolite of APAP (NAPQI), carbon tetrachloride, and bromobenzene). In iron overload, the amount of reactive species formed can overwhelm the ability of the cell to neutralize. The accumulation of iron, with its potential to "redox cycle" and facilitate the formation of free radical species, can accelerate the liver damage already on course by the preexisting liver pathology.

The daily requirement for iron in an adult is generally 10–20 mg and generally comes into the body as Fe^{3+} or Fe^{2+}. Elemental iron gets oxidized by the acidic environment of the stomach, to the ferric, Fe^{3+} form. Iron is absorbed by enterocytes in the small intestine, but only in the ferrous form. Ferric iron gets reduced to the ferrous form by Vitamin C ferrireductase on the surface of the enterocytes and is then transported across the cell membrane via a divalent metal cotransporter (along with H^+) into the enterocytes. Once in the enterocyte, the ferrous iron can be transported out of the cell by the protein ferroportin (Ireg-1) but is then quickly oxidized to the ferric form, which then binds to the transport protein, transferrin (free iron is not transported around the body). Ferrous iron in the enterocyte (and elsewhere in the body) can be sequestered in the storage molecule ferritin. Transferrin-bound iron is transported primarily to bone marrow (~75%) for erythropoiesis and to liver (~10%–20%) for incorporation into biomolecules, or storage (ferritin). Iron concentration in the blood is primarily controlled by hepcidin, produced by the liver, which affects cellular iron release by inhibiting ferroportin. Hepcidin also limits the absorption of iron by the lumen of the intestine. While hepcidin expression is related to plasma transferrin levels, the main control is the HFE protein. It is the mutation of the HFE protein (by the WHO nomenclature, HFE stands for *H*igh *FE*iron) that produces hereditary hemochromatosis and a consequent iron overload in tissues. In the circumstance of iron overload, the protective mechanisms of the body are overwhelmed, resulting in circulating free iron and toxic consequences.

Forensic pathologists will likely encounter decedents with iron overload in whom there is a pathologic condition causing inappropriate iron storage (e.g., hemochromatosis) or with the accidental overingestion of iron-containing tablets. In iron overload (e.g., greater than 60 mg/kg), the liver is dark brown, darker than the usual nutmeg brown. Microscopically, the hepatocytes in zone 1 (periportal) are necrotic without an associated inflammatory reaction. Iron overload at levels >120 mg/kg may be fatal. Because of the lower elimination rate of iron in pediatric patients, this cohort may be at higher risk of iron toxicity.

Iron deposition in the form of hemosiderin can be seen microscopically in a variety of conditions including iron overload, hepatitis, alcoholic liver disease, steatosis, and diabetes mellitus. Hemosiderin (a storage form of iron) is made when iron is released into circulation as red blood cells hemolyze. Iron from hemoglobin is trapped into complexes with lysosomes as hemosiderin and stored in macrophages as well as Kupffer cells. In iron overload, hemosiderin is deposited in hepatocytes, myocytes, and renal tubular cells, potentially damaging them. Iron may also be visible by the H&E stain as chunky golden brown pigment and can be further highlighted with the Prussian blue reaction showing as pale or bright blue globules. As such, iron overload may be readily diagnosed by histologic examination.

Iron is not readily eliminated from the body, and loss via GI and GU tracts amounts to only ~1 mg/day. There is no specific pathway for the natural depletion of accumulated iron from hepatocytes. Pathologic accumulation of iron can be tempered by removing some red blood cells early in the disease by phlebotomy to prevent or minimize the risk of hepatic fibrosis, cirrhosis, and liver failure. Deferoxamine is an iron-chelating agent that can be used when a patient receives an overload of iron from massive or repeated blood transfusions, or toxic ingestion, but will not reverse fibrosis that may have occurred from iron toxicity.

7.5.2 Acetaminophen

Acetaminophen (N-acetyl-para-aminophenol, paracetamolAPAP) remains one of the most widely used analgesic and antipyretic agents, readily available both as an OTC medication and in scheduled drug formulations with several different opiates (e.g., Vicodin, Lortab, and Percocet). In many cases, patients may not be aware of the potential of the drug to be dangerous in overuse. Even when patients are careful not to overuse APAP, they may accidentally administer too much because there are several medications that also contain APAP about which the patient may not be aware (e.g., Percocet). Patients with preexisting liver disease may overdose on the APAP portion of these medications before they succumb to any other effects.

APAP elicits an anti-inflammatory and antipyretic effect by inhibiting the action of the prostaglandin synthesis enzyme "cyclooxygenase" (prostaglandin endoperoxide synthase; COX). Reduced prostaglandin levels correspond with analgesic and antipyretic effects, although APAP is a less effective anti-inflammatory agent than other NSAIDS (e.g., ibuprofen and naproxen). Despite the extensive use of the drug and its relative safety, APAP can be significantly hepatotoxic whether the consequence of an acute dose or accumulation following multiple doses.

APAP is relatively rapidly eliminated by the body, with a half-life of about 2 h in most people. The parent molecule can be conjugated to form either a glucuronide or sulfate form (both inactive) or metabolized by a CYP450 enzyme (CYP2E1) to form an N-hydroxyl compound, which spontaneously dehydrates to form N-acetyl p-quinone amine (NAPQI). Both conjugated species of APAP are highly water-soluble and are readily eliminated in the urine, along with some of the unchanged parent drug; similarly, NAPQI can be conjugated with glutathione (GSH; see Figure 7.6: APAP metabolism).

NAPQI is the toxic species generated from APAP. The degree to which it is formed (generally roughly about 10% of the ingested dose) and subsequently eliminated is what determines the extent of toxicity that will be expressed. NAPQI can form covalent bonds with cellular macromolecules and can also serve as a basis for the formation of "oxygen radical species" leading to

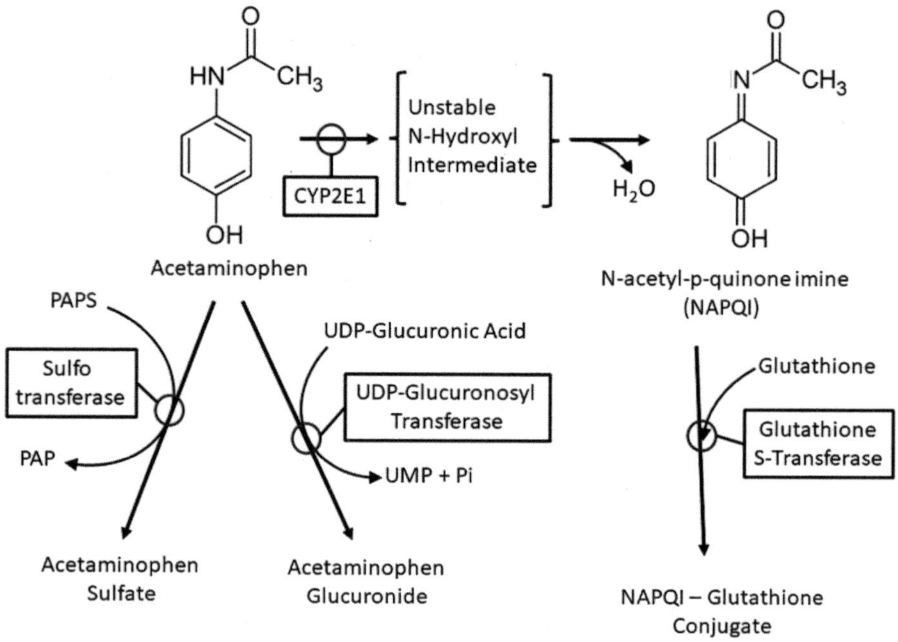

Figure 7.6 APAP metabolism. APAP in the body may be primarily eliminated unchanged in the urine, or conjugated as either a sulfate, by the actions of sulfotransferase utilizing phosphoadenosine phosphosulfate (PAPS) and APAP as cosubstrates, liberating PAP, or as a glucuronide via a UDP-glucuronosyl transferase, with uridine diphospho-glucuronic acid (UDPGA) as an activated cosubstrate and APAP as the aglycone. Uridine monophosphate and inorganic phosphate are products along with the APAP glucuronide. These processes generally account for ~90% of a dose of APAP. A small amount of the drug can be oxidized by a cytochrome P450 isozyme (CYP2E1), to an unstable hydroxylamine, which spontaneously forms the toxic N-acetyl-para-quinon amine (NAPQI). NAPQI can, in turn, be conjugated with a molecule of the tripeptide glutathione, by glutathione-S-tranferase. The ability of the body to synthesize an adequate amount of the molecule to neutralize the NAPQI formed represents the determining factor in APAP toxicity.

lipid peroxidation, membrane damage, and ultimately cellular death. The ability of the molecule to readily donate an electron to the formation of radical oxygen species and then subsequently be reduced by NADH or NADPH allowing repetition of the process is the basis for the toxic response.

The ability of the body to form and eliminate glutathione-conjugated NAPQI is the determining factor in the degree to which APAP toxicity is expressed. In the case of an overdose (e.g., actual overdose, or functional overdose reflecting existing liver damage or other metabolic compromise limiting the metabolism of an otherwise therapeutic dose), generation of NAPQI can be greater than the body's ability to form the water-soluble NAPQI--glutathione conjugate. Subsequent hepatocellular damage will occur on a dose-dependent basis, to the point of causing cellular death. The degree to which the body is able to detoxify a particular amount of NAPQI is related to the ability to synthesize glutathione (GSH), an energy-dependent process. As such, hepatocytes that are energetically limited (e.g., centrilobular (zone 3), corresponding to the lowest pO_2 levels) are most susceptible to the potential for toxic consequences in the case of an overdose. Pathologically, APAP toxicity is therefore characterized by centrilobular hepatic necrosis without an associated inflammatory reaction, reflecting the impact on the cells located furthest from the hepatic artery (see Figure 7.7a and b).

Patients suffering from APAP toxicity may not initially express symptoms beyond mild malaise. Once the liver repairs itself, symptoms resolve. However, depending on the timing and magnitude of the dose, progressively severe symptoms may be expressed as hepatic damage as organ failure proceeds, potentially leading to death in hours to days. In many cases, treatment with the

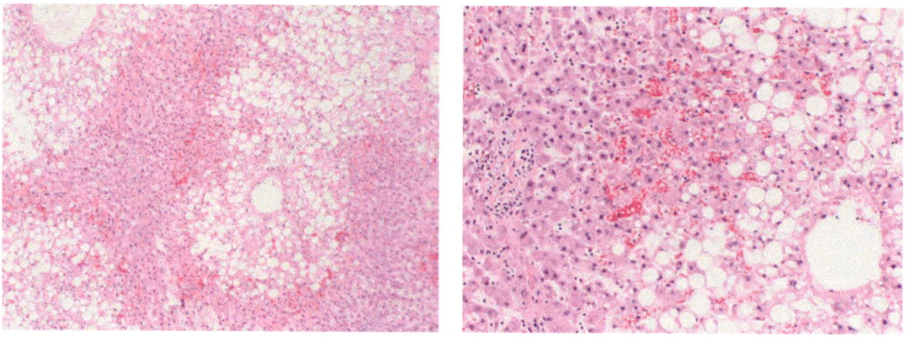

(a) (b)

Figure 7.7 Liver, H&E stain, (a) 2× and (b) 10×. Centrilobular necrosis of the liver. Centrilobular (zone 3) hepatocyte structure is collapsed, and cells in this area have lost their usual cytologic characteristics. The cell membranes are indistinct, and many hepatocyte nuclei are pale or absent with no inflammatory cell infiltrate.

glutathione analogue N-acetylcysteine can be effective, but success will depend on the degree of hepatic damage that has already occurred, and the amount of NAPQI that is generated from the underlying APAP dose. The Rumack–Matthew nomogram, relating the potential for hepatotoxicity as a function of the determined serum APAP levels versus the time elapsed since the exposure occurred, is commonly utilized clinically and in the postmortem setting to evaluate the potential for hepatotoxicity (readily available in multiple texts). An underlying assumption of the nomogram is that the ingestion was acute and does not consider any underlying liver disease or other factors (e.g., co-ingested drugs) that may have exacerbated the APAP toxicity.

Hepatic function tests that had been performed antemortem can also provide an indication of the magnitude of hepatocellular damage (e.g., AST and ALT) and may be useful for the FP in evaluating the extent to which APAP toxicity may have caused or contributed to death. Following an APAP-related death, the liver will typically be soft, enlarged, and pale. As noted above, the classic pathology is centrilobular necrosis, reflecting the death of hepatocytes around the central hepatic vein. The extent of necrosis may extend midzonal, and in cases of major overdose, prolonged survival, underlying or prior damage, drug co-ingestions, etc., bland necrosis can be present throughout the organ.

7.6 UNCOMMON HEPATOTOXINS

There are a wide variety of drugs that can cause some degree of hepatotoxicity, potentially leading to hepatocellular and cholestatic injury. However, the incidence of such toxic effects during regular therapeutic use is relatively low and well-characterized for therapeutic drugs and for various combinations thereof. Circumstances of therapy-associated hepatotoxicity would be expected to be reflected in medical records, as would the drugs utilized in any treatment regimen. Consideration of laboratory findings and clinician notes may provide insight as to the extent to which hepatotoxicity associated with therapeutics may have played a role in a particular death including cases of accidental or deliberate overdose. We recognize that there are a number of compounds capable of causing hepatic toxicity and necrosis, several examples of which are discussed here.

7.6.1 Halothane

Halothane was used as a general anesthetic in the mid to late portion of the last century (1950–1980s) much more than it is used in the United States now. However, this relatively inexpensive and fast acting anesthetic is still in use in other countries. Halothane and other halogenated anesthetic agents are known to cause a hepatitis-like illness occasionally progressing to fulminant hepatic failure. Adverse effects from halothane exposure take two forms: mild, self-limiting hepatitis that may be asymptomatic and fulminant, often fatal, hepatic necrosis. The mild form is seen in the immediate postoperative period and is self-limiting, exhibiting a transient rise in hepatic enzymes from early and brief hepatocyte injury. Patients do not develop jaundice, and serum enzyme levels return to normal within hours.

A more severe form of halothane-related hepatitis is associated with hepatotoxicity and a high mortality rate. Timing of injury is protracted as compared to the mild, subclinical picture. Patients who develop halothane hepatitis become visibly ill anywhere from 1 week to 1 month after exposure. Symptoms may develop earlier in patients who had been previously exposed. Patients become jaundiced and develop a fever from cell injury and cytokine release. They feel generally and nonspecifically unwell. Liver enzymes are tremendously elevated as hepatocyte necrosis develops and progresses.

The hepatotoxicity of halothane has been investigated as an immune-mediated reaction because the effects are often worse with repeated exposures. Halothane is metabolized by cytochrome P450 into reactive intermediate products. Some patients, having first been sensitized to halothane, develop antibodies to halothane metabolites. Being reexposed to halothane appears to cause an immune-mediated reaction. The reaction occurs in genetically susceptible patients, and its potential may be inherited. The immune response is directed against hepatocytes and Kupffer cells.

At autopsy of a patient who died from hepatic failure from halothane, the liver is enlarged, pale, and soft. Microscopically, hepatic necrosis is at first centrilobular progressing to a global pattern. The lesion resembles any other drug-mediated or infectious hepatitis with lymphocytes expanding the portal triads. The histologic picture is indistinguishable from severe viral hepatitis. The incidence of severe hepatotoxicity ranges from 1 in 6,000 to 1 in 35,000 exposures. The incidence of mild hepatitis associated with halothane is difficult to document but is most likely much more common. There is no specific postmortem laboratory test to specifically link the fulminant hepatitis to halothane exposure. The pathologist must infer the diagnosis from the medical record.

7.6.2 Mushroom Toxins

Mushrooms and other forms of fungi are utilized worldwide, and the potential for toxic species to be mistaken for edible forms is well recognized. Nevertheless, many accidental poisonings and deaths have occurred when people have mistakenly collected and eaten a toxic species. The proper identification of mushrooms in the field can be difficult, and many of the significantly toxic species can be mistaken for edible varieties. Most mushroom poisonings occur in mushroom pickers who mistake a poison-containing variety for an edible one in the field. There are a number of folklore "rules" that purport to help distinguish between toxic and nontoxic species; however, none of the rules are reliable with all species (see Sidebar 7.1: Mushroom Folklore).

Sidebar 7.1: Mushroom Folklore

There are a number of "folk truths" about poisonous mushrooms and, more specifically, how to distinguish the poisonous from the nonpoisonous ones. Some examples, in this (noncomprehensive) list, are as follows:

1. Poisonous mushrooms taste bad.
   If true, people simply wouldn't eat them. Unfortunately, it is readily reported that many of the toxic mushrooms taste good, including the examples of the potentially deadly Amanita family.
2. All and only poisonous mushrooms are brightly colored.
   While there are certainly some brightly colored mushrooms (e.g. the toxic/hallucinogenic fly agaric, etc.) some of the most toxic amanitas are just plain white or tan (e.g. the "death cap" and "destroying angel" mushrooms). Many of the mushroom poisonings that have occurred in north America are the consequence of toxic "little brown mushrooms" that resemble an edible species found commonly in Europe.
3. Insects and animals will avoid toxic mushrooms.
   The idea here, evidently, is that if there is evidence that a mushroom has been eaten by something, then that type must be safe (presumably, whatever ate the mushroom isn't already dead).
4. "Fairy ring" mushrooms are edible.
   The growth pattern of a "ring" is a characteristic of the growth of the mycelium in the soil, of which the mushroom is the fruiting body. While there are indeed edible mushrooms that grow in such a circular fashion, so can toxic species, careful (and accurate) identification based other factors would be essential.
5. Mushrooms growing in the vicinity of flowering apple trees are edible.
   Nice idea, and there certainly are edible mushrooms growing near flowering apple trees somewhere, but this is not a reliable method for species identification, and no guarantee that mushrooms around apple tress are not seriously toxic.
6. Poisonous mushrooms blacken silver.
   There is no identified chemical basis for this amongst the known mushroom toxins.
7. All mushrooms are safe if cooked/parboiled/dried/pickled/etc.
   Many fungal toxins are not heat sensitive, so, this is probably not a very reliable approach to render otherwise inedible species to be safe (e.g., alpha-amanitin, the poison produced by the death cap (Amanita phalloides) and others of the genus, is not denatured by heat.

4\. Poisonous mushrooms will turn rice red when boiled.
   Apparently, there are some species that can impart a color to rice when boiled together. However, this is patently unreliable as a means of identifying toxic species.

5\. Poisonous mushrooms have a pointed cap. Edible species have a flat, rounded cap.
   The shape of the mushroom cap does not correlate with presence or absence of mushroom toxins; this is not a reliable method to distinguish between edible and poisonous species.

Basically, there is no uniform test to distinguish between toxic and nontoxic mushrooms, which is, of course, logical based on the multiplicity of toxic compounds that may be contained in the various species of fungi. The best way to identify local edible mushrooms is to learn at the hands of an experienced botanical expert, who is able to identify both toxic and nontoxic species. (Or *"There are old mushroom hunters, and bold mushroom hunters... but there are no old, bold mushroom hunters...."*)

Over 100 species of mushrooms are known to be toxic to humans and other mammals, but only a relatively small number have the potential to be fatal. Symptoms can range from minimal and nonspecific to death from liver or kidney failure. In many cases, no symptoms appear until some significant time after ingestion, and serious organ damage has occurred.

The primary potentially fatal toxins associated with some of the deadliest species of mushrooms are contained in the genus "Amanita" (e.g., the "Death Angel," amanita; the "Death Cap," amanita phalloides; the "Panther Cap," amanita pantherine; and several related species knows as "Destroying Angels."). The characteristic toxins of the group are variations of cyclic polypeptides, known as the "amanitins." The most deadly of these is "α-amanitin," an eight-amino acid cyclic peptide with an oral LD50 estimated at 0.1 mg/kg (the equivalent of one mushroom). Most amanitins are not destroyed by heat, so cooking the mushrooms does not render them safe. Amanita toxins enter the hepatocyte via membrane transport and function by binding to, and inactivating RNA polymerase II, a key enzyme in protein de novo synthesis. The effect is an impairment of generation of overall cellular protein synthesis, in a nonspecific manner. The failure to produce necessary proteins (e.g., enzymes, receptors, and transporters can cause the death of the hepatocyte, although the process can take several days). The pattern of hepatocellular necrosis is initially centrilobular (zone 3), very similar to APAP, reflecting the ability of cells with a slightly higher oxygen availability (periportal, zone 1) to survive the metabolic stress. As the disease progresses, hepatocellular necrosis becomes global.

Symptoms of amanitin intoxication may first be manifested as a gastrointestinal upset after an asymptomatic silent period. GI symptoms include abdominal pain, nausea, vomiting, and diarrhea beginning several hours following exposure. Patients may become dehydrated as vomiting and diarrhea continue. These GI symptoms may be followed by an asymptomatic period, during which hepatic damage begins to unfold. After the initial GI upset, patients become very ill and develop jaundice. Serum hepatic enzymes are very elevated, reflecting the degree of hepatocellular necrosis. As hepatic damage worsens, serum hepatic enzyme levels continue to increase; the patient develops coagulopathy from failure to produce coagulation factors and hepatic encephalopathy with the potential for altered mental state, coma, etc. The untreated patient can progress to fatal hepatic failure with hepatic encephalopathy in about 3–10 days.

This delay between the initial expression of GI symptoms (not present in all species of mushrooms) and the eventual severe hepatic reaction can cause a delay in diagnosis. Because of the nonspecific nature and the delay of the symptoms, patients may not immediately recognize the cause-and-effect relationship between eating poisonous mushrooms and their illness. They may also not report their symptoms to friends and family who would be able to relay a story. There may not be any mushrooms left to examine. In the absence of an example of the suspected plant material coupled with identification by an expert, a causative species may not be determined. If death ensues, determination of the COD may be correspondingly difficult, as mushroom poisoning may not even be suspected. Testing for specific mushroom toxins is not regularly available either clinically or in the postmortem setting (however, HPLC-MSMS methodologies for the analysis of the amanitins are available).

Treatment of suspected mushroom poisoning is multipronged. There is neither a specific antidote nor chelating agent for the toxin. The primary approach to treatment is based on minimizing the absorption of the toxin with gastric lavage and by giving activated charcoal. This treatment is effective only early on after exposure. Once absorption is complete, activated charcoal is not effective. Correcting volume depletion, hypoglycemia, and electrolyte abnormalities are recommended at any time after exposure. Renal dialysis may be used while the patient is in renal failure, but only as an adjunct to the kidney. Amanita toxin is not effectively removed by dialysis. A liver transplant may, in many cases, be the only viable therapeutic option.

7.6.3 Abrin and Ricin

Abrin and ricin are two related plant-derived toxins. Ricin has received considerable notoriety as a potential chemical weapon and used as a homicidal poison. It can be derived from the seed of the castor bean plant or made from the "mash" left over after castor oil is processed from the castor bean. Abrin is a related toxin, but has received less awareness, although is commonly now included in screening procedures for potential chemical toxins. Abrin is contained in the seeds of the rosary pea or jequirity pea plant. The seeds are red with a small black spot and are harmless unless ingested or the powder is inhaled.

Both toxins have an extremely low LD_{50}, in the microgram/kilogram range (the equivalent volume of a few grains of table salt) and are similar two-subunit polypeptides of ~500 amino acid residues. Both compounds act in a functional manner similar to the amanitins, by effectively blocking protein synthesis at the level of the ribosome, albeit with the effect caused by inactivation of the 28s subunit of the ribosome, rather than an effect on RNA polymerase II. The consequence on protein synthesis is the same however, with similar symptoms, disease progression, and pathologic consequences. As with mushroom poisoning, depending on the circumstances of death and the availability of medical or other investigatory information, it may be extremely difficult to definitively determine the underlying source of the hepatotoxicity. As with mushroom poisoning, the absence of regular testing procedures capable of detection of the extremely low levels of toxins that may be present in postmortem samples effectively eliminates the possibility of a direct identification of the causative agent, at least from body fluids.

7.7 OTHER HEPATOTOXINS

There are a wide variety of materials with the potential for causing death via an impact primarily on the liver. The challenge for the FP is threefold: first is simply gaining a recognition or suspicion that the death may reasonably be explained as a toxicologic consequence, rather than as the expression of an acute disease process. Many GI/liver poisons can mimic "the flu" or food poisoning. Some potential disease confounders, for example, infectious hepatitis, can be identified or eliminated by clinical testing; however, such medical history may not always be available. Secondly, the identification of a reasonable possible source of toxicity, be it accidental or deliberate poisoning, coupled with a toxin source, and a possible mechanism of administration can be extremely problematic and will be limited by the amount of information available regarding the decedent and the resources that may be allocated to the task.

Finally, in many cases, the underlying causative agent will not be readily detected by routine toxicologic testing (and indeed, it may not even be detectable by specific testing procedures even if a particular compound is suspected).

Consideration of some examples may serve not so much as to provide a list for evaluation in light of a particular case, but rather as illustrations of the variety of materials that may result in hepatotoxicity that may test and challenge the desired goal of identification of an underlying cause of death.

There are a number of solvents and industrial chemicals that can produce hepatotoxicity, primarily by metabolism to radical species that may then initiate lipid peroxidation, and concomitant membrane damage, in a manner similar to APAP. Chronic exposures to such materials can be particularly problematic to identify and may not be available for detection via postmortem toxicologic testing. Compounds such as carbon tetrachloride, bromobenzene, and other halogenated aromatics and alkanes have been implicated in cases, following acute and chronic exposures. There is a multiplicity of plant-based toxins, sometimes associated with widespread commercial products that may become recognized for hepatotoxic potential. A classic example of this would be "comfrey tea" which, as containing pyrrolizidine alkaloids, has been largely taken off the commercial market but can occasionally be found in herbal preparations. There are a wide variety of fungal toxins, for example, aflatoxins, which may be present in various foodstuffs, although exposure to levels that would reasonably be associated with death would be an unusual circumstance. The potential for recognized medicinals to be hepatotoxic, for example, allopurinol and chlorpromazine, is routinely addressed during medical care, and expression of hepatotoxicity to the extent of contribution to a death would be reasonably expected to be documented in medical records, and drug levels in such cases would likely be determinable by directed toxicologic testing.

Bibliography

Bloomer S.A., Brown K.E. (2019). Iron-induced liver injury: A critical reappraisal. *International Journal of Molecular Sciences*, 20(9):2132. https://doi.org/10.3390/ijms20092132.

Fenton J.J. (2001). *Toxicology: A Case-Oriented Approach*. Boca Raton, FL: CRC Press.

Liver metabolism. In: Lieberman M., Marks A. (eds). *Mark's Basic Medical Biochemistry: A Clinical Approach* (pp. 910–929). 3rd rev. ed. Philadelphia, PA: Wolters Kluwer Health/Lippincott Williams & Wilkins, 2009.

Reichl F.X., Ritter L. (eds) (2011). *Illustrated Handbook of Toxicology*. Stuttgart: Thieme.

Rumack B.H., Matthew H. (1975). Acetaminophen poisoning and toxicity. *Pediatrics*, 55(6):871–876.

SECTION 8

NERVOUS SYSTEM TOXINS

DOI: 10.4324/9781003121060-9

8.1 INTRODUCTION

The central nervous system (CNS) can be thought of as the "switch board" and resident "super-computer" of the body; drugs, toxins, biochemical, pathologic, and physiologic changes that affect the CNS can have far-reaching effects elsewhere. The bulk of the drugs and toxins that forensic pathologists encounter and associate as causative or contributory factors in a death affect the CNS in one way or another. This section highlights some of the major drug classes that are commonly evaluated in that sense. The peripheral nervous system, which is outside the brain and the spinal cord, can also be affected by some of the drugs and toxins discussed here. As with many of the drugs and toxins discussed in this book, the compounds discussed here may impact other organ systems and could reasonably have been included in several different sections. For example, opiates act on the mu receptor located in the brain and brain stem, but mu receptors are also located in the gastrointestinal tract and elsewhere. They could have been included in the section discussing toxins that affect the entire system. Some tricyclic antidepressants (TCAs) have anti-cholinergic activity as well as sodium channel blockade. This class of drugs could have been included in the section discussing cardiac toxins, etc.

8.2 OPIOIDS AND OPIATES

Opiates and opioids represent some of the most important pharmaceutical agents currently in use, both in the medicinal realm and as abused drugs because of their analgesic capability and significant potential for addiction, overdose, and death. The potential pharmacologic benefits from medicinal uses for opiates can hardly be overstated, as this class of drugs represents some of the most effective analgesics available to the physician. Morphine itself has long been the standard to which analgesic efficacy is measured and is often expressed in terms of "morphine" or "morphine equivalent" doses. However, in addition to their widespread use as effective medicinal compounds, the ability of opioids to elicit a euphoric response in users has also been part of the basis for the spread of these drugs in various cultures and societies for thousands of years. The potent euphorigenic potential of the opiates can lead to years or even decades of addiction. It is, however, the significant capability of these drugs to elicit CNS and respiratory depression that is the basis for their significant potential for lethal overdose. Fatal drug overdoses, particularly in light of underlying pathology or an existing medical condition, can represent some of the more significant challenges that the forensic pathologist has to deal with in efforts to understand and properly ascribe cause and manner to a particular deceased person.

The nomenclature of the "Opiate Drugs" can be a source of inconsistency, if not confusion. In a functional sense, it is the ability of a drug to bind to and serve as an agonist of the opiate receptors, which characterizes a particular species as an "opiate" or "opioid," and from this perspective, the distinction is essentially semantic. Historically, the species structurally analogous to morphine and derived directly from the opium poppy (*papaver somniferum*) have been referred to as "opiates" (morphine, codeine, and thebaine primarily). Thebaine is not active in the CNS in the same manner as either morphine or codeine and is utilized primarily as a synthetic basis for a number of "semi-synthetic" opiates agonists, including hydrocodone, hydromorphone, oxycodone, naloxone, buprenorphine, and etorphine (among others), that are commonly called "opioids" rather than opiates. Endogenous biomolecules capable of providing agonist activity (e.g., endorphins and dynorphins) are often referred to as opioids or endogenous opioids. The fully synthetic opiate receptor agonists structurally unrelated to morphine (e.g., methadone, meperidine, fentanyl, analogues, etc.) are commonly distinguished as "synthetic opioids." From a practical perspective, it is however, the functional capability of a drug to act as an opiate agonist that defines membership to the class, regardless of structural similarity to morphine or descriptive nomenclature, as in the examples below:

Opium-derived: morphine, codeine, and thebaine

Semi-synthetics: heroin, ethylmorphine, hydrocodone, hydromorphone, oxycodone, and oxymorphone

Synthetics: tramadol, fentanyl, sufentanil, alfenanil, levorphanol, levomethorphan, propoxyphene, meperidine, fentanyl, acrylfentanyl, acetylfentanyl, furanuylfentanyl, and methadone

The extent to which these opiate drugs can present a potentially lethal overdose threat in either the medicinal or "recreational drug" setting is well recognized and has indeed been a constant factor in postmortem toxicology casework as the fields have developed and evolved. However, in recent years, an increased level of awareness and concern over the degree to which abuse of these drugs has penetrated multiple levels of society has resulted in the recognition of an "opiate crisis." Nevertheless, the level of commonly prescribed opiate deaths has remained relatively constant in the years since ~2007. However, during the years since, the synthetic opiate fentanyl (and several structural analogues) has increasingly become a component of illicit drug mixtures throughout the nation, with a significant corresponding rise in deaths attributed to the synthetic opioids, as shown in Figure 8.1.

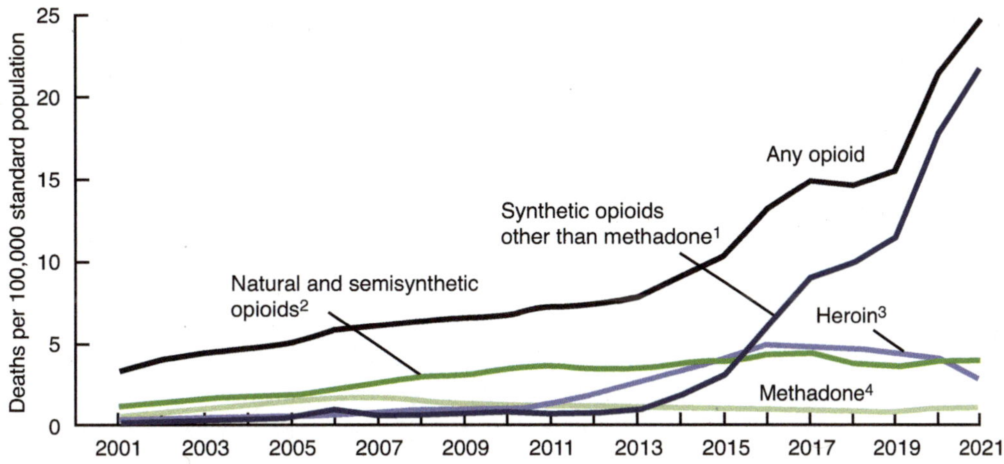

Figure 8.1 Overdose Death Rates Involving Opioids, by Type, United States, 2001–2021. http://www.cdc.gov/nchs/data/databriefs/db457-tables.pdf#4.

In recent decades, there has been an expanded use of opiates as chronic pain medications, commonly utilizing the synthetic morphine structural analogues (e.g., oxy- and hydrocodone and oxy- and hydromorphone). This increased utilization had a significant impact on the number of overdose deaths in the "over 30" age demographic, corresponding to the proliferation of medical practices and offices focused on chronic pain treatment. In many cases, methadone (a synthetic opiate with a relatively long half-life) has been the basis of a chronic pain treatment program. More recently, with the advent of patch delivery systems, morphine and fentanyl patches have begun to be employed for this purpose, with the delivery system itself functioning to effectively prolong the therapeutic levels of the drug in the body. Similarly, indwelling pump systems have been employed, providing a consistent, metered dose of drug for weeks at a time.

In recent years, the increased awareness of the potential for abuse (the "Opiate Crisis") has led to significant efforts to restrict or otherwise limit long-term opiate use for chronic pain patients, and in many states, efficient systems for documentation of prescriptions and utilization levels. Somewhat concurrently, the introduction of newer, highly effective functional analogues of morphine (e.g., fentanyl and related drugs) appearing in and largely supplanting heroin in illicit supplies of that drug has exacerbated the spread of illicit drug use, with a similar impact on the magnitude of "opiate"-related drug deaths. In many cases, opiates from both licit and illicit sources may be present in the same decedent. The effects of opiates are additive, and hence, the total opiate dose that a decedent will have experienced just prior to death can reflect both therapeutic and abused drugs, as well as any analgesic medications the patient may have received during emergency treatment, e.g., fentanyl. The potential for lethality consequential to opiate overdose had made this group of drugs arguably the most significant to the forensic pathologist and toxicologist, regardless of the underlying reason for the drugs to be present. The actual mechanisms by which the opiates are able to elicit their desired pharmacologic effect, pronounced and effective analgesia, as well as the concomitant effects of overdose, being respiratory, CNS, and cardiac depression, are quite well understood, and indeed, with the exception of newly appearing fentanyl (or other opiate) analogues, the therapeutic, toxic, and potentially fatal ranges for the opiates are reasonably well known. In many cases, the circumstances and subsequent designation of the nature of the death are relatively straightforward, as in some cases of IV drug abuse or clearly documented circumstances of opiate overdose, particularly when coupled with relatively unambiguous autopsy and toxicology findings. However, oftentimes, such a clear resolution of a case may be impossible, with potential complicating factors ranging from the potential for the patient to have acquired a tolerance for opiates, complicated underlying medical conditions, the potential contribution of other non-opiate

CNS depressants, to questions regarding the validity of the interpretation of toxicologic findings (opiates are subject to postmortem redistribution). Such cases can be further complicated by the patient's departures from prescription regimens drug-seeking behavior leading to the presence of multiple opiates (or alternate medications) in such illicit forms as heroin and black market fentanyl, oxycodone, or other species.

The importation of illicit fentanyl and analogues, coupled with some degree of in-country synthesis, has taken on significant proportions in the past several years, representing an analytical challenge for many toxicology laboratories. Initially, fentanyl was occasionally used to amend heroin, but that practice has extended to the point of nearly all "street heroin" containing some amount of fentanyl or analogue thereof, primarily as a way of "stretching" or diluting the relatively more expensive heroin, with cheaper materials. Maintaining an analytical capability for new analogue species in terms of validated methods has been a challenge for forensic laboratories. Historically, opiate-related deaths were readily linked to a relatively few opiates, semi-synthetics, and synthetic analogues, primarily heroin, morphine, hydro- and oxycodone, hydro- and oxymorphone, propoxyphene, meperidine, and tramadol, all of which were relatively similar in toxic potency. However, fentanyl and related analogues are generally significantly more potent on a molar basis than their morphine-like functional analogues, resulting in an analytical challenge in terms of the relatively low levels of drug necessary to be determined to provide the FP with an understanding of opiate levels present at the time of death and also in terms of identifying new species being introduced into the illicit market (e.g., carfentanil, sufentanil, etc.).

An additional complication with which FPs must contend is that many of the fentanyl analogues (and fentanyl itself) can be fatal before the classic signs of an opiate overdose are evident at autopsy. This "rapid death" is more likely from fentanyl or a fentanyl analogue than it is with many of the morphine analogues. In such cases, there may not be an adequately long period for the characteristic pathologic findings to develop (e.g., pulmonary and cerebral edema, urinary retention, etc.). Naturally, people who are using these drugs outside the medical setting may do so in unpredictable ways: direct intravenous injection of an unknown concentration and amount, insufflation, ingestion of drugs meant for transdermal use, and other inappropriate uses of transdermal preparations. Often, but not always, there is considerable information regarding the nature of the drugs that were found at the death scene. Evidence of packaging, paraphernalia, prescription bottles, etc., can be very helpful to the FP. As a function of all the variables that may impact the final decisions of the FP, a diagnosis of an opioid overdose, particularly if combined with other potentially CNS-depressant agents, can be challenging.

The use of the opioid Narcan® (generic name, naloxone) as an antidote for opiate toxicity is well known, with the drug being widely available and commonly utilized as first-line treatment in a suspected overdose scenario. The ability of the drug to block opiate effects (receptor antagonist) is based on its structural similarity to morphine, and its ability to compete with active opiates for receptor binding sites. However, while able to bind and thereby preclude the activation of the receptor by an active opiate species, naloxone is unable to functionally activate the receptor, and so binding of this compound does not result in the normal cellular response. To the extent that naloxone is present and is able to compete for binding sites with such opiates as may be present, the binding of those opiates will be limited, and correspondingly, the physiological response will also be attenuated. The onset of action of naloxone is in the range of minutes. The rapidity of the recovery from essentially a comatose state to relatively normal respirations and CNS function can be quite remarkable, depending on the underlying amount of opiate administered and the amount of competing naloxone that has been provided. Conversely, depending on the degree to which a patient is suffering from opiate-induced respiratory depression, acidosis, hypoxia, and bradycardia, naloxone treatment can be "too little too late" for some patients. While the presence of naloxone in PM samples may indicate that upon arrival of medical personnel to treat a patient presumed to be experiencing an opiate overdose, naloxone may be used despite no real expectation that there will be any effect. With the increasing availability of naloxone doses to the general public without medical training, the reliability of an inference regarding the appropriateness of use becomes somewhat questionable. The reversal of opioid toxicity by receptor antagonists such as naloxone could be considered diagnostic of an opioid overdose; however, the converse is not true. If a person does not respond to naloxone, an opioid overdose cannot be excluded. Some opioids have a much stronger affinity for receptors than naloxone, requiring a larger antagonistic concentration, and in some cases, the time-since-administration of the offending drug may have been long enough to cause irreversible anoxic brain injury. In cases of co-ingestion with another CNS-depressant drug, reversal of the opiate effects alone may not be adequate to overcome the overall effects of the combined overdose.

An additional potentially complicating factor that may play into opiate overdose fatalities is the relatively short half-life of naloxone relative to many of the active opiates for which the drug is being administered. While most emergency medical personnel are aware of the implications of an antidote being shorter-lived in the body than the underlying toxin, there are nevertheless cases wherein an apparent recovery from an opiate overdose has been achieved in a patient by using naloxone, who thereafter leaves treatment (occasionally against medical advice). The more rapid loss of the antidote due to metabolism allows the underlying levels of opiate to cause a re-development of toxic effects that may become fatal. While often administered in cases of drug overdose with the expectation that the underlying causative agent is an opiate, there are many other drugs capable of producing "overdose" symptoms reminiscent of opiates, and while not detrimental in any way, naloxone administration will not have any positive effect in such patients.

Interestingly, opiates themselves have been extensively utilized in the treatment of opiate addiction, with the goal of such programs being to provide adequate agonist receptor activity so as to avoid withdrawal symptoms but not enough so as to induce either euphoria or CNS-depressant effects. For several decades, the synthetic agonist methadone was the opiate of choice for this purpose. With a long half-life, daily methadone treatments could provide steady-state levels in treated patients at levels that effectively eliminated symptoms of craving and withdrawal yet produced neither the characteristic CNS depression nor euphoria. Methadone treatment centers, either as stand-alone facilities or associated with hospitals, became one of the primary mechanisms by which opiate abuse was addressed. Such medication-assisted therapy has been proven to be very useful in combination with other forms of addiction treatment and can ameliorate the side effects of heroin withdrawal. Methadone treatment can also be utilized in situations of neonatal abstinence syndrome. Current addiction therapies now include other drugs (e.g., buprenorphine), which, while also acting as opiates, are not as effective as morphine and can also allow for control of cravings and withdrawal symptoms.

8.2.1 Physiological Effects

All of the functional opiates work by binding to specific opiate receptors, which are primarily metabotropic G-coupled protein receptors, of which three (mu, kappa, and delta) are of primary significance in the body. Opiate receptors are found throughout the nervous system, both central and peripheral, with the majority in the brain stem and the cerebral cortex. Opiate effects are additive, in the sense that the CNS and respiratory depression caused by one species will be exacerbated by a co-ingestion with another opioid. Similarly, another drug that causes CNS depression will be essentially additive to the opiate effects, although the other CNS depressants (e.g., barbiturates, benzodiazepines, and "non-opiate sedative/hypnotics") are not as effective at inducing respiratory depression as the opiates.

G-coupled protein receptors are transmembrane receptors with three basic units: an extracellular portion that binds the ligand, an intracellular portion that sends a chemical signal to a guanine nucleotide-binding protein inside the cell, and a portion that joins the two. Opiate receptor ligands, either endogenous opioids such as endorphins or exogenous opioid molecules, bind to the protein loops of the opiate receptor, which extend outside the actual cell membrane. As a consequence of the conformational changes induced in the receptor by the ligand-binding process, G-coupled proteins activate intracellular molecular actions, resulting in various biochemical reactions leading to specific physiological consequences. Functionally, the opiate receptors inhibit presynaptic inhibitory neurons by limiting calcium influx (thereby limiting inhibitory neurotransmitter release) and facilitating potassium efflux (thereby contributing to hyperpolarization).

8.2.1.1 Analgesia

The analgesic effect of the opiates is primarily a function of the agonism of mu receptors. Ligand binding to opiate receptors causes the inhibition of voltage-gated calcium channels on the afferent pre-synaptic nociceptive neuron, along with concomitant activation of inwardly rectifying potassium channels. The net effect of these changes is to diminish the magnitude of neurotransmitter vesicle phosphorylation as a signal for neurotransmitter release, along with a hyperpolarization of the pre-synaptic neuronal membrane, further limiting the potential for signal propagation. The diminished ability to transmit "substance P" (a pain signal neurotransmitter) and glutamate (an excitatory neurotransmitter) are the primary bases for the analgesic effect of the opiates.

8.2.1.2 Euphoria

The euphorigenic effect of the opiates does not seem to be related to toxicity in any manner and primarily impacts the dopaminergic or "pleasure/reward" system of the brain, as a result of the agonism of opiate receptors. As one might expect, there have been significant efforts to find, design, or otherwise identify drugs that might emphasize one aspect of the opiate effect, e.g., analgesia, and minimize the potential for euphoria presumably then, for addiction. No such pure analgesic has yet been discovered.

8.2.1.3 CNS Depression

Opiates function as overall CNS depressants in the brain by the inhibition of neurotransmission as a function of G-coupled protein agonism. Although, from a postmortem perspective, one cannot view this response to the drugs entirely in isolation without considering the contribution of respiratory depression and decreased tissue oxygenation. The actual toxic mechanism of opiates, being combined cardiac/respiratory failure, could easily be considered a consequence of CNS depression, directly impacting essential life processes.

8.2.1.4 Respiratory Depression

As part of the overall CNS depression, opiates cause significant respiratory depression as well, primarily as a function of mu receptors located in the brain stem. As a consequence of this respiratory depression, CO_2 levels in the blood rise, lowering pH by the formation of carbonic acid. In addition, opiates reduce the sensitivity of respiratory neurons to CO_2, thereby facilitating the downward spiral of depressed respiration, hypoxia, respiratory acidosis, and the associated biochemical stress that can ultimately lead to death.

8.2.1.5 Cardiovascular Effects

Overdoses of opiates produce bradycardia, a negative inotropic effect, and hypotension, which, in combination with respiratory depression and the resulting acidosis, become the basis for an opiate-mediated death. The process is not necessarily very quick, and in a hospital setting, the pattern of depressed respiration and other clinical signs of opiate overdose may actually be clearly documented in the medical record.

8.2.1.6 Miosis

Opiate agonists cause a contraction of the iris, producing "pinpoint" pupils or miosis as a consequence of the partial parasympathetic agonism caused by opiates. Miosis is considered a characteristic symptom of opiate overdose and has been used historically as proof of morphine poisoning.

However, miosis is not permanent, and the muscles of the iris eventually relax. As such, while the presence of miosis might well be corroborative of an opiate overdose in a living patient, the absence thereof should not be construed as necessarily suggestive that there was not. Pupils may not remain constricted in a deceased person. It should be noted that miosis is also a characteristic of the cholinergic toxidrome, although the remaining symptomology is, of course, quite distinct.

8.2.1.7 Intestinal Motility/Urinary Retention

Agonism of opioid receptors located in the intestines can slow peristalsis, reduce intestinal motility, and result in constipation. The reduced motility causes delayed transit time, allowing more opportunity for water resorption and allowing the stool to become more solid. Action on the intestinal mu receptors alleviates pain and spasm of the intestines that can be associated with diarrheal diseases. Opiates can, therefore, be effective in the management of diarrhea in patients with chronic intestinal problems such as Crohn's disease and irritable bowel syndrome. At autopsy, the contents of the distal colon of either chronic opioid patients or overdose victims will occasionally be composed of small nuggets of very firm stool. Very rarely, the cause of death of an opioid-tolerant patient is bowel obstruction with ensuing rupture, peritonitis, and sepsis. Loperamide, a synthetic non-lipophilic opiate agonist that is inactive in the CNS because it is not effectively transported across the blood–brain barrier, is commonly used for this purpose.

While used at therapeutic levels, loperamide poses little to no risk of harmful effects. However, when abused, especially at high doses, loperamide can cause fatal cardiac arrythmias because of its effect on potassium and sodium channels. In the clinical setting, the patient may have EKG abnormalities, including widened QRS complex, prolonged QT interval, and/or ventricular dysrhythmias, including torsades de pointes. If the patient was not assessed and treated by a medical professional but dies "on the street," the pathologist will not have any physical clues at autopsy to guide the diagnosis and will need to rely on the investigative information and toxicology findings. In a similar fashion, the effect of opioids on receptors located on the wall and the neck of the urinary bladder can result in urinary retention, particularly in cases of chronic opiate abuse.

8.2.1.8 Cough Suppression

The anti-tussive potential of opiates has long been recognized. Codeine is particularly effective for this purpose and has less euphorigenic potential than morphine and related species. Codeine is metabolized to morphine in the body and is a mu opioid receptor agonist.

8.2.2 Pharmacology and Pharmacokinetics

Opioid elimination is similar to many other drugs in that the primary route of elimination is via the kidney, although there is a degree of biliary excretion as well. Patients developing or with pre-existing renal insufficiency or renal failure may develop some degree of elevated opioid levels and potential toxicity, even with a previously tolerated therapeutic regimen.

In a manner similar to other drugs, some opiate species are subject to the formation of glucuronide conjugates in the liver. These species (e.g., morphine-3- and morphine-6-glucuronide) are large enough to be transported into the bile and then transit into the gastrointestinal tract, where they are eventually eliminated in feces. Bile can be used for screening purposes, although there is currently no defined bile:blood ratio upon which to draw conclusions about the concentration of the drug in blood at the time of death, and the practice is uncommon. Intestinal microflora can hydrolyze the glucuronide bond to some extent, releasing the glucuronic acid as an energy source and the opiate aglycone, which can then be resorbed and re-enter the circulation. This "enterohepatic circulation" can significantly increase the blood level of drugs and may, in some cases, partly explain why a patient exhibits a larger than expected blood level for the prescribed dose.

Heroin (diacetyl morphine) is unique among the opiates with regard to the rapidity with which it is metabolized, first to the mono-acetylated intermediate "6-monoacetylmorphine (6-MAM)" and subsequently to morphine. The half-lives for heroin and 6-MAM in the blood are quite short, being ~5 and ~15 min., respectively, so that in many cases of lethal overdose, heroin itself may be undetected in PM blood samples. 6-MAM is, in such cases, often detectable in the blood, urine, and vitreous fluid. In patients for whom there has been a significant survival time (e.g., hours) following an acute heroin overdose, the parent drug (and often, the intermediate 6-MAM) will not be detectable in blood samples, particularly if there has been a relatively long survival time, but may be detectable in urine. (Demonstration of 6-MAM in urine and/or vitreous is confirmatory of heroin use or exposure since morphine is not acetylated *in vivo* in humans.) This circumstance can complicate determinations regarding the nature of the death and can become an issue in subsequent legal proceedings. With the increasing utilization of triple-quadrupole MS technologies, with lower limits of detection, the ability to determine the presence of 6-MAM is enhanced, allowing the recognition that heroin was the underlying source of the morphine determined to have been present in the patient. While blood is the "go to" sample for nearly all toxicologic analyses, in cases of opiate overdose with suspected heroin, vitreous samples can be of particular value since in the minutes following exposure, a sufficient amount of 6-MAM (and occasionally heroin itself) can be accumulated in the protected space of the vitreous fluid, and therefore remain unhydrolyzed and detectable in postmortem analysis.

8.2.3 Toxicologic Considerations

The actual analysis of opiates as well as the newer synthetic functional analogues is quite reliably accurate, at least in the sense of providing reliable identification and good quantitative values for the specific analytes present in biological materials. With the increasing utilization of triple-quadrupole mass spectrometry techniques, even compounds present at very low levels (e.g., fentanyl analogues) can be reliably quantitated. The issue, as always with postmortem samples, is the degree to which the levels in a particular case can be relied upon to accurately reflect drug levels at the time of death. Current practice commonly utilizes peripheral blood samples for postmortem analytical purposes (meaning outside the central cavities, generally femoral blood, when available). Such samples are generally free from significant artifactual elevation of drug levels due to postmortem redistribution, although there can be some degree of compromise from that process in some circumstances, and postmortem drug levels, even when derived from a peripheral source, should not necessarily be assumed to be accurate, particularly if in conflict with other evidence, e.g., observational or parametric data.

A second consideration regarding toxicologic data is the presumption in many cases that the metabolic products of pharmaceutical agents are themselves innocuous and would not contribute to toxicity. While the potential physiological impact and contribution of some metabolic species is well recognized (e.g., nordiazepam, oxazepam, and temazepam as active metabolites from diazepam), the opiate metabolites tend to be inactive, albeit with the notable exception of morphine-3-glucuronide (M3G). Despite the sizable glucuronic acyl residue, M3G is still able to function as a morphine receptor agonist. As noted above, FP's dealing with heroin/opiate abuse-related fatalities will commonly utilize the rapid and "one-way" metabolism of heroin to 6-MAM and subsequently to morphine itself as a means of differentiation of morphine v. heroin abuse, with the presence of 6-MAM in blood, vitreous, or urine as a diagnostic of heroin use. Another potential confounder is the metabolism of codeine to morphine, which, albeit a rather slow process, can result in detectable levels of morphine in some cases, even after the more rapidly metabolized codeine has disappeared.

Morphine levels (and indeed many drug results) are reported as "free" or "total," and in some cases both, with total values representing the amount of parent drug determined to be present after the hydrolytic or enzymatic liberation from any phase two conjugation (e.g., glycosylation). This information can be particularly useful both in determination as to the potential contribution of an active metabolite (e.g., M3G) and in providing information regarding the length of time a particular analyte has been in the body. The presence of a metabolite at a concentration significantly lower than the parent drug in the suspected circumstance of a single ingestion (e.g., fentanyl and norfentanyl of 4.8 and 2.6 ng/mL, femoral draw) would suggest quite recent ingestion, probably well less than a single half-life of the drug, 3–12 h. Such information with regard to time of use (relative to the death) may be of significant value to the FP attempting to ascribe COD and MOD and might reasonably suggest, even prior to consideration of other factors, an adequate basis for concluding a fentanyl-related overdose. In contrast, the presence of 12.7 ng/mL norfentanyl with that same 4.8 ng/mL fentanyl might suggest, particularly if circumstances were indicative of a single exposure/use event, that the decedent had actually survived the maximal blood level of fentanyl. Further, the ratio between the parent drug and metabolite would be consistent with a time roughly two half-lives past the maximal blood level (and presumably maximal effects of the drug), making the association of the drug with a frank overdose at least a little less straightforward.

Other "opiates" that may be present in postmortem samples and reported in the toxicologic results are naloxone (tradename Narcan®) and, not uncommonly, codeine. Naloxone is widely used and increasingly readily available as an opiate overdose antidote. As a response to the opiate crisis, supplies of Narcan® have been made readily available in many organizations dealing with opiate addiction and are routinely provided directly to both abusers, non-abusing chronic opiate patients, and their families, as well as support structures thereof. Codeine, while much less effective as an analgesic and euphorigenic than morphine, is effective as an antitussive, although with the current level of concern about opiates in general, it is somewhat less utilized for that purpose than it has been in the past. Interestingly, codeine, as the "-3-methoxy" analogue of morphine, is metabolized into morphine, and the half-life of morphine is longer than that of codeine. As such, PM toxicology results may show trace levels of morphine as a result of codeine (only) use and may be somewhat misleading as to the actual source of the drug.

Cases of suspected opiate overdoses, in which the only drug or drug groups present are opiates, certainly present the potential for relatively straightforward interpretation of postmortem drug levels relative to the death. These cases may often be quickly resolved based on confirmation of the drugs present and the concentrations thereof following toxicologic analysis. With the assumption that those PM drug levels provide a relatively accurate reflection of levels at the time of death (as suggested at multiple locations throughout this book, an assumption that should not necessarily be casually or lightly accepted), a quick determination regarding the implication of specific drug levels can be made. There are multiple sources of tabulated ranges for routine therapeutic, toxic, and potentially fatal ranges, and tabulations of case reports collected as drug-specific monographs are commonly relied upon by both FP and toxicologists. Further, different opiate species can readily be correlated in terms of "morphine equivalents" and combined drug ingestions evaluated from that perspective. However, perhaps to a degree unique to opiates, the combination of the potential for tolerance, genetic factors affecting the degree of expression of opiate receptors, and analytical issues (e.g., PMR), a degree of caution regarding the use of such tables may well be in the best interest of the FP.

As noted above, the primary toxic impact of opiates on the body is the combination of CNS and respiratory depression, leading to respiratory acidosis, hypoxia, and ultimately, cardiac failure. Death can occur within a relatively short time period with the rapidly acting synthetics (e.g., fentanyl) or for as long as a couple of hours with morphine or its structural analogues. However, the ability of a respiratory depressant drug to produce significant injury to the brain as a function of hypoxia that is not quickly fatal, or in circumstances where medical intervention has been at least partially successful, can lead to a prolonged period of survival following the actual toxic insult or event. In such cases, depending on the time intervals involved, postmortem toxicologic results may reflect immediate and ongoing therapeutic measures but may not provide any indication of the underlying causative drug. It is standard practice in many offices to request that the hospital reserve and then subsequently acquire samples collected at the time of admission for potential toxicologic analysis in the case of a suspected overdose-related death. The toxicologist or FP will then decide which of the available samples is most appropriate for analysis.

Tolerance to opiates is well recognized as a potentially complicating factor in the interpretation of PM toxicologic values. Tolerance is medically defined as the diminished effects of a drug with increasing use (reduction in the potency of the drug) as well as the need by the patient for an increased level of drug to elicit the same physiological effect as having had a lower dose in the past. The degree to which a particular individual may have acquired and maintained some degree of tolerance to opiates should be borne in mind when considering PM toxicology levels. Tolerance to opioids develops when the total number of cell membrane receptors available to be activated is reduced in response to chronic exposure to opioids. Down-regulation causes a higher concentration of the drug to be needed to attain the same degree of receptor occupation and subsequent intracellular signaling. Receptors that are moved from the cell membrane to the cytoplasm by endocytosis may either become degraded there or return to the cell membrane at a future time. As many practitioners are certainly aware, there can be marked differences in the degree to which individuals respond to opiate exposures based on such tolerance. Simply put, the dose or blood level of an opiate that may be significantly toxic, even fatal, in one naïve individual may be tolerated without any toxic effect in an individual tolerant to that drug.

Related to the above, particularly when considering dosing regimens, is the degree to which the metabolism of a drug may increase over time. While this phenomenon is not "tolerance" in the sense of affecting the magnitude of response to a particular drug level, the induction of metabolic enzymes can increase the dose of drug required to achieve and maintain a particular therapeutic range. As an example, oxycodone is metabolized by two separate Cytochrome P450 enzymes, CYP3A4 and CYP2D6, both of which are "inducible" with the potential to impact the half-life and area under the curve (AUC) for the drug, and in a practical sense, the blood levels achieved following a particular dose. A further complication is the degree of expression of opiate receptors in an individual, driven by genetic factors. Thus, in an "induced tolerant" individual, the level of a particular opiate required to maintain a particular therapeutic level may be significantly higher than in a physically similar, non-induced naïve patient. Correspondingly, the potentially toxic or lethal level of opiates would differ markedly between two such individuals.

The use of PM blood levels as the basis for calculations of estimates of antemortem values is not uncommonly done but is also commonly subjected to (in many cases, well-deserved) criticism and challenge. With the current emphasis and focus on opiate abuse/overdose and the extensive litigation associated with cases (both criminal and civil), there can be significant interest in calculations regarding dose and time. Historically, "back-extrapolation" from a postmortem value to an antemortem level at a particular time has been done using the kinetic calculations commonly utilized in clinical toxicology. Clearly, in these cases, the *critically important* assumption that the postmortem values actually provide a reasonably accurate reflection of drug levels at the time of death should be well-considered and justified prior to calculation using such values. A key value of the process is the rate coefficient k, related to the half-life of the drug and therefore an individual variable, and variations from literature or otherwise tabulated values represent a potential source of considerable uncertainty. However, because of the nature of the exponentially based rate process, the uncertainty of a first-order back extrapolation process can be quite substantial, and inferences (meaning back-extrapolation to points prior to the time of death) from such processes may not be as reliable as the simple calculated values might suggest, particularly if presented without appropriate confidence intervals. Because of the potential for significant uncertainty, forensic toxicologists in general tend to be reluctant in making such calculations. When performed, however, it is important that the underlying assumptions and all the uncertainties contributing to the process be communicated to the end user, medical or legal, such that the potential for any erroneous conclusion to be reached can be minimized.

One of the more commonly utilized equations in clinical toxicology (and occasionally misused in forensic toxicology…) is the "Volume of Distribution" calculation. This equation relates the amount of a specific drug ingestion to the resulting maximal blood value (based on a single-compartment model). Clinically, the equation can be applied to estimating the amount of drug required in a particular patient to achieve a desired blood level. In the forensic arena, the concept is commonly utilized in the determination of the number of "standard drinks" an individual must have consumed to have achieved a particular blood alcohol concentration. The equation can be applied in a postmortem scenario to provide an estimate of the amount of drug an individual must have administered to have achieved the drug levels determined in PM samples. While such information could of course prove potentially valuable, the process can suffer from considerable uncertainty, and similarly, exponentially based back-extrapolation is approached with considerable reluctance by most toxicologists. As is often the case, there will be cases in which such calculations can be useful, and because of the validity of the underlying assumptions, they may have inherently reasonable levels of uncertainty. In contrast, there are many examples where the equation has been applied inappropriately, leading to clearly erroneous conclusions. The failure to appropriately account for and communicate the uncertainties associated with the process (or indeed, that in some circumstances, the calculation would be inappropriate at all) has led some professional organizations to suggest that any such calculation should not be performed or considered. It is our view that a calculation process of such clear value to the practice of clinical toxicology can, in some carefully considered circumstances, be of use and value to the interpretation of postmortem casework. However, the use of the calculations should be performed in such a manner that the uncertainty (or even the validity) of underlying assumptions is critically considered and carefully accounted for in any conclusion drawn.

One basic assumption of the Volume of Distribution equation is that the relationship between the amount administered and subsequent blood level reflects a single dose exposure in a naïve patient. As such, application of the equation to a chronic dose regimen or even a multiple-dose event would not be expected to be valid. A second potential for significant variability lies in the tabulated value for Vd. Values are derived from anecdotal reports, and therefore may, in many cases, be of such a large range as to make any application to a particular case meaningless. Finally, and perhaps one of the largest issues with any utilization of the Vd, is the potential issue in the validity of the actual PM value itself, with the possibility of analytical uncertainty (usually <20%) combined with the potential for (albeit accurately determined PM values) to have been artifactually elevated by PMR.

There can be a significant difference between the manner in which toxicologists consider drugs determined in a PM case as compared to the view of the FP. Specifically, the FP is charged with identifying and indicating as "contributing" all drugs that would have added to the overall physiological effect leading to the death. As such, the cause of death of a person with, for example, PM femoral blood values of 453 ng/mL of oxycodone and 85 ng/mL of lorazepam might reasonably be listed as "combined effects of" both drugs, in that the CNS-depressant activity/effect of lorazepam would be expected to have exacerbated, to some extent, the corresponding effects of the opiate. However, from a toxicologic "but for" perspective, the view might well be that the oxycodone, in the absence of the lorazepam, would have provided an adequate explanation for the death, but the lorazepam, in the absence of the oxycodone, would not. Neither view is wrong; one focuses on the identification of all contributing factors, and the other, in contrast, is directed at identifying a key toxic element. Unfortunately, the appearance of an apparent inconsistency between the two approaches is often misconstrued as disagreement in legal settings.

As noted in the oxycodone-lorazepam example discussed above, there is considerable potential in opiate-related cases for the presence of multiple drugs, and, notwithstanding the interest in identification of contributory causative agents, the challenge in many cases can revolve around recognition of what drug or drugs were actually responsible for the death. While there are a multiplicity of drugs that result in some degree of CNS depression, the association of significant respiratory depression, in addition to CNS depression, is the underlying basis for the toxicity of the opiates as a group. For CNS depressants that do not generate that magnitude of respiratory depression, the potential for lethality in overdose is correspondingly lessened. Similarly, then, considerations of the contributory role non-opiate CNS-depressant agents may have played in a death should take into careful consideration the potentially lower degree of respiratory depression that may be attributable to the drug.

Deaths in hospice care are often accompanied by extensive medical history and documentation and are not commonly considered ME cases. If, however, the patient was involved in an accident or was the victim of an injury whose result would contribute to the cause of death, at least to some degree, the decedent may come into ME jurisdiction. Patients in hospice care are regularly treated with what might normally be considered high doses of opiates, and postmortem levels can be quite high as a consequence of well-established tolerance, a desire on the part of caregivers to provide an adequate level of opiates to alleviate pain, and hepato-renal failure in the final hours of life negatively impacting the ability of the body to metabolize and eliminate morphine and related analgesic species. In some offices, quantitative opiate results are not reported in hospice cases out of concern for misinterpretation, while otherwise such results are understood to represent simply the standard practice in the field of providing adequate analgesic medications for individuals in the final hours of their lives. Clearly, great care should be given to any consideration of opiate concentrations in a deceased person who has been under hospice care.

8.2.4 Pathologic Considerations

Opioid toxicity is characterized by a triad of symptoms consequential to CNS depression at the level of the brain stem. As respiration slows, cardiac output slows, and both pulmonary and cerebral edema begin to develop. Classic autopsy findings in an opiate overdose fatality include pulmonary edema characterized by white or pink-tinged white foam from the nose and mouth (see Figure 8.2), along the tracheobronchial tree (see Figure 8.3), and from the cut sections of the lung parenchyma. The brain can be swollen with flattened gyri and narrow sulci. The ventricular system is very narrow or obliterated. The gray matter will often have a violet hue rather than the typical tan-gray color (see Figure 8.4a and b). A third characteristic of an opiate-related death is urinary retention, with a very full bladder potentially observable at autopsy (see Figure 8.5). There may also be firm stool in the colon due to prolonged or chronic opioid administration. In the case of a death from a rapidly acting opiate, e.g., fentanyl and related analogues, this triad of symptoms may not be as clearly expressed as in the case of a prolonged (e.g., >60 min) process characteristic of morphine and related compounds. Miosis occurs during life and is a well-recognized characteristic

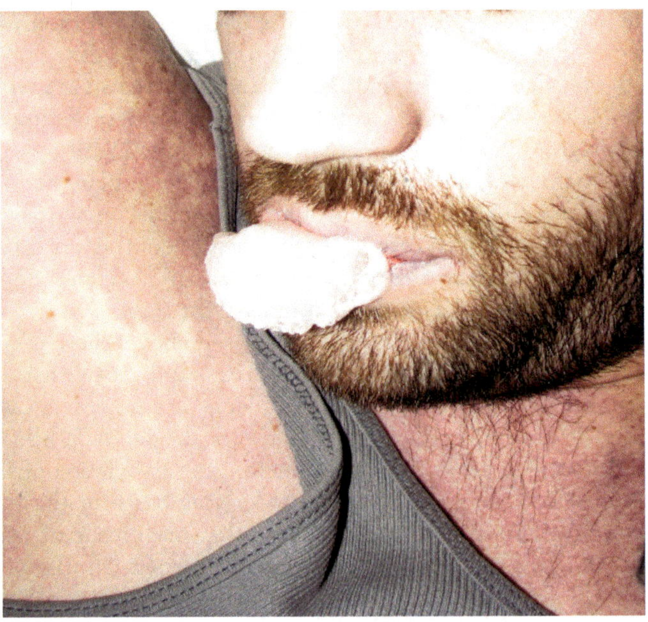

Figure 8.2 The white foam of pulmonary edema from a man who died from heroin administration.

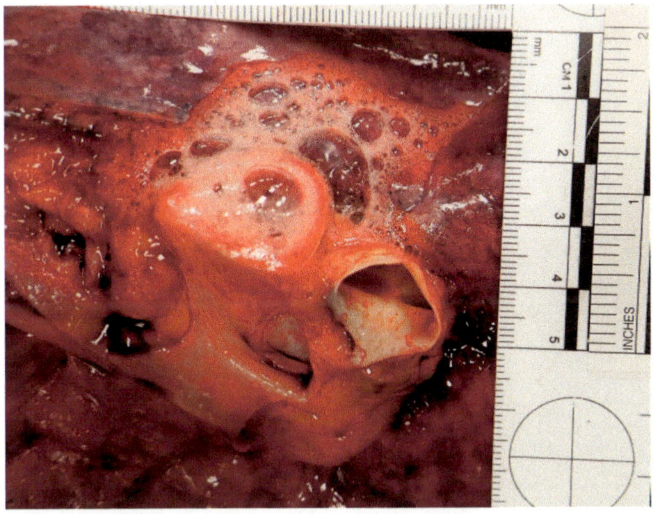

Figure 8.3 The hilum of the right lung from the man in Figure 8.2. The white foam continued to exude during autopsy. Lungs were 2,380 g combined.

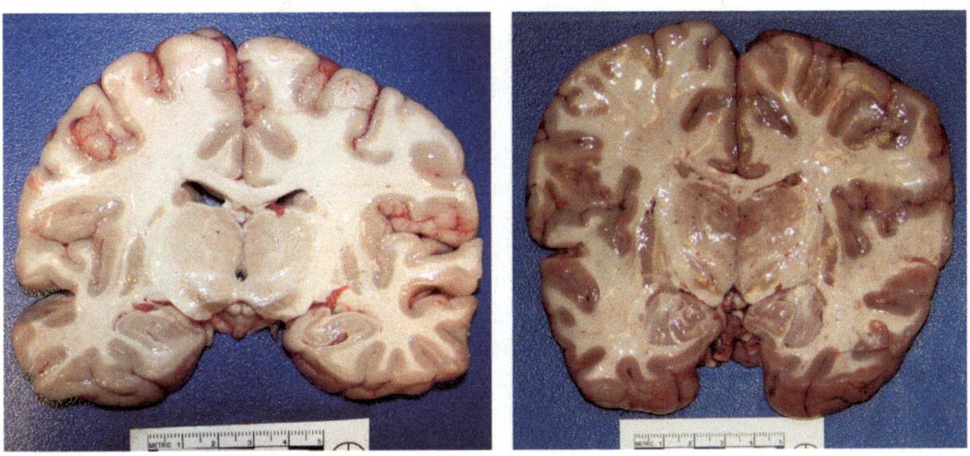

(a) (b)

Figure 8.4 (a).Normal brain; in this case, coronal sections of a person who died rapidly from trauma. (b). Edematous brain from the man in Figure 8.2. Note the violet tinge to the gray matter as well as the cerebral edema. The gyri are flattened, and the sulci are narrowed. The ventricular system is compressed.

of opiate effects on living patients, but the pupillary size in a deceased person can be variable. Dilated pupils in a deceased person do not exclude opioid toxicity.

There are occasional cases in which a person who has apparently died of an opioid overdose does not exhibit the classic triad of opiate overdose signs. Many FPs will have had experience with people who have died "with a needle in the arm" and do not have significant pulmonary or cerebral edema. While the rapidly acting opiates (e.g., fentanyl and analogues) are arguably more prone to a lack of the extensive edema characteristic of morphine structural analogues, the phenomena can also be seen in cases of heroin injection. As a consequence of the quick death, these patients may not have detectable levels of the major metabolites, e.g., norfentanyl in the case of a fentanyl OD morphine glucuronides (M3G and M6G) in the case of heroin, in PM blood samples. The lack of such or analogous metabolites for other opiates, particularly in the absence of marked edema,

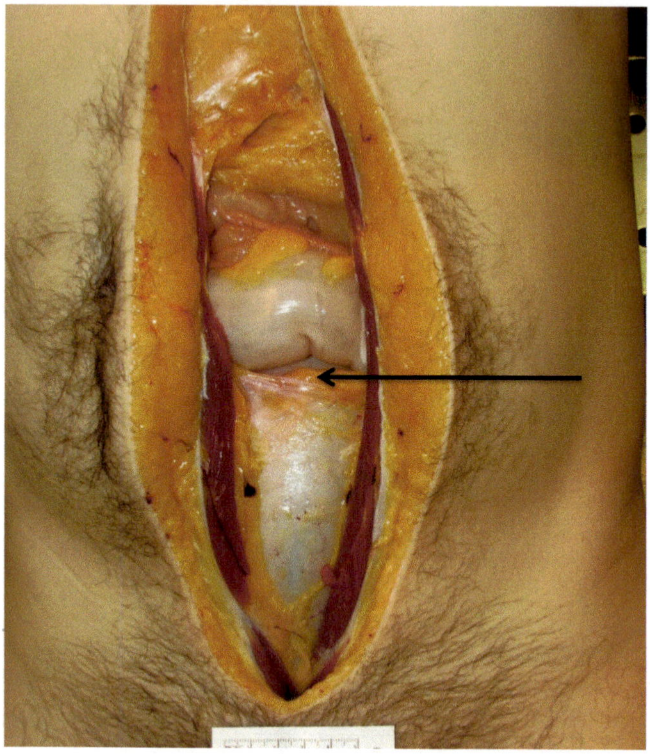

Figure 8.5 This photo shows the level of the dome of the bladder (arrow). Normally, the dome of the bladder is just above, at, or just below the level of the symphysis pubis. The bladder contained 950mL of yellow urine.

would be strongly suggestive of a quick, nearly immediate death. The mechanism for death in patients presenting like this cannot reasonably be the usual CNS-associated, mu receptor-mediated respiratory depression. An alternate suggested mechanism is acute cardiac arrythmia, undetectable at autopsy, having been directly triggered by the arrival of a bolus dose of an IV injection to the heart.

An alternate explanation for an opiate-induced sudden death could be skeletal muscle rigidity following intravenous administration of fentanyl and fentanyl analogues. This phenomenon has been recognized by anesthesiologists for some time, in that intubation following intravenous administration of fentanyl or related analogues for sedation may proceed without problems, but ventilation is subsequently difficult. This phenomenon has been nicknamed "wooden chest syndrome" (WCS), as some patients given one of these drugs develop decreased chest wall compliance and laryngospasm. Clinically, these patients are unable to breathe on their own, and mechanical ventilation is difficult, with laryngospasm and respiratory muscle rigidity developing within a minute or two after dosing. Normally, the vocal cords are relaxed and compliant. Laryngospasm is a sudden, forceful cholinergic-based contraction of the adductor muscles of the vocal cords. It appears that the mechanism for WCS is, at least in part, that fentanyl and analogues may provide some degree of activation of cholinergic and adrenergic receptors in the brain stem and the spinal cord. An overdose of fentanyl is not required for WCS to develop, with reports of WCS occurring in patients given a therapeutic dose of fentanyl and exhibiting laryngospasm and respiratory muscle rigidity within a minute or two after the dose. Treatment by medical professionals is three-fold: mechanical ventilation with supplemental oxygen, reversal of the drug with naloxone, and a neuromuscular blocking agent (e.g., succinylcholine) while stopping the infusion of fentanyl (or analogue). Such measures are unavailable to inadvertent opiate abusers or bystanders outside of the medical environment. Moreover, the rapid onset of WCS may partially explain why opioid reversal drugs such as naloxone, even with repeat dosing, are ineffective following fentanyl administration. (See Sidebar 8.1). Diagnosis of WCS at autopsy is not possible, and the FP is confronted with an apparent opiate overdose, supported by toxicologic findings but without the typical signs of opiate toxicity.

Sidebar 8.1: Sudden Death Following Intravenous Administration of Fentanyl

A 39-year-old man was found dead lying on the floor next to his bed by his brother in his bedroom. He had a well-documented history of intravenous heroin use but no other medical conditions. He had apparently used a belt as a tourniquet, injected some of the drug into a superficial vein, but collapsed before using it all (Figure 8.6).

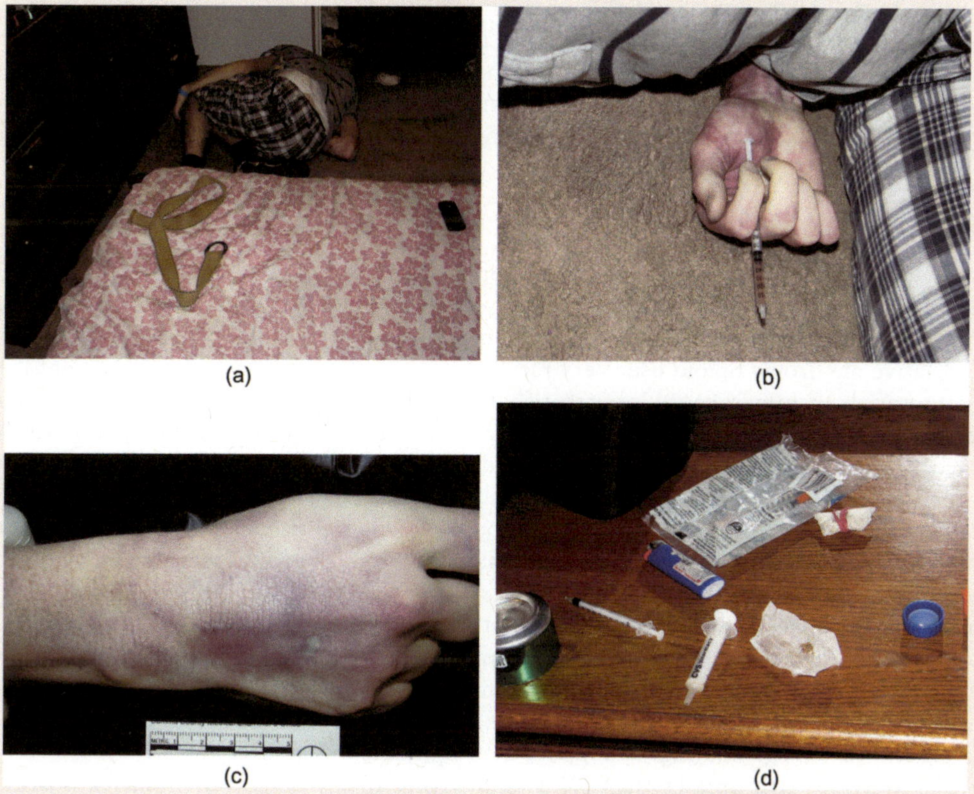

Figure 8.6 (a) The decedent on the floor next to his bed. There is a tan belt on the bedspread, presumably used as a tourniquet. (b). The syringe in the decedent's right hand, with approximately 0.5 mL of light brown liquid remaining in the barrel. The plunger is partially depressed, indicating that some of the liquid has been used. (c) This image shows healing and fresh needle puncture marks in an interrupted linear cluster over a superficial vein in the hand. (d). The top of the dresser is at the left side of the frame in Figure 8.6a. There is a small piece of wax paper with a small brown "rock" on it. The photograph also shows three more syringes; one with a needle, the top of a soda can (inverted), a cigarette lighter, and a bottle cap. Also of interest is what appears to be a bindle of drugs in wax paper secured with a red rubber band. This material could have been removed from the scene and submitted as evidence in the case to a forensic laboratory for analysis. The results may then be compared to the results obtained from autopsy specimens, if necessary. It is also possible for the packaging to be analyzed to determine who was the source of the material (DNA analysis and comparison).

At autopsy, the decedent was 69 inches tall, 178 pounds, with a body mass index of 26.3 kg/m^2. His heart was not enlarged (310g, 1.5cm left ventricular wall thickness). Lungs were 310 and 350g, right and left, respectively. He did not have appreciable pulmonary or cerebral edema. His urinary bladder contained only 3mL of clear, yellow urine. There was no indication that he was incontinent, as he was dying. The toxicology results on postmortem femoral blood were as follows:

Fentanyl 32.6ng/mL
Norfentanyl 12.0ng/mL
Buprenorphine – none detected
Norbuprenorphine 3.1ng/mL

From the pattern of drugs detected in peripheral blood along with the evidence of prior intravenous drug use, this man was a chronic user of opioids. It appears that he died suddenly because he did not have either pulmonary or cerebral edema, and he did not have urinary retention. It is possible that he died from the noradrenergic effect of fentanyl, causing rapid muscle rigidity (WCS). This proposed mechanism is only speculative at autopsy because drug-mediated muscle rigidity cannot be diagnosed postmortem. The cause of death was determined to be "toxic effects of acute fentanyl use," and the manner of death was classified as "accidental."

As noted above, at the autopsy of suspected opiate overdose victims, the contents of the distal colon will often be composed of small nuggets of very firm stool. While such findings may not be of relevance to a COD in a particular case, the information may corroborate suspicions or other findings indicative of chronic opioid use. Very rarely, the cause of death of an opioid patient is bowel obstruction with ensuing rupture, peritonitis, and sepsis. The ability of opiates to slow or reduce intestinal motility is the basis for the function of the effective anti-diarrheal loperamide. While classified as an opiate, the inability of Loperamide to act on opiate receptors in the brain suggests that the drug should not be "added in" to the total opiate load of a decedent when writing the cause of death statement. Similarly, as a function of opiate-mediated urinary retention, the bladder at autopsy of an overdose victim may be greatly distended, with the dome reaching beyond the level of the umbilicus (see Figure 8.4).

The "pinpoint pupils" miotic effect characteristic of opiates is currently considered an important diagnostic parameter of overdose in living people and has historically been utilized to identify morphine poisoning in potential homicide victims. However, current experience suggests that the presence or absence of miosis may not be reliable, and FP's may choose to rely on other pathologic indicators and toxicologic findings to support their opinions.

Perhaps more so with opiates than with many other drugs is the potential for postmortem redistribution to impact the considerations of the FP regarding the contribution of specific species to the cause of death. Because PMR is not related to the structure of the drug and may result in concentrations in blood collected centrally that are as much as ten-fold over peripheral levels, the potential for significant error regarding interpretations of true ante mortem concentrations (and hence, overdose levels) can be made. The current practice of collection of blood from a peripheral source (outside the central core of the body, e.g., femoral vein) is often a reasonable basis for the presumptions that levels are reasonably reflective of true antemortem values. However, in overdose cases, some degree of corroboration from pathologic or circumstantial findings would be desired. Because of the universal nature of the phenomena, consideration as to whether a particular sample has been affected by the process can often be resolved by an evaluation of the levels of other drugs in the system, which would not be expected to have been taken in supratherapeutic levels. In short, if, in a potential opiate overdose, non-psychotropic drugs were elevated to a similar degree as the chronic therapeutic opiate (e.g., 4× therapeutic), then a strong suspicion that the underlying sample was reflective of PMR would be reasonable and could factor into the FP's evaluation of the case. Similarly, a significantly high level of a particular opiate species, with therapeutic levels of prescribed medications would suggest that PMR had not occurred to any significant extent, and that the elevated level was a true reflection of an overdose event.

Sidebar 8.2: Evaluation of Opiate-Related Fatalities

In patients who are suspected to have died of an opiate overdose, there can be a plethora of antemortem medical data, potentially including ER, hospital or other medical records, prescription information, PMH, etc. However, a fatal overdose that has occurred in isolation, in the absence of underlying medical conditions, and in the absence of any relevant or otherwise useful scene or antemortem information, will often result in a relatively unremarkable autopsy, with a couple of notable exceptions. In cases where the death is the consequence of an opiate-induced CNS/respiratory depression, resulting in an eventual terminal cardio/respiratory event, there is an expectation that there will be significant fluid accumulation in the lungs and some degree of cerebral edema. The "foam cone" often found in overdose victims is a consequence of this phenomenon, ultimately deriving from bradycardia and localized pulmonary hypertension, resulting in serosanguinous fluid leakage from the pulmonary vasculature into the alveolar space. Such edema is not only reflected in lung weights (often two or three times the expected values) but also will be readily observed upon sectioning. While not diagnostic of opiate overdose, in cases where a prolonged process of a downward spiral of respiratory depression is presumed to have occurred, such findings are expected, and the absence thereof might well be cause to question the presumption of an opiate-related death. Likewise, cerebral edema is often observed as having resulted from cerebral hypoxia.

Complicating considerations of the expectation of pulmonary edema in opiate-related deaths are those cases, appearing with increasing frequency, of overdoses of high-potency, rapidly acting opiates, such as fentanyl and related analogues. While these drugs may, as a function of dose and administration route, result in a "typical" cycle of CNS and respiratory depression, with the accumulation of fluid in the lungs, there may be such a short time between the onset of CNS/respiratory depression, with concomitant hypoxia, such that death occurs prior to the accumulation of edema fluid. Such cases may represent a challenge for the determination of COD and are somewhat dependent on the ability of the toxicology laboratory to detect not only the traditional opiate formulations used in the community, both by medical personnel and in the illicit drug market, but also to be able to recognize and identify any new analogues appearing in the area.

It is relatively unusual to have a simple, straightforward case, with limited pathology, quick, unambiguous toxicology findings, and circumstances surrounding the death with no inconsistencies. The practical realities are potentially much more complicated, with cases of suspected overdose related to prescription medications being potentially complicated by underlying pathology/medical issues, metabolic changes, multiple or changed medications or dose regimens, etc. In contrast, cases of (apparently clear) illicit drug use can be complicated by such factors as underlying pathology/medical issues, multiple drugs with mixed/overlapping or even contrary actions, etc. There can be some degree of overlap between the situations, in that individuals receiving opiates on a prescription basis can either augment or otherwise misuse their medications or be engaged in frank abuse of illicit opioid materials.

In short, the challenge in opiate deaths lies not so much in the accumulation of data and information from the three main sources, being antemortem (scene/circumstances investigation, medical records, and related information), pathologic findings (autopsy, microscopic, and other evaluations/tests), and toxicologic findings (drugs present, concentrations, and reasonable inferences thereof), but rather in the consideration of the sum total of that information to allow the FP to make the most reasonable determination regarding the cause and manner of death.

1. Are the PM Tox values reliable? As suggested above, one of the first considerations regarding the attribution of a death to an opiate overdose is whether or not the PM tox values are reliably reflective of levels at the time of death. With analytical accuracy not being a significant factor, the key issues then are, "Was the sample drawn from a peripheral site (e.g., femoral vein)?" Was the size and/or position of the decedent such that PMR became a possibility? PMR isa potential for nearly all pharmaceuticals; however, the possibility that, in a questionable death in which opiates may have played a role, the artifactual elevation of a drug level may lead to an erroneous conclusion of the part of the FP is particularly problematic. With the practice of utilizing peripheral draw sites (e.g., femoral), the expectation that PM values do not necessarily reflect PMR is certainly more likely to be valid. However, PMR can result in drug levels as much as 8–10 fold over the underlying antemortem levels, particularly in cases wherein a steady-state of a particular drug has been reached. As such, considerable care should be exercised when utilizing PM values that may have been affected by PMR as uncorroborated (by, e.g., pulmonary edema, scene circumstances, etc.) as necessarily valid reflections of antemortem values.
2. Are the levels of opiates adequate to explain the death? A second consideration in opiate cases, assuming the PM values are reliable, is simply whether the opiates present provide an adequate explanation for the death. With potencies of opiates commonly expressed in "morphine equivalents," it is a relatively straightforward process to simply convert all the various species that may be present into an equivalent concentration of morphine, then deal with the question as to whether or not that level provides an adequate explanation for the death. Recognizing that there can be some degree of difference between the specific receptor affinities of the various opiates, this approach can nevertheless help simplify the overall consideration and may be particularly useful in cases with a combination of prescription and illicit drugs.
3. Are the PM Tox values understandable or consistent in light of prescription information? Related to the above is the question as to whether the drugs present are adequately explained by the prescriptions of the decedent. While far from a straightforward enterprise, a reasonable estimation for an expected therapeutic level can often be generated using a traditional clinical toxicology approach based on body mass as well as therapeutic guidelines. It is of course important to recognize the potential uncertainties associated with this process; nevertheless, in many cases, very useful information can be derived, particularly when coupled with data regarding available medications and usage patterns (e.g., prescription receipt information, pill counts, etc.). A not-uncommon malpractice charge is that a prescribing physician "overprescribed" a particular drug, and in such cases, either the compliance of the decedent with the regimen or departure from can sometimes be clearly demonstrated by the evaluation of records and pill counts.
4. Are the pathology findings consistent with an opiate death? Perhaps most immediately obvious in a suspected overdose death will be the triad of pulmonary edema, cerebral edema, and urinary retention. We recognize that in the case of a rapid opioid-related death, there may not have been a prolonged period of respiratory depression prior to death and, correspondingly, no significant opportunity for the accumulation of edema fluid in the lungs. While not diagnostic of an opiate-related death, this finding is certainly expected, and the absence thereof would require some consideration and potentially an explanation.

5. Differential Diagnosis I: Other explanations, contributory factors? Extensive underlying medical conditions present a significant challenge for opiate-based COD diagnosis. In particular, hypertension-related cardiac hypertrophy is commonly observed and raises the potential of a cardiac event in the abstract. In a more focused sense, the question arises regarding the extent to which the death is actually a function of the underlying potential for a sudden cardiac event, perhaps triggered by a mild hypoxia consequent to opiate use, or indeed even unrelated. Particularly at relatively low levels of opiates, differentiating the degree to which underlying pathology, or, in contrast, the presence of opiates, provides the primary cause and "contributing factors," can represent a serious challenge for the FP. With no clear guidelines or analytical value upon which to base primary v. secondary causation decisions, these questions remain within the knowledge, skill, and experience of the practitioner. (And will, of course, be subject to second-guessing by both knowledgeable and lay personnel.)
6. Differential Diagnosis II: Could other drugs have been contributory? Another complicating factor in many opiate fatalities is the presence of multiple drugs, either prescription or illicit. As noted above, the potential of CNS depressants can and will have some degree of additive effect to an opiate; however, one must be careful not to over-attribute the potential respiratory depressant effect of such drugs when "adding" to opiate-based effects. With that in mind, in a general sense, the GABA-nergic drugs (e.g., benzodiazepines, etc.) would be expected to provide a greater potential for additive effects than drugs not active in a CNS inhibitory sense (e.g., SSRI's and related species). Nevertheless, the potential for the combination of CNS inhibitory drugs to have exacerbated and thereby significantly contributed to an opiate-based death should not be overlooked but considered carefully in light of the potential to mislead eventual consideration of the COD. For example, in the case of a significant prescription overuse/overdose (e.g., oxycodone, PM Fem blood: 480 ng/mL), the presence of a low level of alprazolam (e.g., 22 ng/mL), while certainly "contributory" in a technical sense, would hardly be expected to have had any significant impact on the death.

   While perhaps much harder to sort out, changes in the manner in which a prescription regimen is handled by the body metabolically can have an impact on opiate levels and may impact the interpretation of the manner in which some specific death cases have occurred. Circumstances that affect (as noted above) either the induction or inhibition of metabolic enzymes or inter-hepatic circulation can impact the "steady state" levels of opiates significantly, even in individuals who remain in strict compliance with an unchanged medication regimen.
7. Could metabolism have been ongoing after drug administration? Another potential complicating factor in the interpretation of opioid levels is the patient who became comatose, metabolized some or all of the drug, and died. Blood levels will be nondetectable or very low. Pathologists can only suspect that the patient slipped into a coma, as there are no diagnostic signs of coma at the autopsy. However, the comatose patient at home would have been immobile for a long time. Sometimes those patients have pressure injuries or rhabdomyolysis. Both of these can be seen at autopsy. Rhabdomyolysis can be diagnosed by detecting myoglobin in the kidneys microscopically. Sometimes these patients are transported to the hospital, and the diagnoses are made clinically. Ulcers may also form from pressure on the skin and subcutaneous tissue over bony prominences. In such cases, the sample of choice for toxicologic analysis is not the postmortem blood, urine, or vitreous humor, but the earliest possible antemortem blood that had been drawn upon hospital admission.

8.3 NON-OPIOID SEDATIVE/HYPNOTICS

The "non-opioid sedative/hypnotic" (NOSH) drugs represent a large class of structurally and mechanistically distinct drugs. These are some of the most popularly prescribed drugs worldwide, with multiple medical uses including the treatment of anxiety, sleep disturbance, alcohol withdrawal, seizure disorders, and panic attacks. These drugs are capable of producing similar CNS-depressant effects as the opiates, up to and including a fatal overdose, but the physiologic effects are not mediated via the opiate receptors. Not surprisingly, these drugs are regularly encountered in postmortem forensic toxicology specimens and may, in some cases, have played a causative or contributory role in a death.

Most members of this class act via eliciting an agonist effect on GABA-nergic inhibitory neurotransmission, although a number of species can elicit their physiologic response by different means. As a general rule, the degree of respiratory depression associated with members of this class is not nearly as pronounced as with the opiates, and as such, the potential for lethality as a function of both CNS and respiratory depression/acidosis is considerably less, reflected by a larger corresponding therapeutic index. However, the drugs are certainly not innocuous, either alone or in combination with other drugs (and alcohol in particular), and have a potential for lethality in overdose. These drugs can therefore be a significant factor in ME casework, often seen in multiple drug fatalities, and some consideration regarding the additivity of effects may be warranted based on the mechanism by which the drugs function.

Also, in contrast with the opiates, there is a lack of pronounced euphoria associated with this class of drug, and while some degree of dependance of members of the group can be exhibited by users, the phenomenon of debilitating addiction is not a characteristic of the class. However, these drugs are not uncommonly utilized by patients with a drug addiction (of either opiates or stimulants) to lessen or otherwise ameliorate the dysphoria associated with either withdrawal or the process of "coming down" from a drug-induced "high."

8.3.1 Toxicologic Considerations

Most, if not all the NOSH drugs routinely encountered in a postmortem environment will be medicinals, within the scope of prescribed drugs or commonly used OTC agents, and as such, they will be readily identified and quantitated as appropriate in routine forensic toxicology procedures. As with most pharmaceutical agents, these drugs tend to be readily subject to postmortem redistribution, and indeed, the elevation of long-prescribed pharmaceuticals above expected levels in a postmortem case, particularly when such agents are unlikely to have been utilized in an abuse situation, can be a strong clue that the PMR has been a factor in the concentration of all drugs determined to have been present.

When present in therapeutic levels or even somewhat above therapeutic levels, the presence of such a drug would not reasonably be expected to result in a significant toxicologic result or contribution to the action of a more potent toxic agent, e.g., an opiate or other toxic agent. Significantly toxic levels of NOSH drugs would be expected to be well above therapeutic levels and clearly identifiable as such by reference to tabular data. Specific physiological/toxic effects associated with particular NOSH drugs vary somewhat with the wide variety of agents, but are readily available in such references as Baselt's "Disposition of Toxic Drugs and Chemicals in Man."

8.3.2 Pathologic Considerations

Because of the frequency with which drugs in this class are encountered and the potential they have to serve as contributory agents in death cases, particularly those related to CNS/respiratory depression, one of the recurring challenges faced by the FP is the degree to which specific NOSH agents should be listed as "contributory" agents. From a toxicologic perspective, such questions are not unreasonably resolved by considering if the death would reasonably have occurred even in the absence of the specific agent. However, with current practice generally calling for the identification of drugs that would have played a "contributory" role, determining the degree to which a particular drug (and level) can be ascribed as having played a specific death can present a challenge for both FPs and toxicologists. Confusion regarding this issue is a not uncommon source for many legal actions in the medical malpractice field.

8.3.3 GABA-Nergic CNS-Depressant Drugs

The inhibitory nervous system primarily utilizes the neurotransmitter "GABA" (g-amino butyryl amine) to mediate the degree of inhibition and, thereby, the overall level of CNS activity. The basic mechanism of action is that GABA release at the synapse of inhibitory neurons binds to "$GABA_A$" or "$GABA_B$" receptors on the post-synaptic neuron, resulting in either chloride influx or potassium efflux, respectively. This change in ionic balance "hyperpolarizes" the neuron and makes it less able to propagate an excitatory response.

8.3.3.1 $GABA_A$ Receptor

The $GABA_A$ receptor is a complex molecule with significant structural heterogeneity, but generally, it is a pentamer composed of two alpha subunits, two beta subunits, and one gamma subunit arranged around a potential central core, which is the chloride ion channel. There are two important active sites on the $GABA_A$ receptor, in addition to the GABA-binding site itself. The "barbiturate site" effectively binds barbiturate drugs and structural analogues. Agonism of this site directly activates the receptor and results in the influx of chloride ions into the post-synaptic neuron, with the resulting localized hyperpolarization in the region of the post-synaptic cellular membrane. Similarly, a "Benzodiazepine Site" is able to be agonized by benzodiazepines and structural analogues (e.g., the "Z" drugs, such as zolpidem and zopiclone).

The distinction between the two sites explains the relative toxicity difference between the benzodiazepine and the barbiturate groups, in that the benzodiazepine site acts only as an allosteric activation locus. Binding of the benzodiazepine receptor agonists impacts the magnitude of the receptor response to endogenous GABA and does not result in direct opening of the chloride channel in response to the presence of the drug alone. In contrast, the barbiturate site directly results in chloride channel opening when activated by ligand binding. As such, the magnitude of CNS inhibition elicited by a barbiturate exposure can be greater than with the corresponding benzodiazepine. This slight distinction in the nature of the receptor response is the basis for the difference in therapeutic index between the two types of drugs, with a barbiturates overdose representing a somewhat greater potential for serious toxicologic consequences (particularly in combination with alcohol) than does a benzodiazepine overdose. That is not to suggest that the benzodiazepines are innocuous, but rather that a lethal overdose of a benzodiazepine-type drug will be at a higher multiple of the corresponding therapeutic range than would be the case with a barbiturate-receptor agonist. Similarly, while the lethal potential of the combination of alcohol and barbiturates became well recognized in the general public (and may have contributed to the decline in use of this class in favor of less potentially toxic alternatives), corresponding co-administrations of benzodiazepines and alcohol have proven to be less potentially lethal. Although, as with any CNS depressant combined with alcohol, the corresponding effect on driving capability carries an increased risk as well.

8.3.3.2 Benzodiazepines and "Z-Drugs"

Benzodiazepines and the related "Z-drugs" (e.g., zolpidem and zolpiclone) act, as noted above, as allosteric agonists of the $GABA_A$ receptor and are widely prescribed and extensively utilized as anxiolytic, non-opioid hypnotic, seizure preventative, muscle relaxant, pre-surgical medication, and multiple other uses. Most commonly encountered are lorazepam, clonazepam, diazepam, and alprazolam, although over 20 different benzodiazepines have been approved by the US FDA, differing in speed of onset and duration of action, with many more that have been identified as research chemicals. Some species are approved in other countries but not available in the United States. Consistent with their extensive use within the medical community, benzodiazepines are commonly encountered in postmortem casework. This class of drugs is so named because chemically, they are a combination of a *benzene* ring and a *diazepam* ring. Many of these are the -pam drugs. There are at least ten benzodiazepine drugs available by prescription. While not "drugs of abuse" per se, the benzodiazepines are prescribed for the treatment of anxiety, sleep disturbance, alcohol withdrawal, seizure disorders, and panic attacks. They are also utilized to ameliorate withdrawal, deprivation, or dysphoria associated with either opiate or other recreational/addictive drug use and are therefore commonly encountered in overdose cases. One difficulty facing the FP is clarifying the role, if any, and magnitude thereof, that such drugs would have contributed to a death.

Overdose deaths associated with benzodiazepines as the sole causative agent are relatively unusual, again as a function of the rather large therapeutic index and the need for the decedent to have ingested a significant quantity of a medication to achieve a lethal dose. Co-ingestion with alcohol can result in death at lower levels, but again, significant quantities of a benzodiazepine, along with a substantial alcohol concentration, would be required (this is in marked contrast to the combination of barbiturates and alcohol). There is an antidote for benzodiazepine-site agonists, specifically the (benzodiazepine) flumazinil. However, because of the potential side effects associated with the use of the drug, common practice in the case of suspected benzodiazepine overdose is symptomatic treatment rather than the use of the antidote.

Most of these benzodiazepine drugs are metabolized to some extent by the cytochrome P450 (CYP-) system, with the potential for oxidation (commonly hydroxylation) providing a basis for subsequent conjugation by enzyme-catalyzed glucuronidation. Demethylation can be either a generalized (N-demethylase) or specific (CYP isozyme) reaction. Not uncommonly, urine analysis results will show only metabolites. For example, in the case of diazepam use, oxazepam, temazepam, and nordazepam would be expected in the urine, but the parent diazepam may not be. This apparent discrepancy between prescribed drugs and detected species can be misleading and a source of considerable confusion to interested persons without specific medical training in toxicology.

One side effect of benzodiazepine administration, dependent on dosage, is some degree of amnesia, and this feature can be utilized for minor surgical procedures. Perhaps of more relevance to postmortem casework is that benzodiazepines have often been incorporated as agents of drug-facilitated sexual assault (DFSA), which, like any chemical poisoning, has the potential for the death of the victim. Such DFSAs can be difficult to criminally prosecute as these drugs have a relatively short half-life and are not likely to remain in the blood long enough to be available for analysis.

The "Z" drugs, zolpidem, zopiclone, and zaleplon, are structurally and mechanistically similar to benzodiazepines, acting on the benzodiazepine site on the $GABA_A$ receptor. The Z-drugs are more selective in binding, in that they only bind to the α-1 subunit of the $GABA_A$ receptor. Benzodiazepines bind to any or all of them. Benzodiazepines have a variety of clinical uses, depending on which subtype(s) of the α -subunit they bind to. While they may have some potential as anxiolytics, antiepileptics, and muscle relaxers, the primary medical use of the Z-drugs is to treat insomnia.

The "Z" drugs are most commonly utilized for short-term treatment, usually 1–6 months, and are not usually prescribed for chronic therapy. They have an increased affinity for the receptor, which may explain their higher potency than benzodiazepines. Potential side-effects of the "Z" drugs are hallucinations and poor sleep quality. An alternate explanation, one that is still being developed, is that the activity of these drugs increases levels of the excitatory neurotransmitter serotonin, particularly with zolpidem. Overdoses with Z-drugs have been reported and are manifested by CNS depression. Like the benzodiazepines, fatal overdoses are rare unless they are used in combination with other CNS depressants.

8.3.3.3 Toxicologic Considerations (for the Pathologist)

Analysis of the benzodiazepines and related species in biological materials is straightforward, and even the newer species, given at lower doses, are readily detected, as are the metabolites thereof. As with the opiates, the pattern of metabolic products can provide information regarding timing of exposure, although such considerations are generally not applicable for patients with chronic use or after multiple administrations of the drug.

Tolerance to benzodiazepines appears to be more of a function of induction of metabolic enzymes (e.g., CYP isozymes), rather than down-regulation of a (relatively) specific receptor, as is the case with opiates. Similarly, there can be artefactually elevated levels in blood because of the inhibition of metabolic enzymes in some patients. Because of the rather large therapeutic index of these drugs, such changes are unlikely to provide an explanation for the appearance of a potentially lethal level in an individual who has been maintaining a therapeutic level.

As is the case with all ionizable drugs, benzodiazepines are subject to postmortem redistribution, so some degree of care and consideration should be given to levels that appear to be elevated over what might have been expected, given a particular therapeutic regimen. Similarly, caution regarding the use of clinical toxicology calculations should be exercised, along with the identification of key assumptions and an evaluation of uncertainty.

8.3.3.4 Pathologic Considerations

Deaths due to benzodiazepines alone are unusual. Much more commonly, benzodiazepines play a contributory role in CNS depression in combination with other agents, either opiates, alcohol, or other non-opioid CNS depressants. With this in mind, the tabulated references providing therapeutic, toxic, and potentially fatal levels may be somewhat misleading, particularly if the underlying biochemical mechanism or consequent physiology between two (or more) species is common.

At autopsy, the typical triad of CNS depression can be observed: pulmonary and cerebral edema with urinary retention. The gastric contents may contain pill fragments. The investigative information regarding the medical problems list, prescription history, as well as a pill count of pills remaining can be useful in determining the contribution, if any, of drugs to death. While certainly not diagnostic, this medical and investigative information, along with the subsequent toxicology results, will help the FP formulate a more accurate cause of death statement. Sometimes, FPs are unable to definitively determine how much medication was administered and how much PMR contributed to the postmortem blood level. The manner of death is probably best classified as "undetermined" with an explanatory statement in the autopsy report.

8.3.3.5 Barbiturates

The barbiturate drugs (structural variations of barbituric acid) were introduced for medicinal uses in the early 1900's, and the magnitude of their impact on the treatment of psychoses, neuroses, and perhaps most importantly, epileptic seizures was significant for decades. The barbiturates were extensively utilized in the years prior to the introduction of the benzodiazepines and similar compounds in the early 1960's. While structurally unrelated to the benzodiazepines, these drugs are functionally similar in that they act as GABA-nergic drugs, as noted above. Historically, barbiturates have been used as anxiolytics, antiepileptics, sedatives, and seizure preventive agents. As with the various benzodiazepines, there are multiple species of barbiturates, differing primarily in time to onset and duration of action. Most commonly encountered are the "-al" drugs: phenobarbital, secobarbital, mephobarbital, and amobarbital.

Barbiturates used to be commonly abused, particularly with alcohol, a combination that proved fatal in a number of high-profile deaths (a pattern that has been repeated with cocaine and opiates in the years since). Such use now is quite unusual, and prescription use is mostly restricted to seizure control medications, so abuse is much less of an issue. As such, a key question in deaths with barbiturates is often more of whether the patient was current with their medications, rather than whether or not they were taking too much (with, therefore, the potential for a seizure episode). Therapeutic levels of barbiturates are generally in the mg/L range, and qualitative and quantitative analysis is straightforward in toxicology encountered in a postmortem setting.

Carisoprodol and meprobamate are skeletal muscle relaxants sometimes prescribed for the treatment of chronic back pain, either alone or in combination with other analgesics, e.g., opiates and gabapentin (although gabapentin is used primarily for neuropathic pain). Meprobamate is the primary metabolite of carisoprodol and is itself available as a therapeutic agent. While the mechanism for both species is suspected to be a function of GABA-nergic action similar to barbiturates, a specific mechanism has not been elucidated (e.g., specific $GABA_A$ binding site). As might be expected from a barbiturate functional analogue, both compounds can act as CNS depressants that would be expected to be additive with similar molecules and other CNS sedative/hypnotics, e.g., ethanol, opioids, etc.). The use of carisoprodol and/or meprobamate tends to be somewhat regional, in that in some areas of the US, it is a common finding in postmortem casework while unusual in others. These compounds have little (but not negligible) abuse potential and are not commonly the basis for fatal overdoses.

8.3.3.6 $GABA_B$ Receptor

The $GABA_B$ receptor is a metabotropic receptor with a structure very different from the $GABA_A$ receptor structure. The $GABA_B$ receptor activates "inwardly-rectifying" potassium channels on the post-synaptic neuron, thereby contributing to hyperpolarization by facilitating the efflux of cations (as K^+) in contrast to the influx of anions (as Cl^-) from the $GABA_A$ receptor. The most common agonists encountered in forensic work are baclofen, a skeletal muscle relaxant, and "gamma-hydroxy butyrate" (GHB), a club drug that is also used as a soporific/hypnotic in cases of DFSA (addressed in Section 8.4).

8.3.4 Antihistamines

Histamine receptors are located in the cell membranes of numerous body tissues and expressed in different concentrations in different tissues. They are expressed in the CNS, gastric, bronchial, and vascular smooth muscle in the heart, as well as the immune and endocrine systems. There are four subtypes identified to date, labeled H1, H2, H3, and H4. Sometimes the receptors are called HR1, HR2, HR3, and HR4. They are transmembrane, G-coupled proteins using the extracellular portion for activation and the intracellular portion for sending a secondary messenger for action within the cell. For example, H2 receptors located in the stomach control acid release. H2 blockers are used to treat gastric ulcers by controlling gastric acid release.

Antihistamines (histamine receptor blockers) are available as over-the-counter remedies; usually, a prescription is not required. These drugs are not as tightly controlled as others in this class. Antihistamines, specifically diphenhydramine, are also used to treat allergic reactions and nausea. Antihistamines work by blocking the histamine receptor so that when histamine is released from mast cells following a stimulus, it cannot act on the receptor.

First-generation antihistamines are not trapped by P-glycoprotein and easily cross the blood–brain barrier. These are the ones that cause drowsiness (CNS depression). Examples of these are doxylamine, diphenhydramine, and promethazine. Alone, first-generation antihistamines can be fatal in large amounts, but they can also be fatal if taken in combination with other CNS depressants. Second- and third-generation antihistamines have very little, if any, ability to cross the blood–brain barrier and are much less likely to cause CNS depression. Examples of second- and third-generation antihistamines are desloratadine and fexofenadine.

8.4 DRUG-FACILITATED SEXUAL ASSAULT

DFSA may occasionally result in the death of the victim and thereby fall into the jurisdiction of the medical examiner. Alcohol often plays a significant role in these cases, and a combination of drugs and alcohol, or in some cases, drugs alone, may be the agent utilized. In cases where the COD is to some extent drug-related, the overdose levels encountered are generally marginally into the toxic/fatal range or represent a combination of drugs with additive effects (e.g., a benzodiazepine combined with an opiate). In cases where the amount of drug delivered to the victim has proven fatal, the correct determination of COD and MOD may depend upon the correct interpretation of toxicologic findings and, potentially, autopsy findings as well. While the potential for opiates to be utilized in this type of crime is obvious, and the combination of alcohol and opiates is well-recognized for potential lethality, the ability of benzodiazepines, barbiturates, and other NOSH's to cause, either alone or in combination with alcohol, fatal CNS/respiratory depression is what is commonly associated with such crimes.

Publicity about DFSA has, to an extent, focused on a certain intermediate-acting benzodiazepine (flunitrazepam, "roofies"), which while uncommon in the US (never approved by the FDA), is occasionally referred to as "the date rape drug." Benzodiazepines and functional agonists (e.g., the "Z" drugs) are arguably the most commonly encountered type of drug (after, of course, alcohol) associated with DFSA. There are a variety of drugs that may be encountered in postmortem casework in DFSA cases, including ketamine, xylazine, GHB, chloral hydrate, and a number of other sedative hypnotics that have been utilized in these cases. Mechanistically, ketamine is a dissociative anesthetic and affects the processing of afferent sensory signals. The combination of ketamine and xylazine is a relatively common veterinary anesthetic, with xylazine acting as a potent adrenergic agonist, depressing norepinephrine and dopaminergic neurotransmission. Xylazine is rapidly metabolized in humans, as are several other compounds utilized in this fashion (e.g., alcohol, trichloroethanol (a metabolite of chloral hydrate), and GHB.

Because of the unfortunate increase in the cases of DFSA in the last several decades, forensic laboratories will usually be able to identify the presence of even relatively unusual NOSH's, with no difficulty, and example compounds have been included in proficiency challenges for many years. Nevertheless, several potential agents may require a specific request to the laboratory to evaluate potential DFSA agents and a targeted screen for such compounds as GHB and trichloroethanol.

8.5 SYMPATHOMIMETIC AMINE AND RELATED STIMULANTS

The sympathomimetic amine class (SMA) of drugs are CNS stimulants, meaning that they enhance physical and mental processes. Examples are caffeine, methylphenidate, amphetamine, methamphetamine, cocaine, MDA, MDMA (ecstasy), and a host of structural analogues. These drugs can be, depending on their structure, very potent euphorigenics, with considerable addictive potential. Toxicity in overdose is generally a consequence of CNS stimulation, as opposed to a unique toxic "side effect" analogous to the respiratory depression of the opiates (with the exception of cocaine, as discussed below). However, the potential for the SMAs and related species to be fatal in overdose, either alone or in combination with other drugs, is well recognized.

This large and diverse group of drugs shows varying degrees of abuse potential and can be fatal alone, or in combination with other drugs. The common mechanism for these drugs is interference with the re-uptake of excitatory neurotransmitters at dopamine, serotonin, and epinephrine pre-synaptic neurons, interference with intraneuronal metabolic pathways (e.g., the mono-amine oxidase (MAO) neurotransmitter catabolism), and transport into pre-synaptic neurotransmitter vesicles. The consequential elevation of excitatory neurotransmitters at the synapse is the basis for the "toxic" response, with the pattern and magnitude of expression being the basis for the differential expression of psychotropic effects between different drugs. The addictive nature of these drugs is presumed to be primarily a function of their ability to increase dopamine levels available at the synapse of dopaminergic neurons. Because of their similarity to endogenous biomolecules, many members of this group are readily able to cross the blood–brain barrier.

The archetypal compounds for this group would be amphetamine, its methyl analogue, methamphetamine, and cocaine, each with a long history of medical applications and each also having been extensively utilized and abused as an addictive drug. In contrast to cocaine (a complex tri-cyclic structure), amphetamine is structurally quite simplistic, being the de-hydroxylated analogue of the excitatory neurotransmitter nor-ephedrine. The methylated version (methamphetamine) is structurally analogous to ephedrine. The simple "backbone" of the molecule has led to a whole host of pharmacologically active synthetic analogues, including MDA (methylenedioxy amphetamine) and MDMA (methylenedioxy methamphetamine), also commonly referred to as "Ecstasy" among recreational drug users. There are quite literally thousands of structural analogues of this group, many of which have been evaluated for the magnitude and nature of psychotropic effects.

The archetypal compounds of this group have been in use for over a century (amphetamine was synthesized in the late 1800's; cocaine was similarly popularized in Europe at roughly the same time; however, it has been utilized as an herbal-based drug since pre-Columbian times). While the general population currently views cocaine almost exclusively as a drug of abuse, and nearly so with amphetamine and methamphetamine, these drugs were extensively utilized, albeit for markedly different purposes, in the 20th century. Cocaine has long been used as a local anesthetic for nasopharyngeal surgery, and amphetamine and methamphetamine have been utilized by militaries around the world as adjuncts to pilot alertness and combat capability, starting in World War II (both sides) and continuing through conflicts since that time. After WWII, amphetamine became a common stimulant and "diet pill," but its use and access became increasingly restricted in the 1960's, primarily as a function of motor vehicle accidents associated with excessive use by drivers attempting to stay awake for long periods of time. Currently, amphetamine, methamphetamine, and a number of functional analogues (e.g., methylphenidate) are utilized for the paradoxical calming and "focus ability" enhancing effects of these drugs for both adolescents and adults suffering from hyperactivity/attention deficit disorder. SMAs and analogues are also not uncommonly utilized in the treatment of narcolepsy and as appetite suppressants.

The SMAs in general, when present in physiologically significant concentrations, are readily detected and identified in biological matrices and, as such, do not generally present an analytical challenge to the same degree as would (e.g.) a new, highly potent fentanyl analogue. From a toxicologic perspective, the levels routinely maintained for such uses are generally far less, by nearly an order of magnitude, than those seen in acute abuse scenarios. As such, differentiation between abuse and a therapeutic presence of the drug is often relatively straightforward, and considerable caution should be associated with drawing an inference regarding abuse in cases where a prescribed SMA is present, albeit at low levels, in a postmortem case.

From a pathologic perspective, the toxic mechanism for these drugs is a consequence of ancillary physiologic effects, primarily related to cardiac and thermoregulatory alterations; as such, arrhythmias, acute hypertensive crises (and the potential for cardiac consequences thereof), and acute hyperthermia, reminiscent of "serotonin syndrome," with the potential for seizures as well. As noted above, when one of these species is an underlying cause of death, there is a reasonable expectation of relatively high levels of drug. As an example, the "psychotropic" levels normally seen for amphetamine and methamphetamine tend to be ~1 mg/L or higher, while cocaine tends to be ~700–900 ng/mL.

8.5.1 Amphetamine, Methamphetamine, and Related Drugs

Amphetamine, methamphetamine, and many of the SMAs are structurally related to the excitatory neurotransmitters dopamine and norepinephrine and their N-methyl analogue, epinephrine. The underlying core structure is "*p*henyl*e*thyl*a*mine," and members of the group are occasionally referred to as "PEA's." As noted above, the "psychotropic" dose levels for these drugs are well above therapeutic, and the toxic consequences of toxicity can be fatal. The clinical presentation of overdose is fever, psychosis, hypertension, and cardiac arrythmia, similar to serotonin syndrome. In fatal cases, records of medical intervention may indicate antemortem hyperthermia, sometimes reaching a core temperature of 105^0 F. Rigor mortis advances more quickly than usual in patients who have died with significant hyperthermia. Depending on the nature of the case and the immediate antemortem circumstance, vitreous chemistry may document dehydration, and there may be pigment in the renal tubules from rhabdomyolysis. Toxicologically significant levels of an SMA analogue would be expected to be readily demonstrated in routine postmortem samples. In the case of N-methyl analogue use (e.g., methamphetamine and MDMA), there would be expected to be a significant quantity of the N-demethylated analogue (amphetamine and MDA, respectively), as might be expected, with the predominant metabolic pathway being rapid N-demethylation. However, the converse is not true, and while there may be small amounts of methylation of amphetamine and analogues occurring (as a function of the enzyme phenylethanolamine N-methyl transferase), there is no expectation that the methyl analogue would ever approach the concentration of the un-methylated precursor, and indeed, would not generally be an expected finding, even at low levels.

Methamphetamine use represents one of the serious addictive drug problems currently being dealt with worldwide, easily synthesized by even inexperienced chemists from readily available precursors (e.g., pseudoephedrine). Synthetic methamphetamine may contain significant quantities of byproducts and be either caustic or acidic, with the resulting potential for tissue damage. The drug is potently euphorigenic and addictive. Methamphetamine is available as the dextro- and levo- enantiomers. The d-isomer is psychotropically active, while the l-isomer is contained in a number of over-the-counter decongestants having no psychotropic effect. This distinction is not often an issue in PM cases but can become important in other legal issues, e.g., DUI, assault, etc. While not generally a routine procedure, optically specific analysis is readily available should there be a question regarding the actual nature of the methamphetamine isomer present.

Despite its highly addictive nature, methamphetamine seemingly presents a somewhat lower risk for fatality than cocaine, probably as a function of a comparatively lower cardiac/cardiovascular effect. Chronic users of illicit methamphetamine can develop dental carries and eroded tooth enamel quickly. This so-called "meth mouth" probably develops from multiple exposures to the acidic or basic residues of the synthetic process, exacerbated by a combination of a consistently dry mouth and poor oral hygiene (see Figure 8.7). Figure 8.7 also shows some slightly darker areas on the right cheek, resembling healing injuries. These may represent excoriations caused by scratching, an itching sensation that some chronic methamphetamine users experience. These "meth mites" can resemble acne on the face but can be anywhere on the body within reach of the patient. At autopsy, a decedent may have many such lesions in various stages of inflammation and healing, as some of them may have progressed to abscess formation.

As might be suspected, considering the relatively simplistic structure of amphetamine, with the possibility for structural alterations on the phenyl ring, the aliphatic side chain, and the amine function itself, there are thousands of analogues of amphetamine and methamphetamine that have been synthesized and evaluated for their psychotropic potential. The nature and intensity of effects vary as a function of the different structural alterations; however, the common nature of (non-psychotropic) toxicity seems to remain as noted above, similar to "serotonin syndrome" with hypertension, hyperthermia, arrhythmogenic, intracerebral hemorrhage, and seizure potential as well.

A number of these synthetic analogues have become popular among the younger demographic and were (and remain) popular in the recreational "Club Drug" scene. While there can be variations on specific drugs available in a particular locality, the "methylene dioxy" analogues of amphetamine and methamphetamine (MDA and MDMA, respectively), also known as "ecstasy," are commonly encountered. The psychotropic pattern of these drugs seems to be less oriented toward aggression and is commonly experienced by users as enhancing social contact. As such, drugs in this category are often referred to as "entactogens" or "entheogens." While there is not a significant expectation of acute toxicity associated with use, the potential for overdose, with the typical SMA pattern of symptoms and potential for death remains, particularly when combined with other drugs (e.g., opiates, cocaine, and alcohol). These drugs are usually available as pills or tablets, and as such, the onset of action is not immediate, with users reporting effects 30 min or so after administration. There are no specific findings at autopsy for a death related to methamphetamine or a related compound. The history or prior use and the physical deterioration of the body as described above are helpful but not diagnostic.

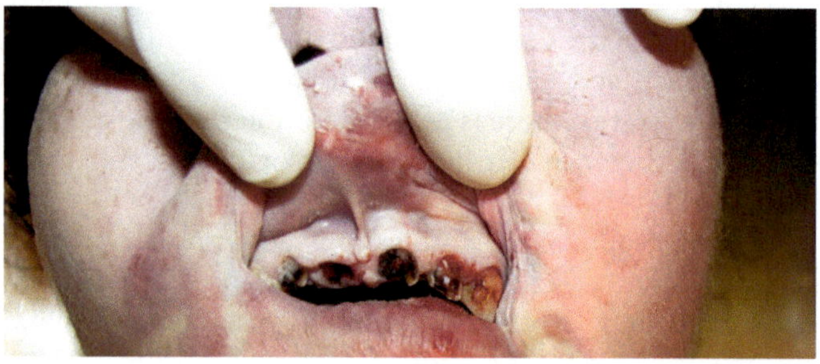

Figure 8.7 Poor dentition in a person who used methamphetamine chronically retraction of the upper lip of a patient reveals tooth decay in the anterior and left lateral mandibular teeth as well as possible excoriations on the right cheek of the face of a patient who died with methamphetamine in the blood. Note that the anterior and left lateral maxillary teeth are chipped to, almost to, and below the gingiva. The residual portions of the teeth are brown to black. The tooth enamel has worn and chipped off. The fragile dentin and pulp chambers are exposed, leading to additional loss of tooth structure. The overlying gingiva becomes inflamed. Teeth in this condition are not restorable. This condition seems to develop regardless of the route of admiration: intravenous, insufflation, or ingestion.

8.5.2 Cocaine

Cocaine remains one of the most popular abused drugs in our society as a pronounced euphorigenic/stimulant with, as might be expected, significant addictive potential. Despite historical medical and commercial use local anesthetic, food additive (the "coca" in Coca-Cola), the primary use of the drug is predominantly as an illicit, recreational drug. Cocaine plays a role in many ME cases, from causing deleterious changes to the cardiovascular system (e.g., cardiac hypertrophy, atherosclerosis, and microvascular disease) to acute hypertensive crises and terminal cardiac events (MI, arrhythmias, CHF, aortic dissection, etc.). As such, cocaine remains a significant factor in many ME cases, if not as an acute toxin, with quantifiable levels in toxicologic specimens, then as an underlying factor affecting the body in general and the cardiovascular system in particular.

The psychotropic aspects of the drug cannot be overlooked, as albeit unusual, users can enter into a state of agitation and delirium and "act out" in ways that can either result in their own physical harm or even death or can result in interactions with law enforcement. In such cases, there can be a sudden cardiac event, which may then circumstantially be associated with actions and activities rather than the recognition of a cardiac-related crisis.

Cocaine is distinct from the other SMAs in that it is structurally unrelated to the excitatory neurotransmitters. However, cocaine does function as a neurotransmitter reuptake inhibitor (primarily serotonin and dopamine), but unlike amphetamine analogues, it does not affect intracellular processes or MAO-based metabolism. The euphorigenic effects of the drug are well known, as are the corresponding effects of acute hypertension associated with psychotropic concentrations (~700 ng/mL and higher). The pronounced hypertension seems to be a function of both CNS stimulation, with the heart beating faster and stronger, coupled with an effect on peripheral and coronary artery vasoconstriction. As a function of acute hypertension, cocaine-associated cerebral hemorrhages, occurring preferentially in the basal ganglia, may be observed in acute cocaine-related fatalities.

Cocaine is rapidly metabolized into the psychotropically inactive "benzoylecgonine;" however, this compound has been shown to have vasoconstrictive activity and may therefore play a contributory role in cocaine-related cardiac death. When cocaine is co-ingested with alcohol, there can be some degree of trans-esterification in the liver, producing cocaethylene (the "ethyl ester" of cocaine, or the methyl ester, cocamethylene). Cocaethylene is also a potent sympathomimetic amine drug that has the same, if not greater, stimulant property than cocaine. Cocaethylene is readily detected in toxicologic specimens, and PM samples containing cocaethylene would reasonably indicate acute use of cocaine, even if the parent drug is not detected.

The administration of the combination of an SMA, usually cocaine, with heroin, a so-called "Speedball," has resulted in the deaths of a number of people, including celebrities. In such cases, the death can be cardiac in nature, directly related to the cocaine, or, if enough time passes, a respiratory depression/cardiac death as the opiate symptomology becomes increasingly expressed. With the increasing influx of fentanyl into the heroin market, the potentially equally lethal combination with cocaine is not uncommonly encountered in PM casework.

8.5.3 Cathinones and Tryptamines

The cathinones represent a large family of drugs, including the basic cathinone structure, plus hundreds of synthetic modifications. Cathinone can be thought of as the b-keto analogue of amphetamine and occurs naturally in the Khat plant (the leaves of which are chewed to release the active ingredient). Cathinone itself and a wide variety of synthetic analogues have been utilized in the club drug culture, often erroneously described as "bath salts." Mechanistically, these compounds act generally more like MDMA than amphetamine or methamphetamine, but nevertheless have the potential, in overdose to produce the characteristic serotonin-syndrome-like symptoms characterizing the class. Despite the wide variety of potential structures, when present in overdose levels, the detection and resolution of specific species are readily accomplished by toxicology laboratories.

Like the cathinones, the "tryptamines" (structural analogues of 5-hydroxytryptamine; serotonin, 5-HT) are mechanistically related to the other sympathomimetic amines and have the same physiologic effects. The tryptamine structure has also been subjected to multiple synthetic modifications, leading to hundreds of potentially psychotropically active compounds and their incorporation into many variations and formulations of "bath salts." Also similar to the cathinones, these compounds are readily detected and identified in PM samples.

8.5.4 Ephedrine and Related Compounds

Ephedrine and related compounds (e.g., pseudoephedrine and beta-hydroxyphenylethylamines) are stimulants used for appetite suppressants, decongestants, and anti-asthmatics. They act by increasing the release of norepinephrine from the presynaptic neuron into the synaptic space, activating adrenergic receptors. These receptors are located throughout the body on the walls of blood vessels, the bronchial tree, as well as the CNS. Stimulation of adrenergic receptors on vessel walls causes vasoconstriction. Conversely, bronchial relaxation is caused by stimulation of adrenergic receptors on the smooth muscle of the bronchial tree. These drugs do not appear to significantly affect dopamine or serotonin. The majority of these compounds are excreted unchanged in the urine. Blood, urine, and vitreous humor are adequate matrices for analysis. Ephedrine represents one of a number of "herbal medications" that actually have significant and consistent physiological effects and has been used as a medicinal for thousands of years. However, in the early 2000's, a number of deaths were associated with the use of the drug as a dietary supplement, suggesting some degree of cardiotoxicity, and the FDA banned supplements with ephedrine at that time. The drug remains in use for medical purposes.

8.6 SEROTONERGIC ANTIDEPRESSANTS

The group of antidepressants affecting the monoamine neurotransmitters (serotonin, norepinephrine, and dopamine) is composed of three classes of relatively commonly prescribed antidepressant drugs, selective serotonin reuptake inhibitors (SSRI's), serotonin/norepinephrine reuptake inhibitors (SNRI's), and TCA's, and a less popular class, the MAO inhibitors (MAOI's), used for a fairly broad group of depression, anxiety, and other psychological problems. While often detected and reported during routine toxicologic evaluations, toxicity associated with the SSRI's and SNRI's is relatively unusual unless present at levels well above therapeutic. Both the TCA's and the MAOI's have a greater potential for significant toxicity than the SSRI's and SNRI's.

SRIs function based on the neurotransmitter's ability to modulate mood. Serotonin also partially affects thermoregulation and enhances bronchoconstriction- and vasoconstriction. The "SSRI's" function at the level of the presynaptic excitatory neuron, inhibiting the reuptake of serotonin from the synapse by specific transport proteins, thereby increasing the background concentration in the synapse and decreasing the magnitude of serotonin release by the pre-synaptic neuron required to induce depolarization in the post-synaptic neuron. Related compounds may exhibit some degree of effect on norepinephrine reuptake transport proteins as well (and hence, "SNRI's"). The common SSRIs are citalopram, sertraline, fluoxetine, and paroxetine. The SNRI's include duloxetine and venlafaxine. Fatal overdoses with SSRIs are related to the increased level of serotonin in the synapse: hyperthermia, tachycardia, and muscle rigidity. Rigor mortis may develop earlier, and the body temperature may be elevated in the deceased person, particularly if the postmortem interval is short.

The functionally analogous TCAs have been, to a great extent, replaced by the SSRI's, SNRI's, and benzodiazepines, although the drugs (primarily amitriptyline and imipramine) are still not uncommonly encountered in postmortem toxicology along with their metabolites (nortriptyline and desipramine, respectively). In contrast to the SSRIs and SNRIs, TCAs in overdose levels can have an effect on both sodium and potassium channels in the heart, effecting the action potential and resulting in a QRS prolongation, bradycardia, and prolonged QT interval, potentially leading to a fatal arrhythmia. Because of the potential for cardiac effects, TCA's have a narrower therapeutic window than the other reuptake inhibitor-type drugs.

In mechanistic contrast to the SSRIs, SNRIs, and TCAs, the MAOIs limit the activity of the catabolic enzyme MAO, a mitochondrial enzyme that functions to oxidize the monoamine neurotransmitters (norepinephrine, serotonin, and dopamine), as well as tyramine, a metabolite of the amino acid tyrosine (tyramine is a catecholamine-releasing agent). Inhibition of MAO then increases the concentration of these neurotransmitters in the pre-synaptic neuron, resulting in a correspondingly higher synaptic concentration following release during the neurotransmission process. Commonly, MAOI toxicity is a function of increased adrenergic activity consequential to the ingestion of tyramine-containing foods. The combination of MAO inhibition with serotonin reuptake inhibition can result in serotonin syndrome, with the potential for fatality related to seizures, coma, or cardiac effects. Because MAO inhibitors tend to irreversibly bind to the enzyme and recovery to pre-treatment levels may take a couple of weeks, the transition between an MAO inhibitor to a serotonin re-uptake inhibitor is a well-recognized risk for significant toxic consequences.

8.7 ANTIPSYCHOTICS

There are numerous antipsychotic or "neuroleptic" medications available by prescription that primarily function as sedative/hypnotics used to treat conditions including agitation, psychosis, schizophrenia and related conditions, the manic phase of bipolar disorder, dementia, delirium, etc. The "First Generation" or "typical antipsychotics" (e.g., phenothiazines, butyrophenones, etc.) work as dopamine receptor agonists and also have some degree of noradrenergic, cholinergic, and histaminergic receptor blocking action. Typical examples that can be encountered in forensic samples include chlorpromazine and haloperidol. While typical antipsychotics can cause a number of side effects, of particular concern from a forensic perspective is their potential to cause a lowered seizure threshold as well as to cause arrhythmias, prolonged QT interval, and other cardiac conduction issues. Also of note is the potential for neuroleptic malignant syndrome, which can result in fatality as a function of hyperthermia, cardiac issues, seizures, or kidney failure. Neuroleptic malignant syndrome is usually seen within the first several weeks of use, however, it can occur at any time. Symptoms include fever, labile blood pressure, muscle rigidity, and autonomic dysfunction. Evidence of hyperthermia may be noted at autopsy, sometimes with decomposition out of proportion to the postmortem interval.

The "Second Generation" or "atypical antipsychotics" function as dopaminergic receptor antagonists, but also exhibit serotonin receptor blocking action and some degree of antidepressant activity, presumably associated with serotonin/norepinephrine reuptake inhibition. The atypical antipsychotics have become the drug of choice for many clinicians, and the degree of efficacy of these drugs, with fewer side effects, has significantly improved the effectiveness of treatment for many individuals with psychosis. While there are generally fewer side effects, there remains some risk of neuroleptic malignant syndrome. Typical second generation neuroleptic drugs are clozapine, olanzapine, quetiapine, and risperidone. The detection and quantitation of neuroleptic drugs is readily accomplished by current analytical procedures.

One issue with the neuroleptic drugs can be whether the patient was actually compliant with the medication prescription, with questions of overdose or failure to maintain therapeutic levels, both being potentially of significance in a death investigation. As noted in other sections of this book, such calculations based on PM values may indeed be of value, but any such data should be critically scrutinized regarding the validity of the underlying assumptions, and the appropriate expression of confidence intervals.

8.8 NEURONAL CELL BODY TOXINS

Drugs that are directly toxic to the cell body of neurons are not commonly encountered in the forensic setting, other than drugs that are systemically active, such as chemical asphyxiants or general metabolic poisons (e.g., electron-transport system poisons, ATP synthesis inhibitors, etc.) (addressed in Sections 3 and 5).

One can draw an important distinction between toxins that merely inhibit or limit the functional capacity of neurons, with those that are directly toxic to the neuron itself, although, of course, such effects may in the long term, be fatal as a function of the CNS and/or respiratory depression. Similarly, the stimulation of inappropriate neuronal transmission may also be fatal (causing a seizure or muscle paralysis), but not neurotoxic in the sense of causing the death of the neuron and, subsequently, the death of the body. In the postmortem setting, acute toxic agents causing an inappropriate neuronal response (either inappropriately limiting or stimulating function) tend to be cardiotoxins, affecting sodium or potassium channels, and hence cardiac function (and are discussed in Section 6), and causing muscle spasms or seizures.

True "neurotoxic" agents, which elicit a toxic response as a direct function of killing neurons, tend to be chronic and often environmental in nature, e.g., chronic metal exposure (lead, tin, tellurium, etc.), shellfish poisoning (domoic and kainic acid), acrylamide, etc. However, examples have arisen from deliberate homicidal poisoning (e.g., colchicine, a neuronal microtubule poison) and drugs of abuse (e.g., MPP+, see Sidebar 8.3). In a practical sense, deaths caused by this type of agent will often have a significant documented medical history and, in many cases, even the identification or suspicion of a reasonable underlying toxic agent. Pathologically, autopsy findings will be expected to corroborate antemortem symptoms such as paresthesia, hypoesthesia, or partial paralysis. Determination of the underlying causative agent may, in such cases, have been achieved well prior to death, although the complexity associated with the task of correctly diagnosing a neurotoxin-based illness can be challenging both at the level of the physician and at the toxicology laboratory challenged with actually identifying a toxic agent. Often, the course of diagnosis, either ante-mortem- or postmortem, will involve analysis for agents not routinely tested for in a forensic toxicology laboratory (e.g., heavy metals, large molecular-weight biological toxins, such as the "Red Tide" agent, saxitoxin).

Sidebar 8.3: MPP+, MPPP, MPTP, Desmethylprodine, and Meperidine

One example of a drug that is directly toxic to the nerve cell body is a precursor to the actual toxic species. Biochemically, it is methylphenyl tetrahydropyridine, or MPTP for short. MPTP is an accidental byproduct in the manufacture of the synthetic opiate methylphenylpropionylpiperidine (MPPP, "desmethylprodine," a meperidine analogue) that was used as a legal (at the time) opiate analogue. MPTP is able to cross the blood–brain barrier and enter cells, in particular astrocytes, where it can be oxidized by MAO in two steps to N-methyl-4-phenylpyridin-1-ium (MPP+). MPP+, which is a substrate for the dopamine reuptake site on the neurons in the substantia nigra of the brain stem, is able to readily be reduced by complex I of the mitochondrial electron transport chain and subsequently form reactive oxygen species, leading to free-radical-type membrane damage and ultimately cellular death. The net effect is a permanent loss of dopaminergic neurons of the substantia nigra, and an irreversible expression of the symptoms of Parkinson's disease.

8.9 CHOLINERGICS AND ANTICHOLINERGICS

The neurotransmitter acetylcholine (ACh) acts within the nervous system in cholinergic synapses, at neuromuscular junctions throughout the body, and also on some glands, including the pituitary and adrenal medulla. The two types of ACh receptors are "muscarinic" and "nicotinic," named for their iconic agonists. Muscarinic receptors are concentrated more in the brain, with nicotinic receptors located at the neuromuscular junction. Stimulation of nicotinic cholinergic receptors on the adrenal medulla release norepinephrine. The fate of ACh following release from that of the pre-synaptic neuron is somewhat different from other neurotransmitters. Typically, NTs are released from the presynaptic neuron, diffuse across the synaptic space, bind to receptors on the post-synaptic neural surface, and are then removed from the synapse, primarily by the action of pre-synaptic re-uptake transport proteins. (e.g., dopamine, serotonin, and norepinephrine re-uptake proteins). ACh is not taken directly back into the pre-synaptic cell body; rather, it is metabolized in the synapse by the enzyme acetylcholinesterase. Because of the close physical proximity between ACh and the enzyme that degrades it, the half-life of ACh is very short.

8.9.1 Cholinergics

Cholinergics are those drugs and toxins that increase the level of ACh in the synapse by directly inhibiting or inactivating acetylcholinesterase or by agonizing ACh receptors in the glands, smooth muscles, and motor neurons. Symptoms are determined by how much of each type of receptor is affected. Because muscarinic and nicotinic receptors have *both* excitatory and inhibitory potential, both types of symptoms are produced in various proportions. With cholinergic toxicity, ACh receptors remain activated because of adequate localized concentrations of ACh to occupy the receptor, resulting in a depolarized membrane that is refractory to further signal transmission.

Cholinergic toxicity results in overstimulation of the parasympathetic nervous system, resulting in the classic cholinergic toxidrome, SLUDGE-M: salivation, lacrimation, urination, defecation, gastric sounds, emesis, and miosis with blurred vision. Examples of toxins causing cholinergic toxicity are organophosphate fertilizers, insecticides (e.g., malathion), pesticides (e.g., parathion), and Sarin gas. The route of exposure of these toxins is either inhalation of vapors or direct dermal absorption. Rarely, patients ingest these toxins as the taste is very unpleasant. Examples of drugs that can cause cholinergic toxicity are bethanechol (for urinary retention), pilocarpine (for radiation therapy-associated dry mouth), neostigmine (for treatment of myasthenia gravis and urinary retention), and donepezil (used to treat dementia in patients with organic brain diseases).

One of the primary sources of cholinergic toxicity resulting in death is inadvertent exposure to organophosphate insecticides or their nerve-gas analogues, such as sarin. The mechanism of toxicity of organophosphates and nerve gases is the direct inhibition of the enzyme acetylcholinesterase, as the organophosphate forms a covalent bond with it, inactivating the enzyme. With the limitation in the amount of functional acetylcholinesterase able to break down ACh, the concentration of ACh remains elevated in the synapse. Both types of cholinergic receptors will be stimulated (muscarinic and nicotinic).

8.9.2 Anticholinergics

Anticholinergics are drugs and toxins that prevent the release of ACh from the presynaptic neuron or block the action of ACh on the postsynaptic receptor. Patients with irritable bowel syndrome, insomnia, Parkinson's disease, and motion sickness may be treated with these medications to ameliorate the symptoms. Therapy is aimed at blocking the receptor or minimizing the concentration of ACh at the receptor. Drugs in this class can be sedating but do not produce euphoria. There are numerous drugs that can cause an anticholinergic effect, including atropine, scopolamine, hydroxyzine, doxylamine, and diphenhydramine. There is low potential for chronic abuse, but suicidal ingestions as well as accidental poisonings have occurred. Elderly patients may have lower levels of ACh as part of the aging process and may be especially vulnerable to these medications. Patients with multiple medical problems are also at risk for synergistic effects.

Plants that contain anticholinergic toxins include belladonna (atropine) and those in the Solanaceae family. Living patients will generally exhibit symptoms of the anticholinergic toxidrome, with a dry mouth, hyperthermia, dry skin, urinary retention, and constipation. Severe exposures may progress to seizures and death. There are no diagnostic findings at autopsy, so the scene investigation and toxicologic analyses may be necessary to facilitate a determination of COD.

Curare is an interesting example of an anticholinergic toxin, originally used for hunting but later prepared for clinical use. The curare toxin acts as a cholinergic receptor antagonist and was originally extracted by boiling plants that contain it, most typically large tropical vines of the Chondrodendron genus. The resulting paste was then painted onto the tips of arrows and spears for hunting. Curare has a short duration of action, killing quickly by completely relaxing the diaphragm. Curare had been used in surgery as a muscle relaxant, causing complete immobility. Curare has no anesthetizing ability and a rapid onset of action, so an anesthetic agent must be used, and the patient must be intubated for respiratory protection. Curare has been supplanted for use in surgery by the similarly functioning neuromuscular blocking agents, pancuronium, vecuronium, and rocuronium.

In contrast to direct antagonism of the cholinergic receptors, the botulinum toxin, produced by the anaerobic bacteria *Clostridium botulinum*, is taken up by the presynaptic cholinergic neuron, where it subsequently blocks neurotransmitter vesicle binding and release of ACh. The result is flaccid muscular paralysis. Therapeutically, botulinum toxin is used to treat spastic muscle activity (e.g., post-stroke, cerebral palsy, and post-traumatic spasticity), chronic migraine headaches, and for cosmetic dermatology. There are no specific autopsy findings; the diagnosis is suspected based on investigative information. C. *botulinum* forms encapsulated spores that are resistant to breakdown. However, the toxin is heat sensitive and is destroyed by properly heating the food by boiling. People who can their own food are at risk of ingesting the toxin if the food has not been heated to a high enough temperature. C. *botulinum* cannot multiply at pH levels below 4.6, so high-acidity foods (fruit, tomatoes, and cucumbers) are safe to leave at room temperature. Low-acid foods, such as cooked green vegetables, may allow the bacteria to grow. C. *botulinum* can also multiply at room temperature and release toxins into unrefrigerated food. It does not impart an "off" odor or unpleasant taste, so people may not be aware that they are eating contaminated food. Honey is a good medium for bacterial growth and is usually stored at room temperature because it crystallizes with refrigeration. Re-warming does not return honey to its original consistency. The forensic pathologist can be alerted to fatal intoxication if multiple people at the same event or household become ill.

8.10 TETANUS AND STRYCHNINE

The tetanus toxin comes from another Clostridium bacteria, *Clostridium tetani*. C. *tetani* is a soil-borne contaminant that produces the tetanus toxin when the bacteria enter the body. When the toxin is released, it is taken up by neurons and transported retrograde into the CNS, ultimately to the inhibitory interneurons in the spinal cord. The toxin blocks the release of the inhibitory neurotransmitters GABA and glycine by interfering with neurotransmitter vesicle binding to the synaptic membrane during a depolarization event. The clinical picture is spastic paralysis of the diaphragm and skeletal muscles. The condition, tetanus, or colloquially "lock jaw," is not common in the US because a vaccine is given in childhood and after puncture wounds.

With an effect similar to tetanus toxin, strychnine functions as an antagonist of the (CNS) inhibitory neurotransmitter glycine, thereby eliciting spastic paralysis, with the potential for an asphyxial death, in a manner similar to tetanus.

Bibliography

Brodal. P. (2004). *The Central Nervous System: Structure and Function*. 3rd rev. ed. New York: Oxford University Press.

Conn M.P. (ed) (2008). *Neuroscience in Medicine*. 3rd rev. ed. Totowa, NJ: Humana Press.

Gilman A.G., Rall T.W., Nies A.S., Taylor P. (eds) (1990). *Goodman and Gilman's The Pharmacological Basis of Therapeutics*. 8th ed. New York: McGraw-Hill.

McCorry L.K. (2009). *Essentials of Human Physiology for Pharmacy*. 2nd ed. Boca Raton, FL: CRC Press.

Barile F.A. (2010). *Clinical Toxicology: Principles and Mechanisms*. 2nd ed. New York: Informa Healthcare.

Drummer O.H. (2001). *The Forensic Pharmacology of Drugs of Abuse*. London: Arnold.

Fenton J.J. (2002). *Toxicology: A Case-Oriented Approach*. Boca Raton, FL: CRC Press.

Gunja N. (2013). The clinical and forensic toxicology of Z-drugs. *Journal of Medical Toxicology: Official Journal of the American College of Medical Toxicology*, 9(2):155–162. https://doi.org/10.1007/s13181-013-0292-0.

Klassen C.D. (2013). *Casarett and Doull's Toxicology: The Basic Science of Poisons*. 8th rev. ed. New York: McGraw-Hill.

Reichl F.X., Ritter L. (eds) (2011). *Illustrated Handbook of Toxicology*. Stuttgart: Thieme.

Langston, J.W. (2007). The MPTP story. *Journal of Parkinson's Disease*, 7(1):S11–S19. https://doi.org/10.3233/JPD-179006.

Levine R, Veliz S, Singer, D. (2020). Wooden chest syndrome: Beware of opioid antagonists, not just agonists. *The American Journal of Emergency Medicine*, 38(2):411.e5–411.e6. https://doi.org/10.1016/j.ajem.2019.09.009.

Pergolizzi J.V., Webster L.R., Vortsman E., LeQuang J.A., Raffa R.B. (2021). Wooden chest syndrome: the atypical pharmacology of fentanyl overdose. *Journal of Clinical Pharmacology and Therapeutics*, 46(6):1485–1803.

Squire L.R., Berg D., Bloom F.E., Du Lac S., Ghosh A., Spitzer N.C. (eds) (2008). *Fundamental Neuroscience*. 3rd rev. ed. Boston, MA: Elsevier.

INDEX

Note: **Bold** page numbers refer to tables and *italic* page numbers refer to figures.